BRIGHOUSE'S
PRECEDENTS OF WILLS

AUSTRALIA
Law Book Co.
Sydney

CANADA and USA
Carswell
Toronto

HONG KONG
Sweet & Maxwell Asia

NEW ZEALAND
Brookers
Wellington

SINGAPORE and MALAYSIA
Sweet & Maxwell Asia
Singapore and Kuala Lumpur

BRIGHOUSE'S
PRECEDENTS OF WILLS

thirteenth edition
by

DAVID ENDICOTT

and

ANDREW JONES

*both of Spratt Endicott
Banbury*

THOMSON

™

SWEET & MAXWELL

2002

First Edition 1910	Seventh Edition 1958
Second Edition 1919	Eighth Edition 1964
Third Edition 1927	Ninth Edition 1971
Fourth Edition 1938	Tenth Edition 1978
Fifth Edition 1945	Eleventh Edition 1986
Sixth Edition 1951	Twelth Edition 1997

Published in 2002 by
Sweet & Maxwell Limited of
100 Avenue Road, Swiss Cottage, London NW3 3PF
www.sweetandmaxwell.co.uk
Typeset by J.P. Price, Chilcompton, Somerset
Printed and bound in Great Britain by
MPG Books Ltd, Bodmin, Cornwall.

Whilst all reasonable care has been taken to ensure the accuracy of the
contents of this book, no responsibility for loss occasioned to any person
acting or refraining from action as a result of any statement in it can be
accepted by the author or the publisher.

No natural forests were destroyed to make this product;
only farmed timber was used and replanted

A CIP catalogue record for this book is available from the British Library.

ISBN 0421 787 104

To Jill and Alexandra

PREFACE TO THE 13TH EDITION

It was a privilege to be asked by Sweet and Maxwell in 1997 to prepare the 12th edition of this book. Earlier this year I was approached and asked to prepare the 13th edition. I agreed to do so on two conditions: first, that the book would be the joint effort of me and my colleague, Andrew Jones, and secondly, that the only rationale that we could think of for a new edition was that it would take a fresh approach at the drafting of wills, and attempt to draft wills which are both in plain English and, more importantly, understandable by the client.

This we have attempted to do.

We are now in the second term of the Labour Government which, in Opposition, complained that Inheritance Tax was voluntary, and as a consequence we all feared the worst. In fact, there have been no dramatic changes to the tax. The nil-rate band continues to increase and is currently £250,000. Thus, now to write a nil-rate band discretionary trust in a will can save £100,000 in tax. The reliefs available to farmers and businessmen continue, as does the surviving spouse exemption, and reliefs for gifts into charities and certain political parties.

Somewhat surprisingly the deed of variation regime remains intact, and so, as before, this book contains precedents for both deeds of variation and disclaimers. There must be a health warning, however, and I would continue to urge practitioners to be cautious and not to rely too much on the continued availability of deeds of variation.

Two major pieces of legislation that affect trust and estate practitioners are, of course, the Trustee Act 2001 and the Trustee Delegation Act 1999, but these are for the most part outside the scope of this book.

As before, a wills questionnaire is included, and once again I am indebted to James Kessler for his permission to incorporate the STEP standard provisions and his own commentary thereon.

Finally, a word of thanks to my co-author. When we agreed to take on this job I did not realise that I would shortly be in de-merger talks with my practice, and founding a new practice all within the space of six weeks. As a consequence Andrew Jones has done the lion's share of the work. Thus, much of the inspired drafting is his. He assures me that it is based upon the previous edition, which is probably designed to ease my conscience.

David Endicott
Banbury

August 2002

CONTENTS AT A GLANCE

TABLE OF CONTENTS

PART 2

Common Form Clauses

PART 3

PART 4

Trustees' Powers Collected

PART 5

PART 6

PART 7

PART 8

Codicils

PART 9

PART 10

APPENDICES

TABLE OF CASES

TABLE OF STATUTES

PART 1

INTRODUCTION

It is five years since the previous edition of this book was published, and since **1–001** then the event of great moment was the new Millennium. With that in mind we have attempted in this edition to bring will drafting up to date in plain and modern English which we hope will be accessible to the practitioner and understandable by the client.

It is not our wish to reinvent the wheel. This is by definition a book of precedents and that should probably be its focus. As a consequence, purchasers of the 12th Edition may find that much of this introduction is familiar to them.

In the introduction to the 11th edition, E.F. George and A. George **1–002** conceived as a context for a will a chain of acts, events and instruments whereby the property of one person is transferred, otherwise than by a transaction at arms length, by him or her to another or others, whether by way of gift or settlement or otherwise. They commented that the place of the will in the chain was sometimes the last, or the only link, but quite often the penultimate one; the last being a disclaimer, deed of variation or appointment.

They identified quite correctly that the will differed from the other instruments in the chain because it took effect at a future time when the testator's estate might be quite different from that at the time of execution, the contemplated beneficiaries different or in altered circumstances and the law changed. They commented "the solicitor's task may be a delicate one". How true that is.

It is, no doubt, the experience of many solicitors when taking instructions **1–003** for a will to be told "keep it simple and cheap, everything to the wife and then to the kids". It is then that the solicitor becomes part prophet of doom and part tax planner. What will happen if none of them survive you? What will happen if your wife remarries? What about trying to save some tax? If the solicitor is to do his job properly, then these and many other questions must be answered before a draft is prepared.

It is, of course, all too tempting to reassure the client and oneself that "it **1–004** will be all right on the night" by throwing into the conversation at a suitable time the availability of a deed of variation, which in effect may rewrite the will within two years of the date of death. It should be noted, however, that deeds of variation are not always appropriate, and may not always be available. Indeed, it was the then Chancellor Norman Lamont who in the 1989 Finance Bill sought to abolish deeds of variation. The proposal was only dropped after intense lobbying by, amongst others, the Law Society and the Institute of Chartered Accountants.It is many years since the wills draftsman had to consider the impact of capital gains tax on death, but the implication of other

3

taxes, principally income tax and inheritance tax, must be carefully considered, and it is surely wise to take full effect of available reliefs, such as agricultural property and business property relief (currently at 100 per cent).

1–005   Since the publication of the 11th edition in 1986 much has changed. During this time we have witnessed a tightening up of checks and controls by virtue of the Financial Services Act 1986, but at the same time a loosening of the monopoly formerly enjoyed by the legal profession. It is not uncommon to see will writing agencies selling their computer-based wares in shopping arcades alongside computer horoscopes and double glazing. Banks and Building Societies (now hardly distinguishable) are writing wills for customers at an increasing rate. Whilst the "testate" proportion of the population is still in the minority, with sales of council houses and privatisation of nationalised utilities, more and more people perceive that they have a need to pass assets on, and that they require a will.

In society too, changes are happening. Marriage seems to be declining whilst divorce increases. There are many more one-parent families, more cohabitees and more couples with extended families as a result of a second marriage. Coupled with these ever more complex family scenarios is the demand that legal documents, including wills, are written in a language that the client understands. How many of us have in the past produced a beautifully bound and drafted will to have the client, who had dutifully read it, ask the question "yes, but what does it say?"

1–006   Cost is another issue. The draftsman knows that the document that he or she produces is perhaps one of the most important documents that the client will ever sign. It will save tax, it will ensure the devolution of the family business or farm, it will even ensure that the children are looked after through the appointment of guardians. There remains however, a resistance to pay a lot of money for what looks to be a relatively simple document. More and more practitioners are utilising information technology and standard precedent clauses to reduce the costs involved.

1–007   This book concentrates on wills, codicils and related documents. For the first time we have incorporated, albeit briefly, a chapter and some precedents on living wills, otherwise referred to as Advance Directives. For precedents on lifetime giving the reader is referred to the current edition of James Kessler's excellent book "Drafting Trusts and Will Trusts — A Modern Approach."

Appendix 1 contains a wills questionnaire for use when taking instructions. Use of it or a similar questionnaire is recommended because it is also easy to miss something when taking instructions, and the courts are tending to find against the will draftsman.

1–008   It is important that once instructed the will is completed and executed as soon as possible. Delays can be very expensive — see *e.g. Ross v. Caunters*[1] and *White v. Jones*.[2] If the testator has, or you believe the testator has foreign property, then ensure that any foreign will which might deal with that property is not accidentally revoked. If the testator does not have a will in the country in which any property is situated then the client should be

---

[1] [1980] Ch. 297; [1979] 3 All E.R. 580; [1979] 3 W.L.R. 605; 123 S.J. 605.
[2] [1993] 3 All E.R. 481; [1993] 3 W.L.R. 730; (1993) 23 L.S. Gaz. R. 43; [1993] NLJR 473; C.A.; *affirmed* [1995] 1 All E.R. 691; [1995] 2 W.L.R. 187; [1995] NCJR 251; 139 S.J. L.B.83, H.L.

encouraged to prepare a local will, which will save both time and expense on death. It is equally necessary however, to ensure that the foreign will does not accidentally revoke the U.K. will.

It is equally important, in these ever more litigious days, to keep a full record of both the instructions received and the advice given. This is particularly important when the client chooses to ignore the advice given and is advised of potential problems or rights, *e.g.* a claim against the estate. It is advisable to store the will file for at least twenty years.

INHERITANCE TAX

Inheritance tax (IHT) was introduced by the Finance Act 1986 which **1–009** renamed the Capital Transfer Act 1984 as "the Inheritance Tax Act 1984". To its predecessor, capital transfer tax, the 1986 Act made two major alterations:

(1) The introduction of potentially exempt transfers (PETs). A potentially exempt transfer is a transfer of value made by way of gift to an individual or into an interest in possession settlement or an accumulation and maintenance, or a disabled trust. Provided the transferor survives for seven years then no tax is payable. If the transferor dies within seven years of the gift but more than four years, then taper relief is available.

(2) Reservation of benefit. When a donor makes a gift and either the donee does not assume possession and enjoyment of the property given, or the donor is not virtually entirely excluded from the enjoyment of the property or any benefit, whether by way of contract or otherwise, on his death the property is treated as part of the donor's estate.

Thus, inheritance tax is payable on property passing on death, including **1–010** failed PETs and property whenever gifted where there was a reservation of benefit which lasted to the date of death or seven years before death, but not on any other property except settled property (other than under an accumulation and maintenance trust or a disabled trust).

The nil-rate band (currently £250,000) should increase each year. It is available both to husband and wife and should not be wasted (see Part 5; nil-rate band discretionary trust and accompanying note). With PETs falling out of charge after seven years, the nil-rate band is a useful tax planning tool. The rate of tax fixed by the Finance Act 1988 is currently 40 per cent.

GROSSING UP

In essence, inheritance tax is a tax based upon the loss to the person giving **1–011** rather than the benefit received. The tax may be paid by the donor or the donee.

On death, and subject to any contrary provision in the will, the tax will be borne out of the residuary estate. There are two, arguably three, exceptions to this rule:

(1) Where foreign property passes on the death, in which case the foreign property itself bears tax (and any foreign tax).

(2) Where tax is payable in respect of settled property (other than that settled by the will) which bears its own tax.

1–012 Arguably the third exception to the rule arises in the case of tax on a failed PET, but this is not quite so straightforward. The primary liability for the payment of tax in respect of a failed PET effectively falls on the transferee within a period of 12 months from the date of death. Thereafter it falls on the transferor's estate. Section 119(2) of the Inheritance Tax Act 1984 imposes primary liability on the transferor but section 204(8)(b) effectively postpones this for 12 months from the date of death. If the tax is not paid within 12 months of the date of death, then the Inland Revenue may have recourse to the transferor's personal representatives. Liability is limited to the assets within the estate. Strictly, therefore, this imposes on the personal representatives absolute liability for tax on transfers made by the deceased within seven years preceding the death. In circumstances where the personal representatives pay the inheritance tax, the question arises as to whether they can recover the tax they have paid from the donee. There are in fact no statutory provisions which enable the personal representatives to recover tax in these circumstances, but it has been argued that the personal representatives may have a quasi-contractual claim against the donee, although such claim is far from certain.

1–013 This does not mean that the testator should ignore the incidence of tax. He may be content for the tax to come from the residuary estate; alternatively, he may wish beneficiaries or some of them to pay their own tax. When the residue passes wholly to exempt persons, or wholly to non-exempt persons, grossing up may be ignored. Where part of the residue goes to exempt persons and part to non-exempt persons, then grossing up must be considered. It is preferable to avoid grossing up, by making such gifts bear their own tax, increasing them if necessary. The most appropriate action is to ask the testator to think about what he actually wants the effect of his will to be where there are exempt and non-exempt beneficiaries. This is even more relevant after the decision in *Re Benham's Will Trusts (Lockhart v. Harker, Reed and The Royal National Lifeboat Institution)*.[3] See also section 41 of the Inheritance Tax Act 1984 which provides that:

> "notwithstanding the terms of any disposition . . . none of the tax attributable to the value of the property comprised in residue shall fall on any gift of a share of residue if or to the extent that the transfer is exempt with respect to the gift".

[3] [1995] S.T.C. 210.

To avoid the problems created by the *Benham* decision, it is advisable to state in a will, where there is both exempt and non-exempt residue, that the non-exempt residue is to bear its own tax. Failure to do so will mean that the tax bite will be greater.

EXEMPT GIFTS

There are a number of exemptions from inheritance tax, many of which apply **1–014** only in respect of a transfer *inter vivos*. Those that are applicable in the case of testamentary gifts as well as *inter vivos* gifts are:

(1) gifts between spouses;

(2) gifts to charity without limit;

(3) gifts to specified named bodies, certain other gifts for public benefit, and subject to certain qualifications, gifts to political parties.

SETTLED PROPERTY

LIFE INTERESTS

Where property passes on the death of a life tenant, that property is treated for **1–015** inheritance tax purposes as part of his estate and is aggregated with his free estate. The tax charged is apportioned between the settled assets and the free estate and tax claimed from the trustees and executors respectively. A reversionary interest (unless acquired at any time for consideration, or one to which the settlor or his spouse was beneficially entitled, or one expectant on a lease for life or lives other than a commercial lease), is excluded from liability (Inheritance Tax Act 1984, sections 43 and 48(1)). Thus to give a life interest to a widow does not serve any particular tax purpose other than in the negative sense of potentially wasting the deceased's spouse nil rate band and a potential tax saving of £100,000 at current rates. On the death of the surviving spouse, the life interest will aggregate with her free estate with only one nil rate band available. There may be good reason for giving a surviving spouse a life interest rather than an absolute interest. For example, there is what the distinguished author, Ralph Ray, refers to as the "milkman syndrome" and the "barmaid syndrome," where the surviving spouse remarries, often with the result that the estate passes out of the family on the death of the surviving spouse. So far as the tax disadvantages are concerned, these can be remedied by creating a nil rate band discretionary trust with the residue thereafter being gifted to the spouse either absolutely or in trust so as to take full advantage of the availability of the nil rate band which otherwise would be lost.

There is, of course, no fiscal disadvantage in creating life interests for non- **1–016** spouses. Thus, if the testator has a spinster daughter or a spendthrift son, a life interest with power to advance capital might be appropriate. In the case of the spendthrift son, it might be even more appropriate to create a protective life interest under section 33 of the Wills Act 1837. In any case, it is appropriate to give powers to the trustees to advance capital, to the extent that the trust may be brought to a close. Where property is held on the statutory protective trusts or trusts "to the like effect," inheritance tax is not chargeable on the termination during the trust period of the tenant's life interest in the property, nor in respect of a distribution payment made out of the of settled property for the benefit of the life tenant. On a life tenant's interest coming to an end as a result of a disabling act or event, a discretionary trust comes into existence and accordingly, apart from special provisions, the trust fund would become subject to the 10-year periodic charge for inheritance tax purposes. For the purpose of the tax, the disabling act or event is ignored, and the beneficiary is still treated as a life tenant. If a payment of capital is made to anyone other than a beneficiary or spouse, there is a potential charge to tax, and on the death of the beneficiary there will be a transfer of value of capital remaining in the fund.

DISCRETIONARY TRUSTS

1–017 The only fiscal drawback to discretionary trusts is the 10-year periodic charge, and there are five exceptional cases:

(1) protective trusts;

(2) discretionary trusts within the nil-rate band;

(3) trusts for the handicapped;

(4) discretionary trusts which the testator intends are to be brought to an end within two years of his death;

(5) statutory accumulation and maintenance settlements.

Trusts for the handicapped

1–018 Section 89 of the Inheritance Tax Act 1984 provides that where a discretionary trust is created for the benefit of a disabled person he is treated as though he had a life interest and consequently the 10-year periodic charge does not apply. To come within the section:

(1) the beneficiary has to be a disabled person, *i.e.* one who, when the property was transferred into settlement (death in the case of a testamentary trust), was:

(a) incapable by reason of mental disorder within the meaning of the Mental Health Act 1983 of administering his property or managing his affairs, or

(b) in receipt of an attendance allowance under Social Security Contributions and Benefits Act 1992, section 64, or Social Security (Northern Ireland) Act 1975, section 35, or

(c) in receipt of a disability living allowance under Social Security Contributions and Benefits Act 1992, section 71, by virtue of entitlement to the care component at the highest or middle rate;

8

(2) the settled property is held on trusts under which, during the life of the beneficiary, no interest in possession subsists and which secure that not less than half the settled property which is applied during his life is applied for his benefit.

If the above conditions are complied with the trust fund is treated on the same footing as property held on protective trusts.

Two-year discretionary trusts

Although the Inheritance Tax Act 1984 does not refer to a two-year **1–019** discretionary trust, it does provide in section 144 that where a discretionary trust is established under a will and within two years from the testator's death, the discretion is exercised so that, apart from special provision, inheritance tax would be eligible (or potentially eligible) on the exercise, the exercise does not give rise to inheritance tax and the taxing provisions apply as if the will provided for devolution of the property in accordance with the exercise.

This provision can be particularly important to a testator who has children under the age of 18 who could not join in a deed of variation (assuming that they survive for very much longer). Given that the testator has no way of calculating the fiscal impact of his death, it provides a two-year breathing space for the trustees (one of whom should preferably be the surviving spouse) to let the dust settle and then appoint as necessary.

Accumulation and maintenance settlements

A number of conditions must be fulfilled to qualify as a "statutory" **1–020** accumulation and maintenance settlement:

(1) one or more persons must on or before attaining an age not exceeding 25 years become entitled to either the capital fund or an interest in possession in the fund;

(2) there must be a beneficiary in existence when the settlement is established;

(3) there is no interest in possession in the fund and the income is to be accumulated (*i.e.* there must be a trust, not merely a power involved to accumulate), so far as not applied for maintenance, education or benefit of a beneficiary; and

(4) either:

(a) not more than 25 years have elapsed from whichever is the later of the date of the settlement and the date when the conditions in sub-paragraphs (1) and (3) were satisfied; or

(b) all the beneficiaries are either grandchildren of a common grand-parent or children or spouses of the beneficiaries who have died before the time when, had they survived, they would have become entitled under sub-paragraph (1).

1–021 A number of points arise which are worthy of note:

(1) The settlement may be established by will or *inter vivos*.

(2) Where a person is entitled contingently on attaining any age, and section 31 of the Trustee Act 1925 applies, the legacy complies with the conditions because the whole income belongs to the child on majority and then he has a life interest.

(3) The conditions will apply even if the contingency fails.

(4) If there is no beneficiary when the settlement commences, there is a liability to inheritance tax on a beneficiary coming into existence. It is however, irrelevant if a beneficiary dies leaving no beneficiary.

(5) In practice the 25-year rule under sub-paragraph (4)(a) may be quite sufficient in many cases, and therefore the draftsman may disregard the limitation of beneficiaries under sub-paragraph (4)(b).

(6) A settlement will not be excluded merely because there are remainders over, if no beneficiary lives to attain a vested interest.

(7) Under sub-paragraph (4)(b) children and spouses of grandchildren cannot be included as beneficiaries unless the grandchild in question must have taken a vested interest in some part of the trust fund had he survived. If a power of appointment could have excluded him, he would not have been a beneficiary who "will have become entitled" under paragraph (1) above but merely someone who might have become entitled.

When the conditions are complied with:

(1) the payment to a beneficiary out of settled property is not a capital distribution liable to tax;

(2) there is no periodic charge to inheritance tax during the period in which the income is to be accumulated;

(3) there is no charge to inheritance tax on the beneficiaries becoming entitled.

TRUSTS OF LAND AND APPOINTMENT OF TRUSTEES ACT 1996

1–022 This Act (which came into force on January 1, 1997) is "An Act to make new provision about trusts of land including provision phasing out the Settled Land Act 1925 abolishing the doctrine of conversion and otherwise amending the law about trusts for sale of land; to amend the law about the appointment and retirement of trustees of any trusts; and for connected purposes".

The Act has abolished statutory trusts for sale. Strict settlements under the Settled Land Act 1925 may no longer be created and existing settlements are to be phased out over a period of time. It replaces with a single system the previous dual system of trusts for sale and strict settlements under the Settled Land Act. The Act also widens the powers of trustees, permitting them to delegate to a tenant for life or any other qualifying beneficiary; it gives to certain beneficiaries the right to be consulted by trustees in the exercise of any function relating to the land subject to a trust and for their wishes to be given effect to, and it confers new rights on beneficiaries both to appoint and to remove trustees. As stated in the preamble above it also abolished the doctrine of conversion. Practitioners will be familiar with the doctrine, the effects of which have been mitigated over the years by the courts, not least in *Williams and Glyn's Bank Limited v. Boland.*[4]

A "trust of land" is defined in section 1 of the Act as meaning any trust of **1–023** property which consists of or includes land other than land which is settled land or to which the Universities and College Estates Act 1925 applies. "Trustees of land" means trustees of a trust of land. It is the trust of land which replaces the statutory trust for sale. Although it is still possible to create an express trust for sale, which a testator may wish to do, trustees now have a power to sell, which is balanced by a power to retain, and there is no overriding duty to sell. An express trust for sale may be appropriate in some circumstances, tipping the scales in favour of sale over retention, possibly in the event of a dispute between beneficiaries. If an express trust for sale is created, then there is implied a power to postpone without liability on the part of the trustees.

Section 6(1) provides that "for the purpose of exercising their function as **1–024** trustees, the trustees of land have in relation to the land subject to the trust, all the powers of an absolute owner". Note, however, that the powers are only conferred "in relation to the land". The powers must be exercised having regard to the rights of beneficiaries and section 6(4) gives the trustees a specific power to buy land in England and Wales by way of investment, for occupation by any beneficiary or for any other reason. It has been suggested that as a consequence *Re Power, Public Trustees v. Hastings*[5] is overruled. This is not necessarily the case. Remember this is a power for trustees of land and if there were never any land in the trust then the power does not exist. Furthermore, it is debatable as to whether trustees of land, having sold land may invest more than the net proceeds of sale in acquiring land. For this reason, it is appropriate to retain the power for trustees to invest in land, see, *e.g.,* para. **3–003**.

The trustees of land are given additional powers under sections 6 and 7 of **1–025** the Act, including a power to convey the land to beneficiaries, even though they are not required to do so. Land may also be partitioned between beneficiaries, but only with their consent. The powers given to trustees under sections 6 and 7 may by virtue of section 8(2) be excluded by the disposition creating the trust.

[4] [1981] A.C. 487; [1980] 3 W.L.R. 138; (1980) 124 S.J. 443; [1980] 2 All E.R. 408; (1980) 40 P.&C.R. 451, H.4.; *affirming* [1979] Ch. 312; [1979] 2 W.L.R. 550; (1979) S.J. 183; [1979] 2 All E.R. 697, C.A.
[5] [1947] Ch. 572; [1947] 2 All E.R. 282.

Trustees also have, by virtue of section 9, authority to delegate by power of attorney to any beneficiary or beneficiaries of full age and beneficially entitled to an interest in possession in the land, subject to the trusts any of their trust functions which relate to the land.

It was common for testators to provide that a sale required consent, *e.g.* of the life tenant, or indeed that the exercise of all statutory powers required the consent of one or more third parties. Where the consent of more than two persons was required, section 26(1) of the Law of Property Act 1925 provided that the consent of any two such persons was sufficient for a purchaser, even though as against beneficiaries it might still be a breach of trust. Section 10(1) TLATA makes similar provisions in relation to trusts of land. It does not apply, however, to personal representatives (section 18(1)).

1–026 Section 11(1) requires trustees to consult with beneficiaries in the exercise of any function relating to land subject to the trust. The beneficiary must be of full age and beneficially entitled to an interest in possession (not defined) in the land. Again, section 18(1) provides that section 11 does not apply to personal representatives.

Subject to the provisions of section 13, section 12 gives to a beneficiary entitled to an interest in possession in land subject to a trust of land an entitlement by reason of his interest to occupy the land, if the purpose of the trust included making the land available for his occupation (or beneficiaries of the class of which he is a member or of beneficiaries in general), or the land is held by the trustees so as to be so available. The entitlements of a beneficiary under section 12 may be limited or excluded by the trust instrument.

1–027 Part II of the Act is concerned with the appointment and retirement of trustees, and confers upon beneficiaries certain rights in relation to both the appointment of trustees and their removal. These provisions extend to trusts generally and are not limited to trusts of land. They apply where (section 19) there is no person nominated for the purpose of appointing new trustees by the instrument (if any) creating a trust, and also (section 20) to the appointment of a substitute trustee for an incapable trustee where there is no person who is entitled, willing and able to appoint a trustee under section 36(1) of the Trustee Act 1925. These powers may be excluded and it is for the testator to decide as to whether they should or not.

Section 22 to be found in Part III of the Act, defines, in subsection (1), "Beneficiary" in relation to a trust as being any person who under the trust has an interest in property subject to the trust (including a person who has such an interest as a trustee or a personal representative); clearly this would not extend to a beneficiary under a discretionary trust.[6]

1–028 Additional common form clauses have been inserted in this edition, limiting or excluding certain rights and powers under the Act, of both trustees and beneficiaries, for use in appropriate cases.

---

[6] *Gartside v. I.R.C.* [1968] A.C. 553; [1967] 2 All E.R. 173; [1967] 3 W.L.R. 671; 46 ATC 25.

FAMILY PROVISION

INHERITANCE (PROVISION FOR FAMILY AND DEPENDANTS) ACT 1975, AS AMENDED BY THE LAW REFORM (SUCCESSION) ACT 1995

The Inheritance (Provision for Family and Dependants) Act 1975 which **1–029** repealed the Inheritance (Family Provision) Act 1938 and sections 26–28 of the Matrimonial Causes Act 1965, as subsequently amended by section 2 of the Law Reform (Succession) Act 1995, now governs the situation where a dependant claims that the disposition of the deceased's estate either by will or on intestacy fails to make adequate provision for him or her. Dependants under the 1975 Act are a spouse, a former spouse (provided he or she has not remarried — whether or not the later marriage still subsists at the date of the testator's death), a child of the testator, a person treated by the testator as a child of the family, and any other person who immediately before the death of the testator was being maintained, either wholly or partly, by the testator. The Law Reform (Succession) Act 1995 inserted, in relation to persons dying on or after January 1, 1996, a new category of applicant who, not a spouse or unremarried former spouse of the deceased, has during the whole of the period of two years preceding the deceased's death, lived in the same household and as husband or wife of the deceased.

In all cases, other than the surviving spouse, provision is for what is **1–030** reasonable in all the circumstances for dependants to receive by way of maintenance, whereas in respect of the spouse of the deceased, the court must order what is reasonable in all the circumstances whether or not that provision is required for the surviving spouse's maintenance. Applications under the Act should be made before the end of the period of six months from the date on which representation to the estate of the deceased is first taken out, and the Act only applies to the estates of deceased persons dying domiciled in England and Wales.

An order under the Act made by the court can take almost any conceivable **1–031** form; periodical payments, a transfer or settlement of property, or a variation of a previous settlement. For the purpose of proceedings under the Act the testator's estate is treated as including property comprised in a *donatio mortis causa*. The court can make an order that the deceased's share in a joint tenancy or part of it, shall be treated as part of the testator's net estate, and furthermore, where within six years of the death the testator made a disposition "with the intention of defeating an application for financial provision" under the Act, the donor shall pay up to the net amount of money or property received under the dispositions. For inheritance tax purposes any order made by the court is treated as though made by the deceased.

Perhaps predictably when first introduced the Act was hailed by the tabloid press as "the mistresses charter". However, by including a mistress as a dependant, the Act underlines that she has rights which may be just as great as or indeed greater than those of a wife, from whom perhaps the testator has been separated for some considerable time, even though not judicially separated. Advising clients in these circumstances is often difficult. Case law on the Act is quite limited, possibly because the vast majority of cases commenced under the Act are settled.

1–032 The Act itself provides that a statement made by the deceased, whether orally or in a document or otherwise, shall be admissible as evidence of any facts stated therein of which direct oral evidence by him would be admissible (section 21).

It should be noted that whether a provision is reasonable or not is to be determined on the facts known at the date of the hearing, and not the date of death, and the test is objective rather than subjective.

DIVORCE AND SEPARATION

1–033 The Administration of Justice Act 1982, section 18(2), inserted section 18A into the Wills Act 1837 and provided that a decree of divorce or nullity, subject to a contrary intention appearing in the will, would take effect as if the appointment of the spouse as executor or executor and trustee were omitted, that any testamentary gift to him or her would lapse, and if she or he were given a life interest then that would accelerate the remainder interests.

1–034 In *Re Sinclair*[7] the Court of Appeal held that this provision did not have the effect of treating the former spouse as predeceasing the testator so as to give effect to any alternative gift in the will. This defect was remedied by section 3(1) of the Law Reform (Succession) Act 1995, amending section 18A(1) for deaths on or after January 1, 1996. The amended section 18A(1) deems the former spouse to have died when the marriage was dissolved or annulled. The provision is subject to a contrary intention appearing in the will.

Separation will have no effect on the dispositions under a will. However, in such circumstances, it would seem sensible to review any existing will or advise a client as to the application of the rules of intestacy.

THE FAMILY, CHILDREN AND ISSUE

1–035 We live in an age not uncommonly referred to as that of the "nuclear family". Amongst the issues confronting the solicitor in advising a client are second, and subsequent, marriages and the resulting second and subsequent families, increased cohabitation and same-sex relationships.

In advising testators who are divorced and remarried, it is important to deal first with the impact, if any, of the Inheritance (Provision for Family and Dependants) Act 1975. Claims under the Act may have been excluded under the terms of the divorce, but it is essential to find out and advise on the potential consequences if claims under that Act have not been excluded and remain a threat.

Where two or more families are involved, it is important to clarify whether the spouses wish to ring-fence their own estates, passing them ultimately to

[7] [1984] 3 All E.R. 362; [1984] 1 W.L.R. 1240; [1985] F.L.R. 229; 15 Fam. Law. 94; 128 S.J. 753; 81 L.S. Gaz. R. 3254; *affirmed* [1985] Ch. 446; [1985] 1 All E.R. 1066; [1985] 2 W.L.R. 795; [1985] F.L.R. 965; 15 Fam. Law 227, C.A.

their own children. If so, then a life interest trust for the surviving spouse will be the appropriate vehicle with remainders onto the deceased spouse's children. The position of cohabitees has been considered particularly in relation to the Inheritance (Provision for Family and Dependants) Act 1975 as extended. Certainly, so far as the Law Reform (Succession) Act 1995 is concerned, a person of the same sex as the deceased would be unable to claim under that Act and would be dependent upon the 1975 Act as a person who immediately before the death of the testator was being maintained either wholly or partly by the testator.

The Family Law Reform Act 1987 replaced Part 2 of the Family Law **1–036** Reform Act 1969 which governed the entitlement of illegitimate persons. Section 1 of the 1987 Act provides that, unless a contrary intention appears, references (however expressed) to any relationship between two persons shall be construed without regard as to whether or not the father and mother of either of them, or the father and mother of any persons for whom the relationship is deduced have or had been married to each other at any time. Thus illegitimate children are put on the same footing as legitimate children and the same rule applies to other relationships. The protection previously enjoyed by personal representatives by virtue of section 17 of the Family Law Reform Act 1969 has ceased to have effect and for the future personal representatives will have to rely on the protection afforded by notice under section 27 of the Trustee Act 1925.

Decisions need to be taken as to the age upon which a child or children of **1–037** the testator will attain an entitlement to capital. Notwithstanding the legal age of majority being 18, testators often prefer to delay an entitlement until 21 or 25, and on occasions even later. If the beneficiary is an infant, the gift will generally constitute an accumulation and maintenance trust until the beneficiary becomes entitled to the income or capital. A power of advancement should be given to the trustees.

WILLS ACT 1837, SECTION 33

The Administration of Justice Act 1982 substituted a new section 33 in place **1–038** of the old section 33 of the Wills Act 1837. The section deals with a gift by will to a child or other issue of the testator and the new section extends the class gifts to children "or remoter descendants of the testator". Then, subject to a contrary intention appearing in the will, if, in the case of a gift other than a class gift, the donee dies before the testator, his issue living at his death take according to the stocks in his place. In the case of a class gift, if a member of the class dies, the gift is presumed to take effect as if the class included the issue of the deceased member living at the testator's death according to the stocks.

The effect of the new section is not wholly satisfactory. If a testator makes a gift to his son and the son predeceases him, leaving a widow and child, and under the son's will or intestacy his estate passes to his widow, under the old section 33 the widow took. Under the new section the child takes, even if he or she is a minor.

The old section 33 did not apply to class gifts, as in such a case the share of **1–039** the deceased member of the class did not lapse but accrued to the other members of the class. Thus, in the case of a gift to children, where one child died, his or her share passed to his siblings, whether or not the deceased child had children of his own. The new section 33 remedies this defect by providing in such circumstances that the gift "shall take effect as if the class included the issue of its deceased member living at the testator's death". Section 33 will apply unless a contrary intention appears in the will.

SPECIAL PROPERTIES

AGRICULTURAL PROPERTY

1–040 Agricultural property means agricultural land or pasture, and includes woodlands and any building used in connection with the intensive rearing of livestock or fish, if the woodland or building is occupied with agricultural land or pasture and the occupation is ancillary to that of agricultural land or pasture. It also includes such cottages, farm buildings and farmhouses, together with land occupied with them, as are of a character appropriate to the property.

Agricultural value is the value of agricultural property on the assumption that it is subject to a perpetual covenant prohibiting its use other than as agricultural property.

1–041 To obtain agricultural property relief the testator or transferor must either occupy the property for the purposes of agriculture throughout the period of two years ending with the date of the transfer, or have owned the property for a period of seven years ending with the date of transfer, during which period it must have been occupied by someone for the purpose of agriculture.

1–042 For agricultural property relief to apply to buildings they must be occupied. The relief is a percentage reduction of the value transferred by a transfer of value. The appropriate percentage is:

(1) 100 per cent in relation to the transfers of value made, and other events occurring after March 9, 1992 of the agricultural value of the property transferred, if either

(a) the transferor immediately before the transfer enjoyed either the right to vacant possession or the right to obtain it within the next 12 months; or

(b) the transferor has been beneficially entitled to his interest since before March 10, 1981; and

(i) if he had disposed of it by a transfer of value immediately before that date he would have been entitled to claim the 50 per cent relief available after April 6, 1976 and before March 10, 1981; and

(ii) that relief would not have been restricted by reference to the limits of £250,000 or 1,000 acres (whichever was the more favourable to the tax payer) applying between those dates; and

(iii) the interest did not in the period from March 10, 1981 to the date of transfer give the vacant possession rights in (1)(a) above and did not fail to give him those rights because of any Act or deliberate omission by him during that period;

(2) 100 per cent in relation to transfers of value of farmland let for periods exceeding 12 months which is let on or after September 1, 1995 (to coincide with the commencement of the Agricultural Tenancies Act 1995);

(3) 50 per cent in relation to transfers of value made and other events occurring after March 9, 1992 in cases not covered by (1) or (2) above.

An Inland Revenue press release dated February 13, 1995 published an **1–043** extra-statutory concession which extends to 100 per cent from 50 per cent the agricultural property relief where the transferor's interest in the property either:

(1) carries the right to vacant possession within 24 months from the date of transfer, or

(2) is notwithstanding the terms of the tenancy, valued at an amount broadly equivalent to vacant possession value. In purely tax planning terms it is inappropriate to leave property subject to 100 per cent relief to a surviving spouse. Generally speaking farm assets, *e.g.* plant and machinery, live and dead stock which would not qualify for agricultural property relief will qualify for business property relief.

The Agricultural Tenancies Act 1995 has introduced a new type of tenancy **1–044** and these will run along side the old-style Agricultural Holdings Act 1986 tenancies for some years to come.

Under the 1986 Act, tenancies of agricultural holdings do not necessarily come to an end on the death of a farming tenant. In circumstances where a 1986 Act tenancy acquires rights of succession, it is a valuable asset for which a tenant farmer will need to make specific provision in his will.

He may by will designate a member of his family as the person he wishes to succeed him as tenant of his holding. Members of the family consist of the tenant's spouse, brother, sister and child (including a person treated by the tenant as a child of his family). To be eligible to claim a tenancy, the nominee must not be a farmer of another holding and must have worked on the tenant's holding, normally for a period of five years.

Even assuming these conditions are fulfilled, an application must be made within three months of the death to the agricultural land tribunal, which must be satisfied that the applicant is suitable. There are certain cases where these provisions do not apply, *e.g.* when the tenant has a fixed term of which more than 27 months remain unexpired at the date of death.

The importance of nomination is that the nominee must be confirmed if he **1–045** is eligible and suitable. The nomination can be by specific bequest of the tenancy of the holding, or a statement mentioning the holding or the deceased's tenancy of it and exclusively designating a person whether by name or description, as the person the testator wishes to succeed him as tenant. The nomination may be of different persons in different circumstances if (in the events which happen) the statement exclusively designates a particular person. With the consent of the landlord but only with such consent, the tribunal may specify 2, 3 or 4 applicants and thus entitle them to a joint tenancy. It seems clear that a testator cannot by will specify joint nominees directly, but he can do so indirectly. Thus:

> "In relation to my tenancy of Ten Pounder Farm Spalding Lincolnshire I designate my son Peter as the person I wish to succeed me as tenant of the holding and I request that, if the landlord consents, a tenancy of the holding shall be granted jointly to my son and my wife Hilda".

1–046 When designating someone as successor to agricultural tenancy it must not be overlooked that the tribunal may not find him eligible or suitable and the legacy of the live and dead stock should have regard to this, *e.g.* by providing that if someone else is appointed successor he shall have an option to purchase it.

Under the 1995 Act, which controls new farming tenancies created on or after September 1, 1995, there are no statutory rights of succession, but the tenancy can in some circumstances still be an asset of a deceased farmer's estate. Farm business tenancies, unlike the Agricultural Holdings Act 1986 tenancies, have little statutory regulation and the parties are largely free to negotiate the terms of their tenancy contract.

1–047 One of the fundamentals of the farm business tenancy is that the landlord will be able to regain possession on termination of the contractual term. Unless the farm business tenancy is for a long period of years, it is highly unlikely that its value will be anywhere near as high as a yearly tenancy of a 1986 Act agricultural holding with potential succession rights. Indeed, there may well be specific provision in the tenancy agreement itself for termination on the death or incapacity of the tenant.

That aside, the 1995 Act does not limit the tenant's choice of beneficiary, though again there could be some limitation in the tenancy agreement; and it would appear to be the case that an assignment of a farming tenancy on the death of a tenant will not, in itself, constitute a breach of a prohibition against assignment in the tenancy agreement. It follows therefore that the farming tenant will, in appropriate circumstances, still be concerned to see that arrangements are made on his death for the transmission of the tenancy for the remaining period of the contractual term.

BUSINESS PROPERTY

1–048 There are certain practical considerations when dealing with the gift of business by will. Thus it is prudent to include within the will powers for the trustees to borrow. Redundancy can be a problem, though if the business is sold as a going concern then there is likely to be a transfer of undertakings. If the beneficial interest in the business devolves in a different way from the rest of the estate, then the beneficiary of the business should normally be required to bear any expenses of compensation for redundancy or unfair dismissal, and these liabilities will be taken into account when valuing the business.

Where certain conditions are satisfied, relief from inheritance tax is available on the transfer of relevant business property, and as with agricultural property relief, the relief is a percentage reduction in the value transferred. For business property relief to be available, the business must be a qualifying business, the assets must be relevant business property and there is a minimum period of ownership.

A qualifying business includes a business carried on by way of profession or **1–049** vocation. Where the business consists wholly or mainly in dealing in securities, stocks or shares, land or buildings, or making or holding investments the relief does not apply unless the business is wholly that of a market maker or that of a discount house (in either case carried on in the United Kingdom) or that of a holding company for one or more companies whose business does qualify.

Relevant business property falls into two categories: (a) unincorporated businesses or interests in such businesses, which would include sole traders, professionals and shares in partnership and include assets deposited with Lloyds by individual underwriters, and (b) quoted or unquoted shares or securities in a company carrying on a qualifying business.

The minimum period of ownership is two years immediately preceding the **1–050** transfer or, where the property replaced other property which qualified (apart from the two-year period) immediately before the replacement, and both properties together (or all properties if other qualifying property had been previously replaced directly or indirectly) were owned by the transferor, for at least two years out of the five years immediately preceding the transfer.

Where the appropriate conditions apply then relief is available either at 100 per cent or 50 per cent, depending upon the class of relevant property.

Partnership shares are included within the definition of a qualifying business. In many cases the deceased's partnership share will pass under the Deed of Partnership and in such a case, assuming that full consideration is given for the provision, the testator and his estate are concerned only with the consideration which still gets the relief, and not the actual value of the assets. Investment companies, companies subject to a contract for sale and companies in liquidation (save for the purpose of reconstruction on amalgamation), do not qualify for the relief. Where tax is payable, it is subject to the benefit of the instalment option over 10 years and the instalments do not bear interest if duly paid. If the business or part thereof, or the deceased's interest or part thereof, is sold, the balance of the tax or of the appropriate proportion becomes payable and, in the case of a partnership, the payment out of the deceased's share (in whole or in part) is treated as a sale.

It is appropriate to mention here, albeit briefly, the potential tax trap created **1–051** by section 39A of the Inheritance Tax Act 1984, introduced by the Finance Act 1986. Where the whole of an estate passes either to an exempt beneficiary, *e.g.* a spouse, or to a non-exempt beneficiary then section 39A will not apply. It does apply where there are gifts to exempt and non-exempt beneficiaries and business property relief or agricultural property relief is available. If there is a specific gift of property which qualifies for the relief, *e.g.* the gift by a trader of his grocery business to his son, then under the present rules the effect of business property relief will be to reduce the value transferred by the appropriate percentage, presently 100 per cent, and so the asset will pass tax-free. By contrast, if the business were taken by the son as part of his share of residue, then it is not a specific gift within section 39A and the gross estate has the business property relief applied rateably, thereby creating an unnecessary charge to tax.

1–052   It is questionable whether a gift of a relevant business or agricultural property to one person (which could conceivably take the form of a gift of residue to a surviving spouse) subject to a testamentary option, *e.g.* to her son (a non-exempt beneficiary) is a specific gift of the property within section 39A. It is not possible with any certainty to answer that question, and given the element of doubt, a discretionary trust might be the preferred solution.

ANNUITIES

1–053   My own experience in drafting wills over a number of years leads me to conclude that annuities are less than fashionable. There may, however, be circumstances when an annuity is appropriate. One of the difficulties is that for inheritance tax purposes the annuitant is treated as having a life interest in the underlying capital, which may result in a charge on the death of the annuitant. Where the will contains a direction to purchase, the beneficiary is entitled to demand the purchase money instead of the annuity.[8]

Of course, a fixed annuity will take no account of inflation, which may cause difficulty for an annuitant who survives the testator for a number of years.

ADMINISTRATIVE MACHINERY

1–054   Whilst it is sometimes difficult to persuade testators that lawyers do not in fact charge by the word or the page for a will, there is resistance to lengthy documents, particularly where one is instructed to keep it simple. It is worth taking the time to explain to testators that the various administrative provisions are required to avoid complications in the future, *e.g.* apportionment, to give the trustees power properly to invest the trust funds by giving the trustees the widest possible powers and to deal with such everyday matters as insurance.

The cost of delivery of chattels is borne by the donee unless there is a contrary provision in the will. The testator may wish this expense to fall on his estate and include a power to insure the chattels until delivery.

There is always a temptation these days to run off a computer print-out of an extraordinarily lengthy document containing all sorts of esoteric provisions, most of which might never affect the estate in question. If that temptation exists, then be prepared to be interrogated by the client who unexpectedly reads every word and seeks an explanation.

---

[8] *Stokes v. Cheek (1860) 28 beav. 620; 29 L.J.Ch. 922.*

VARIATIONS AND DISCLAIMERS

DEEDS OF VARIATION

A deed of variation may be made within two years of an individual's death, to **1–055** vary the destination of property passing on that death without incurring additional inheritance tax. Such a variation may be of the deceased's will, in whole or in part, or of the disposition on intestacy. The range of persons to whom benefits may be directed is wide, and includes parties benefiting under the will or intestacy, members of the family and strangers.

It is a most useful tax-planning tool, but be warned. An attempt was made by the previous government to abolish deeds of variation and when that failed they pledged to review the situation. Since that time there has been silence on the subject, but doubts over the long-term availability of deeds of variation remain.

In respect of variations, as opposed to disclaimers, it is necessary to elect to **1–056** the Board of Inland Revenue, normally within six months of the instrument effecting variation, if it is wished to take advantage of the relief. It no longer matters that the beneficiary who effects the variation has received some benefit, *e.g.* dividends, interest or a right of occupation, in contrast to disclaimers. A variation can take effect as to part of the gift of residue or a specific gift, but not in the case of a disclaimer unless specifically authorised by the will. It is not possible to reduce a minor's interest without the court's consent, and care should be taken when *per stirpes* provisions are included in the will. There is a similar relief for capital gains tax purposes,[9] as well as stamp duty,[10] but not relief for income tax liability.

Following the recent decision in *Russell v. IRC,*[11] beware of trying to take **1–057** two bites of the cherry. The case decided that once the deed of variation had been entered into, a further purported redirection to be treated as made by the deceased was not valid in respect of the assets in question, and that further redirections did not have this retrospective effect. For example, if a pecuniary legacy is increased by a deed of variation and later increased again by another deed of variation, the Revenue would not allow the second variation because the residue is merely reduced by both deeds. However, contrast this with the decision in the *Lake v. Lake and Others*[12] in which the court allowed a rectification of a deed of variation to achieve a legitimate tax advantage where the document contained errors and the rectification gave effect to the intention of the parties. Variations also apply for capital gains tax purposes (TCGA 1992, section 62) but where a settlement is involved the beneficiary effecting the variation is likely to be the settlor.[13]

[9] TCGA, s.62(6).
[10] Finance Act 1985, s. 84.
[11] [1988] 2 All E.R. 405; [1988] 1 W.L.R. 834.
[12] [1989] S.T.C. 865.
[13] *Marshall (Inspector of Taxes) v. Kerr* [1995] 1 A.C. 148; [1994] 3 W.L.R. 299.

DISCLAIMERS

1–058 In a case of variation, the beneficiary redirects the dispositions as he chooses; in the case of a disclaimer, the beneficiary normally has no choice and the disclaimer merely accelerates the subsequent interest, *e.g.* a legacy disclaimed may fall into residue. So far as variation is concerned, part of a specific gift or share of residue can be redirected, but in the case of a disclaimer it appears that the whole interest must be disclaimed. For this reason it may be appropriate to leave an individual a series of legacies (or shares of residue). However, under current practice a partial disclaimer is permissible if the will includes a power to this effect. This has been confirmed by the Capital Taxes Office.[14]

STEP AND THE STANDARD PROVISIONS

1–059 The Society of Trust and Estate Practitioners (STEP) was founded in 1991.The governing body is the Council, all the members of which sit on other specialist committees. One of the first proposals of the Technical Committee was for the publication of standard administrative clauses which could be incorporated in settlements or wills by reference, to enable such documents to be both shorter and simpler. A practice direction allows wills which incorporate the STEP provisions to be proved in the normal way without separately proving the text of the provisions.

1–060 A book such as this would be incomplete without these provisions. They are largely the work of James Kessler and he has also prepared a separate commentary upon them. Both the provisions and the newly updated commentary are reproduced in full in Appendices II and III. I am deeply indebted to the Society and to James Kessler for their generosity (and encouragement) in permitting me to reproduce the standard provisions and commentary.

ADVANCE DIRECTIVES (LIVING WILLS)

1–061 We have incorporated just one precedent, giving a variety of options. Certain organisations, notably the Terence Higgins Trust and the Volunatry Euthenasia Society, offer alternatives. People are living longer, and the combination of advances in medical science and the sanctity of life mean that more and more of us can look forward to being kept going when perhaps we would rather not. These documents are not binding and can therefore be nothing more than an indication to both the medical profession and the family of an individual's wishes as to the limits of medical treatment that they think appropriate.

---

[14] See exchange of correspondence in Tolley's Practical tax, June 28, 1989, page 102.10.

PRINCIPLES FOR REDRAFTING THE 13TH EDITION

1 Fundamentals

(a) The basic aim of the revised precedents is that they should always be **1–062** understood by the testator. They should therefore always be in plain modern English.

   We have not failed if the testator needs an explanation of the effect of technical clauses, but we have failed if a testator needs explanatory notes on what the will actually means.

(b) What differentiates *Brighouse* from other will drafting books is that it focuses on complete wills, rather than working clause-by-clause. Nevertheless, in drafting we should work clause-by-clause, and make it easy, when using our precedents disc, for a solicitor and secretary to do the same.

2 Drafting Policy

Plain English

(a) Every clause should have a heading, to give structure to the will and **1–063** enable the testator to understand and navigate it easily.

(b) We should consistently draft in present tense, saving the future for those circumstances where it is clearly required by the sense.

(c) Every word we use should be either:

   (i) an everyday modern English word; or
   (ii) a term of art (in which case we should consider whether it can be replaced by modern English or explained there-and-then in a few words of modern English); or
   (iii) a term defined in the will itself.

(d) we should apply the "under 15 word average sentence length" rule, but amend it so that it's "under 15 unbroken words average" instead. That will allow us to use colons and semi-colons with carriage returns, and treat them as if they were sentence breaks for the purposes of the 15-word rule.

(e) Wills should be punctuated.

Practical

(a) Ease of use for the solicitor and secretary should be a primary **1–064** consideration.

(b) Clauses should be drafted, so far as possible, to reduce the possibility of careless error by the drafting solicitor.

(c) Clauses should always say what they mean. They should never rely on a legal fiction, nor on a form of words which has been held in such-and-such a case to have such-and-such an effect.

(d) Throughout the book, whenever saying the same thing, we should always say it the same way.

(e) We should purge all alternative versions of the same thing. We should definitely never have a "long form" and a "short form" for the same thing.

(f) Defined terms should have their definition at the start of the clause where they are needed. A long definition clause is very difficult for a solicitor and secretary to keep track of, and encourages errors. The advantage of a definition clause is obvious in a very long document like a commercial contract, but in a relatively short document like a will there is no such advantage.

(g) Statutory provisions, and rules from case law, should never be referred to without the clause explaining *what* is being referred to.

(h) We should avoid tautology while trying to give the impression of thoroughness, in phrases such as "release and forgive" or "give, devise and bequeath".

(i) We should use shorter forms where no meaning is added by a longer form. For example, "legacies" is better than "legacies given by this Will or any codicil to it".

(j) The will should not contain a provision to the effect that the clause headings are to be ignored in interpreting the will. Clause headings should be meaningful and integrated into the drafting.

(k) The will should not contain a provision that defined terms apply "only where the context so admits." If well drafted, the context should always admit. Even if a mistake is made, the law is not such an ass that it will impose a meaning in a place where the context does not admit it. Besides, if such a dilemma does come before a judge, a "context so admits" clause will not help him to solve it.

(l) We should express numbers as numbers, not words, and without trailing decimals unless they are significant. We should not repeat amounts of money. Therefore "£50" not "fifty pounds (£50)".

(m) We should abandon Latin forms which have not found acceptance in modern English. "Executors", for example, is the English word for that particular office, and it should not be expressed as "executrices" even where the office holders are plural and female. ("Testatrix" has not been used, for the same reason.)

3 Computer Issues

Drafting

(a) To help the secretary who has to use our precedents, we should use **1–065**
Word stop-codes on the precedents disc. That gave us a policy decision
to make for the text of the book — *i.e.* whether to express those things
in the traditional way:

> "I give £(x) to [name] absolutely."

Or use stop-codes there also:

> "I give £$/ to $/ absolutely."

The second looks more clumsy on the page, but it could be said to
have the advantage that the lawyer would be seeing the same as her
secretary, and (using the explanations in the text) could use that fact to
guide the secretary through the precedents while dictating.

(b) Again for ease of use, we should develop a "Word outline", along the
lines of:

Body Text

1   CLAUSE HEADING

Text
(a) Sub-clause text
   (i) Sub-sub-clause text
      (A) Sub-sub-sub-clause text
         (I) Sub-sub-sub-sub-clause text

. . . with a kind of informal rule that we try not to go beyond small
romans without good reason.

In the text of the book, we might, for brevity, feel the desire to write things **1–066**
like "[insert clauses 2–4 from precedent 91]". We should resist that temptation, and instead set out such text, in full, since only then will the precedents
disk be truly useful to a solicitor and secretary who want to use it in practice.

4 Trustees' powers

The twelfth edition of *Brighouse* gives the user: **1–067**

(i) the wording of individual trustees' powers; and

(ii) complete wills;

but not a set of trustees' powers to insert into wills of specific kinds. The
problem is that to use it in practice you have to go through the whole section

dictating something like "add clauses 19, 20, 24, 25, 26, 29, 30, 32, 34, 37, 40, 41, 42, 45, 46, and 48", whereas if you build one set of powers which is right for such-and-such a type of will, the solicitor only has to dictate "add clause 86" and the job is done.

1–068 The word "shall" presents grammatical problems. The consensus among writers on grammar is that the usage of the words "shall" and "will" is so inconsistent that even where they are used correctly readers will not necessarily understand them in their grammatically correct sense, nor assume that they have been used correctly, nor even recognise the problems (on which we refer you to any text book on the subject). The word "shall" is obsolescent in everyday English, but is widely used by lawyers. We have tried, where possible, to use "may" where a person is being given a power, "must" where a person is being given a duty, and have tried to write consistently in present tense, avoiding the future unless the context absolutely requires it.

1–069 We have, very reluctantly, abandoned the practice of giving initial capitals to defined terms. Although widely used by lawyers, we nevertheless had to accept that:

(a) the practice is not standard English;

(b) it does not aid clarity to have documents where "property" means something different from "Property"; and

(c) in any event capitalisation is generally not used properly. Indeed, in the field of wills the word "Executor" is almost always given a capital initial whether it is being used in its defined sense, or merely as a common noun.

1–070 Our approach has been to avoid defining terms, and instead to use terms as common nouns wherever this creates no ambiguity. Where necessary we have defined terms, but have used lower-case initials.

1–071 We have included many fewer notes than previous editions. Our feeling was that the plainer English of the text made accompanying notes less necessary.

PART 2

COMMON FORM CLAUSES

COMMON FORM CLAUSES

COMMENCEMENT & APPOINTMENTS

1 Commencement

This is the last will of me $/ of $/.   2–001

1 REVOCATION

I revoke all former wills.

2 Appointing private executors

1 APPOINTMENT OF EXECUTOR   2–002

(a) I appoint $/ $/[and $/$/] to be my $/{executor$//executors$/}.
(b) References to "my executors" include anyone who acts as my personal representative.

3 Appointing private executors with substitutes

1 APPOINTMENT OF EXECUTORS   2–003

(a) I appoint $/ $/[and $/$/] to be my $/{executor$//executors$/} but if $/{he is$//she is$//both of them are$//either of them is$//all of them are$//any of them is$/} unable or unwilling to act then I appoint $/ instead.
(b) References to "my executors" include anyone who acts as my personal representative.

4 Appointing public trustee as executor

1 APPOINTMENT OF EXECUTOR   2–004

(a) I appoint the Public Trustee to be my executor.
(b) I wish the firm of $/ (solicitors) of $/ to be employed in connection with my estate.
(c) References to "my executors" include anyone who acts as my personal representative.

5 Appointing a firm of solicitors as executor

2–005 1 APPOINTMENT OF EXECUTORS

(a) I appoint as my executors the partners at my death in the firm of $/ (solicitors) of $/.

(b) If at my death that firm no longer exists, I appoint the firm which carries on its practice.

(c) I wish no more than two people to act as my executors.

(d) References to "my executors" include anyone who acts as my personal representative.

6 Appointing a bank as executor

2–006 1 APPOINTMENT OF EXECUTOR

(a) I appoint $/ Bank $/[PLC$/] to be my executor.

(b) The bank is appointed on its terms and conditions in force at the date of my death.

(c) The bank may act by its proper officers.

(d) The bank may charge under its published scale of fees, as amended from time to time.

(e) The bank's charges are payable out of capital or income, at the bank's discretion.

(f) I wish the firm of $/ (solicitors) of $/ to be employed in connection with my estate.

(g) References to "my executors" include anyone who acts as my personal representative.

7 Appointing executors of foreign property

2–007 1 APPOINTMENT OF SPECIAL EXECUTORS

(a) I appoint $/ $/[and $/$/] ("my special $/{executor$//executors$/}") to be the $/{executor$//executors$/} of all my property in the United States of America.

(b) "My property in the United States of America" means property which is situated in any part of the United States of America according to the laws of any state of the United States of America.

(c) This appointment takes precedence over the appointment of my general $/{executor$//executors$/}.

8 Appointing special executors of a business

2–008 1 APPOINTMENT OF SPECIAL EXECUTORS

(a) I appoint $/ $/[and $/$/] ("my special $/{executor$//executors$/}") to be the $/{executor$//executors$/} of my business assets.

(b) "my business assets" means:

(i) all the assets which form part of my business known as $/ $/[(now carried on by me at $/) $/] including its:

(A) goodwill;
(B) bank accounts;
(C) chattels; and
(D) leaseholds and other property interests; and

(ii) all the assets of any other business carried on by me at my death.

(c) This appointment takes precedence over the appointment of my general $/{executor$//executors$/}.

9 Appointing literary executors

1 APPOINTMENT OF LITERARY EXECUTORS   2–009

(a) I appoint $/ $/[and $/$/] ("my literary $/{executor$//executors$/}") to be the $/{executor$//executors$/} of my literary estate.
(b) "My literary estate" means:

(i) my published works;
(ii) my unpublished works and those in the course of publication;
(iii) all my literary notes and memoranda.

(c) This appointment takes precedence over the appointment of my general $/{executor$//executors$/}.
(d) $/[I give to my literary $/{executor$//executors$/}:

(i) £$/ (free of inheritance tax) if $/{he accepts$//she accepts$//they accept$/} office; and
(ii) $/% of all royalties and other income received by $/{him$//her$// them$/} in respect of my literary estate.$/]

10 Power to appoint new trustees

1 POWER TO APPOINT NEW TRUSTEES   2–010

$/ has the power to appoint new trustees during $/{his$//her$/} life$/[and after $/{his$//her$/} death $/ has the power to appoint new trustees$/].

11 Appointing guardians

1 APPOINTMENT OF GUARDIANS   2–011

$/[If at my death I am the sole surviving parent, $/] I appoint $/ $/[and $/ $/] to be the $/{guardian$//guardians$/} of any of my children who are under 18.

12 Appointing guardians with substitutes

1 APPOINTMENT OF GUARDIANS   2–012

(a) $/[If at my death I am the sole surviving parent, $/] I appoint $/ $/[and $/ $/] to be the $/{guardian$//guardians$/} of any of my children who are under 18.
(b) If $/{he is$//she is$//either of them is$//both of them are$//any of them is$//all of them are$/} unable or unwilling to act then I appoint $/ $/[and $/ $/] instead.

PRELIMINARY MATTERS

13 Desire for cremation

2–013 1 FUNERAL WISHES

(a) I wish to be cremated$/[following a funeral service at $/$/].
(b) I would like my ashes to be $/{scattered at $/ $//buried at $/$//buried in the grave of $/ at $/$/}.

14 Desire for burial

2–014 1 FUNERAL WISHES

(a) I wish to be buried $/[at $/$/] $/[in the grave of $/ at $/$/] $/[following a funeral service at $/ $/].
(b) My Executors may pay any amount they think fit to erect a memorial over my grave.

15 Desire for body to be used for medical purposes

2–015 1 DISPOSAL OF MY BODY

(a) I request (without imposing any binding legal obligation) that my body be used for medical education or research as permitted by law.
(b) My estate must pay the cost of transporting my body to the institution receiving it.
(c) I would like the institution receiving my body to eventually have it cremated.
(d) $/[In the first instance my body must be offered to the Department of Anatomy, $/ Medical School, $/. $/]

16 Expectation of marriage

2–016 1 EXPECTATION OF MARRIAGE

(a) My will is not revoked if I marry $/.

CHATTELS

17 Gift of chattels

2–017 1 PERSONAL CHATTELS

(a) I give my personal chattels, free of inheritance tax, to $/.
(b) "Personal chattels" has the meaning given in section 55(1)(x) of the Administration of Estates Act 1925, but does not include chattels which are the subject of specific gifts.

18 Precatory trust of chattels (individual precatory trustee)

1 PERSONAL CHATTELS

2–018

(a) In this clause, "personal chattels" has the meaning given in section 55(1)(x) of the Administration of Estates Act 1925, but does not include chattels which are the subject of specific gifts.

(b) I give my personal chattels to $/ absolutely.

(c) I request $/{him$//her$/}:

    (i) to dispose of my personal chattels in accordance with any wishes of mine which come to $/{his$//her$/} attention; and

    (ii) to keep any remaining personal chattels for $/{himself$//herself$/} absolutely.

(d) This clause does not impose any legal obligation on $/{him$//her$/}, nor does it confer any legal entitlement on any other person.

19 Precatory trust of chattels (executors precatory trustees)

1 PERSONAL CHATTELS

2–19

(a) In this clause, "personal chattels" has the meaning given in section 55(1)(x) of the Administration of Estates Act 1925, but does not include chattels which are the subject of specific gifts.

(b) I give my personal chattels to my executors.

(c) I request them:

    (i) to dispose of my personal chattels in accordance with any wishes of mine which come to their attention; and

    (ii) to divide any remaining personal chattels among my family and beneficiaries in any manner they think fit.

(d) This clause does not confer any legal entitlement on any person.

LEGACIES

20 Class legacies

21a Class legacies ("each")

1 CLASS LEGACY

2–020

I give, free of inheritance tax, £$/ to each of my $/{children$//grandchildren$//nieces$//nephews$//nieces and nephews$//cousins$/} who is living at my death $/[and attains $/{18$//21$//25$/}$/].

20b Class legacies ("each") with substitutions

Note: 25 is not included as an option in sub-clause (c) of this clause because a contingency age over 21 would create perpetuity problems. For an alternative solution to those problems, see clause 33d.

2–021 1 CLASS LEGACY

    (a) I give, free of inheritance tax, £$/ to each of my $/{children$// grandchildren$//nieces$//nephews$//nieces and nephews$//cousins$/} who is living at my death $/[and attains $/{18$//21$//25$/}$/];

    (b) if any of them dies before me, then to divide his or her share equally between those of his or her children who are living at my death and attain $/{18$//21$//25$/};

    (c) if any of them dies after me, but before attaining $/{18$//21$/}, then to divide his or her share equally between those of his or her children who are living at his or her death and attain $/{18$//21$/}.

20c Class legacies ("equally")

2–022 1 CLASS LEGACY

I give, free of inheritance tax, £$/ to those of my $/{children$// grandchildren$//nieces$//nephews$//nieces and nephews$//cousins$/} who are living at my death $/[and attain $/{18$//21$//25$/}$/] equally.

20d Class legacies ("equally") with substitution

2–023 1 CLASS LEGACY

    (a) I give, free of inheritance tax, £$/ to those of my $/{children$// grandchildren$//nieces$//nephews$//nieces and nephews$//cousins$/} who are living at my death $/[and attain $/{18$//21$//25$/}$/] equally.

    (b) if any of them dies before me, then to divide his or her share equally between those of his or her children who are living at my death and attain $/{18$//21$//25$/};

    (c) if any of them dies after me, but before attaining $/{18$//21$/}, then to divide his or her share equally between those of his or her children who are living at his or her death and attain $/{18$//21$/}.

21 Various legacies

21a Pecuniary Legacy

2–024 1 LEGACY

I give, free of inheritance tax, £$/ to $/.

21b List of pecuniary legacies

2–025 1 LEGACIES

I give, free of inheritance tax:

    (a) £$/ to $/;

    (b) £$/ to $/;

    (c) £$/ to $/; and

    (d) £$/ to $/.

21c List of legacies with sub-leaders

1 LEGACIES   2–026

I give, free of inheritance tax:
  (a) to $/:

  (i) $/
  (ii) $/; and
  (iii) £$/;

  (b) to $/:

  (i) $/
  (ii) $/; and
  (iii) £$/; and

  (c) to $/:

  (i) $/
  (ii) $/; and
  (iii) £$/.

22 Split legacies

Note: These clauses are included for the benefit of those readers who like to work "building block style"!

22a Leader

1 LEGACIES   2–027

I give, free of inheritance tax:

22b Basic cash legacy

  (a) £$/ to $/;

22c Basic sub-leader

  (a) to $/:

22d Contingent cash legacy

  (a) £$/ to $/ if $/{he$//she$/} attains $/{18$//21$//25$/};

22e Contingent sub-leader

  (a) to $/ if $/{he$//she$/} attains $/{18$//21$//25$/}:

22f Charity cash legacy

  (b) £$/ to $/ of $/ (registered charity number $/);

35

22g Charity sub-leader

(c) to $/ of $/ (registered charity number $/):

22h Cash legacy following sub-leader

(i) £$/;

22i "My . . ." following sub-leader

(i) my $/;

22j Jewellery following sub-leader

(i) my jewellery;

22k Jewellery and articles of personal use and adornment following sub-leader

(i) my jewellery and articles of personal use and adornment;

22l Books following sub-leader

(i) my books;

22m Car following sub-leader

(i) any car(s) which I own at my death;

22n Real property following sub-leader

(i) all my interest in the property known as $/$/[(registered at HM Land Registry in title number $/)$/];

22o Whole interest in company following sub-leader

(i) all my shares in $/ Limited ("the company");
(ii) the benefit of any loans due to me from the company;
(iii) any assets owned by me but used by the company;

22p Specified shares in company following sub-leader

(i) $/ ordinary shares in $/ Limited;

23 Annuity

Note: If using this clause, specific powers are required also. Please refer to clause 91. We recommend including the specific powers listed there even in a will which incorporates the STEP provisions.

2–028 1 GIFT OF ANNUITY

(d) I give to $/, free of inheritance tax, a gross annuity of £$/ per annum.

(e) The annuity is to be paid net of any applicable taxes.

(f) The annuity will be paid by equal $/{monthly$//quarterly$//annual$/} payments, commencing on the date three months after my death.

(g) The annuity is not to be apportioned on $/{his$//her$/} death (and accordingly the final payment will be the last one to fall due during $/{his$//her$/} lifetime).

24 Legacy of business (with charges)

1 LEGACY OF BUSINESS SUBJECT TO CHARGES   2–029

In this clause:

(a) "the business" means;

    (i) $/{my business of $/ carried on by me at $/$//$/ Ltd.$//all my shares in $/ Ltd.$/};

    (ii) all assets of mine used in the business;

    (iii) $/[all my interest in the premesis at $/$/]; and

    (iv) all loans due to my from the $/{business$//company$/}

(b) "the charges on the business" means

    (v) a gross annuity of £$/ per annum payable to $/.

    (vi) the sum of £$/ payable to $/ within $/ $/{months$//years$/} of my death.

    (vii) a sum equal to $/% of the net value of the business at the date of payment, payable to $/ within $/ $/{months$//years$/} of my death.

    (viii) a sum equal to $/% of the net value of the business at the date of payment, payable to $/ if $/{he$//she$/} attains $/{18$//21$//25$/}.

    (ix) a sum equal to $/% of the net value of the business at the date of payment, payable to $/ if $/{he$//she$/} attains $/{18$//21$//25$/} or, at $/'s discretion, the option for $/ to enter the business as an $/{equal$//$/%$/} $/{partner$//shareholder$/}.

I give the business to $/ absolutely if (and only if) $/{he enters$//she enters$// they enter$/} into a deed of covenant or contract which will, to the reasonable satisfaction of my executors, secure the charges on the business.

25 Forgiveness of debt

1 FORGIVENESS OF DEBT   2–030

I forgive, free of inheritance tax:

(a) all sums owing to me by $/ at my death; and

(b) any interest on (a).

INHERITANCE TAX

We have preferred to include specific clauses dealing with the burden of **2–031** inheritance tax, rather than listing inheritance tax among testamentary expenses, and it follows that when using this edition of *Brighouse* you should incorporate one of the following clauses in any estate that is, or could be, inheritance taxable. (Our recommendation, naturally, is that it is in every will. Any estate "could be" inheritance taxable, for example if the testator won the Football Pools, or the charity exemption was abolished.)

The case called *Re Benham* created, for a time, very real dilemmas for the executors of estates which were "partially exempt" (that is, inheritance tax was payable because some of the estate went to non-exempt beneficiaries, yet other parts of the estate went to exempt beneficiaries). While not wanting to go into a discussion of that case, here, we do recognise that there are two ways of dealing with a partially exempt estate, which we have described as "pro-*Benham*" and "anti-*Benham*". The difference is best explained by example.

2–032   Imagine a Mr Smith dies leaving £1 million equally between his nephew, Derrick, and the RSPCA:

(a) *Anti-Benham*
In this distribution, the estate is divided into two halves. The RSPCA receive £500,000, without suffering any inheritance tax because of their charitable status. Derrick receives £500,000 less inheritance tax of £100,000, leaving him with £400,000.

(b) *Pro-Benham*
The gift to Derrick is "grossed-up" to £562,500 on which he bears tax of £125,000, and therefore receives £437,500. This leaves £437,500 for the RSPCA. The two beneficiaries have *actually received* the same amount after payment of inheritance tax.

Generally, an "anti-*Benham*" distribution is to be preferred. Although the pro-*Benham* distribution can appear fairer, there is more tax to pay so the ultimate losers are the charities who have been denied part of their tax exemption. From the point of view of the solicitor who has to make the calculations, the only thing that can be said for it is that it takes chargeable time!

26 Incidence of inheritance tax — residue pays

2–033 1 BURDEN OF INHERITANCE TAX

If inheritance tax, or any other form of death duty, is payable on my free estate then my executors must pay it from the residue of my estate.

27 Incidence of inheritance tax — legatees pay

2–034 1 BURDEN OF INHERITANCE TAX

If inheritance tax, or any other form of death duty, is payable on my free estate then:

(a) Legatees must bear the tax on their legacies.
(b) My executors must pay the balance from the residue of my estate.

28 Incidence of inheritance tax — legatees have time to pay

1 BURDEN OF INHERITANCE TAX   2–035

If inheritance tax, or any other form of death duty, is payable on my free estate then:

(a) Legatees must bear the tax on their legacies.
(b) My executors must pay the balance from the residue of my estate.
(c) My executors may:

   (i) pay the legacies in full;
   (ii) pay the tax on those legacies from the residue of my estate; and
   (iii) give the legatees time to pay, with or without taking security.

(d) If my executors allow a legatee time to pay, my executors are not liable to my residuary beneficiaries if, in the event, the legatee does not pay on time or at all.

29 Anti-*Benham* Clause

1 BURDEN OF INHERITANCE TAX   2–036

(a) If inheritance tax, or any other form of death duty, is payable on my free estate then my executors must pay it from the residue of my estate.
(b) If some parts of the residue of my estate are exempt from inheritance tax, and other parts are chargeable to inheritance tax, then the non-exempt parts must bear that inheritance tax (even though the beneficiaries will then receive unequal amounts).

30 Pro-*Benham* clause

1 BURDEN OF INHERITANCE TAX   2–037

(a) If inheritance tax, or any other form of death duty, is payable on my free estate then my executors must pay it from the residue of my estate.
(b) If some parts of the residue of my estate are exempt from inheritance tax, and other parts are chargeable to inheritance tax, then the gifts made in my will are adjusted such that, after payment of inheritance tax, the amounts actually received by my beneficiaries have the proportions to each other stated in my will.

RESIDUE

31 Residue introduction

1 RESIDUE   2–038

I give to my executors:

(I) $/[the rest of $/]my estate, anywhere in the world; and
(II) any property over which I have a general power of appointment;
to hold it on trust:

(a) to pay my debts, taxes and funeral and testamentary expenses;

32 Residue continuation — spouse

2–039   (a) to pay the residue to my $/{husband$//wife$/} $/ absolutely if $/{he$// she$/} survives me by 28 days $/[; but if this gift fails$/]

33 Residue continuation for children

2–040 *33a Residue continuation for children (no substitution)*

(a) to divide the residue equally between those of my children who are living at my death $/[and attain $/{18$//21$//25$/}$/] (without substituting their children if their shares fail); $/[but if this gift fails entirely:$/]

33b Residue for children (with substitution, children of age)

(a) to divide the residue equally between those of my children who are living at my death; except:
(b) if any of my children dies before me, then to divide that child's share equally between those of $/{his$//her$//his or her$/} children who are living at my death $/[and attain $/{18$//21$//25$/}$/]$/[; but if the above trusts fail:$/]

33c Residue continuation for children (with substitution, children not of age, contingency age 21 or under)

(a) to divide the residue equally between those of my children who are living at my death and attain $/{18$//21$/}; except:
(i) if any of my children dies before me, then to divide that child's share equally between those of $/{his$//her$//his or her$/} children who are living at my death and attain $/{18$//21$/}; and
(ii) if any of my children dies after me, but before attaining $/{18$//21$/}, then to divide that child's share equally between those of $/{his$//her$//his or her$/} children who are living at $/{his$//her$//his or her$/} death and attain $/{18$//21$/}$/.
[if the above trusts fail, then:$/]

33d Residue continuation for children (with substitution, children not of age, contingency age over 21)

(a) to divide the residue equally between those of my children who are living at my death and attain 25; except:
(i) if any of my children dies before me, then to divide that child's share equally between those of $/{his$//her$//his or her$/} children who are living at my death and attain 25; and

40

(ii) if any of my children dies after me, but before attaining 25, then to divide that child's share equally between those of $/{his$//her$//his or her$/} children who are living at $/{his$//her$//his or her$/} death and who either:

   (A) attain 25; or

   (B) are living, and under 25, 21 years after the death of the last survivor of those of my descendants who are living at my death.

[if the above trusts fail, then:$/]

34 Residue continuation for classes

Note: The "those of . . . who" construction (more traditionally seen as the **2–041** "such of . . . as shall" construction) is the draftsman's friend. It is short and to the point, it generally conveniently closes classes, and it never needs to be followed by an accrual clause.

34a *Those of . . . who*

(a) to divide the residue equally between those of my $/{children$// grandchildren$//nieces$//nephews$//nieces and nephews$//cousins$/} who are living at my death $/[and attain $/{18$//21$//25$/}$/] $/[; but if the above trusts fail, then:$/]

34b *Those of (a), (b), (c) who*

(b) to divide the residue equally between those of the following who are living at my death $/[and attain $/{18$//21$//25$/}$/]:

   (i) $/;

   (ii) $/; and

   (iii) $/;

   $/[if the above trusts fail, then:$/]

34c *Shares with accrual*

(a) to divide the residue into $/ equal shares and to pay:

   (i) $/ $/{share$//shares$/} to $/;

   (ii) $/ $/{share$//shares$/} to $/; and

   (iii) $/ $/{share$//shares$/} to $/.

(b) $/{If any of the above shares fail, the failed share accrues proportionately to the shares which do not fail.$//If either of the above shares fail, the failed share accrues to the other.$/}

(c) $/[If the above trusts fail entirely, then:$/]

41

34d Percentages with accrual

(a) to pay the residue:

   (i) $/% to $/;
   (ii) $/% to $/; and
   (iii) $/% to $/.

(b) $/{if any of the above shares fail, the failed share accrues proportionately to the shares which do not fail;$//if either of the above shares fail, the failed share accrues to the other;$/}

(c) $/[if the above trusts fail entirely, then:$/]

35 Residue continuation for individual absolutely

2–042   (a) to pay the residue to $/ absolutely $/[; but if this gift fails$/]

36 Residue continuation — divisions between families

2–043 *36a Division between both sets of parents*

(a) to divide the residue into two equal shares and to pay:

   (i) one share to those of my parents who survive me, jointly; and
   (ii) one share to those of my $/{husband's$//wife's$/} parents who survive me, jointly.

(b) If either of the above shares fail, the failed share accrues to the other.

(c) $/[If the above trusts fail entirely, then:$/]

36b Division between both sets of parents, substituting siblings

(a) to divide the residue into two equal shares and to pay:

   (i) one share:

      (A) to those of my parents who survive me, jointly, but if this gift fails:
      (B) to those of my brothers and sisters who survive me equally; and

   (ii) one share:

      (C) to those of my $/{husband's$//wife's$/} parents who survive me, jointly, but if this gift fails:
      (D) to those of my $/{husband's$//wife's$/} brothers and sisters who survive me equally.

(b) If either of the above shares fail, the failed share accrues to the other.

(c) $/[If the above trusts fail entirely, then:$/]

36c Division between two sets of children (where there is a second family)

(a) to divide the residue into two equal shares and to pay:

    (i) one share to those of my children who are living at my death$/ [and attain $/{18$//21$/}$/]; and

    (ii) one share to those of the children of my $/{husband$//wife$/} who are living at my death $/[and attain $/{18$//21$/}$/]; except

(b) if any of the beneficiaries above die before me, then to divide his or her share equally between those of his or her children who are living at my death and attain $/{18$//21$/}; and

(c) if any of them dies after me, but before attaining $/{18$//21$/}then to divide his or her share equally between those of her or her children who are living at his or her death and attain $/{18$//21$/}

(d) if either of the above shares fails entirely then the failed share accrues to the other;

(e) $/[If the above trusts fail entirely then:$/]

MISCELLANEOUS

37 Forfeiture clause

1 FORFEITURE   2–044

All benefits given to $/ by this will are forfeited (and my estate divided as if $/{he$//she$/} had died before me) if

(a) $/[$/{he$//she$/} is remarried at my death; or$/]

(b) $/{he$//she$/} makes any application to the court, whether:

    (i) under the Inheritance (Provision for Family and Dependants) Act 1975; or

    (ii) relying on any other ground;

the effect of which, if successful, would be to alter any of the terms of my will.

My executors must not pay any benefits to $/{him$//her$/} until either:

(a) $/{he$//she$/} has given a binding undertaking to accept the terms of my will; or

(b) the last date upon which $/{he$//she$/} could make a claim under the Inheritance (Provision for Family and Dependants) Act 1975 has passed, without a claim being made.

38 Mutual wills

Note: It is not our intention to encourage the use of mutual wills, and the matter is discussed at more length in the "Second Families" section of Part 6.

In this clause we have introduced an innovation which we hope will underline to testators the seriousness and binding nature of the mutual will agreement — and that is a declaration made by each party, on the face of the other's will. We believe that the existence of this signature, on the publicly available probate copy of the will of the first to die, would make it more likely that the mutual will agreement would be honoured on the second death, even where the survivor has changed his or her will.

2–045 1 MUTUAL WILLS

I have made this will on the same day as $/ has made $/{his$//her$/} will. It is our intention that the wills should be mutual. That is, we agree that if the first of us dies without having changed the will made today, the survivor will be bound to stand by the terms of his or her will made today. We agree that this agreement is to be enforceable against the survivor of us, and his or her executors. $/ has acknowledged this agreement by signing the following declaration on the face of my will.

DECLARATION

I, $/, acknowledge the agreement set out above. I agree that if $/ dies before me without having changed this will, I am bound to honour the terms of my will signed today. This agreement binds me and my executors.

. . . .
Signature of $/

---

39 Definition of "children"

2–046 1 DEFINITION OF "CHILDREN"

In my will, "children":

(a) includes those who are legitimate, illegitimate or adopted; but
(b) does not include step-children, nor natural children who have been adopted by another person;

and other terms describing family relationships are to be interpreted accordingly.

ATTESTATIONS

40 Attestation for blind testator

SIGNATURES

Signed by me on the .... 20$/
Signature on behalf of testator

Signed by .... with the name of the testator, $/, (who is $/{blind$//partially sighted$/}) in $/{his$//her$/} presence and ours, and at $/{his$//her$/} direction, after the will had been read over to $/{him$//her$/} in our joint presence when $/{he$//she$/} appeared to thoroughly understand and approve it, and then signed by us in $/{his$//her$/} presence.

| Witness 1 | Witness 2 |

Signature:

Full name:

Address:

Occupation:

41 Attestation (by mark) for illiterate testator

SIGNATURES

Signed by me on the .... 20$/
Mark of Testator

Signed by $/ by $/{his$//her$/} mark in our joint presence, after the will had been read over to $/{him$//her$/} in our joint presence when $/{he$//she$/} appeared to thoroughly understand and approve it, and then signed by us in $/{his$//her$/} presence.

| Witness 1 | Witness 2 |

Signature:

Full name:

Address:

Occupation:

42 Usual Attestation

2–049 SIGNATURES

Signed by me on . . . . 20$/

Signature of Testator

Signed by $/ in our joint presence and then by us in $/{his$//hers$/}

                 Witness 1   Witness 2

Signature:

Full name:

Address:

Occupation:

PART 3

TRUSTEES' POWERS

TRUSTEES' POWERS

43 STEP provisions (basic version)

1 EXECUTORS' POWERS
3–001

The Standard Provisions of the Society of Trust and Estate Practitioners (1st edition) apply.

44 STEP provisions (updated version)

Note: See also clauses 84a to 84d

1 EXECUTORS' POWERS
3–002

(a) The Standard Provisions of the Society of Trust and Estate Practitioners (1st edition) apply, amended as follows:

  (i) Standard provision 5 ("trust for sale") does not apply.
  (ii) My executors may exercise their powers without consulting beneficiaries, so section 11 of the Trusts of Land and Appointment of Trustees Act 1996 does not apply.

45 Power to invest

1 POWER OF INVESTMENT
3–003

My executors may invest my estate in any investments they could make if they owned my estate personally. In particular, they may:

(a) invest in unsecured loans, including interest-free loans to a beneficiary;
(b) invest in land, whether as an investment or as a residence for a beneficiary, and may improve and maintain it;
(c) invest jointly with another person;
(d) invest in wasting or non-income-producing assets;
(e) invest anywhere in the world; and
(f) choose not to diversify investments.

46 Excluding apportionment

1 EXCLUSION OF THE APPORTIONMENT RULES
3–004

(a) My executors may treat income as arising on the day it is paid.

(b) The Apportionment Act 1870 does not apply.

(c) The rules known as "the rule in *Howe v. Dartmouth*" and "the rule in *Allhusen v. Whittell*" do not apply.

47 Excluding section 11 of the trusts of land and appointment of trustees act 1996

3–005 1 EXCLUSION OF S.11 TLATA

My executors may exercise their powers without consulting beneficiaries, so section 11 of the Trusts of Land and Appointment of Trustees Act 1996 does not apply.

48 Power of advancement

3–006 1 POWER OF ADVANCEMENT

My executors may apply the share of any beneficiary for $/{his$//her$//his or her$/} benefit, and this power:

(a) is in addition to any other powers my executors may have, in particular section 32 of the Trustee Act 1925;

(b) applies to the whole or part of the beneficiary's share;

(c) applies whether the beneficiary's right is vested, contingent, expectant or presumptive, but not where another person is entitled in priority;

(d) may be used for advancement, maintenance, education or any other benefit;

(e) may be exercised by paying the share to a third party or, where appropriate, to the beneficiary direct.

49 Power to advance capital to life tenant

Note: While we have included powers to advance capital in this section, our recommendation is to include the power in the trust itself. Accordingly you will see that paras **3–007** and **3–008** are not reproduced anywhere in parts 4 or 6, and you will see examples in Part 5 of equivalent provisions being incorporated directly into the substantive trusts.

3–007 1 POWER TO ADVANCE CAPITAL TO LIFE TENANT

My executors may apply the capital of my estate for the benefit of the life tenant, and this power may apply to the whole or part of that capital in which $/{he$//she$/} has an interest.

50 Power to advance capital to life tenant and children

3–008 1 POWER TO ADVANCE CAPITAL TO LIFE TENANT AND CHILDREN

My executors may apply the capital of my estate for the benefit of the life tenant, or any of $/{his$//her$/} children, and this power:

(a) may apply to the whole or part of that capital in which $/{he$//she$/} has an interest;

(b) may be used for advancement, maintenance, education or any other benefit;

(c) may be exercised by paying the share to a third party or, where appropriate, to the recipient direct;

but the recipient, if one of the children, must bring into account any benefit received under this clause on any later distribution of my estate.

51 Parents' receipt clause

1 POWER TO ACCEPT RECEIPT OF PARENT OR GUARDIAN

3–009

My executors may accept the receipt of the parent or guardian of any beneficiary who is under 18 for money applied for the benefit of that beneficiary. If they do so my executors are discharged from the trusts of that money and are not obliged to supervise how it is used.

52 Power to appropriate annuity fund

1 POWER TO APPROPRIATE ANNUITY FUND

3–010

My executors may appropriate from my estate the sum which, in their view, is sufficient to satisfy the $/{annuity$//annuities$/} given in my will. If they do so:

(a) My executors must take appropriate professional advice on the size and composition of the annuity fund.

(b) My executors may use the income and capital of the annuity fund to pay the annuity.

(c) If they believe that the annuity fund is, at any time, larger than is necessary to satisfy the $/{annuity$//annuities$/}, my executors may hold the surplus as part of the residue of my estate.

(d) The $/{annuitant has$//annuitants have$/} no further claim on my estate if, in the event, the annuity fund is inadequate to pay the $/{annuity$//annuities$/} in full.

(e) On the death of the $/[last$/] annuitant, my executors must hold any balance of the annuity fund as part of the residue of my estate.

53 Power to purchase annuity

1 POWER TO PURCHASE ANNUITY

3–011

My executors may purchase an annuity from any insurance office, company or corporation as they think fit to satisfy the $/{annuity$//annuities$/} given in my will. If they do so the $/{annuitant has$//annuitants have$/} no further claim against my estate.

54 Direction to purchase annuity

3–012 1 DIRECTION TO PURCHASE ANNUITY

My executors must purchase an annuity, from any insurance office, company or corporation as they think fit, to satisfy the $/{annuity$//annuities$/} given in my will. Once they have done so the $/{annuitant has$//annuitants have$/} no further claim against my estate.

55 Power to commute annuity

3–013 1 POWER TO COMMUTE AN ANNUITY

My executors may commute the $/{annuity$//annuities$/} given in my will, by paying to the $/{annuitant$//annuitants$/} the capital amount which my executors consider reasonable. If they do so:

(a) My executors must take appropriate professional advice on the capital amount.

(b) The $/{annuitant has$//annuitants have$/} no further claim on my estate.

56 Power of appropriation

3–014 1 POWER OF APPROPRIATION

My executors may appropriate assets to beneficiaries without requiring consent. (Section 41 of the Administration of Estates Act 1925 therefore applies subject to that amendment.)

57 Power to insure (with restriction on source of premiums)

3–015 1 POWER OF INSURANCE

My executors may:

(a) keep any assets of my estate insured, against any risk and in any amount;

(b) pay insurance premiums from the income or capital of that part of my estate which is held on the same trusts as the insured property; and

(c) treat any insurance money received as though it were the proceeds of sale of the insured property.

58 Power to insure (without restriction)

3–016 1 POWER OF INSURANCE

My executors may:

(a) keep any assets of my estate insured, against any risk and in any amount;

(b) pay insurance premiums from the income or capital of any part of my estate; and

(c) treat any insurance money received as though it were the proceeds of sale of the insured property.

59 Exclusion of liability

1 EXCLUSION OF EXECUTORS' LIABILITY 3–017

No executor, or trustee, is liable for any loss arising from:

(a) exercising, or failing to exercise, any discretion or power;
(b) any improper investment made in good faith;
(c) the negligence or fraud of any agent employed by him, or by any other executor or trustee, even if the employment was not strictly necessary or expedient;
(d) any mistake or omission made in good faith;
(e) any other matter, except wilful and individual fraud on the part of the executor or trustee who is sought to be made liable.

60 Exclusion of liability — restricted but with protection

1 EXCLUSION OF EXECUTORS' LIABILITY 3–018

(a) Only a professional executor or trustee can be liable for any loss arising from:

(i) exercising, or failing to exercise, any discretion or power;
(ii) any improper investment made in good faith;
(iii) the negligence or fraud of any agent employed by him, or by any other executor or trustee, even if the employment was not strictly necessary or expedient;
(iv) any mistake or omission made in good faith;
(v) any other matter or thing, except wilful and individual fraud on the part of the executor or trustee who is sought to be made liable.

(b) No executor can be liable for any loss, of any kind, if he has acted in accordance with the advice of Counsel of at least five years' standing.

61 Power not to interfere in management

1 POWER NOT TO INTERFERE IN THE MANAGEMENT OF A BUSINESS 3–019

My executors may choose not to interfere in the management (or conduct) of any business, company or corporation over which my executors have any level of control. If they are not aware of any wrongdoing on the part of the directors of a company, my executors may leave:

(a) the conduct of the business; and
(b) the decision whether to declare a dividend, and its amount;

to those directors. My executors are not liable to my estate for any action they take, or fail to take, in reliance on this clause.

62 Power to purchase

3–020 1 POWER TO PURCHASE ASSETS

My executors may personally purchase assets from my estate if (and only if):

    (a) there is at least one other executor or trustee for the time being who does not have a personal interest in the transaction; and

    (b) in the case of:

        (i) investments quoted on any stock exchange in the United Kingdom — the purchase price is not less than the current middle market price at the time of the execution of the transfer.

        (ii) property of any other description—

            (A) my executors must obtain (at the cost of the proposed purchaser) an independent valuation and report on the proposed sale by a competent, properly qualified and independent person appointed by my trustees

            (B) the purchase price is not less than the amount of that valuation; and

            (C) the report does not advise against the sale for any reason.

63 Power to act as officer or employee

3–021 1 POWER TO ACT AS OFFICER OR EMPLOYEE

Any executor may act personally as an officer, or employee, of any company in which my estate is interested. An executor who does so may retain personally any remuneration received. This is so even if:

    (a) my executor having chosen to exercise (or not to exercise) rights over shares in my estate may have been instrumental in procuring the position as officer or employee; or

    (b) my executor's qualifications for the position may be constituted (in part or in whole) by the holding in my estate.

64 Trust corporation

3–022 1 TRUST CORPORATIONS

If a trust corporation is appointed as executor or trustee, it may:

    (a) act by its proper officers;

    (b) exercise all the powers given to executors or trustees by my will;

    (c) charge under its published scale of fees, as amended from time to time;

    (d) meet its charges out of capital or income, at its discretion.

65 Power to run a business

3–023 1 POWER TO RUN A BUSINESS

My executors may carry on any business in which I am engaged at my death. If they do so then they may:

(a) carry on the business either alone or in partnership with any other people (and whether as general partners or limited partners);

(b) act upon such terms as they think fit, and as if they were the beneficial owners absolutely entitled;

(c) employ any of the capital of my estate in the business, including capitalising financing (by loans, guarantees or otherwise);

(d) employ anyone in connection with the business on such terms as they think fit;

(e) promote a company or corporation in any part of the world to acquire the business (or part of it) by the issue to my trustees of shares or securities or otherwise;

(f) pay, out of any property held upon the same trusts as the business, the cost of promoting such a company or corporation, and of the transfer of the business to it;

and my executors are indemnified, out of any property held upon the same trusts as the business, against any personal liability which they incur in connection with the business (unless that liability arose by reason of their own willful and individual fraud or wrongdoing).

2 TREATMENT OF BUSINESS PROFITS 3–024

The net profits of any business in my estate are to be treated as if they were the income which would arise from investments representing the proceeds of sale of the business, if it were sold.

66 Power to use nominees

1 POWER TO USE NOMINEES 3–025

My executors may vest any asset of my estate in the name of, or under the control of:

(a) one or more of their number; or

(b) any person (which may include a trust corporation), or people, as nominee(s).

67 Charging clause

1 POWER TO CHARGE FOR PROFESSIONAL SERVICES 3–026

Any of my executors who is engaged in a profession or business may charge fees for work done by him or her, or by his or her firm, in connection with my estate and its trusts, including acts which an executor or trustee not being in any profession or business could have done personally, and those charges shall be a first charge against my estate, without abatement.

68 Power to distribute to known beneficiaries only

1 POWER TO DISTRIBUTE AMONG KNOWN BENEFICIARIES ONLY 3–027

My executors may distribute my estate among the beneficiaries of whom they are aware at the later of:

(a) the date of that distribution; and

(b) six months from my death;

and accordingly no person who is described in my will (as distinct from being named in it) has any claim against my estate if he or she was not known to my executors at that time. This is so whether or not my executors have placed advertisements or taken other steps to trace unknown beneficiaries.

69 Minimum of two trustees

3–028 1 MINIMUM OF TWO TRUSTEES

(a) I intend that at all times there must be at least two executors or trustees of my will.

(b) If at any time the number of trustees falls below two:

(i) the number of trustees must be made up to two or more as soon as practicable; and

(ii) the only power exercisable by a sole trustee is the power to appoint new trustees.

70 Minimum two trustees or a trust corporation

3–029 1 MINIMUM OF TWO TRUSTEES OR A TRUST CORPORATION

(a) I intend that at all times there must be at least two executors or trustees of my will, or a trust corporation.

(b) If at any time a trust corporation is not an executor or trustee, and the number of trustees falls below two:

(i) the number of trustees must be made up to two or more as soon as practicable; and

(ii) the only power exercisable by a sole individual trustee is the power to appoint new trustees.

71 Commorientes clause

3–030 1 COMMORIENTES

My estate is to be divided as if any person who dies within one month of my death had predeceased me.

72 Jurisdiction clause

3–031 1 JURISDICTION

My will shall be construed in accordance with the laws of England and Wales. All the powers and rights implied by English law apply.

73 Accumulations of income

1 ACCUMULATIONS OF INCOME 3–032

My executors may:

    (a) within 21 years of my death, accumulate income to the extent that it is not paid to, or applied for the benefit of, any beneficiary; and

    (b) apply accumulated income as if it were the income of the current year.

74 Power to borrow

1 POWER TO BORROW 3–033

    (a) My executors may borrow money for any purpose.

    (b) My executors may charge any assets of my estate as security for any liability.

75 Power to delegate

1 POWER OF DELEGATION 3–034

My executors may delegate any of their functions, in writing, to:

    (a) one or more of their number; or

    (b) any other person;

and if they do so my executors are not personally liable to my estate for the defaults of that delegate.

76 Power to administer offshore

1 POWER TO ADMINISTER OFFSHORE 3–035

    (a) Any person with a power to appoint trustees may appoint a person who has no connection with the United Kingdom;

    (b) My executors may administer the trusts of my estate outside the United Kingdom.

77 Power to give indemnities

1 INDEMNITIES 3–036

My executors may indemnify a retiring trustee, or any other person, against any liability concerning my estate. If they do so, then my estate (not my executors personally) will bear the liability of that indemnity. My executors may charge the indemnity on assets of my estate.

78 Charities' receipt clause

1 CHARITIES' RECEIPT 3–037

My executors may accept, as a complete discharge, the receipt of any person who appears to be a proper officer of a charity.

79 Minor's receipt clause

3–038 **1 MINOR'S RECEIPT**

where a person is a minor (that is:

    (a) under 18; or

    (b) 18 or over, but not of an age to be entitled to capital outright);

my executors may pay money to which he or she becomes entitled, whether:

      (i) income or capital; or

      (ii) as of right or under a power

to any the following, and in each case their receipt is a complete discharge:

        (A) the minor, if he or she has attained 16;

        (B) the minor's parent or guardian, in which case my executors are under no further obligation to enquire into the use of the money; or

        (C) a third party for the benefit of the minor;

or my executors may resolve to hold the money on trust for the minor absolutely (in which case the administrative provisions of my will continue to apply to the money).

80 Conflicts of interest

3–039 **1 CONFLICTS OF INTEREST**

My executors may exercise (or fail to exercise) any powers in my will, even if one or more of them has a personal interest in the outcome.

81 Use of trustees' powers

3–040 **1 USE OF EXECUTORS' POWERS**

My executors may exercise any of their powers:

    (a) from time to time; and

    (b) at their absolute discretion.

PART 4

TRUSTEES' POWERS COLLECTED

TRUSTEES' POWERS COLLECTED

"COMPLETE" POWERS

82 Trustees' powers complete set

Note: There are *absolutely no circumstances* in which this clause is appropriate **4–001** by itself. We have included it for the benefit of our many peers who like to start with a complete set which they can "blue pencil" in each individual will. We should perhaps sound a word of warning where that is done using a dictating machine. The *Brighouse* clauses on disc are specifically written so as to automatically renumber. If you start with the list:

(a) apples
(b) pears
(c) oranges
(d) bananas
(e) cherries

and you dictate, to a secretary who is not used to automatic numbering, that you want to delete clauses b and d, you are likely to end up with:

(a) apples
(b) oranges
(c) bananas

because on deleting "(b) pears", "(e) cherries" automatically renumbered itself as "(d)". This may seem like a silly example, but in a 9-page precedent like this one, your poor long-suffering secretary will have real difficulties if you dictate by clause number alone. It will be even worse in a real will, as "1. POWER OF INVESTMENT" will itself renumber depending upon the number of clauses you have already dictated.

1 POWER OF INVESTMENT

4–002

My executors may invest my estate in any investments they could make if they owned my estate personally. In particular, they may:

(a) invest in unsecured loans, including interest-free loans to a beneficiary;
(b) invest in land, whether as an investment or as a residence for a beneficiary, and may improve and maintain it;
(c) invest jointly with another person;
(d) invest in wasting or non-income-producing assets;

(e) invest anywhere in the world; and

(f) choose not to diversify investments.

4–003 2 EXCLUSION OF THE APPORTIONMENT RULES

(a) My executors may treat income as arising on the day it is received.

(b) The Apportionment Act 1870 does not apply.

(c) The rules known as "the rule in *Howe v. Dartmouth*" and "the rule in *Allhusen v. Whittell*" do not apply.

3 EXCLUSION OF S.11 TLATA

My executors may exercise their powers without consulting beneficiaries, so section 11 of the Trusts of Land and Appointment of Trustees Act 1996 does not apply.

4–004 4 POWER OF ADVANCEMENT

My executors may apply the share of any beneficiary for $/{his$//her$//his or her$/} benefit, and this power:

(a) is in addition to any other powers my executors may have, in particular section 32 of the Trustee Act 1925;

(b) applies to the whole or part of the beneficiary's share;

(c) applies whether the beneficiary's right is vested, contingent, expectant or presumptive but not where another person is entitled in priority;

(d) may be used for advancement, maintenance, education or any other benefit;

(e) may be exercised by paying the share to a third party or, where appropriate, to the beneficiary direct.

4–005 5 POWER TO ADVANCE CAPITAL TO LIFE TENANT

My executors may apply the capital of my estate for the benefit of the life tenant, and this power may apply to the whole or part of that capital in which $/{he$//she$/} has an interest.

4–006 6 POWER TO ADVANCE CAPITAL TO LIFE TENANT AND CHILDREN

My executors may apply the capital of my estate for the benefit of the life tenant, or any of $/{his$//her$/} children, and this power:

(a) may apply to the whole or part of that capital in which $/{he$//she$/} has an interest;

(b) may be used for advancement, maintenance, education or any other benefit;

(c) may be exercised by paying the share to a third party or, where appropriate, to the recipient direct;

but the recipient, if one of the children, shall bring into account any benefit received under this clause on any later distribution of my estate.

7 POWER TO ACCEPT RECEIPT OF PARENT OR GUARDIAN

My executors may accept the receipt of the parent or guardian of any beneficiary who is under 18 for money applied for the benefit of that beneficiary. If they do, so my executors are discharged from the trusts of that money and are not under any obligation to supervise how it is applied.

8 POWER TO APPROPRIATE ANNUITY FUND

My executors may appropriate from my estate the sum which, in their view, is sufficient to satisfy the $/{annuity$//annuities$/} given in my will. If they do so:

(a) My executors must take appropriate professional advice on the size and composition of the annuity fund.
(b) The $/{annuitant has$//annuitants have$/} no further claim on my estate if, in the event, the annuity fund is inadequate to pay the $/{annuity$//annuities$/} in full.
(c) My executors may use the income and capital of the annuity fund to pay the annuity.
(d) If they believe that the annuity fund is, at any time, larger than is necessary to satisfy the $/{annuity$//annuities$/}, my executors may hold the surplus as part of the residue of my estate.
(e) On the death of the $/[last$/] annuitant, my executors must hold any balance of the annuity fund as part of the residue of my estate.

9 POWER TO PURCHASE ANNUITY

My executors may purchase an annuity from any insurance office, company or corporation as they think fit to satisfy the $/{annuity$//annuities$/} given in my will. If they do so the $/{annuitant has$//annuitants have$/} no further claim against my estate.

10 DIRECTION TO PURCHASE ANNUITY

My executors must purchase an annuity, from any insurance office, company or corporation as they think fit, to satisfy the $/{annuity$//annuities$/} given in my will. Once they have done so the $/{annuitant has$//annuitants have$/} no further claim against my estate.

11 POWER TO COMMUTE AN ANNUITY

My executors may commute the $/{annuity$//annuities$/} given in my will, by paying to the $/{annuitant$//annuitants$/} the capital amount which my executors consider reasonable. If they do so:

(a) My executors must take appropriate professional advice on the capital amount.
(b) The $/{annuitant has$//annuitants have$/}/} no further claim on my estate.

4–012 12 POWER OF APPROPRIATION

My executors may give specific assets of my estate to beneficiaries without requiring consent. (Section 41 of the Administration of Estates Act 1925 therefore applies subject to that amendment.)

4–013 13 POWER OF INSURANCE

My executors may:

(a) keep any assets of my estate insured, against any risk and in any amount;

(b) pay insurance premiums from the income or capital of that part of my estate which is held on the same trusts as the insured property; and

(c) treat any insurance money received as though it were the proceeds of sale of the insured property.

4–014 14 POWER OF INSURANCE

My executors may:

(a) keep any assets of my estate insured, against any risk and in any amount;

(b) pay insurance premiums from the income or capital of any part of my estate; and

(c) treat any insurance money received as though it were the proceeds of sale of the insured property.

4–015 15 EXCLUSION OF EXECUTORS' LIABILITY

No executor, or trustee, is liable for any loss arising from:

(a) exercising, or failing to exercise, any discretion or power;

(b) any improper investment made in good faith;

(c) the negligence or fraud of any agent employed by him, or by any other executor or trustee, even if the employment was not strictly necessary or expedient;

(d) any mistake or omission made in good faith;

(e) any other matter, except willful and individual fraud on the part of the executor or trustee who is sought to be made liable.

4–016 16 EXCLUSION OF EXECUTORS' LIABILITY

(a) Only a professional executor or trustee can be liable for any loss arising from:

(i) exercising, or failing to exercise, any discretion or power;

(ii) any improper investment made in good faith;

(iii) the negligence or fraud of any agent employed by him, or by any other executor or trustee, even if the employment was not strictly necessary or expedient;

(iv) any mistake or omission made in good faith;

(v) any other matter, except willful and individual fraud on the part of the executor or trustee who is sought to be made liable.

(b) No executor can be liable for any loss, of any kind, if he has acted in accordance with the advice of Counsel of at least five years' standing.

17 POWER NOT TO INTERFERE IN THE MANAGEMENT OF A BUSINESS 4–017

My executors may choose not to interfere in the management (or conduct) of any business, company or corporation over which my executors have any level of control. If they are not aware of any wrongdoing on the part of the directors of a company, my executors may leave:

(a) the conduct of the business; and
(b) the decision whether to declare a dividend, and its amount;

to those directors. My executors are not liable to my estate for any action they take, or fail to take, in reliance on this clause.

18 POWER TO PURCHASE ASSETS 4–018

My executors may personally purchase assets of my estate if (and only if):

(a) there is at least one other executor or trustee for the time being who does not have a personal interest in the transaction; and
(b) in the case of:

    (i) investments quoted on any stock exchange in the United Kingdom — the purchase price is not less than the current middle market price at the time of the execution of the transfer.
    (ii) any other property:

        (A) my executors must obtain (at the cost of the proposed purchaser) an independent valuation and report on the proposed sale by a competent, properly qualified and independent person;
        (B) the purchase price is not less than the amount of that valuation; and
        (C) the report does not advise against the sale for any reason.

19 POWER TO ACT AS OFFICER OR EMPLOYEE 4–019

Any executor may act personally as an officer, or employee, of any company in which my estate is interested. An executor who does so may retain personally any remuneration received. This is so even if:

(a) my executor having chosen to exercise (or not to exercise) rights over shares in my estate may have been instrumental in procuring the position as officer or employee; or
(b) my executor's qualifications for the position may be constituted (in part or in whole) by the holding in my estate.

20 TRUST CORPORATIONS 4–020

If a trust corporation is appointed as executor or trustee, it may:

(a) act by its proper officers;

(b) exercise all the powers given to executors or trustees by my will;

(c) charge under its published scale of fees, as amended from time to time;

(d) meet its charges out of capital or income, at its discretion.

4-021   21   POWER TO RUN A BUSINESS

My executors may carry on any business in which I am engaged at my death. If they do so then they may:

(a) carry on the business either alone or in partnership with any other people (and whether as general partners or limited partners);

(b) act upon such terms as they think fit, and as if they were the beneficial owners absolutely entitled;

(c) employ any of the capital of my estate in the business, including capitalising financing (by loans, guarantees or otherwise);

(d) employ anyone in connection with the business on such terms as they think fit;

(e) promote a company or corporation in any part of the world to acquire the business (or part of it) by the issue to my trustees of shares or securities or otherwise;

(f) pay, out of any property held upon the same trusts as the business, the cost of promoting such a company or corporation, and of the transfer of the business to it;

and my executors are indemnified, out of any property held upon the same trusts as the business, against any personal liability which they incur in connection with the business (unless that liability arose by reason of their own wilful and individual fraud or wrongdoing)

4-022   22   TREATMENT OF BUSINESS PROFITS

The net profits of any business in my estate are to be treated as if they were the income which would arise from investments representing the proceeds of sale of the business, if it were sold.

4-023   23   POWER TO USE NOMINEES

My executors may vest any asset of my estate in the name of, or under the control of:

(a) one or more of their number; or

(b) any person (which may include a trust corporation), or people, as nominee(s).

4-024   24   POWER TO CHARGE FOR PROFESSIONAL SERVICES

Any of my executors who is engaged in a profession or business may charge fees for work done by him or her, or by his or her firm, in connection with my estate and its trusts, including acts which an executor or trustee not being in any profession or business could have done personally, and those charges shall be a first charge against my estate, without abatement.

25 POWER TO DISTRIBUTE AMONG KNOWN BENEFICIARIES ONLY

4–025

My executors may distribute my estate among the beneficiaries of whom they are aware at the later of:

(a) the date of that distribution; and
(b) six months from my death;

and accordingly no person who is described in my will (as distinct from being named in it) has any claim against my estate if he or she was not known to my executors at that time. This is so whether or not my executors have placed advertisements or taken other steps to trace unknown beneficiaries.

26 MINIMUM OF TWO TRUSTEES

4–026

(a) I intend that at all times there must be at least two executors or trustees of my will.
(b) If at any time the number of trustees falls below two:

(i) the number of trustees must be made up to two or more as soon as practicable; and
(ii) the only power exercisable by a sole trustee is the power to appoint new trustees.

27 MINIMUM OF TWO TRUSTEES OR A TRUST CORPORATION

4–027

(a) I intend that at all times there must be at least two executors or trustees of my will, or a trust corporation.
(b) If at any time a trust corporation is not an executor or trustee, and the number of trustees falls below two:

(i) the number of trustees must be made up to two or more as soon as practicable; and
(ii) the only power exercisable by a sole individual trustee is the power to appoint new trustees.

28 COMMORIENTES

4–028

My estate is to be divided as if any person who dies within one month of my death had predeceased me.

29 JURISDICTION

4–029

My will shall be construed in accordance with the laws of England and Wales. All the powers and rights implied by English law apply.

30 ACCUMULATIONS OF INCOME

4–030

My executors may:

(a) within 21 years of my death, accumulate income to the extent that it is not paid to, or applied for the benefit of, any beneficiary; and
(b) apply accumulated income as if it were the income of the current year.

4–031 31 POWER TO BORROW

    (a) My executors may borrow money for any purpose.

    (b) My executors may charge any assets of my estate as security for any liability.

4–032 32 POWER OF DELEGATION

My executors may delegate any of their functions, in writing, to:

    (a) one or more of their number; or

    (b) any other person;

and if they do so my executors are not personally liable to my estate for the defaults of that delegate.

4–033 33 POWER TO ADMINISTER OFFSHORE

    (a) Any person with a power to appoint trustees may appoint a person who has no connection with the United Kingdom;

    (b) My executors may administer the trusts of my estate outside the United Kingdom.

4–034 34 INDEMNITIES

My executors may indemnify a retiring trustee, or any other person, against any liability concerning my estate. If they do so, then my estate (not my executors personally) will bear the liability of that indemnity. My executors may charge the indemnity on assets of my estate.

4–035 35 CHARITIES' RECEIPT

My executors may accept, as a complete discharge, the receipt of any person who appears to be a proper officer of a charity.

4–036 36 MINOR'S RECEIPT

where a person is a minor (that is:

    (a) under 18; or

    (b) 18 or over, but not of an age to be entitled to capital outright);

my executors may pay money to which he or she becomes entitled, whether:

    (i) income or capital; or

    (ii) as of right or under a power;

to any the following, and in each case their receipt is a complete discharge:

    (A) the minor, if he or she has attained 16;

    (B) the minor's parent or guardian, in which case my executors are under no further obligation to enquire into the use of the money; or

    (C) a third party for the benefit of the minor;

or my executors may resolve to hold the money on trust for the minor absolutely (in which case the administrative provisions of my will continue to apply to the money).

37 CONFLICTS OF INTEREST

4–037

My executors may exercise (or fail to exercise) any powers in my will, even if one or more of them has a personal interest in the outcome.

38 USE OF EXECUTORS' POWERS

4–038

My executors may exercise any of their powers:

(a) from time to time; and
(a) at their absolute discretion.

COLLECTED "SHORT FORM" POWERS

83 STEP powers

4–039

83a Basic STEP powers (amended in accordance with James Kessler's recommendations)

1 EXECUTORS' POWERS

The Standard Provisions of the Society of Trust and Estate Practitioners (1st edition) apply, amended as follows:

(a) Standard provision 5 ("trust for sale") does not apply.
(b) My executors may exercise their powers without consulting beneficiaries, so section 11 of the Trusts of Land and Appointment of Trustees Act 1996 does not apply.

83b Basic STEP powers (further amended for "interested" executors)

1 EXECUTORS' POWERS

The Standard Provisions of the Society of Trust and Estate Practitioners (1st edition) apply, amended as follows:

(a) Standard provision 5 ("trust for sale") does not apply.
(b) I have deliberately chosen executors who are interested in my estate. I wish them to be the only decision makers in my estate, and to be adequately protected. Accordingly:

    (i) standard provision 9 ("conflicts of interest") applies without the provisos to 9.2 and 9.3 (which would require formal disclosure of any interest in a decision, and the existence of an independent trustee).

    (ii) standard provision 12 ("liability of trustees") does not apply, and the next clause (2) applies in its place.

(c) My executors may exercise their powers without consulting beneficiaries, so section 11 of the Trusts of Land and Appointment of Trustees Act 1996 does not apply.

2 EXCLUSION OF EXECUTORS' LIABILITY

No executor, or trustee, is liable for any loss arising from:

(a) exercising, or failing to exercise, any discretion or power;

(b) any improper investment made in good faith;

(c) the negligence or fraud of any agent employed by him, or by any other executor or trustee, even if the employment was not strictly necessary or expedient;

(d) any mistake or omission made in good faith;

(e) any other matter, except wilful and individual fraud on the part of the executor or trustee who is sought to be made liable.

84 Recommended technical clauses for shorter wills

4–040 *Note*: One of the main themes of the redrafting between the 12th and 13th Editions of *Brighouse* has been to produce wills which are shorter, and more directly to the point, than traditional ones.

To that end, we strongly favour the use of the STEP Standard Provisions (which are reproduced in Appendix II) in place of detailed provisions in the will itself. As you will see, we have provided precedents in the longer and shorter form. However, our recommendation is for shorter form endings to wills, and accordingly we recommend one of the following endings in place of most technical endings. Where an estate includes a business, however, we recommend adding clause 92 and where a will contains an annuity it is necessary to make the appropriate choice from clauses 91a to 91c, in addition to the following. Our favourite is 84a, which you will see has been widely used in Part 6.

84a Ending for most common situations

4–041 **1 TECHNICAL CLAUSES**

(a) The Standard Provisions of the Society of Trust and Estate Practitioners (1st edition) apply, amended as follows:

(i) Standard provision 5 ("trust for sale") does not apply.

(ii) My executors may exercise their powers without consulting beneficiaries, so section 11 of the Trusts of Land and Appointment of Trustees Act 1996 does not apply.

(b) In my will, "children":

(i) includes those who are legitimate, illegitimate or adopted; but

(ii) does not include step-children, nor natural children who have been adopted by another person;

and other terms describing family relationships are to be interpreted accordingly.

(c) My estate is to be divided as if any person who dies within one month of my death had predeceased me.

84b Similar to 84a, but provisions relaxed for "interested" executors

1 TECHNICAL CLAUSES   4–042

(a) In my will, "children":

   (i) includes those who are legitimate, illegitimate or adopted; but
   (ii) does not include step-children, nor natural children who have been adopted by another person;

   and other terms describing family relationships are to be interpreted accordingly.

(b) My estate is to be divided as if any person who dies within one month of my death had predeceased me.

2 EXECUTORS' POWERS   4–043

The Standard Provisions of the Society of Trust and Estate Practitioners (1st edition) apply, amended as follows:

(a) Standard provision 5 ("trust for sale") does not apply.

(b) I have deliberately chosen executors who are interested in my estate. I wish them to be the only decision makers in my estate, and to be adequately protected. Accordingly:

   (i) standard provision 9 ("conflicts of interest") applies without the provisos to 9.2 and 9.3 (which would require formal disclosure of any interest in a decision, and the existence of an independent trustee).
   (ii) standard provision 12 ("liability of trustees") does not apply, and the next clause (3) applies in its place.

(c) My executors may exercise their powers without consulting beneficiaries, so section 11 of the Trusts of Land and Appointment of Trustees Act 1996 does not apply.

3 EXCLUSION OF EXECUTORS' LIABILITY   4–044

No executor, or trustee, is liable for any loss arising from:

(a) exercising, or failing to exercise, any discretion or power;
(b) any improper investment made in good faith;
(c) the negligence or fraud of any agent employed by him, or by any other executor or trustee, even if the employment was not strictly necessary or expedient;
(d) any mistake or omission made in good faith;
(e) any other matter, except wilful and individual fraud on the part of the executor or trustee who is sought to be made liable.

84c Same as 84a, but definition of "children" not required

Note: Our precedents are structured so that the "children" definition is useful *not only* in every will that uses the word children, *but also* in any will that refers to another family relationship (except, of course, just

71

husband/wife/widow(er)/spouse), and is therefore needed in any will containing one of the more flexible trusts.

4-045 1 TECHNICAL CLAUSES

(a) The Standard Provisions of the Society of Trust and Estate Practitioners (1st edition) apply, amended as follows:

  (i) Standard provision 5 ("trust for sale") does not apply.
  (ii) My executors may exercise their powers without consulting beneficiaries, so section 11 of the Trusts of Land and Appointment of Trustees Act 1996 does not apply.

(b) My estate is to be divided as if any person who dies within one month of my death had predeceased me.

84d Same as 84b, but definition of "children" not required

Note: See note to 84c.

4-046 1 COMMORIENTES

My estate is to be divided as if any person who dies within one month of my death had predeceased me.

4-047 2 EXECUTORS' POWERS

The Standard Provisions of the Society of Trust and Estate Practitioners (1st edition) apply, amended as follows:

(a) Standard provision 5 ("trust for sale") does not apply.
(b) I have deliberately chosen executors who are interested in my estate. I wish them to be the only decision makers in my estate, and to be adequately protected. Accordingly:

  (i) standard provision 9 ("conflicts of interest") applies without the provisos to 9.2 and 9.3 (which would require formal disclosure of any interest in a decision, and the existence of an independent trustee).
  (ii) standard provision 12 ("liability of trustees") does not apply, and the next clause (3) applies in its place.

(c) My executors may exercise their powers without consulting beneficiaries, so section 11 of the Trusts of Land and Appointment of Trustees Act 1996 does not apply.

4-048 3 EXCLUSION OF EXECUTORS' LIABILITY

No executor, or trustee, is liable for any loss arising from:

(a) exercising, or failing to exercise, any discretion or power;
(b) any improper investment made in good faith;
(c) the negligence or fraud of any agent employed by him, or by any other executor or trustee, even if the employment was not strictly necessary or expedient;

(d) any mistake or omission made in good faith;

(e) any other matter, except wilful and individual fraud on the part of the executor or trustee who is sought to be made liable.

COLLECTED "FULL FORM" POWERS

Note: The following clauses (85 to 90) are collected trustees' powers for different types of will. Broadly, the trusts in this book can be divided into four kinds: minorities, life interests, discretionary and annuities. Annuities are something of a law unto themselves and are dealt with in clause 91. It is quite possible to have more than one trust in a will, so the following table sets out the clause to use for each circumstance:

No ongoing trusts	85
Minorities	86
Life Interests	87
Discretionary	88
Minority + life interest	89
Minority + discretionary	90
Life Interest + discretionary	88
Minority + life interest + discretionary	90

In addition, you make the appropriate choice from 91a to 91c where the will contains an annuity, and you add 92 where the estate contains, or may contain, a business.

85 Trustees' powers where no ongoing trusts

1 POWER OF INVESTMENT 4–049

My executors may invest my estate in any investments they could make if they owned my estate personally. In particular, they may:

(a) invest in unsecured loans, including interest-free loans to a beneficiary;

(b) invest in land, whether as an investment or as a residence for a beneficiary, and may improve and maintain it;

(c) invest jointly with another person;

(d) invest in wasting or non-income-producing assets;

(e) invest anywhere in the world; and

(f) choose not to diversify investments.

2 EXCLUSION OF S.11 TLATA 4–050

My executors may exercise their powers without consulting beneficiaries, so section 11 of the Trusts of Land and Appointment of Trustees Act 1996 does not apply.

3 POWER OF APPROPRIATION 4–051

My executors may give specific assets of my estate to beneficiaries without requiring consent. (Section 41 of the Administration of Estates Act 1925 therefore applies subject to that amendment.)

4–052 4 POWER OF INSURANCE

My executors may:

(a) keep any assets of my estate insured, against any risk and in any amount;

(b) pay insurance premiums from the income or capital of that part of my estate which is held on the same trusts as the insured property; and

(c) treat any insurance money received as though it were the proceeds of sale of the insured property.

4–053 5 EXCLUSION OF EXECUTORS' LIABILITY

(a) Only a professional executor or trustee can be liable for any loss arising from:

    (i) exercising, or failing to exercise, any discretion or power;

    (ii) any improper investment made in good faith;

    (iii) the negligence or fraud of any agent employed by him, or by any other executor or trustee, even if the employment was not strictly necessary or expedient;

    (iv) any mistake or omission made in good faith;

    (v) any other matter, except willful and individual fraud on the part of the executor or trustee who is sought to be made liable.

(b) No executor can be liable for any loss, of any kind, if he has acted in accordance with the advice of Counsel of at least five years' standing.

4–054 6 POWER TO USE NOMINEES

My executors may vest any asset of my estate in the name of, or under the control of:

(a) one or more of their number; or

(b) any person (which may include a trust corporation), or people, as nominee(s).

4–055 7 POWER TO CHARGE FOR PROFESSIONAL SERVICES

Any of my executors who is engaged in a profession or business may charge fees for work done by him or her, or by his or her firm, in connection with my estate and its trusts, including acts which an executor or trustee not being in any profession or business could have done personally, and those charges shall be a first charge against my estate, without abatement.

4–056 8 COMMORIENTES

My estate is to be divided as if any person who dies within one month of my death had predeceased me.

4–057 9 CONFLICTS OF INTEREST

My executors may exercise (or fail to exercise) any powers in my will, even if one or more of them has a personal interest in the outcome.

10 USE OF EXECUTORS' POWERS 4–058

My executors may exercise any of their powers:

    (a) from time to time; and
    (b) at their absolute discretion.

86 Trustees' powers for minorities

1 POWER OF INVESTMENT 4–059

My executors may invest my estate in any investments they could make if they owned my estate personally. In particular, they may:

    (a) invest in unsecured loans, including interest-free loans to a beneficiary;
    (b) invest in land, whether as an investment or as a residence for a beneficiary, and may improve and maintain it;
    (c) invest jointly with another person;
    (d) invest in wasting or non-income-producing assets;
    (e) invest anywhere in the world; and
    (f) choose not to diversify investments.

2 EXCLUSION OF S.11 TLATA 4–060

My executors may exercise their powers without consulting beneficiaries, so section 11 of the Trusts of Land and Appointment of Trustees Act 1996 does not apply.

3 POWER OF ADVANCEMENT 4–061

My executors may apply the share of any beneficiary for $/{his$//her$//his or her$/} benefit, and this power:

    (a) is in addition to any other powers my executors may have, in particular section 32 of the Trustee Act 1925;
    (b) applies to the whole or part of the beneficiary's share;
    (c) applies whether the beneficiary's right is vested, contingent, expectant or presumptive but not where another person is entitled in priority;
    (d) may be used for advancement, maintenance, education or any other benefit;
    (e) may be exercised by paying the share to a third party or, where appropriate, to the beneficiary direct.

4 POWER OF APPROPRIATION 4–062

My executors may give specific assets of my estate to beneficiaries without requiring consent. (Section 41 of the Administration of Estates Act 1925 therefore applies subject to that amendment.)

5 POWER OF INSURANCE 4–063

My executors may:

    (a) keep any assets of my estate insured, against any risk and in any amount;

    (b) pay insurance premiums from the income or capital of that part of my estate which is held on the same trusts as the insured property; and

    (c) treat any insurance money received as though it were the proceeds of sale of the insured property.

4–064 6 EXCLUSION OF EXECUTORS' LIABILITY

    (a) Only a professional executor or trustee can be liable for any loss arising from:

        (i) exercising, or failing to exercise, any discretion or power;

        (ii) any improper investment made in good faith;

        (iii) the negligence or fraud of any agent employed by him, or by any other executor or trustee, even if the employment was not strictly necessary or expedient;

        (vi) any mistake or omission made in good faith;

        (v) any other matter, except willful and individual fraud on the part of the executor or trustee who is sought to be made liable.

    (b) No executor can be liable for any loss, of any kind, if he has acted in accordance with the advice of Counsel of at least five years' standing.

4–065 7 TRUST CORPORATIONS

If a trust corporation is appointed as executor or trustee, it may:

    (a) act by its proper officers;

    (b) exercise all the powers given to executors or trustees by my will;

    (c) charge under its published scale of fees, as amended from time to time;

    (d) meet its charges out of capital or income, at its discretion.

4–066 8 POWER TO USE NOMINEES

My executors may vest any asset of my estate in the name of, or under the control of:

    (a) one or more of their number; or

    (b) any person (which may include a trust corporation), or people, as nominee(s).

4–067 9 POWER TO CHARGE FOR PROFESSIONAL SERVICES

Any of my executors who is engaged in a profession or business may charge fees for work done by him or her, or by his or her firm, in connection with my estate and its trusts, including acts which an executor or trustee not being in any profession or business could have done personally, and those charges shall be a first charge against my estate, without abatement.

4–068 10 COMMORIENTES

My estate is to be divided as if any person who dies within one month of my death had predeceased me.

11 ACCUMULATIONS OF INCOME 4–069

My executors may:

(a) within 21 years of my death, accumulate income to the extent that it is not paid to, or applied for the benefit of, any beneficiary; and

(b) apply accumulated income as if it were the income of the current year.

12 POWER OF DELEGATION 4–070

My executors may delegate any of their functions, in writing, to:

(a) one or more of their number; or

(b) any other person;

and if they do so my executors are not personally liable to my estate for the defaults of that delegate.

13 INDEMNITIES 4–071

My executors may indemnify a retiring trustee, or any other person, against any liability concerning my estate. If they do so, then my estate (not my executors personally) will bear the liability of that indemnity. My executors may charge the indemnity on assets of my estate.

14 MINOR'S RECEIPT 4–072

where a person is a minor (that is:

(a) under 18; or

(b) 18 or over, but not of an age to be entitled to capital outright);

my executors may pay money to which he or she becomes entitled, whether:

(i) income or capital; or

(ii) as of right or under a power;

to any the following, and in each case their receipt is a complete discharge:

(A) the minor, if he or she has attained 16;

(B) the minor's parent or guardian, in which case my executors are under no further obligation to enquire into the use of the money; or

(C) a third party for the benefit of the minor;

or my executors may resolve to hold the money on trust for the minor absolutely (in which case the administrative provisions of my will continue to apply to the money).

15 CONFLICTS OF INTEREST 4–073

My executors may exercise (or fail to exercise) any powers in my will, even if one or more of them has a personal interest in the outcome.

4–074 16 USE OF EXECUTORS' POWERS

My executors may exercise any of their powers:

    (a) from time to time; and

    (b) at their absolute discretion.

87 Trustees' powers for life interest trusts

4–075 1 POWER OF INVESTMENT

My executors may invest my estate in any investments they could make if they owned my estate personally. In particular, they may:

    (a) invest in unsecured loans, including interest-free loans to a beneficiary;

    (b) invest in land, whether as an investment or as a residence for a beneficiary, and may improve and maintain it;

    (c) invest jointly with another person;

    (d) invest in wasting or non-income-producing assets;

    (e) invest anywhere in the world; and

    (f) choose not to diversify investments.

4–076 2 EXCLUSION OF THE APPORTIONMENT RULES

    (a) My executors may treat income as arising on the day it is received.

    (b) The Apportionment Act 1870 does not apply.

    (c) The rules known as "the rule in *Howe v. Dartmouth*" and "the rule in *Allhusen v. Whittell*" do not apply.

4–077 3 EXCLUSION OF S.11 TLATA

My executors may exercise their powers without consulting beneficiaries, so section 11 of the Trusts of Land and Appointment of Trustees Act 1996 does not apply.

4–078 4 POWER OF APPROPRIATION

My executors may give specific assets of my estate to beneficiaries without requiring consent. (Section 41 of the Administration of Estates Act 1925 therefore applies subject to that amendment.)

4–079 5 POWER OF INSURANCE

My executors may:

    (a) keep any assets of my estate insured, against any risk and in any amount;

    (b) pay insurance premiums from the income or capital of that part of my estate which is held on the same trusts as the insured property; and

    (c) treat any insurance money received as though it were the proceeds of sale of the insured property.

6 EXCLUSION OF EXECUTORS' LIABILITY   4–080

(a) Only a professional executor or trustee can be liable for any loss arising from:

  (i) exercising, or failing to exercise, any discretion or power;
  (ii) any improper investment made in good faith;
  (iii) the negligence or fraud of any agent employed by him, or by any other executor or trustee, even if the employment was not strictly necessary or expedient;
  (iv) any mistake or omission made in good faith;
  (v) any other matter, except willful and individual fraud on the part of the executor or trustee who is sought to be made liable.

(b) No executor can be liable for any loss, of any kind, if he has acted in accordance with the advice of Counsel of at least five years' standing.

7 TRUST CORPORATIONS   4–081

If a trust corporation is appointed as executor or trustee, it may:

(a) act by its proper officers;
(b) exercise all the powers given to executors or trustees by my will;
(c) charge under its published scale of fees, as amended from time to time;
(d) meet its charges out of capital or income, at its discretion.

8 POWER TO USE NOMINEES   4–082

My executors may vest any asset of my estate in the name of, or under the control of:

(a) one or more of their number; or
(b) any person (which may include a trust corporation), or people, as nominee(s).

9 POWER TO CHARGE FOR PROFESSIONAL SERVICES   4–083

Any of my executors who is engaged in a profession or business may charge fees for work done by him or her, or by his or her firm, in connection with my estate and its trusts, including acts which an executor or trustee not being in any profession or business could have done personally, and those charges shall be a first charge against my estate, without abatement.

10 COMMORIENTES   4–084

My estate is to be divided as if any person who dies within one month of my death had predeceased me.

11 POWER TO BORROW   4–085

(a) My executors may borrow money for any purpose.
(b) My executors may charge any assets of my estate as security for any liability.

4–086 12 POWER OF DELEGATION

My executors may delegate any of their functions, in writing, to:

(a) one or more of their number; or
(b) any other person;

and if they do so my executors are not personally liable to my estate for the defaults of that delegate.

4–087 13 INDEMNITIES

My executors may indemnify a retiring trustee, or any other person, against any liability concerning my estate. If they do so, then my estate (not my executors personally) will bear the liability of that indemnity. My executors may charge the indemnity on assets of my estate.

4–088 14 CONFLICTS OF INTEREST

My executors may exercise (or fail to exercise) any powers in my will, even if one or more of them has a personal interest in the outcome.

4–089 15 USE OF EXECUTORS' POWERS

My executors may exercise any of their powers:

(a) from time to time; and
(b) at their absolute discretion.

88 Trustees' powers for discretionary trusts (also for life interest + discretionary trusts)

4–090 1 POWER OF INVESTMENT

My executors may invest my estate in any investments they could make if they owned my estate personally. In particular, they may:

(a) invest in unsecured loans, including interest-free loans to a beneficiary;
(b) invest in land, whether as an investment or as a residence for a beneficiary, and may improve and maintain it;
(c) invest jointly with another person;
(d) invest in wasting or non-income-producing assets;
(e) invest anywhere in the world; and
(f) choose not to diversify investments.

4–091 2 EXCLUSION OF THE APPORTIONMENT RULES

(a) My executors may treat income as arising on the day it is received.
(b) The Apportionment Act 1870 does not apply.
(c) The rules known as "the rule in *Howe v. Dartmouth*" and "the rule in *Allhusen v. Whittell*" do not apply.

4–092 3 EXCLUSION OF S.11 TLATA

My executors may exercise their powers without consulting beneficiaries, so section 11 of the Trusts of Land and Appointment of Trustees Act 1996 does not apply.

4 POWER OF APPROPRIATION   4–093

My executors may give specific assets of my estate to beneficiaries without requiring consent. (Section 41 of the Administration of Estates Act 1925 therefore applies subject to that amendment.)

5 POWER OF INSURANCE   4–094

My executors may:
- (a) keep any assets of my estate insured, against any risk and in any amount;
- (b) pay insurance premiums from the income or capital of that part of my estate which is held on the same trusts as the insured property; and
- (c) treat any insurance money received as though it were the proceeds of sale of the insured property.

6 EXCLUSION OF EXECUTORS' LIABILITY   4–095

- (a) Only a professional executor or trustee can be liable for any loss arising from:

  - (i) exercising, or failing to exercise, any discretion or power;
  - (ii) any improper investment made in good faith;
  - (iii) the negligence or fraud of any agent employed by him, or by any other executor or trustee, even if the employment was not strictly necessary or expedient;
  - (iv) any mistake or omission made in good faith;
  - (v) any other matter, except willful and individual fraud on the part of the executor or trustee who is sought to be made liable.

- (b) No executor can be liable for any loss, of any kind, if he has acted in accordance with the advice of Counsel of at least five years' standing.

7 TRUST CORPORATIONS   4–096

If a trust corporation is appointed as executor or trustee, it may:

- (a) act by its proper officers;
- (b) exercise all the powers given to executors or trustees by my will;
- (c) charge under its published scale of fees, as amended from time to time;
- (d) meet its charges out of capital or income, at its discretion.

8 POWER TO USE NOMINEES   4–097

My executors may vest any asset of my estate in the name of, or under the control of:

- (a) one or more of their number; or
- (b) any person (which may include a trust corporation), or people, as nominee(s).

4–098 9 POWER TO CHARGE FOR PROFESSIONAL SERVICES

Any of my executors who is engaged in a profession or business may charge fees for work done by him or her, or by his or her firm, in connection with my estate and its trusts, including acts which an executor or trustee not being in any profession or business could have done personally, and those charges shall be a first charge against my estate, without abatement.

4–099 10 COMMORIENTES

My estate is to be divided as if any person who dies within one month of my death had predeceased me.

4–100 11 POWER TO BORROW

    (a) My executors may borrow money for any purpose.

    (b) My executors may charge any assets of my estate as security for any liability.

4–101 12 POWER OF DELEGATION

My executors may delegate any of their functions, in writing, to:

    (a) one or more of their number; or

    (b) any other person;

and if they do so my executors are not personally liable to my estate for the defaults of that delegate.

4–102 13 INDEMNITIES

My executors may indemnify a retiring trustee, or any other person, against any liability concerning my estate. If they do so, then my estate (not my executors personally) will bear the liability of that indemnity. My executors may charge the indemnity on assets of my estate.

4–103 14 MINOR'S RECEIPT

where a person is a minor (that is:

    (a) under 18; or

    (b) 18 or over, but not of an age to be entitled to capital outright);

my executors may pay money to which he or she becomes entitled, whether:

        (i) income or capital; or

        (ii) as of right or under a power;

to any the following, and in each case their receipt is a complete discharge:

        (A) the minor, if he or she has attained 16;

        (B) the minor's parent or guardian, in which case my executors are under no further obligation to enquire into the use of the money; or

        (C) a third party for the benefit of the minor;

or my executors may resolve to hold the money on trust for the minor absolutely (in which case the administrative provisions of my will continue to apply to the money).

15 CONFLICTS OF INTEREST 4–104

My executors may exercise (or fail to exercise) any powers in my will, even if one or more of them has a personal interest in the outcome.

16 USE OF EXECUTORS' POWERS 4–105

My executors may exercise any of their powers:

(a) from time to time; and
(b) at their absolute discretion.

89 Trustees' powers for minority + life interest trusts

1 POWER OF INVESTMENT 4–106

My executors may invest my estate in any investments they could make if they owned my estate personally. In particular, they may:

(a) invest in unsecured loans, including interest-free loans to a beneficiary;
(b) invest in land, whether as an investment or as a residence for a beneficiary, and may improve and maintain it;
(c) invest jointly with another person;
(d) invest in wasting or non-income-producing assets;
(e) invest anywhere in the world; and
(f) choose not to diversify investments.

2 EXCLUSION OF THE APPORTIONMENT RULES 4–107

(a) My executors may treat income as arising on the day it is received.
(b) The Apportionment Act 1870 does not apply.
(c) The rules known as "the rule in *Howe v. Dartmouth*" and "the rule in *Allhusen v. Whittell*" do not apply.

3 EXCLUSION OF S.11 TLATA 4–108

My executors may exercise their powers without consulting beneficiaries, so section 11 of the Trusts of Land and Appointment of Trustees Act 1996 does not apply.

4 POWER OF ADVANCEMENT 4–109

My executors may apply the share of any beneficiary for $/{his$//her$//his or her$/} benefit, and this power:

(a) is in addition to any other powers my executors may have, in particular section 32 of the Trustee Act 1925;
(b) applies to the whole or part of the beneficiary's share;
(c) applies whether the beneficiary's right is vested, contingent, expectant or presumptive but not where another person is entitled in priority;
(d) may be used for advancement, maintenance, education or any other benefit;
(e) may be exercised by paying the share to a third party or, where appropriate, to the beneficiary direct.

4–110 5 POWER OF APPROPRIATION

My executors may give specific assets of my estate to beneficiaries without requiring consent. (Section 41 of the Administration of Estates Act 1925 therefore applies subject to that amendment.)

4–111 6 POWER OF INSURANCE

My executors may:

(a) keep any assets of my estate insured, against any risk and in any amount;

(b) pay insurance premiums from the income or capital of that part of my estate which is held on the same trusts as the insured property; and

(c) treat any insurance money received as though it were the proceeds of sale of the insured property.

4–112 7 EXCLUSION OF EXECUTORS' LIABILITY

(a) Only a professional executor or trustee can be liable for any loss arising from:

(i) exercising, or failing to exercise, any discretion or power;

(ii) any improper investment made in good faith;

(iii) the negligence or fraud of any agent employed by him, or by any other executor or trustee, even if the employment was not strictly necessary or expedient;

(iv) any mistake or omission made in good faith;

(v) any other matter, except willful and individual fraud on the part of the executor or trustee who is sought to be made liable.

(b) No executor can be liable for any loss, of any kind, if he has acted in accordance with the advice of Counsel of at least five years' standing.

4–113 8 TRUST CORPORATIONS

If a trust corporation is appointed as executor or trustee, it may:

(a) act by its proper officers;

(b) exercise all the powers given to executors or trustees by my will;

(c) charge under its published scale of fees, as amended from time to time;

(d) meet its charges out of capital or income, at its discretion.

4–114 9 POWER TO USE NOMINEES

My executors may vest any asset of my estate in the name of, or under the control of:

(a) one or more of their number; or

(b) any person (which may include a trust corporation), or people, as nominee(s).

4–115 10 POWER TO CHARGE FOR PROFESSIONAL SERVICES

Any of my executors who is engaged in a profession or business may charge fees for work done by him or her, or by his or her firm, in connection with my estate and its trusts, including acts which an executor or trustee not being in any profession or business could have done personally, and those charges shall be a first charge against my estate, without abatement.

11 COMMORIENTES 4–116

My estate is to be divided as if any person who dies within one month of my death had predeceased me.

12 ACCUMULATIONS OF INCOME 4–117

My executors may:

- (a) within 21 years of my death, accumulate income to the extent that it is not paid to, or applied for the benefit of, any beneficiary; and
- (b) apply accumulated income as if it were the income of the current year.

13 POWER TO BORROW 4–118

- (a) My executors may borrow money for any purpose.
- (b) My executors may charge any assets of my estate as security for any liability.

14 POWER OF DELEGATION 4–119

My executors may delegate any of their functions, in writing, to:

- (a) one or more of their number; or
- (b) any other person;

and if they do so my executors are not personally liable to my estate for the defaults of that delegate.

15 INDEMNITIES 4–120

My executors may indemnify a retiring trustee, or any other person, against any liability concerning my estate. If they do so, then my estate (not my executors personally) will bear the liability of that indemnity. My executors may charge the indemnity on assets of my estate.

16 MINOR'S RECEIPT 4–121

where a person is a minor (that is:

- (a) under 18; or
- (b) 18 or over, but not of an age to be entitled to capital outright);

my executors may pay money to which he or she becomes entitled, whether:

- (i) income or capital; or
- (ii) as of right or under a power;

to any the following, and in each case their receipt is a complete discharge:

(A) the minor, if he or she has attained 16;

    (B) the minor's parent or guardian, in which case my executors are under no further obligation to enquire into the use of the money; or

    (C) a third party for the benefit of the minor;

or my executors may resolve to hold the money on trust for the minor absolutely (in which case the administrative provisions of my will continue to apply to the money).

4–122 17 CONFLICTS OF INTEREST

My executors may exercise (or fail to exercise) any powers in my will, even if one or more of them has a personal interest in the outcome.

4–123 18 USE OF EXECUTORS' POWERS

My executors may exercise any of their powers:
  (a) from time to time; and
  (b) at their absolute discretion.

90 Trustees' powers for minority and discretionary trusts (also for minority + life interest + discretionary trusts)

4–124 1 POWER OF INVESTMENT

My executors may invest my estate in any investments they could make if they owned my estate personally. In particular, they may:

  (a) invest in unsecured loans, including interest-free loans to a beneficiary;
  (b) invest in land, whether as an investment or as a residence for a beneficiary, and may improve and maintain it;
  (c) invest jointly with another person;
  (d) invest in wasting or non-income-producing assets;
  (e) invest anywhere in the world; and
  (f) choose not to diversify investments.

4–125 2 EXCLUSION OF THE APPORTIONMENT RULES

  (a) My executors may treat income as arising on the day it is received.
  (b) The Apportionment Act 1870 does not apply.
  (c) The rules known as "the rule in *Howe v. Dartmouth*" and "the rule in *Allhusen v. Whittell*" do not apply.

4–126 3 EXCLUSION OF S.11 TLATA

My executors may exercise their powers without consulting beneficiaries, so section 11 of the Trusts of Land and Appointment of Trustees Act 1996 does not apply.

4 POWER OF ADVANCEMENT

4–127

My executors may apply the share of any beneficiary for $/{his$//her$//his or her$/} benefit, and this power:

(a) is in addition to any other powers my executors may have, in particular section 32 of the Trustee Act 1925;

(b) applies to the whole or part of the beneficiary's share;

(c) applies whether the beneficiary's right is vested, contingent, expectant or presumptive but not where another person is entitled in priority;

(d) may be used for advancement, maintenance, education or any other benefit;

(e) may be exercised by paying the share to a third party or, where appropriate, to the beneficiary direct.

5 POWER OF APPROPRIATION

4–128

My executors may give specific assets of my estate to beneficiaries without requiring consent. (Section 41 of the Administration of Estates Act 1925 therefore applies subject to that amendment.)

6 POWER OF INSURANCE

4–129

My executors may:

(a) keep any assets of my estate insured, against any risk and in any amount;

(b) pay insurance premiums from the income or capital of that part of my estate which is held on the same trusts as the insured property; and

(c) treat any insurance money received as though it were the proceeds of sale of the insured property.

7 EXCLUSION OF EXECUTORS' LIABILITY

4–130

(a) Only a professional executor or trustee can be liable for any loss arising from:

(i) exercising, or failing to exercise, any discretion or power;

(ii) any improper investment made in good faith;

(iii) the negligence or fraud of any agent employed by him, or by any other executor or trustee, even if the employment was not strictly necessary or expedient;

(iv) any mistake or omission made in good faith;

(v) any other matter, except willful and individual fraud on the part of the executor or trustee who is sought to be made liable.

(b) No executor can be liable for any loss, of any kind, if he has acted in accordance with the advice of Counsel of at least five years' standing.

8 TRUST CORPORATIONS

4–131

If a trust corporation is appointed as executor or trustee, it may:

(a) act by its proper officers;

(b) exercise all the powers given to executors or trustees by my will;

(c) charge under its published scale of fees, as amended from time to time;

(d) meet its charges out of capital or income, at its discretion.

4–132 9 POWER TO USE NOMINEES

My executors may vest any asset of my estate in the name of, or under the control of:

(a) one or more of their number; or

(b) any person (which may include a trust corporation), or people, as nominee(s).

4–133 10 POWER TO CHARGE FOR PROFESSIONAL SERVICES

Any of my executors who is engaged in a profession or business may charge fees for work done by him or her, or by his or her firm, in connection with my estate and its trusts, including acts which an executor or trustee not being in any profession or business could have done personally, and those charges shall be a first charge against my estate, without abatement.

4–134 11 COMMORIENTES

My estate is to be divided as if any person who dies within one month of my death had predeceased me.

4–135 12 ACCUMULATIONS OF INCOME

My executors may:

(a) within 21 years of my death, accumulate income to the extent that it is not paid to, or applied for the benefit of, any beneficiary; and

(b) apply accumulated income as if it were the income of the current year.

4–136 13 POWER TO BORROW

(a) My executors may borrow money for any purpose.

(b) My executors may charge any assets of my estate as security for any liability.

4–137 14 POWER OF DELEGATION

My executors may delegate any of their functions, in writing, to:

(a) one or more of their number; or

(b) any other person;

and if they do so my executors are not personally liable to my estate for the defaults of that delegate.

4–138 15 INDEMNITIES

My executors may indemnify a retiring trustee, or any other person, against any liability concerning my estate. If they do so, then my estate (not my executors personally) will bear the liability of that indemnity. My executors may charge the indemnity on assets of my estate.

16 MINOR'S RECEIPT   4–139

where a person is a minor (that is:

(a) under 18; or
(b) 18 or over, but not of an age to be entitled to capital outright);

my executors may pay money to which he or she becomes entitled, whether:

(i) income or capital; or
(ii) as of right or under a power;

to any the following, and in each case their receipt is a complete discharge:

(A) the minor, if he or she has attained 16;
(B) the minor's parent or guardian, in which case my executors are under no further obligation to enquire into the use of the money; or
(C) a third party for the benefit of the minor;

or my executors may resolve to hold the money on trust for the minor absolutely (in which case the administrative provisions of my will continue to apply to the money).

17 CONFLICTS OF INTEREST   4–140

My executors may exercise (or fail to exercise) any powers in my will, even if one or more of them has a personal interest in the outcome.

18 USE OF EXECUTORS' POWERS   4–141

My executors may exercise any of their powers:

(a) from time to time; and
(b) at their absolute discretion.

91 Additional Powers for annuities

91a Full Powers

1 POWER TO APPROPRIATE ANNUITY FUND   4–142

My executors may appropriate from my estate the sum which, in their view, is sufficient to satisfy the $/{annuity$//annuities$/} given in my will. If they do so:

(a) My executors must take appropriate professional advice on the size and composition of the annuity fund.
(b) The $/{annuitant has$//annuitants have$/} no further claim on my estate if, in the event, the annuity fund is inadequate to pay the $/{annuity$//annuities$/} in full.

(c) My executors may use the income and capital of the annuity fund to pay the annuity.

(d) If they believe that the annuity fund is, at any time, larger than is necessary to satisfy the $/{annuity$//annuities$/}, my executors may hold the surplus as part of the residue of my estate.

(e) On the death of the $/[last$/] annuitant, my executors must hold any balance of the annuity fund as part of the residue of my estate.

4–143 2 POWER TO PURCHASE ANNUITY

My executors may purchase an annuity from any insurance office, company or corporation as they think fit to satisfy the $/{annuity$//annuities$/} given in my will. If they do so the $/{annuitant has$//annuitants have$/} no further claim against my estate.

4–144 3 POWER TO COMMUTE AN ANNUITY

My executors may commute the $/{annuity$//annuities$/} given in my will, by paying to the $/{annuitant$//annuitants$/} the capital amount which my executors consider reasonable. If they do so:

(a) My executors must take appropriate professional advice on the capital amount.

(b) The $/{annuitant has$//annuitants have$/} no further claim on my estate.

91b Full powers except without power to commute

4–145 1 POWER TO APPROPRIATE ANNUITY FUND

My executors may appropriate from my estate the sum which, in their view, is sufficient to satisfy the $/{annuity$//annuities$/} given in my will. If they do so:

(a) My executors must take appropriate professional advice on the size and composition of the annuity fund.

(b) The $/{annuitant has$//annuitants have$/} no further claim on my estate if, in the event, the annuity fund is inadequate to pay the $/{annuity$//annuities$/} in full.

(c) My executors may use the income and capital of the annuity fund to pay the annuity.

(d) If they believe that the annuity fund is, at any time, larger than is necessary to satisfy the $/{annuity$//annuities$/}, my executors may hold the surplus as part of the residue of my estate.

(e) On the death of the $/[last$/] annuitant, my executors must hold any balance of the annuity fund as part of the residue of my estate.

4–146 2 POWER TO PURCHASE ANNUITY

My executors may purchase an annuity from any insurance office, company or corporation as they think fit to satisfy the $/{annuity$//annuities$/} given in my will. If they do so the $/{annuitant has$//annuitants have$/} no further claim against my estate.

91c Direction to purchase

Note: We have included it here for ease of reference, but in fact this clause is the same as clause 54.

1 DIRECTION TO PURCHASE ANNUITY 4–147

My executors must purchase an annuity, from any insurance office, company or corporation as they think fit, to satisfy the $/{annuity$//annuities$/} given in my will. Once they have done so the $/{annuitant has$//annuitants have$/} no further claim against my estate.

92 Additional trustees' powers for businesses

1 POWER NOT TO INTERFERE IN THE MANAGEMENT OF A BUSINESS 4–148

My executors may choose not to interfere in the management (or conduct) of any business, company or corporation over which my executors have any level of control. If they are not aware of any wrongdoing on the part of the directors of a company, my executors may leave:

(a) the conduct of the business; and
(b) the decision whether to declare a dividend, and its amount;

to those directors. My executors are not liable to my estate for any action they take, or fail to take, in reliance on this clause.

2 POWER TO ACT AS OFFICER OR EMPLOYEE 4–149

Any executor may act personally as an officer, or employee, of any company in which my estate is interested. An executor who does so may retain personally any remuneration received. This is so even if:

(a) my executor having chosen to exercise (or not to exercise) rights over shares in my estate may have been instrumental in procuring the position as officer or employee; or
(b) my executor's qualifications for the position may be constituted (in part or in whole) by the holding in my estate.

3 POWER TO RUN A BUSINESS 4–150

My executors may carry on any business in which I am engaged at my death. If they do so then they may:

(a) carry on the business either alone or in partnership with any other people (and whether as general partners or limited partners);
(b) act upon such terms as they think fit, and as if they were the beneficial owners absolutely entitled;
(c) employ any of the capital of my estate in the business, including capitalising financing (by loans, guarantees or otherwise);
(d) employ anyone in connection with the business on such terms as they think fit;

(e) promote a company or corporation in any part of the world to acquire the business (or part of it) by the issue to my trustees of shares or securities or otherwise;

(f) pay, out of any property held upon the same trusts as the business, the cost of promoting such a company or corporation, and of the transfer of the business to it;

and my executors are indemnified, out of any property held upon the same trusts as the business, against any personal liability which they incur in connection with the business (unless that liability arose by reason of their own wilful and individual fraud or wrongdoing).

4–151 4 TREATMENT OF BUSINESS PROFITS

The net profits of any business in my estate are to be treated *as if* they were the income which would arise from investments representing the proceeds of sale of the business, if it were sold.

Part 5

TRUSTS

TRUSTS

Note: Most of the trusts in this chapter have been provided in two different **5–001** forms:

(a) as "residue continuation", that is — clauses which are intended to slip into a will in the same way as clauses 32 to 36 in Part 2; or

(b) as "settled legacies", that is — trusts which stand alone in the Will and not as part of residue.

Precedents in the sections "the home", "life interests" and "protective trusts" all have remainders (or quasi-remainders). Because almost any remainder can follow on from any of those trusts, remainders are dealt with separately in their own section (Precedents 97a to 97n). Each of the substantive trusts ends with a short leader along the lines of "subject to the above:" or "on the death of the life tenant:" which must be followed by a tail in order to complete the clause.

THE HOME

93 Right of residence in home

1 GIFT OF CONTENTS
5–002

(a) In this clause and the next (2):

(i) "the resident" means $/;

(ii) "the property" means $/ $/[or any other property which I own as my main residence at my death$/]; and

(iii) "personal chattels" has the meaning given in section 55(1)(x) of the Administration of Estates Act 1925, but does not include chattels which are the subject of specific gifts.

(b) I give all my personal chattels which are situated in the property at my death to the resident.

2 RIGHT OF RESIDENCE IN HOUSE
5–003

(a) In this clause "my trustees" means my executors or the trustees for the time being of this clause. My trustees have all the powers given to executors by my will.

(b) The resident has the right to reside at the property until the earliest of the following events:

(i) $/[the resident marries;$/]
(ii) $/[$/ $/{months$//years$/} from the date of my death;$/]
(iii) the resident dies;
(iv) the resident ceases to reside permanently at the property;
(v) the resident ceases to comply with any of the following conditions:

    (A) the resident must pay all outgoings;
    (B) the resident must keep the dwelling in good repair;
    (C) the resident must keep the dwelling insured to its full reinstatement value, with an insurance company approved by my trustees, at the resident's expense.

(c) The decision of my trustees as to whether an event has occurred, or a condition has been fulfilled, is binding.
(d) My trustees are not obliged to ensure that the resident's obligations set out in this clause have been complied with.
(e) At the resident's request, my trustees may sell the property and buy another to be held on the same terms as the property. Any surplus arising from the sale and purchase forms part of the residue of my estate.

Subject to the above:

94 Life interest in home

5–004 1 GIFT OF CONTENTS

(a) In this clause and the next (2):

    (i) "the life tenant" means $/;
    (ii) "the property" means $/ $/[or any other property which I own as my main residence at my death$/]; and
    (iii) "personal chattels" has the meaning given in section 55(1)(x) of the Administration of Estates Act 1925, but does not include chattels which are the subject of specific gifts.

(b) I give all my personal chattels which are situated in the property at my death to the life tenant.

5–005 2 LIFE INTERST IN HOUSE

(a) In this clause:

    (i) "my trustees" means my executors or the trustees for the time being of this clause; and
    (ii) "the trust fund" means all my interest in the property, and the assets representing it from time to time.

(b) My trustees have all the powers given to executors by my will.
(c) I give the trust fund to my trustees on trust to pay the income to the life tenant during $/{his$//her$/} lifetime $/[or until $/{he$//she$/} remarries$/].

(d) While the trust fund contains a dwelling occupied by the life tenant as a home, the life tenant must:

    (i) pay all outgoings;

    (ii) keep the dwelling in good repair;

    (iii) keep the dwelling insured to its full reinstatement value, with an insurance company approved by my trustees, at the life tenant's expense.

Subject to the above:

LIFE INTERESTS

Note: There are a great many permutations on a life interest trust, and for **5–006** ease of use this chapter presents twelve of those permutations. They are broken down as follows, and the table at the end of this note should assist you in choosing which precedent clause is the one you wish to draw into any particular will.

Type

A life interest trust can be of three types:

(a) for a single life tenant;

(b) for a class of life tenants equally, on their joint lives, so that as each of them dies the income continues to be paid equally to the survivors until none are left; or

(c) for a class in equal shares, so that on the death of one of the life tenants that share passes immediately to the remainderman while the other shares continue.

Advances of Capital

You can either have a true life interest where the capital is protected for the benefit of the remainderman, or you can have a more flexible life interest where advances of capital to the life tenant are permitted.

Style

As with all the trusts in this chapter, it might be formatted either as:

(a) a residue continuation; or

(b) a settled legacy;

and those concepts are explained in the note at the start of Part 5.

In addition we have also included precedents for a fully flexible life interest trust, which we have provided in both "residue continuation" and "settled legacy" format.

The following table shows all these permutations, and matching the ticks to the clause number on the left should indicate which clause is best for your circumstances.

Note that all these trusts (except the flexible ones) will require a "tail" to deal with the remainder interests — see clause 97a onwards.

Table of Life Interest Clauses

Clause Number	TYPE			ADVANCES OF CAPITAL		STYLE	
	One Life Tenant	Class (Equal & Joint)	Class (Shares)	No Power to Advance	Power to Advance	Residue Continuation	Settled Legacy
95a	✓			✓		✓	
95b	✓			✓			✓
95c	✓				✓	✓	
95d	✓				✓		✓
95e		✓		✓		✓	
95f		✓		✓			✓
95g			✓	✓		✓	
95h			✓	✓			✓
95i		✓			✓	✓	
95j		✓			✓		✓
95k			✓		✓	✓	
95l			✓		✓		✓
96a	FLEXIBLE TRUST					✓	
96b	FLEXIBLE TRUST						✓

95 Basic life interests

95a Basic life interest (residue continuation)

(a) to pay the residue ("the trust fund") to the trustees of the settlement **5–007**
declared in clause (1) below.

1 LIFE INTEREST TRUST   5–008

(a) In this clause, "my trustees" means my executors or the trustees for
the time being of this clause.
(b) My trustees have all the powers given to executors by my will.
(c) I give the trust fund to my trustees on trust to pay the income to $/
during ${his$//her$/} lifetime $/[or until ${he$//she$/} remarries$/];
and subject to that:

95b Basic life interest (settled legacy)

1 LIFE INTEREST TRUST   5–009

(a) In this clause, "my trustees" means my executors or the trustees for
the time being of this clause.
(b) My trustees have all the powers given to executors by my will.
(c) I give £$/ ("the trust fund") to my trustees on trust to pay the income
to $/ ("the life tenant") during ${his$//her$/} lifetime $/[or until
${he$//she$/} remarries$/]; and subject to that:

95c Life interest with power to advance (residue continuation)

(a) to pay the residue ("the trust fund") to the trustees of the settlement **5–010**
declared in clause (1) below.

1 LIFE INTEREST TRUST   5–011

(a) In this clause, "my trustees" means my executors or the trustees for
the time being of this clause.
(b) My trustees have all the powers given to executors by my will.
(c) I give the trust fund to my trustees on trust to pay the income to $/
("the life tenant") during ${his$//her$/} lifetime $/[or until ${he$//
she$/} remarries$/].
(d) My trustees may apply the capital of my estate for the benefit of the
life tenant. This power may apply to the whole or part of that capital in
which ${he$//she$/} has an interest.

subject to the above:

95d Life interest with power to advance (settled legacy)

5–012 1 LIFE INTEREST TRUST

> (a) In this clause, "my trustees" means my executors or the trustees for the time being of this clause.
> (b) My trustees have all the powers given to executors by my will.
> (c) I give £$/ ("the trust fund") to my trustees on trust to pay the income to $/ ("the life tenant") during $/{his$//her$/} lifetime $/[or until $/{he$//she$/} remarries$/].
> (d) My trustees may apply the capital of the trust fund for the benefit of the life tenant. This power may apply to the whole or part of that capital in which $/{he$//she$/} has an interest.

Subject to the above:

95e Life interest to class — equal & joint (residue continuation)

5–013   (a) to pay the residue ("the trust fund") to the trustees of the settlement declared in clause (1) below.

5–014 1 LIFE INTEREST TRUST

> (a) In this clause, "my trustees" means my executors or the trustees for the time being of this clause.
> (b) My trustees have all the powers given to executors by my will.
> (c) I give the trust fund to my trustees on trust to pay the income, jointly, to those of $/ who are living from time to time, and on the death of the survivor of them:

95f Life interest to class — equal & joint (settled legacy)

5–015 1 LIFE INTEREST TRUST

> (a) In this clause, "my trustees" means my executors or the trustees for the time being of this clause.
> (b) My trustees have all the powers given to executors by my will.
> (c) I give £$/ ("the trust fund") to my trustees on trust to pay the income, jointly, to those of $/ who are living from time to time, and on the death of the survivor of them:

95g Life interest to class — shares (residue continuation)

5–016   (a) to pay the residue ("the trust fund") to the trustees of the settlement declared in clause (1) below.

5–017 1 LIFE INTEREST TRUST

> (a) In this clause, "my trustees" means my executors or the trustees for the time being of this clause.
> (b) My trustees have all the powers given to executors by my will.
> (c) I give the trust fund to my trustees to divide it into $/ equal shares, and:

(i) to pay the income from $/ shares to $/ during ${his$//her$/} lifetime $/[or until ${he$//she$/} remarries$/];

(ii) to pay the income from $/ shares to $/ during ${his$//her$/} lifetime; and

(iii) to pay the income from $/ shares to $/ during ${his$//her$/} lifetime;

(d) and on the failure of each share, to hold it:

95h Life interest to class — shares (settled legacy)

1 LIFE INTEREST TRUST   5–018

(a) In this clause, "my trustees" means my executors or the trustees for the time being of this clause.

(b) My trustees have all the powers given to executors by my will.

(c) I give £$/ ("the trust fund") to my trustees to divide it into $/ equal shares, and:

(i) to pay the income from $/ shares to $/ during ${his$//her$/} lifetime $/[or until ${he$//she$/} remarries$/];

(ii) to pay the income from $/ shares to $/ during ${his$//her$/} lifetime; and

(iii) to pay the income from $/ shares to $/ during ${his$//her$/} lifetime;

(d) and on the failure of each share, to hold it:

95i Life interest to class — equal & joint — power to advance (residue continuation)

(a) to pay the residue ("the trust fund") to the trustees of the settlement **5–019** declared in clause (1) below.

1 LIFE INTEREST TRUST   5–020

(a) In this clause, "my trustees" means my executors or the trustees for the time being of this clause.

(b) My trustees have all the powers given to executors by my will.

(c) I give the trust fund to my trustees on trust to pay the income, jointly, to those of $/ ("the life tenants") who are living from time to time.

(d) My trustees may apply the capital of my estate for the benefit of the life tenants. This power may apply to the whole or part of that capital in which each respective life tenant has an interest.

on the death of the survivor of the life tenants:

95j Life interest to class — equal & joint — power to advance (settled legacy)

1 LIFE INTEREST TRUST   5–021

(a) In this clause, "my trustees" means my executors or the trustees for the time being of this clause.

101

(b) My trustees have all the powers given to executors by my will.

(c) I give £$/ ("the trust fund") to my trustees on trust to pay the income, jointly, to those of $/ ("the life tenants") who are living from time to time.

(d) My trustees may apply the capital of the trust fund for the benefit of the life tenants. This power may apply to the whole or part of that capital in which each respective life tenant has an interest.

(e) On the death of the survivor of the life tenants:

95k Life interest to class — shares — power to advance (residue continuation)

5–022   (a) to pay the residue ("the trust fund") to the trustees of the settlement declared in clause (1) below.

5–023   1 LIFE INTEREST TRUST

(a) In this clause, "my trustees" means my executors or the trustees for the time being of this clause.

(b) My trustees have all the powers given to executors by my will.

(c) I give the trust fund to my trustees to divide it into $/ equal shares, and:

    (i) to pay the income from $/ shares to $/ during ${his$//her$/} lifetime $/[or until ${he$//she$/} remarries$/];

    (ii) to pay the income from $/ shares to $/ during ${his$//her$/} lifetime; and

    (iii) to pay the income from $/ shares to $/ during ${his$//her$/} lifetime.

(d) My trustees may apply the capital of my estate for the benefit of the life tenants. This power may apply to the whole or part of that capital in which each respective life tenant has an interest.

On the failure of each share, to hold it:

95l Life interest to class — shares — power to advance (settled legacy)

5–024   1 LIFE INTEREST TRUST

(a) In this clause, "my trustees" means my executors or the trustees for the time being of this clause.

(b) My trustees have all the powers given to executors by my will.

(c) I give £$/ ("the trust fund") to my trustees to divide it into $/ equal shares, and:

    (i) to pay the income from $/ shares to $/ during ${his$//her$/} lifetime $/[or until ${he$//she$/} remarries$/];

    (ii) to pay the income from $/ shares to $/ during ${his$//her$/} lifetime; and

    (iii) to pay the income from $/ shares to $/ during ${his$//her$/} lifetime.

(d) My trustees may apply the capital of the trust fund for the benefit of the life tenants. This power may apply to the whole or part of that capital in which each respective life tenant has an interest.

(e) On the failure of each share:

96 Flexible life interest trust

96a Flexible life interest trust (residue continuation)   5–025

(a) to pay the residue ("the trust fund") to the trustees of the settlement declared in clause (1) below.

1 FLEXIBLE LIFE INTEREST TRUST   5–026

(a) In this clause:
"my trustees" means my executors or the trustees for the time being of this clause;
"beneficiaries" means:

   (i) my $/{husband$//wife$/};
   (ii) all descendants of any of my grandparents;
   (iii) all descendants of any of my $/{husband's$//wife's$/} grandparents;
   (iv) the spouses and former spouses of (ii) and (iii);
   (v) charities

(b) I give the trust fund to my trustees on the following trusts:

   (i) to pay the income to my $/{husband$//wife$/} for his or her lifetime;
   (ii) subject to that, to divide the trust fund equally between those of my children who are living at the death of the survivor of me and my $/{husband$//wife$/} and attain 25; except:

   (A) if any of my children dies before the survivor of me and my $/{husband$//wife$/}, then to divide that child's share equally between those of $/{his$//her$//his or her$/} children who are living at the death of the survivor of me and my $/{husband$//wife$/}, and attain 25; and

   (B) if any of my children dies after the survivor of me and my $/{husband$//wife$/}, but before attaining 25, then to divide that child's share equally between those of $/{his$//her$//his or her$/} children who are living at $/{his$//her$//his or her$/} death and who either:

   (I) attain 25; or
   (II) are living, and under 25, 21 years after the death of the last survivor of those of my descendants who are living at my death.

(c) While my $/{husband$//wife$/} is alive, and after $/{his$//her$/} death in respect of any part of the trust fund which has not yet been paid to a beneficiary outright, my trustees may:

    (i) bring to an end the right to income granted to my $/{husband$// wife$/};

   (ii) pay the capital to (or use it for the benefit of) any beneficiaries they think fit;

  (iii) pay the income to (or use it for the benefit of) any beneficiaries they think fit;

  (iv) create (revocably or irrevocably) any trusts that they think fit over the trust fund, in favour of any beneficiaries they think fit;

   (v) bring to an end revocable trusts created under (iv);

  (vi) while any beneficiary is under 25, resolve that they hold the trust fund (or a specified share in it) on trusts which will be an accumulation and maintenance settlement (as defined in section 71 of the Inheritance Tax Act 1984);

 (vii) while any beneficiary is under 25, resolve that they hold the trust fund (or a specified share in it) on trust for the beneficiary absolutely (in which case the administrative provisions of my will continue to apply to it).

(d) My trustees must not exercise their powers under (c) so as to breach:

    (i) the rule against perpetuities;

   (ii) the rule against excessive accumulations of income.

(e) My trustees must exercise their discretions by deed of appointment. A deed of appointment may be revocable or irrevocable.

 (f) My trustees have all the powers given to executors by my will.

96b Flexible life interest trust (settled legacy)

5–027 1 FLEXIBLE LIFE INTEREST TRUST

(a) In this clause:

"my trustees" means my executors or the trustees for the time being of this clause;

"beneficiaries" means:

    (i) my $/{husband$//wife$/};

   (ii) all descendants of any of my grandparents;

  (iii) all descendants of any of my $/{husband's$//wife's$/} grandparents;

  (iv) the spouses and former spouses of (ii) and (iii);

   (v) charities

(b) I give £$/ ("the trust fund") to my trustees on the following trusts:

    (i) to pay the income to my $/{husband$//wife$/} for his or her lifetime;

   (ii) subject to that, to divide the trust fund equally between those of my children who are living at the death of the survivor of me and my $/{husband$//wife$/} and attain 25; except:

      (A) if any of my children dies before the survivor of me and my $/{husband$//wife$/}, then to divide that child's share equally between those of $/{his$//her$//his or her$/} children who are living at the death of the survivor of me and my $/{husband$//wife$/}, and attain 25; and

(B) if any of my children dies after the survivor of me and my $/{husband$//wife$/}, but before attaining 25, then to divide that child's share equally between those of $/{his$//her$//his or her$/} children who are living at $/{his$//her$//his or her$/} death and who either:

(I) attain 25; or

(II) are living, and under 25, 21 years after the death of the last survivor of those of my descendants who are living at my death.

(c) While my $/{husband$//wife$/} is alive, and after $/{his$//her$/} death in respect of any part of the trust fund which has not yet been paid to a beneficiary outright, my trustees may:

(i) bring to an end the right to income granted to my $/{husband$// wife$/};

(ii) pay the capital to (or use it for the benefit of) any beneficiaries they think fit;

(iii) pay the income to (or use it for the benefit of) any beneficiaries they think fit;

(iv) create (revocably or irrevocably) any trusts that they think fit over the trust fund, in favour of any beneficiaries they think fit;

(v) bring to an end revocable trusts created under (iv);

(vi) while any beneficiary is under 25, resolve that they hold the trust fund (or a specified share in it) on trusts which will be an accumulation and maintenance settlement (as defined in section 71 of the Inheritance Tax Act 1984);

(vii) while any beneficiary is under 25, resolve that they hold the trust fund (or a specified share in it) on trust for the beneficiary absolutely (in which case the administrative provisions of my will continue to apply to it).

(d) My trustees must not exercise their powers under (c) so as to breach:
(i) the rule against perpetuities;
(ii) the rule against excessive accumulations of income.

(e) My trustees must exercise their discretions by deed of appointment. A deed of appointment may be revocable or irrevocable.

(f) My trustees have all the powers given to executors by my will.

REMAINDERS

97 "Tails"

Note: See the note under the heading "life interests", preceding clause 95.   **5–028**
Note that where *remarriage* is a determining event, the tail must be followed by a tail-on-a-tail (see clause 97m). There is a similar tail-on-a-tail (in 305n) which is particularly useful to follow *protective trusts, or rights-of-residence.*

Just like the residue continuations in Part 2, these tails are written such that they can follow on one from the other, to give several levels of substitution if needed.

97a Children (no substitutions)

5–029   (a) to divide the residue equally between those of my children who are living at the death of the survivor of:

> (i) me; and
> (ii) $/{my wife$// my husband$//the life tenant$//each respective life tenant$//the last of the life tenants to die$/};

$/[and attain $/{18$//21$//25$/}$/] (without substituting their children if their shares fail); $/[but if this gift fails entirely$/]

97b Children — substituting grandchildren — children of age

5–030   (a) to divide the residue equally between those of my children who are living at the death of the survivor of:

> (i) me; and
> (ii) $/{my wife ("the life tenant")$// my husband ("the life tenant")$// the life tenant$//each respective life tenant$//the last of the life tenants to die$/};

except:

(b) if any of my children dies before the survivor of me and the life tenant, then to divide that child's share equally between those of $/{his$//her$//his or her$/} children who are living at the death of the survivor of me and the life tenant $/[and attain $/{18$//21$//25$/}$/]$/[; but if the above trusts fail$/]

97c Children — substituting grandchildren — children not of age — contingency age 21 or under

5–031   (a) to divide the residue equally between those of my children who are living at the death of the survivor of:

> (i) me; and
> (ii) $/{my wife ("the life tenant")$// my husband ("the life tenant")$// the life tenant$//each respective life tenant$//the last of the life tenants to die$/};

and attain $/{18$//21$/}; except:

> (A) if any of my children dies before the survivor of me and the life tenant, then to divide that child's share equally between those of $/{his$//her$//his or her$/} children who are living at the death of the survivor of me and the life tenant, and attain $/{18$//21$/}; and
> (B) if any of my children dies after the survivor of me and the life tenant, but before attaining $/{18$//21$/}, then to divide

that child's share equally between those of $/{his$//her$//his or her$/} children who are living at $/{his$//her$//his or her$/} death and attain $/{18$//21$/}$/.

[if the above trusts fail, then:$/]

97d Children — substituting grandchildren — children not of age — contingency age over 21

(a) to divide the residue equally between those of my children who are **5–032** living at the death of the survivor of:

(i) me; and

(ii) $/{my wife ("the life tenant")$// my husband ("the life tenant")$// the life tenant$//each respective life tenant$//the last of the life tenants to die$/};

and attain 25; except:

(A) if any of my children dies before the survivor of me and the life tenant, then to divide that child's share equally between those of $/{his$//her$//his or her$/} children who are living at the death of the survivor of me and the life tenant, and attain 25; and

(B) if any of my children dies after the survivor of me and the life tenant, but before attaining 25, then to divide that child's share equally between those of $/{his$//her$//his or her$/} children who are living at $/{his$//her$//his or her$/} death and who either:

(I) attain 25; or

(II) are living, and under 25, 21 years after the death of the last survivor of those of my descendants who are living at my death.

[if the above trusts fail, then:$/]

97e Class — those of . . . Who . . .

(a) to divide the residue equally between those of my $/{children$// **5–033** grandchildren$//nieces$//nephews$//nieces and nephews$//cousins$/} who are living at the death of the survivor of:

(i) me; and

(ii) $/{my wife$// my husband$//the life tenant$//each respective life tenant$//the last of the life tenants to die$/};

$/[and attain $/{18$//21$//25$/}$/] $/[; but if the above trusts fail, then:$/]

97f Class — those of (a), (b), (c) who . . .

(a) to divide the residue equally between those of the following who are **5–034** living at the death of the survivor of:

(i) me; and

(ii) $/{my wife$// my husband$//the life tenant$//each respective life tenant$//the last of the life tenants to die$/};

$/[and attain $/{18$//21$//25$/} $/]namely:

(A) $/;
(B) $/; and
(C) $/;

$/[if the above trusts fail, then:$/]

97g Class — shares

5–035   (a) to divide the residue into $/ equal shares and to pay:

(i) $/ $/{share$//shares$/} to $/;
(ii) $/ $/{share$//shares$/} to $/; and
(iii) $/ $/{share$//shares$/} to $/;

if each of them respectively is living at the death of the survivor of:

(A) me; and
(B) $/{my wife$// my husband$//the life tenant$//each respective life tenant$//the last of the life tenants to die$/}.

(b) $/{If any of the above shares fail, the failed share accrues proportionately to the shares which do not fail.$//If either of the above shares fail, the failed share accrues to the other.$/}

(c) $/[If the above trusts fail entirely, then:$/]

97h Class — percentage

5–036   (a) to pay the residue:

(i) $/% to $/;
(ii) $/% to $/; and
(iii) $/% to $/;

if each of them respectively is living at the death of the survivor of:

(A) me; and
(B) $/{my wife$// my husband$//the life tenant$//each respective life tenant$//the last of the life tenants to die$/}.

(b) $/{If any of the above shares fail, the failed share accrues proportionately to the shares which do not fail.$//If either of the above shares fail, the failed share accrues to the other.$/}

(c) $/[If the above trusts fail entirely, then:$/]

97i Individual

5–037   (a) to pay the residue to $/ if $/{he$//she$/} is living at the death of the survivor of:

(i) me; and

(ii) $/{my wife$// my husband$//the life tenant$//each respective life tenant$//the last of the life tenants to die$/};
$/[but if this gift fails:$/]

97j Individual (backstop)

Note: It is impossible for this trust to fail, so that possibility is not covered. **5–038**

(a) My backstop beneficiary is $/. When the above trusts fail my trustees must pay the trust fund to $/{him$//her$/} (or $/{his$//her$/} estate) absolutely.

97k "Residue"

Note: This clause and the next (97l) are only for use as tails to settled **5–039** legacies. If you ask the executors to hold residue on the trusts of residue, the Judge will not thank you for it! It is impossible for this trust to fail, so that possibility is not covered.

(a) to hold the trust fund as part of the residue of my estate.

97l "Residue as if . . ."

Note: See the note to clause 97k. **5–040**

(a) to hold the trust fund on the trusts of the residue of my estate as they would apply if references to my death were references to the death of the survivor of:

(i) me; and

(ii) $/{my wife$// my husband$//the life tenant$//each respective life tenant$//the last of the life tenants to die$/};

97m Tail-on-a-tail where remarriage is a determining event

(a) If the determining event was the remarriage of $/{my husband$//my **5–041** wife$//the life tenant$/}, then the provisions describing the remainder interest are to be interpreted as if $/{my husband$//my wife$//the life tenant$/} had died at the date of that remarriage.

97n Tail-on-a-tail where death is not the only determining event

Note: This tail is particularly important for rights-of-residence, and for **5–042** protective trusts.

(a) If the determining event was anything other than the death of $/{my husband$//my wife$//the life tenant$/}, then the provisions describing the remainder interest are to be interpreted as if $/{my husband$//my wife$//the life tenant$/} had died at the date of that determining event.

PROTECTIVE TRUSTS

98 Various protective trusts

Note: Like life interest trusts, these protective trust precedents need to be followed by "tails" (See clauses 97a *et seq,* and particularly clause 97n).

98a Unmodified protective trust (residue continuation)

5–043 (a) to pay the residue ("the trust fund") to the trustees of the settlement declared in clause (1) below.

5–044 1 PROTECTIVE TRUST

  (a) In this clause, "my trustees" means my executors or the trustees for the time being of this clause.
  (b) My trustees have all the powers given to executors by my will.
  (c) I give the trust fund to my trustees, for the benefit of $/ during $/{his$//her$/} lifetime, on protective trusts (as set out in section 33 of the Trustee Act 1925); and subject to that:

98b Unmodified protective trust (settled legacy)

5–045 1 PROTECTIVE TRUST

  (a) In this clause, "my trustees" means my executors or the trustees for the time being of this clause.
  (b) My trustees have all the powers given to executors by my will.
  (c) I give £$/ ("the trust fund") to my trustees, for the benefit of $/ ("the life tenant") during $/{his$//her$/} lifetime, on protective trusts (as set out in section 33 of the Trustee Act 1925); and subject to that:

98c Modified protective trust (residue continuation)

5–046 (a) to pay the residue ("the trust fund") to the trustees of the settlement declared in clause (1) below.

5–047 1 PROTECTIVE TRUST

  (a) In this clause, "my trustees" means my executors or the trustees for the time being of this clause.
  (b) My trustees have all the powers given to executors by my will.
  (c) I give the trust fund to my trustees, for the benefit of $/ ("the life tenant") during $/{his$//her$/} lifetime, on protective trusts (as set out in section 33 of the Trustee Act 1925) modified as follows:

   (i) my trustees may apply the capital of my estate for the benefit of the life tenant. This power may apply to the whole or part of that capital in which $/{he$//she$/} has an interest.
   (ii) the life tenant may, with the written consent of the trustees, surrender $/{his$//her$/} interest under this clause. If $/{he$// she$/} does so then the trust devolves as if $/{he$//she$/} had died at the date of the surrender.

Subject to the above:

98d modified protective trust (settled legacy)

5–048 1 PROTECTIVE TRUST

  (a) In this clause, "my trustees" means my executors or the trustees for the time being of this clause.

(b) My trustees have all the powers given to executors by my will.

(c) I give £$/ ("the trust fund") to my trustees, for the benefit of $/ ("the life tenant") during $/{his$//her$/} lifetime, on protective trusts (as set out in section 33 of the Trustee Act 1925) modified as follows:

  (i) my trustees may apply the capital of my estate for the benefit of the life tenant. This power may apply to the whole or part of that capital in which $/{he$//she$/} has an interest.

  (ii) the life tenant may, with the written consent of the trustees, surrender $/{his$//her$/} interest under this clause. If $/{he$//she$/} does so then the trust devolves as if $/{he$//she$/} had died at the date of the surrender.

(d) Subject to the above:

ACCUMULATION AND MAINTENANCE TRUSTS

99 Flexible accumulation and maintenance trusts

Note: The technical rules for accumulation and maintenance ("A&M") settlements are discussed briefly in the introduction.

Our practice has been to create most interests for children in Part 2 of this book, without using the term "trustees" nor creating any formal-looking trusts. Nevertheless, the minority interests which we have created in Part 2 do normally take effect as A&M settlements. The only A&M settlement included in this part is this fully flexible A&M trust which (as usual for this book) comes in two forms — residue continuation or settled legacy. Also, because there is slightly greater flexibility where the "common grandparent rule" is satisfied (again, see the introduction) we have provided separate forms where that rule is, and is not, satisfied by the intended beneficiaries. An alternative recommended by some writers is to create more than one A&M trust, each one for the benefit of a group of beneficiaries who do have a common grandparent.

99a Flexible A&M trust — common grandparent rule satisfied (residue continuation)

Note: It is essential to choose only one of the definitions of "primary **5–050** beneficiaries" in this clause

(a) to pay the residue ("the trust fund") to the trustees of the settlement declared in clause (1) below.

1 FLEXIBLE ACCUMULATION AND MAINTENANCE TRUST   5–051

(a) In this clause:

"my trustees" means my executors or the trustees for the time being of this clause;

"the primary beneficiaries" means those of my children who are living at my death;

"the primary beneficiaries" means those of my grandchildren who are either:

(i) living at my death; or

(ii) born after me but before the eldest living primary beneficiary attains 25;

"the primary beneficiaries" means my following $/{children$// grandchildren$/}:

(i) $/;

(ii) $/; and

(iii) $/;

"the primary beneficiaries" means:

(i) $/;

(ii) $/; and

(iii) $/;

being grandchildren of a common grandparent, namely $/ $/[late$/] of $/;

"the beneficiaries" means:

(i) the primary beneficiaries;

(ii) all descendants of the primary beneficiaries;

(iii) the spouses and former spouses of (i) and (ii);

(iv) my $/{widow$//widower$/}; and

(v) charities;

"interest-in-possession" means the right to receive the current income from a share in the trust fund.

(b) I give the trust fund to my trustees on the following trusts:

(i) to divide the trust fund into one equal share for each primary beneficiary;

(ii) while a primary beneficiary is under 25:

(A) to apply the income from his or her share for his or her maintenance, education or benefit; or

(B) within 21 years of my death, to accumulate any income not so applied;

(iii) as each primary beneficiary attains 25, to grant an interest-in-possession in his or her share, to him or her.

(c) The above trusts are subject to the following powers:

(i) while a primary beneficiary is under 25 my trustees may apply the income of his or her share for the benefit of any other primary beneficiary who is for the time being under 25;

(ii) my trustees may grant a primary beneficiary an interest-in-possession in his or her share at any age below 25;

    (iii) if a primary beneficiary dies before attaining an interest-in-possession then my trustees may hold his or her share for the benefit of any of the beneficiaries they think fit.

    (iv) once a primary beneficiary has attained an interest-in-possession, my trustees may hold his or her share for the benefit of any of the beneficiaries they think fit.

    (v) if my trustees have the power to benefit any of the beneficiaries they think fit, their powers include:

        (A) the power to pay to a primary beneficiary the capital of his or her share outright;

        (B) the power to bring an interest-in-possession to an end, or to transfer it to another beneficiary;

        (C) the power to use a share for the benefit of (or pay the capital from it to) a beneficiary other than the primary beneficiary whose share it was;

        (D) the power to settle any part of the trust fund on the trustees of a separate trust if (and only if) the only possible beneficiaries of that trust are also beneficiaries of this clause;

        (E) where a primary beneficiary has died, the power to redistribute his share among the shares of surviving primary beneficiaries.

(d) My trustees must exercise their discretions by deed of appointment. A deed of appointment may be revocable or irrevocable.

(e) My trustees have all the powers given to executors by my will.

99b Flexible A&M trust — common grandparent rule satisfied (settled legacy)

Note: It is essential to choose *only one* of the definitions of "primary beneficiaries" in this clause.   **5–052**

1 FLEXIBLE ACCUMULATION AND MAINTENANCE TRUST   5–053

(a) In this clause:

    "the trust fund" means £$/ and the property from time to time representing it;

    "my trustees" means my executors or the trustees for the time being of this clause;

    "the primary beneficiaries" means those of my children who are living at my death;

    "the primary beneficiaries" means those of my grandchildren who are either:

    (i) living at my death; or

    (ii) born after me but before the eldest living primary beneficiary attains 25;

"the primary beneficiaries" means my following $/{children$//grandchildren$/}:

(i) $/;
(ii) $/; and
(iii) $/;

"the primary beneficiaries" means:
(i) $/;
(ii) $/; and
(iii) $/;

being grandchildren of a common grandparent, namely $/ $/[late$/] of $/;

"the beneficiaries" means:

(i) the primary beneficiaries;
(ii) all descendants of the primary beneficiaries;
(iii) the spouses and former spouses of (i) and (ii);
(iv) my $/{widow$//widower$/}; and
(v) charities;

"interest-in-possession" means the right to receive the current income produced by a share in the trust fund.

(b) I give the trust fund to my trustees on the following trusts:

(i) to divide the trust fund into one equal share for each primary beneficiary;
(ii) while a primary beneficiary is under 25:

(A) to apply the income from his or her share for his or her maintenance, education or benefit; or
(B) within 21 years of my death, to accumulate any income not so applied;

(iii) as each primary beneficiary attains 25, to grant an interest-in-possession in his or her share, to him or her.

(c) The above trusts are subject to the following powers:

(i) while a primary beneficiary is under 25 my trustees may apply the income of his or her share for the benefit of any other primary beneficiary who is for the time being under 25;
(ii) my trustees may grant a primary beneficiary an interest-in-possession in his or her share at any age below 25;
(iii) if a primary beneficiary dies before attaining an interest-in-possession then my trustees may hold his or her share for the benefit of any of the beneficiaries they think fit.
(iv) once a primary beneficiary has attained an interest-in-possession, my trustees may hold his or her share for the benefit of any of the beneficiaries they think fit.
(v) if my trustees have the power to benefit any of the beneficiaries they think fit, their powers include:

(A) the power to pay to a primary beneficiary the capital of his or her share outright;

(B) the power to bring an interest-in-possession to an end, or to transfer it to another beneficiary;

(C) the power to use a share for the benefit of (or pay the capital from it to) a beneficiary other than the primary beneficiary whose share it was;

(D) the power to settle any part of the trust fund on the trustees of a separate trust if (and only if) the only possible beneficiaries of that trust are also beneficiaries of this clause;

(E) where a primary beneficiary has died, the power to redistribute his share among the shares of surviving primary beneficiaries.

(d) My trustees must exercise their discretions by deed of appointment. A deed of appointment may be revocable or irrevocable.

(e) My trustees have all the powers given to executors by my will.

99c Flexible A&M trust — common grandparent rule not satisfied (residue continuation)

Note: Unlike 99a and 99b, you may have as many elements as you wish in the "primary beneficiaries" section of this precedent.   **5–054**

(a) to pay the residue ("the trust fund") to the trustees of the settlement declared in clause (1) below.

1 FLEXIBLE ACCUMULATION AND MAINTENANCE TRUST   5–055

(a) In this clause:

"my trustees" means my executors or the trustees for the time being of this clause;

"the primary beneficiaries" means:

(i) those of my children who are living at my death;

(ii) those of my $/{husband's$//wife's$/} children who are living at my death;

(iii) those of my $/{grandchildren$//nieces$//nephews$//nieces and nephews$//cousins$/} who are either:

(A) living at my death; or

(B) born after me but before the eldest living primary beneficiary attains 25;

(iv) $/;

(v) $/; and

(vi) $/;

"the beneficiaries" means:

(i) the primary beneficiaries;

(ii) all descendants of the primary beneficiaries;

(iii) the spouses and former spouses of (i) and (ii);

(iv) my ${widow$//widower$/}; and

(v) charities;

"interest-in-possession" means the right to receive the current income from a share in the trust fund.

(b) I give the trust fund to my trustees on the following trusts:

(i) to divide the trust fund into one equal share for each primary beneficiary;

(ii) while a primary beneficiary is under 25:

(A) to apply the income from his or her share for his or her maintenance, education or benefit; or

(B) within 21 years of my death, to accumulate any income not so applied;

(iii) as each primary beneficiary attains 25, to grant an interest-in-possession in his or her share, to him or her.

(iv) *except* that if the trust fund is still in existence 25 years less 1 day from my death, then to immediately grant an interest-in-possession in their share to every principal beneficiary.

(c) The above trusts are subject to the following powers:

(i) while a primary beneficiary is under 25 my trustees may apply the income of his or her share for the benefit of any other primary beneficiary who is for the time being under 25;

(ii) my trustees may grant a primary beneficiary an interest-in-possession in his or her share at any age below 25;

(iii) if a primary beneficiary dies before attaining an interest-in-possession then my trustees may hold his or her share for the benefit of any of the beneficiaries they think fit.

(iv) once a primary beneficiary has attained an interest-in-possession, my trustees may hold his or her share for the benefit of any of the beneficiaries they think fit.

(v) if my trustees have the power to benefit any of the beneficiaries they think fit, their powers include:

(A) the power to pay to a primary beneficiary the capital of his or her share outright;

(B) the power to bring an interest-in-possession to an end, or to transfer it to another beneficiary;

(C) the power to use a share for the benefit of (or pay the capital from it to) a beneficiary other than the primary beneficiary whose share it was;

(D) the power to settle any part of the trust fund on the trustees of a separate trust if (and only if) the only possible beneficiaries of that trust are also beneficiaries of this clause;

(E) where a primary beneficiary has died, the power to redistribute his share among the shares of surviving primary beneficiaries.

(d) My trustees must exercise their discretions by deed of appointment. A deed of appointment may be revocable or irrevocable.

(e) My trustees have all the powers given to executors by my will.

99d Flexible A&M trust — common grandparent rule not satisfied (settled legacy)

Note: Unlike 99a and 99b, you may have as many elements as you wish in the "primary beneficiaries" section of this precedent.

1 FLEXIBLE ACCUMULATION AND MAINTENANCE TRUST   5–056

(a) In this clause:

"the trust fund" means £$/ and the property from time to time representing it;

"my trustees" means my executors or the trustees for the time being of this clause;

"the primary beneficiaries" means:

(i) those of my children who are living at my death;

(ii) those of my $/{husband's$//wife's$/} children who are living at my death;

(iii) those of my my $/{children$//grandchildren$//nieces$//nephews$//nieces and nephews$//cousins$/} who are either:

    (A) living at my death; or

    (B) born after me but before the eldest living primary beneficiary attains 25;

(iv) $/;

(v) $/; and

(vi) $/;

"the beneficiaries" means:

(i) the primary beneficiaries;

(ii) all descendants of the primary beneficiaries;

(iii) the spouses and former spouses of (i) and (ii);

(iv) my $/{widow$//widower$/}; and

(v) charities;

"interest-in-possession" means the right to receive the current income from a share in the trust fund.

(b) I give the trust fund to my trustees on the following trusts:

(i) to divide the trust fund into one equal share for each primary beneficiary;

(ii) while a primary beneficiary is under 25:

    (A) to apply the income from his or her share for his or her maintenance, education or benefit; or

    (B) within 21 years of my death, to accumulate any income not so applied;

(iii) as each primary beneficiary attains 25, to grant an interest-in-possession in his or her share, to him or her.

(iv) *except* that if the trust fund is still in existence 25 years less 1 day from my death, then to immediately grant an interest-in-possession in their share to every principal beneficiary.

(c) The above trusts are subject to the following powers:

  (i) while a primary beneficiary is under 25 my trustees may apply the income of his or her share for the benefit of any other primary beneficiary who is for the time being under 25;

  (ii) my trustees may grant a primary beneficiary an interest-in-possession in his or her share at any age below 25;

  (iii) if a primary beneficiary dies before attaining an interest-in-possession then my trustees may hold his or her share for the benefit of any of the beneficiaries they think fit.

  (iv) once a primary beneficiary has attained an interest-in-possession, my trustees may hold his or her share for the benefit of any of the beneficiaries they think fit.

  (v) if my trustees have the power to benefit any of the beneficiaries they think fit, their powers include:

     (A) the power to pay to a primary beneficiary the capital of his or her share outright;

     (B) the power to bring an interest-in-possession to an end, or to transfer it to another beneficiary;

     (C) the power to use a share for the benefit of (or pay the capital from it to) a beneficiary other than the primary beneficiary whose share it was;

     (D) the power to settle any part of the trust fund on the trustees of a separate trust if (and only if) the only possible beneficiaries of that trust are also beneficiaries of this clause;

     (E) where a primary beneficiary has died, the power to redistribute his share among the shares of surviving primary beneficiaries.

(d) My trustees must exercise their discretions by deed of appointment. A deed of appointment may be revocable or irrevocable.

(e) My trustees have all the powers given to executors by my will.

DISCRETIONARY TRUSTS

100 General discretionary trust

100a General discretionary trust (residue continuation)

5–057   (a) to pay the residue ("the trust fund") to the trustees of the settlement declared in clause (1) below.

5–058 1 DISCRETIONARY TRUST

(a) In this clause, "my trustees" means my executors or the trustees for the time being of this clause.

(b) My trustees have all the powers given to executors by my will.

(c) In this clause "the beneficiaries" means:

    (i) my $/{husband$//wife$/};

    (ii) all descendants of any of my grandparents;

    (iii) all descendants of any of my $/{husband's$//wife's$/} grandparents;

    (iv) the spouses and former spouses of (ii) and (iii); and

    (v) charities

(d) I give the trust fund to my trustees on the following trusts:

    (i) within 80 years of my death, to pay the capital to (or use it for the benefit of) any beneficiaries they think fit;

    (ii) within 80 years of my death, to pay the income to (or use it for the benefit of) any beneficiaries they think fit, or within 21 years of my death to accumulate some or all of it.

    (iii) my trustees must distribute the whole fund within 80 years of my death (which is the perpetuity period of this trust);

    (iv) my trustees need not ensure equality among the beneficiaries, and are not liable to any beneficiary who they choose not to benefit;

(e) My trustees must exercise their discretions by deed of appointment. A deed of appointment may be revocable within 80 years of my death, or irrevocable.

(f) My backstop beneficiary is $/. If the above trusts fail entirely then my trustees must pay the trust fund to $/{him$//her$/} (or $/{his$//her$/} estate) absolutely.

100b General discretionary trust (settled legacy)

1 DISCRETIONARY TRUST   5–059

(a) In this clause, "my trustees" means my executors or the trustees for the time being of this clause.

(b) My trustees have all the powers given to executors by my will.

(c) In this clause "the beneficiaries" means:

    (i) my $/{husband$//wife$/};

    (ii) all descendants of any of my grandparents;

    (iii) all descendants of any of my $/{husband's$//wife's$/} grandparents;

    (iv) the spouses and former spouses of (ii) and (iii); and

    (v) charities

(d) I give £$/ ("the trust fund") to my trustees on the following trusts:

    (i) within 80 years of my death, to pay the capital to (or use it for the benefit of) any beneficiaries they think fit;

    (ii) within 80 years of my death, to pay the income to (or use it for the benefit of) any beneficiaries they think fit, or within 21 years of my death to accumulate some or all of it.

    (iii) my trustees must distribute the whole fund within 80 years of my death (which is the perpetuity period of this trust);

    (iv) my trustees need not ensure equality among the beneficiaries, and are not liable to any beneficiary who they choose not to benefit;

(e) My trustees must exercise their discretions by deed of appointment. A deed of appointment may be revocable within 80 years of my death, or irrevocable.

(f) My backstop beneficiary is $/. If the above trusts fail entirely then my trustees must pay the trust fund to $/{him$//her$/} (or $/{his$//her$/} estate) absolutely.

101 Trust for disabled beneficiary

101a Trust for disabled beneficiary (residue continuation)

5–060   (a) to pay the residue ("the trust fund") to the trustees of the settlement declared in clause (1) below.

5–061 **1 DISCRETIONARY TRUST**

(a) In this clause:
"my trustees" means my executors or the trustees for the time being of this clause.
"the primary beneficiary" means $/.
"the beneficiaries" means:

   (i) the primary beneficiary;
   (ii) all descendants of the primary beneficiary;
   (iii) the spouses and former spouses of (i) and (ii); and
   (iv) charities

(b) I give the trust fund to my trustees on the following trusts:

   (i) during the lifetime of the primary beneficiary, and within 2 years of his death, to pay the capital to (or use it for the benefit of) any beneficiaries they think fit;
   (ii) during the lifetime of the primary beneficiary, and within 2 years of his death, to pay the income to (or use it for the benefit of) any beneficiaries they think fit, or until the earlier of:
      (A) 21 years from my death; and
      (B) 2 years from the death of the primary beneficiary;
      to accumulate some or all of it.
   (iii) my trustees must distribute the whole fund within 2 years of the death of the primary beneficiary (which is the perpetuity period of this trust);
   (iv) my trustees need not ensure equality among the beneficiaries, and are not liable to any beneficiary who they choose not to benefit;

(c) My trustees must exercise their discretions by deed of appointment. A deed of appointment may be revocable or irrevocable.

(d) My trustees have all the powers given to executors by my will.

(e) My backstop beneficiary is $/. If the above trusts fail entirely then my trustees must pay the trust fund to $/{him$//her$/} (or $/{his$//her$/} estate) absolutely.

101b Trust for disabled beneficiary (settled legacy)

1 DISCRETIONARY TRUST

5–062

(a) In this clause:
"my trustees" means my executors or the trustees for the time being of this clause.
"the primary beneficiary" means $/.
"the beneficiaries" means:

    (i) the primary beneficiary;
    (ii) all descendants of the primary beneficiary;
    (iii) the spouses and former spouses of (i) and (ii); and
    (iv) charities

(b) I give £$/ ("the trust fund") to my trustees on the following trusts:
    (i) during the lifetime of the primary beneficiary, and within 2 years of his death, to pay the capital to (or use it for the benefit of) any beneficiaries they think fit;
    (ii) during the lifetime of the primary beneficiary, and within 2 years of his death, to pay the income to (or use it for the benefit of) any beneficiaries they think fit, or until the earlier of:

        (A) 21 years from my death; and
        (B) 2 years from the death of the primary beneficiary;

    to accumulate some or all of it.

    (iii) my trustees must distribute the whole fund within 2 years of the death of the primary beneficiary (which is the perpetuity period of this trust);
    (iv) my trustees need not ensure equality among the beneficiaries, and are not liable to any beneficiary who they choose not to benefit;

(c) My trustees must exercise their discretions by deed of appointment. A deed of appointment may be revocable or irrevocable.
(d) My trustees have all the powers given to executors by my will.
(e) My backstop beneficiary is $/. If the above trusts fail entirely then my trustees must pay the trust fund to $/{him$//her$/} (or $/{his$//her$/} estate) absolutely.

102 Nil-band discretionary trust

1 GIFT OF CHATTELS

5–063

(a) In this clause, "personal chattels" has the meaning given in section 55(1)(x) of the Administration of Estates Act 1925, but does not include chattels which are the subject of specific gifts.
(b) I give all my personal chattels to my $/{husband$//wife$/}.

5–064 2 NIL-BAND DISCRETIONARY TRUST

(a) In this clause and the next (3):

"the nil-band sum" means the lower of:

(i) the maximum sum which I could give to a non-exempt benefici-ary by this clause, without inheritance tax becoming payable on my death;

(ii) $/[the upper limit of the nil per cent rate band in Schedule 1 to the Inheritance Tax Act 1984, as it is applicable on my death; or$/]

(iii) nil if:

(A) inheritance tax has been abolished at my death;

(B) I am not married at my death; or

(C) the nil-band sum would otherwise be less than £10,000;

"the nil-band fund" means:

(i) the nil-band sum; and

(ii) the assets from time to time representing it.

"my trustees" means:

(i) my executors; and

(ii) the trustees for the time being of this clause

"the beneficiaries" means:

(i) my $/{husband$//wife$/};

(ii) all descendants of any of my grandparents;

(iii) all descendants of any of my $/{husband's$//wife's$/} grandparents;

(iv) the spouses and former spouses of (ii) and (iii);

(v) charities

(b) I give the nil-band sum to my trustees on the following trusts:

(i) within 80 years of my death, to pay the capital to (or use it for the benefit of) any beneficiaries they think fit;

(ii) within 80 years of my death, to pay the income to (or use it for the benefit of) any beneficiaries they think fit, or within 21 years of my death to accumulate some or all of it.

(iii) my trustees must distribute the whole fund within 80 years of my death (which is the perpetuity period of this trust);

(iv) my trustees need not ensure equality among the beneficiaries, and are not liable to any beneficiary who they choose not to benefit;

(c) My backstop beneficiary is $/. If the above trusts fail entirely then my trustees must pay the nil-band fund to $/{him$//her$/} (or $/{his$//her$/} estate) absolutely.

5–065 3 TRUSTEES' POWERS ANCILLARY TO THE NIL-BAND DISCRETIONARY TRUST

(a) My trustees have all the powers given to executors by my will.

(b) My trustees must exercise their discretions by deed of appointment. A deed of appointment may be revocable within 80 years of my death, or irrevocable.

(c) My executors may require my trustees to accept:

    (i) a binding promise of payment made by my $/{husband$//wife$/}; or

    (ii) a charge over any property given to my $/{husband$//wife$/} by my will or any codicil;

in place of all or part of the nil-band fund, and this power may be exercised even if my executors and my trustees are, at that time, the same people. My executors are under no further liability to ensure that the trustees receive the sum promised or charged.

(d) If my executors exercise their power to charge property given to my $/{husband$//wife$/} they may make an assent of the property, subject to the charge, without my $/{husband$//wife$/} becoming personally liable for the sum charged.

(e) My trustees may lend any of the nil-band fund to my $/{husband$//wife$/}.

(f) Any promise made by my $/{husband$//wife$/}, or loan made to my $/{husband$//wife$/}, may be made subject to such terms as to repayment and security as my trustees think fit.

103 Expression of wishes

To: the executors of my will dated . . . . 20$/   **5–066**

As you know, I have appointed you as the executors and trustees of my will.

Under the terms of my will, you are the trustees of a discretionary fund equal to the inheritance tax "nil rate band", which will take effect if my $/{husband$//wife$/} survives to take my residuary estate.

In the hope that this may be of help to you in exercising your powers (but not so as to impose any binding obligation, nor to deter you from acting as you think best in the light of changing circumstances) I would like you to know that my wishes are:

(a) The primary purpose of the discretionary trust is tax planning.

(b) You should regard my $/{husband$//wife$/} as the primary beneficiary while $/{he$//she$/} is alive, augmenting $/{his$//her$/} resources out of income or capital to any extent that may be necessary to ensure that $/{he$//she$/} is able to live in full comfort for the rest of $/{his$//her$/} life.

(c) I want my $/{husband$//wife$/} to continue living at $/ for so long as $/{he$//she$/} wishes.

(d) I would like you to follow my $/{husband's$//wife's$/} wishes regarding the assets of the discretionary trust.

(e) Subject to (b), (c) and (d) above, and in any event after my $/{husband$//wife$/} has died, I would like you to deal with the fund in accordance with the residuary terms of my Will, although taking into account any changes of circumstances since my death.

(f) Subject to my wishes set out above, I will leave it to you to deal with the fund as you see fit, taking into account all circumstances, including the changing circumstances of my family, and the taxation rules in force from time to time.

I know that you will deal with the matter to the best advantage of all concerned.

Signed . . . .

Dated . . . .

104 Two-year discretionary trust

104a Two-year discretionary trust (residue continuation)

5–067   (a) to pay the residue ("the trust fund") to the trustees of the settlement declared in clause (1) below.

5–068 1 TWO YEAR DISCRETIONARY TRUST

(a) In this clause, "my trustees" means my executors or the trustees for the time being of this clause.

(b) My trustees have all the powers given to executors by my will.

(c) In this clause "the beneficiaries" means:

    (i) my $/{husband$//wife$/};

    (ii) all descendants of any of my grandparents;

    (iii) all descendants of any of my $/{husband's$//wife's$/} grandparents;

    (iv) the spouses and former spouses of (ii) and (iii); and

    (v) charities

(d) I give the trust fund to my trustees on the following trusts:

    (i) within 2 years of my death, to pay the capital to (or use it for the benefit of) any beneficiaries they think fit;

    (ii) within 2 years of my death, to pay the income to (or use it for the benefit of) any beneficiaries they think fit, or to accumulate some or all of it.

    (iii) my trustees must distribute the whole fund within 2 years of my death;

    (iv) my trustees need not ensure equality among the beneficiaries, and are not liable to any beneficiary who they choose not to benefit;

(e) My trustees must exercise their discretions by deed of appointment. A deed of appointment may be revocable within 2 years of my death, or irrevocable.

(f) My backstop beneficiary is $/. If the above trusts fail entirely then my trustees must pay the trust fund to $/{him$//her$/} (or $/{his$//her$/} estate) absolutely.

104b Two-year discretionary trust (settled legacy)

1 TWO YEAR DISCRETIONARY TRUST 5–069

(a) In this clause, "my trustees" means my executors or the trustees for the time being of this clause.

(b) My trustees have all the powers given to executors by my will.

(c) In this clause "the beneficiaries" means:

    (i) my $/{husband$//wife$/};

    (ii) all descendants of any of my grandparents;

    (iii) all descendants of any of my $/{husband's$//wife's$/} grandparents;

    (iv) the spouses and former spouses of (ii) and (iii); and

    (v) charities

(d) I give £$/ to my trustees on the following trusts:

    (i) within 2 years of my death, to pay the capital to (or use it for the benefit of) any beneficiaries they think fit;

    (ii) within 2 years of my death, to pay the income to (or use it for the benefit of) any beneficiaries they think fit, or to accumulate some or all of it;

    (iii) my trustees must distribute the whole fund within 2 years of my death;

    (iv) my trustees need not ensure equality among the beneficiaries, and are not liable to any beneficiary who they choose not to benefit.

(e) My trustees must exercise their discretions by deed of appointment. A deed of appointment may be revocable within 2 years of my death, or irrevocable.

(f) My backstop beneficiary is $/. If the above trusts fail entirely then my trustees must pay the trust fund to $/{him$//her$/} (or $/{his$//her$/} estate) absolutely.

105 Testamentary trust of pension benefits

1 TESTAMENTARY TRUST OF PENSION BENEFITS 5–070

(a) In this clause and the next (2):
"the trust fund" means:

    (i) £5;

    (ii) any sums paid to the trustees of this clause from any source; and

    (iii) the assets from time to time representing them.

"my trustees" means:

    (i) my executors; and

    (ii) the trustees for the time being of this clause

"the beneficiaries" means:

    (i) my $/{husband$//wife$/};

    (ii) all descendants of any of my grandparents;

    (iii) all descendants of any of my $/{husband's$//wife's$/} grandparents;

    (iv) the spouses and former spouses of (ii) and (iii);

    (v) charities

(b) I give the trust fund to my trustees on the following trusts:

    (i) within 80 years of my death, to pay the capital to (or use it for the benefit of) any beneficiaries they think fit;

    (ii) within 80 years of my death, to pay the income to (or use it for the benefit of) any beneficiaries they think fit, or within 21 years of my death to accumulate some or all of it.

    (iii) my trustees must distribute the whole fund within 80 years of my death (which is the perpetuity period of this trust);

    (iv) my trustees need not ensure equality among the beneficiaries, and are not liable to any beneficiary who they choose not to benefit;

(c) My backstop beneficiary is $/. If the above trusts fail entirely then my trustees must pay the trust fund to $/{him$//her$/} (or $/{his$//her$/} estate) absolutely.

5–071 2 TRUSTEES' POWERS ANCILLARY TO THE TESTAMENTARY TRUST

(a) My trustees have all the powers given to executors by my will.

(b) My trustees must exercise their discretions by deed of appointment. A deed of appointment may be revocable within 80 years of my death, or irrevocable.

(c) My trustees may lend any of the trust fund to my $/{husband$//wife$/}.

(d) Any loan made to my $/{husband$//wife$/} may be made subject to such terms as to repayment and security as my trustees think fit.

106 Nomination

5–072 To: The secretary to the trustees of the $/ pension scheme.

Without fettering your discretion, I express the wish that you will pay any lump sum benefits payable from the scheme on my death to the trustees of the "Testamentary Trust of Pension Benefits" contained in clause $/ of my will dated $/ 20$/.

Part 6

GENERAL WILLS

GENERAL WILLS

Our attitude is to encourage the use of the STEP standard provisions **6–001** wherever they are appropriate (that is, in most wills). Accordingly, every precedent in this book comes in two formats — one which incorporates trustees' powers in full in the body of the Will, and one which incorporates the STEP provisions.

Although it produces a longer book, we have set out the text in full. In the following chapters you will not find any cross references along the lines of "continue as in form 36", or "insert clauses 3–6 from precedent 27". We realise readers of the book might find this approach quite pedestrian, but your secretary will love us for it!

UNMARRIED TESTATOR

107 Basic will for single adult beneficiary

It is very rare for a will of this kind to be adequate, but we must accept that it **6–002** is occasionally what the testator wants to do. It is the only will in this book where we felt you could get by without incorporating any trustees' powers. However, we felt that the possibility of the assets of the estate proving complicated made it desirable to have trustees' powers, even here. Of the three precedents which follow, therefore, we *prefer* the third (with the STEP provisions); *quite like* the second (with trustees' powers set out in full) and *are ambivalent* about the first, although it is likely to be adequate in many simple cases.

107a Basic will — single adult beneficiary — no Powers

This is the last will of me $/ of $/.   **6–003**

1 REVOCATION   **6–004**

I revoke all former wills.

2 APPOINTMENT OF EXECUTOR   **6–005**

I appoint $/ to be my executor.

3 RESIDUE   **6–006**

I give to my executors:

    (i) my estate, anywhere in the world; and

(ii) any property over which I have a general power of appointment;

to hold it on trust:

(a) to pay my debts, taxes and funeral and testamentary expenses;
(b) to pay the residue to $/ absolutely.

6–007 SIGNATURES

Signed by me on .... 20$/
Signature of Testator

Signed by $/ in our joint presence and then by us in $/{his$//hers$/}
          Witness 1   Witness 2

Signature:

Full name:

Address:

Occupation:

107b Basic will — single adult beneficiary — complete powers

6–008 This is the last will of me $/ of $/.

6–009 1 REVOCATION

I revoke all former wills.

6–010 2 APPOINTMENT OF EXECUTOR

I appoint $/ to be my executor.

6–011 3 RESIDUE

I give to my executors:
(I) my estate, anywhere in the world; and
(II) any property over which I have a general power of appointment;

to hold it on trust:

(a) to pay my debts, taxes and funeral and testamentary expenses;
(b) to pay the residue to $/ absolutely.

6–012 4 POWER OF INVESTMENT

My executors may invest my estate in any investments they could make if they owned my estate personally. In particular, they may:

(a) invest in unsecured loans, including interest-free loans to a beneficiary;

(b) invest in land, whether as an investment or as a residence for a beneficiary, and may improve and maintain it;

(c) invest jointly with another person;

(d) invest in wasting or non-income-producing assets;

(e) invest anywhere in the world; and

(f) choose not to diversify investments.

5 EXCLUSION OF S.11 TLATA 6–013

My executors may exercise their powers without consulting beneficiaries, so section 11 of the Trusts of Land and Appointment of Trustees Act 1996 does not apply.

6 POWER OF APPROPRIATION 6–014

My executors may give specific assets of my estate to beneficiaries without requiring consent. (Section 41 of the Administration of Estates Act 1925 therefore applies subject to that amendment.)

7 POWER OF INSURANCE 6–015

My executors may:

(a) keep any assets of my estate insured, against any risk and in any amount;

(b) pay insurance premiums from the income or capital of that part of my estate which is held on the same trusts as the insured property; and

(c) treat any insurance money received as though it were the proceeds of sale of the insured property.

8 EXCLUSION OF EXECUTORS' LIABILITY 6–016

(a) Only a professional executor or trustee can be liable for any loss arising from:

　(i) exercising, or failing to exercise, any discretion or power;

　(ii) any improper investment made in good faith;

　(iii) the negligence or fraud of any agent employed by him, or by any other executor or trustee, even if the employment was not strictly necessary or expedient;

　(iv) any mistake or omission made in good faith;

　(v) any other matter, except willful and individual fraud on the part of the executor or trustee who is sought to be made liable.

(b) No executor can be liable for any loss, of any kind, if he has acted in accordance with the advice of Counsel of at least five years' standing.

9 POWER TO USE NOMINEES 6–017

My executors may vest any asset of my estate in the name of, or under the control of:

(a) one or more of their number; or

(b) any person (which may include a trust corporation), or people, as nominee(s).

6–018 10 POWER TO CHARGE FOR PROFESSIONAL SERVICES

Any of my executors who is engaged in a profession or business may charge fees for work done by him or her, or by his or her firm, in connection with my estate and its trusts, including acts which an executor or trustee not being in any profession or business could have done personally, and those charges shall be a first charge against my estate, without abatement.

6–019 11 COMMORIENTES

My estate is to be divided as if any person who dies within one month of my death had predeceased me.

6–020 12 CONFLICTS OF INTEREST

My executors may exercise (or fail to exercise) any powers in my will, even if one or more of them has a personal interest in the outcome.

6–021 13 USE OF EXECUTORS' POWERS

My executors may exercise any of their powers:

    (a) from time to time; and
    (b) at their absolute discretion.

6–022 SIGNATURES

Signed by me on . . . . 20$/

Signature of Testator

Signed by $/ in our joint presence and then by us in $/{his$//hers$/}
               Witness 1   Witness 2

Signature:

Full name:

Address:

Occupation:

107c Basic will — single adult beneficiary — step powers

6–023 This is the last will of me $/ of $/.

6–024 1 REVOCATION

I revoke all former wills.

6–025 2 APPOINTMENT OF EXECUTOR

I appoint $/ to be my executor.

1 RESIDUE 6–026

I give to my executors:
- (I) my estate, anywhere in the world; and
- (II) any property over which I have a general power of appointment;

to hold it on trust:

- (a) to pay my debts, taxes and funeral and testamentary expenses;
- (a) to pay the residue to $/ absolutely.

1 TECHNICAL CLAUSES 6–027

- (a) The Standard Provisions of the Society of Trust and Estate Practitioners (1st edition) apply, amended as follows:

    - (i) Standard provision 5 ("trust for sale") does not apply.
    - (ii) My executors may exercise their powers without consulting beneficiaries, so section 11 of the Trusts of Land and Appointment of Trustees Act 1996 does not apply.

- (b) My estate is to be divided as if any person who dies within one month of my death had predeceased me.

SIGNATURES 6–028

Signed by me on .... 20$/

Signature of Testator

Signed by $/ in our joint presence and then by us in $/{his$//hers$/}

        Witness 1   Witness 2

Signature:

Full name:

Address:

Occupation:

108 Chattels on precatory trust, residue to brothers and sisters with accrual

108a Complete powers

This is the last will of me $/ of $/. 6–029

1 REVOCATION 6–030

I revoke all former wills.

6–031 2 APPOINTMENT OF EXECUTORS

I appoint $/ $/[and $/$/] to be my $/{executor$//executors$/} but if $/{he is$// she is$//both of them are$//either of them is$//all of them are$//any of them is$/} unable or unwilling to act then I appoint $/ instead.

6–032 3 PERSONAL CHATTELS

(a) In this clause, "personal chattels" has the meaning given in section 55(1)(x) of the Administration of Estates Act 1925, but does not include chattels which are the subject of specific gifts.

(b) I give my personal chattels to $/ absolutely.

(c) I request $/{him$//her$/}:

  (i) to dispose of my personal chattels in accordance with any wishes of mine which come to $/{his$//her$/} attention; and

  (ii) to keep any remaining personal chattels for $/{himself$//herself$/} absolutely.

(d) This clause does not impose any legal obligation on $/{him$//her$/}, nor does it confer any legal entitlement on any other person.

6–033 4 BURDEN OF INHERITANCE TAX

If inheritance tax, or any other form of death duty, is payable on my free estate then my executors must pay it from the residue of my estate.

6–034 5 RESIDUE

I give to my executors:

  (I) the rest of my estate, anywhere in the world; and

  (II) any property over which I have a general power of appointment;

to hold it on trust:

  (a) to pay my debts, taxes and funeral and testamentary expenses;

  (b) to divide the residue equally between those of my brothers and sisters who are living at my death (but without substituting their children if any of them dies before me)

6–035 6 POWER OF INVESTMENT

My executors may invest my estate in any investments they could make if they owned my estate personally. In particular, they may:

  (a) invest in unsecured loans, including interest-free loans to a beneficiary;

  (b) invest in land, whether as an investment or as a residence for a beneficiary, and may improve and maintain it;

  (c) invest jointly with another person;

  (d) invest in wasting or non-income-producing assets;

  (e) invest anywhere in the world; and

  (f) choose not to diversify investments.

6–036 7 EXCLUSION OF S.11 TLATA

My executors may exercise their powers without consulting beneficiaries, so section 11 of the Trusts of Land and Appointment of Trustees Act 1996 does not apply.

8 POWER OF APPROPRIATION   6–037

My executors may give specific assets of my estate to beneficiaries without requiring consent. (Section 41 of the Administration of Estates Act 1925 therefore applies subject to that amendment.)

9 POWER OF INSURANCE   6–038

My executors may:

(a) keep any assets of my estate insured, against any risk and in any amount;

(b) pay insurance premiums from the income or capital of that part of my estate which is held on the same trusts as the insured property; and

(c) treat any insurance money received as though it were the proceeds of sale of the insured property.

10 EXCLUSION OF EXECUTORS' LIABILITY   6–039

(a) Only a professional executor or trustee can be liable for any loss arising from:

  (i) exercising, or failing to exercise, any discretion or power;

  (ii) any improper investment made in good faith;

  (iii) the negligence or fraud of any agent employed by him, or by any other executor or trustee, even if the employment was not strictly necessary or expedient;

  (iv) any mistake or omission made in good faith;

  (v) any other matter, except willful and individual fraud on the part of the executor or trustee who is sought to be made liable.

(b) No executor can be liable for any loss, of any kind, if he has acted in accordance with the advice of Counsel of at least five years' standing.

11 POWER TO USE NOMINEES   6–040

My executors may vest any asset of my estate in the name of, or under the control of:

(a) one or more of their number; or

(b) any person (which may include a trust corporation), or people, as nominee(s).

12 POWER TO CHARGE FOR PROFESSIONAL SERVICES   6–041

Any of my executors who is engaged in a profession or business may charge fees for work done by him or her, or by his or her firm, in connection with my estate and its trusts, including acts which an executor or trustee not being in any profession or business could have done personally, and those charges shall be a first charge against my estate, without abatement.

13 COMMORIENTES   6–042

My estate is to be divided as if any person who dies within one month of my death had predeceased me.

6–043 14 CONFLICTS OF INTEREST

My executors may exercise (or fail to exercise) any powers in my will, even if one or more of them has a personal interest in the outcome.

6–044 15 USE OF EXECUTORS' POWERS

My executors may exercise any of their powers:

(a) from time to time; and
(b) at their absolute discretion.

6–045 16 DEFINITION OF "CHILDREN"

In my will, "children":

(a) includes those who are legitimate, illegitimate or adopted; but does not include step-children, nor natural children who have been adopted by another person;
(b) and other terms describing family relationships are to be interpreted accordingly.

6–046 SIGNATURES

Signed by me on . . . . 20$/

Signature of Testator

Signed by $/ in our joint presence and then by us in $/{his$//hers$/}

         Witness 1   Witness 2

Signature:

Full name:

Address:

Occupation:

108b — Chattels on precatory trust, residue to brothers and sisters with accrual (STEP powers)

6–047 This is the last will of me $/ of $/.

6–048 1 REVOCATION

I revoke all former wills.

6–049 2 APPOINTMENT OF EXECUTORS

I appoint $/ $/[and $/$/] to be my $/{executor$//executors$/} but if $/{he is$// she is$//both of them are$//either of them is$//all of them are$//any of them is$/} unable or unwilling to act then I appoint $/ instead.

136

3 PERSONAL CHATTELS 6–050

(a) In this clause, "personal chattels" has the meaning given in section 55(1)(x) of the Administration of Estates Act 1925, but does not include chattels which are the subject of specific gifts.

(b) I give my personal chattels to $/ absolutely.

(c) I request $/{him$//her$/}:

  (i) to dispose of my personal chattels in accordance with any wishes of mine which come to $/{his$//her$/} attention; and

  (ii) to keep any remaining personal chattels for $/{himself$//herself$/} absolutely.

(d) This clause does not impose any legal obligation on $/{him$//her$/}, nor does it confer any legal entitlement on any other person.

4 BURDEN OF INHERITANCE TAX 6–051

If inheritance tax, or any other form of death duty, is payable on my free estate then my executors must pay it from the residue of my estate.

5 RESIDUE 6–052

I give to my executors:

  (I) the rest of my estate, anywhere in the world; and

  (II) any property over which I have a general power of appointment;

to hold it on trust:

(a) to pay my debts, taxes and funeral and testamentary expenses;

(b) to divide the residue equally between those of my brothers and sisters who are living at my death (but without substituting their children if any of them dies before me)

6 TECHNICAL CLAUSES 6–053

(a) The Standard Provisions of the Society of Trust and Estate Practitioners (1st edition) apply, amended as

  (i) Standard provision 5 ("trust for sale") does not apply.

  (ii) My executors may exercise their powers without consulting beneficiaries, so section 11 of the Trusts of Land and Appointment of Trustees Act 1996 does not apply.

(b) In my will, "children":

  (i) includes those who are legitimate, illegitimate or adopted; but

  (ii) does not include step-children, nor natural children who have been adopted by another person;

and other terms describing family relationships are to be interpreted accordingly.

(c) My estate is to be divided as if any person who dies within one month of my death had predeceased me.

6–054 SIGNATURES

Signed by me on .... 20$/

Signature of Testator

Signed by $/ in our joint presence and then by us in $/{his$//hers$/}

Witness 1   Witness 2

Signature:

Full name:

Address:

Occupation:

109 Chattels on precatory trust, residue to brothers and sisters with substitutions of their children

109a Complete powers

6–055 This is the last will of me $/ of $/.

6–056 1 REVOCATION

I revoke all former wills.

6–057 2 APPOINTMENT OF EXECUTORS

I appoint $/ $/[and $/$/] to be my $/{executor$//executors$/} but if $/{he is$//she is$//both of them are$//either of them is$//all of them are$//any of them is$/} unable or unwilling to act then I appoint $/ instead.

6–058 3 PERSONAL CHATTELS

    (a) In this clause, "personal chattels" has the meaning given in section 55(1)(x) of the Administration of Estates Act 1925, but does not include chattels which are the subject of specific gifts.

    (b) I give my personal chattels to $/ absolutely.

    (c) I request $/{him$//her$/}:

       (i) to dispose of my personal chattels in accordance with any wishes of mine which come to $/{his$//her$/} attention; and

      (ii) to keep any remaining personal chattels for $/{himself$//herself$/} absolutely.

    (d) This clause does not impose any legal obligation on $/{him$//her$/}, nor does it confer any legal entitlement on any other person.

6–059 4 BURDEN OF INHERITANCE TAX

If inheritance tax, or any other form of death duty, is payable on my free estate then my executors must pay it from the residue of my estate.

5 RESIDUE 6–060

I give to my executors:

    (I) the rest of my estate, anywhere in the world; and
    (II) any property over which I have a general power of appointment;

to hold it on trust:

        (a) to pay my debts, taxes and funeral and testamentary expenses;
        (b) to divide the residue equally between those of my brothers and sisters who are living at my death; except:
        (c) if any of them dies before me, then to divide his or her share equally between those of his or her children who are living at my death and attain $/{18$//21$/}.

6 POWER OF INVESTMENT 6–061

My executors may invest my estate in any investments they could make if they owned my estate personally. In particular, they may:

    (a) invest in unsecured loans, including interest-free loans to a beneficiary;
    (b) invest in land, whether as an investment or as a residence for a beneficiary, and may improve and maintain it;
    (c) invest jointly with another person;
    (d) invest in wasting or non-income-producing assets;
    (e) invest anywhere in the world; and
    (f) choose not to diversify investments.

7 EXCLUSION OF S.11 TLATA 6–062

My executors may exercise their powers without consulting beneficiaries, so section 11 of the Trusts of Land and Appointment of Trustees Act 1996 does not apply.

8 POWER OF ADVANCEMENT 6–063

My executors may apply the share of any beneficiary for $/{his$//her$//his or her$/} benefit, and this power:

    (a) is in addition to any other powers my executors may have, in particular section 32 of the Trustee Act 1925;
    (b) applies to the whole or part of the beneficiary's share;
    (c) applies whether the beneficiary's right is vested, contingent, expectant or presumptive but not where another person is entitled in priority;
    (d) may be used for advancement, maintenance, education or any other benefit;
    (e) may be exercised by paying the share to a third party or, where appropriate, to the beneficiary direct.

9 POWER OF APPROPRIATION 6–064

My executors may give specific assets of my estate to beneficiaries without requiring consent. (Section 41 of the Administration of Estates Act 1925 therefore applies subject to that amendment.)

6–065 10 POWER OF INSURANCE

My executors may:

    (a) keep any assets of my estate insured, against any risk and in any amount;

    (b) pay insurance premiums from the income or capital of that part of my estate which is held on the same trusts as the insured property; and

    (c) treat any insurance money received as though it were the proceeds of sale of the insured property.

6–066 11 EXCLUSION OF EXECUTORS' LIABILITY

    (a) Only a professional executor or trustee can be liable for any loss arising from:

        (i) exercising, or failing to exercise, any discretion or power;

        (ii) any improper investment made in good faith;

        (iii) the negligence or fraud of any agent employed by him, or by any other executor or trustee, even if the employment was not strictly necessary or expedient;

        (iv) any mistake or omission made in good faith;

        (v) any other matter, except wilful and individual fraud on the part of the executor or trustee who is sought to be made liable.

    (b) No executor can be liable for any loss, of any kind, if he has acted in accordance with the advice of Counsel of at least five years' standing.

6–067 12 TRUST CORPORATIONS

If a trust corporation is appointed as executor or trustee, it may:

    (a) act by its proper officers;

    (b) exercise all the powers given to executors or trustees by my will;

    (c) charge under its published scale of fees, as amended from time to time;

    (d) meet its charges out of capital or income, at its discretion.

6–068 13 POWER TO USE NOMINEES

My executors may vest any asset of my estate in the name of, or under the control of:

    (a) one or more of their number; or

    (b) any person (which may include a trust corporation), or people, as nominee(s).

6–069 14 POWER TO CHARGE FOR PROFESSIONAL SERVICES

Any of my executors who is engaged in a profession or business may charge fees for work done by him or her, or by his or her firm, in connection with my estate and its trusts, including acts which an executor or trustee not being in any profession or business could have done personally, and those charges shall be a first charge against my estate, without abatement.

15 COMMORIENTES 6–070

My estate is to be divided as if any person who dies within one month of my death had predeceased me.

16 ACCUMULATIONS OF INCOME 6–071

My executors may:

(a) within 21 years of my death, accumulate income to the extent that it is not paid to, or applied for the benefit of, any beneficiary; and
(b) apply accumulated income as if it were the income of the current year.

17 POWER OF DELEGATION 6–072

My executors may delegate any of their functions, in writing, to:

(a) one or more of their number; or
(b) any other person;

and if they do so my executors are not personally liable to my estate for the defaults of that delegate.

18 INDEMNITIES 6–073

My executors may indemnify a retiring trustee, or any other person, against any liability concerning my estate. If they do so, then my estate (not my executors personally) will bear the liability of that indemnity. My executors may charge the indemnity on the trust fund.

19 MINOR'S RECEIPT 6–074

where a person is a minor (that is:

(a) under 18; or
(b) 18 or over, but not of an age to be entitled to capital outright);

my executors may pay money to which he or she becomes entitled, whether:

(i) income or capital; or
(ii) as of right or under a power;

to any the following, and in each case their receipt is a complete discharge:

(A) the minor, if he or she has attained 16;
(B) the minor's parent or guardian, in which case my executors are under no further obligation to enquire into the use of the money; or
(C) a third party for the benefit of the minor;

or my executors may resolve to hold the money on trust for the minor absolutely (in which case the administrative provisions of my will continue to apply to the money).

20 CONFLICTS OF INTEREST 6–075

My executors may exercise (or fail to exercise) any powers in my will, even if one or more of them has a personal interest in the outcome.

6–076 21 USE OF EXECUTORS' POWERS

My executors may exercise any of their powers:

    (a) from time to time; and

    (b) at their absolute discretion.

6–077 22 DEFINITION OF "CHILDREN"

In my will, "children":

    (a) includes those who are legitimate, illegitimate or adopted; but

    (b) does not include step-children, nor natural children who have been adopted by another person;

and other terms describing family relationships are to be interpreted accordingly.

6–078 SIGNATURES

Signed by me on .... 20$/

Signature of Testator

Signed by $/ in our joint presence and then by us in $/{his$///hers$/}

           Witness 1   Witness 2

Signature:

Full name:

Address:

Occupation:

109b chattels on precatory trust, residue to brothers and sisters with substitutions of their children (STEP powers)

6–079 This is the last will of me $/ of $/.

6–080 1 REVOCATION

I revoke all former wills.

6–081 2 APPOINTMENT OF EXECUTORS

I appoint $/ $/[and $/$/] to be my $/{executor$///executors$/} but if $/{he is$//she is$//both of them are$//either of them is$//all of them are$//any of them is$/} unable or unwilling to act then I appoint $/ instead.

6–082 3 PERSONAL CHATTELS

    (a) In this clause, "personal chattels" has the meaning given in section 55(1)(x) of the Administration of Estates Act 1925, but does not include chattels which are the subject of specific gifts.

(b) I give my personal chattels to $/ absolutely.
(c) I request $/{him$//her$/}:

(i) to dispose of my personal chattels in accordance with any wishes of mine which come to $/{his$//her$/} attention; and
(ii) to keep any remaining personal chattels for $/{himself$//herself$/} absolutely.

(d) This clause does not impose any legal obligation on $/{him$//her$/}, nor does it confer any legal entitlement on any other person.

4 BURDEN OF INHERITANCE TAX 6–083

If inheritance tax, or any other form of death duty, is payable on my free estate then my executors must pay it from the residue of my estate.

5 RESIDUE 6–084

I give to my executors:

(I)   the rest of my estate, anywhere in the world; and
(II) any property over which I have a general power of appointment;

to hold it on trust:

(a) to pay my debts, taxes and funeral and testamentary expenses;
(b) to divide the residue equally between those of my brothers and sisters who are living at my death; except that if any of them dies before me, then to divide his or her share equally between those of his or her children who are living at my death and attain $/{18$//21$/}.

6 TECHNICAL CLAUSES 6–085

(a) The Standard Provisions of the Society of Trust and Estate Practitioners (1st edition) apply, amended as follows:

(i) Standard provision 5 ("trust for sale") does not apply.
(ii) My executors may exercise their powers without consulting beneficiaries, so section 11 of the Trusts of Land and Appointment of Trustees Act 1996 does not apply.

(b) In my will, "children":

(i) includes those who are legitimate, illegitimate or adopted; but
(ii) does not include step-children, nor natural children who have been adopted by another person;

and other terms describing family relationships are to be interpreted accordingly.
(c) My estate is to be divided as if any person who dies within one month of my death had predeceased me.

6–086 SIGNATURES

Signed by me on .... 20$/

Signature of Testator

Signed by $/ in our joint presence and then by us in $/{his$//hers$/}

Witness 1   Witness 2

Signature:

Full name:

Address:

Occupation:

110 Discretionary trust for parents — residue to brothers and sisters equally

6–087 *Note*:   The next six clauses (110a and b, 111a and b, 112a and b) work on the premise that for tax-saving purposes it is unattractive to allow assets to pass *up* a generation outright. Accordingly, in clause 110 we have provided a discretionary settlement of residue for parents with a remainder to siblings after the parents' death, in clause 111 we have provided a settled legacy to parents (again, on a discretionary basis) with remainder and residue to siblings, and in clause 112 we have provided an annuity for parents with residue to siblings.

    There are, however, clients for whom tax planning is simply not an issue, and others who prefer simple structures to more complex ones. We have therefore included an outright gift to parents (with gift over to siblings) in precedents 113a and 113b.

110a Discretionary trust for parents — residue to brothers and sisters equally (complete powers)

6–088 This is the last will of me $/ of $/.

6–089 1 REVOCATION

I revoke all former wills.

6–090 2 APPOINTMENT OF EXECUTORS

I appoint $/ $/[and $/$/] to be my $/{executor$//executors$/} but if $/{he is$// she is$//both of them are$//either of them is$//all of them are$//any of them is$/} unable or unwilling to act then I appoint $/ instead.

6–091 3 BURDEN OF INHERITANCE TAX

If inheritance tax, or any other form of death duty, is payable on my free estate then my executors must pay it from the residue of my estate.

4 RESIDUE 6–092

I give to my executors:
  (I) my estate, anywhere in the world; and
  (II) any property over which I have a general power of appointment;

to hold it on trust:

> (a) to pay my debts, taxes and funeral and testamentary expenses;
> (b) to pay the residue ("the trust fund") to the trustees of the settlement declared in clause (5) below.

5 DISCRETIONARY TRUST 6–093

(a) In this clause, "my trustees" means my executors or the trustees for the time being of this clause.

(b) My trustees have all the powers given to executors by my will.

(c) In this clause "the beneficiaries" means:

  (i) my parents;
  (ii) all descendants of my parents;
  (iii) the spouses and former spouses of anyone in (ii);

(d) I give the trust fund to my trustees on the following trusts:

  (i) during the lifetime of the survivor of my parents, to pay the capital to (or use it for the benefit of) any beneficiaries they think fit;
  (ii) within the lifetime of the survivor of my parents, to pay the income to (or use it for the benefit of) any beneficiaries they think fit, or within 21 years of my death to accumulate some or all of it.
  (iii) my trustees need not ensure equality among the beneficiaries, and are not liable to any beneficiary who they choose not to benefit;
  (iv) I express the wish (without imposing any binding legal obligation) that my trustees will treat my parents as the primary beneficiaries of this settlement during their lifetimes.

(e) My trustees must exercise their discretions by deed of appointment. A deed of appointment may be revocable within 80 years of my death, or irrevocable.

(f) after the death of the survivor of my parents to divide the residue equally between those of my brothers and sisters who are living at my death; except:

(g) if any brother or sister of mine dies before the survivor of me and my parents, then to divide his or her share equally between those of his or her children who are living at the time of such death, $/[and attain $/{18$//21$//25$/}$/].

6 POWER OF INVESTMENT 6–094

My executors may invest my estate in any investments they could make if they owned my estate personally. In particular, they may:

> (a) invest in unsecured loans, including interest-free loans to a beneficiary;

(b) invest in land, whether as an investment or as a residence for a beneficiary, and may improve and maintain it;

(c) invest jointly with another person;

(d) invest in wasting or non-income-producing assets;

(e) invest anywhere in the world; and

(f) choose not to diversify investments.

6–095 7 EXCLUSION OF THE APPORTIONMENT RULES

(a) My executors may treat income as arising on the day it is received.

(b) The Apportionment Act 1870 does not apply.

(c) The rules known as "the rule in *Howe v. Dartmouth*" and "the rule in *Allhusen v. Whittell*" do not apply.

6–096 8 EXCLUSION OF S.11 TLATA

My executors may exercise their powers without consulting beneficiaries, so section 11 of the Trusts of Land and Appointment of Trustees Act 1996 does not apply.

6–097 9 POWER OF ADVANCEMENT

My executors may apply the share of any beneficiary for $/{his$//her$//his or her$/} benefit, and this power:

(a) is in addition to any other powers my executors may have, in particular section 32 of the Trustee Act 1925;

(b) applies to the whole or part of the beneficiary's share;

(c) applies whether the beneficiary's right is vested, contingent, expectant or presumptive but not where another person is entitled in priority;

(d) may be used for advancement, maintenance, education or any other benefit;

(e) may be exercised by paying the share to a third party or, where appropriate, to the beneficiary direct.

6–098 10 POWER OF APPROPRIATION

My executors may give specific assets of my estate to beneficiaries without requiring consent. (Section 41 of the Administration of Estates Act 1925 therefore applies subject to that amendment.)

6–099 11 POWER OF INSURANCE

My executors may:

(a) keep any assets of my estate insured, against any risk and in any amount;

(b) pay insurance premiums from the income or capital of that part of my estate which is held on the same trusts as the insured property; and

(c) treat any insurance money received as though it were the proceeds of sale of the insured property.

6–100 12 EXCLUSION OF EXECUTORS' LIABILITY

(a) Only a professional executor or trustee can be liable for any loss arising from:

(i) exercising, or failing to exercise, any discretion or power;

(ii) any improper investment made in good faith;

(iii) the negligence or fraud of any agent employed by him, or by any other executor or trustee, even if the employment was not strictly necessary or expedient;

(iv) any mistake or omission made in good faith;

(v) any other matter, except willful and individual fraud on the part of the executor or trustee who is sought to be made liable.

(b) No executor can be liable for any loss, of any kind, if he has acted in accordance with the advice of Counsel of at least five years' standing.

13 TRUST CORPORATIONS 6–101

If a trust corporation is appointed as executor or trustee, it may:

(a) act by its proper officers;

(b) exercise all the powers given to executors or trustees by my will;

(c) charge under its published scale of fees, as amended from time to time;

(d) meet its charges out of capital or income, at its discretion.

14 POWER TO USE NOMINEES 6–102

My executors may vest any asset of my estate in the name of, or under the control of:

(a) one or more of their number; or

(b) any person (which may include a trust corporation), or people, as nominee(s).

15 POWER TO CHARGE FOR PROFESSIONAL SERVICES 6–103

Any of my executors who is engaged in a profession or business may charge fees for work done by him or her, or by his or her firm, in connection with my estate and its trusts, including acts which an executor or trustee not being in any profession or business could have done personally, and those charges shall be a first charge against my estate, without abatement.

16 COMMORIENTES 6–104

My estate is to be divided as if any person who dies within one month of my death had predeceased me.

17 ACCUMULATIONS OF INCOME 6–105

My executors may:

(a) within 21 years of my death, accumulate income to the extent that it is not paid to, or applied for the benefit of, any beneficiary; and

(b) apply accumulated income as if it were the income of the current year.

18 POWER TO BORROW 6–106

(a) My executors may borrow money for any purpose.

(b) My executors may charge any assets of my estate as security for any liability.

6–107 19 POWER OF DELEGATION

My executors may delegate any of their functions, in writing, to:

(a) one or more of their number; or

(b) any other person;

and if they do so my executors are not personally liable to my estate for the defaults of that delegate.

6–108 20 INDEMNITIES

My executors may indemnify a retiring trustee, or any other person, against any liability concerning my estate. If they do so, then my estate (not my executors personally) will bear the liability of that indemnity. My executors may charge the indemnity on assets of my estate.

6–109 21 MINOR'S RECEIPT

where a person is a minor (that is:

(a) under 18; or

(b) 18 or over, but not of an age to be entitled to capital outright);

my executors may pay money to which he or she becomes entitled, whether:

(i) income or capital; or

(ii) as of right or under a power;

to any the following, and in each case their receipt is a complete discharge:

(A) the minor, if he or she has attained 16;

(B) the minor's parent or guardian, in which case my executors are under no further obligation to enquire into the use of the money; or

(C) a third party for the benefit of the minor;

or my executors may resolve to hold the money on trust for the minor absolutely (in which case the administrative provisions of my will continue to apply to the money).

6–110 22 CONFLICTS OF INTEREST

My executors may exercise (or fail to exercise) any powers in my will, even if one or more of them has a personal interest in the outcome.

6–111 23 USE OF EXECUTORS' POWERS

My executors may exercise any of their powers:

(a) from time to time; and

(b) at their absolute discretion.

24 DEFINITION OF "CHILDREN" 6–112

In my will, "children":

(a) includes those who are legitimate, illegitimate or adopted; but
(b) does not include step-children, nor natural children who have been adopted by another person;

and other terms describing family relationships are to be interpreted accordingly.

SIGNATURES 6–113

Signed by me on .... 20$/

Signature of Testator

Signed by $/ in our joint presence and then by us in $/{his$///hers$/}
        Witness 1   Witness 2

Signature:

Full name:

Address:

Occupation:

110b discretionary trust for parents — residue to brothers and sisters equally (step powers)

This is the last will of me $/ of $/.   6–114

1 REVOCATION 6–115

I revoke all former wills.

2 APPOINTMENT OF EXECUTORS 6–116

I appoint $/ $/[and $/$/] to be my $/{executor$///executors$/} but if $/{he is$// she is$//both of them are$//either of them is$//all of them are$//any of them is$/} unable or unwilling to act then I appoint $/ instead.

3 BURDEN OF INHERITANCE TAX 6–117

If inheritance tax, or any other form of death duty, is payable on my free estate then my executors must pay it from the residue of my estate.

4 RESIDUE 6–118

I give to my executors:

(I) my estate, anywhere in the world; and

(II) any property over which I have a general power of appointment;

to hold it on trust:

    (a) to pay my debts, taxes and funeral and testamentary expenses;

    (b) to pay the residue ("the trust fund") to the trustees of the settlement declared in clause (5) below.

6–119 5 DISCRETIONARY TRUST

(a) In this clause, "my trustees" means my executors or the trustees for the time being of this clause.

(b) My trustees have all the powers given to executors by my will.

(c) In this clause "the beneficiaries" means:

    (i) my parents;

    (ii) all descendants of my parents;

    (iii) the spouses and former spouses of anyone in (ii);

(d) I give the trust fund to my trustees on the following trusts:

    (i) during the lifetime of the survivor of my parents, to pay the capital to (or use it for the benefit of) any beneficiaries they think fit;

    (ii) within the lifetime of the survivor of my parents, to pay the income to (or use it for the benefit of) any beneficiaries they think fit, or within 21 years of my death to accumulate some or all of it.

    (iii) my trustees need not ensure equality among the beneficiaries, and are not liable to any beneficiary who they choose not to benefit;

    (iv) I express the wish (without imposing any binding legal obligation) that my trustees will treat my parents as the primary beneficiaries of this settlement during their lifetimes.

(e) My trustees must exercise their discretions by deed of appointment. A deed of appointment may be revocable within 80 years of my death, or irrevocable.

(e) after the death of the survivor of my parents to divide the residue equally between those of my brothers and sisters who are living at my death; except:

(g) if any brother or sister of mine dies before the survivor of me and my parents, then to divide his or her share equally between those of his or her children who are living at the time of such death, $/[and attain $/{18$//21$//25$/}$/].

6–120 6 TECHNICAL CLAUSES

(a) The Standard Provisions of the Society of Trust and Estate Practitioners (1st edition) apply, amended as follows:

    (i) Standard provision 5 ("trust for sale") does not apply.

    (ii) My executors may exercise their powers without consulting beneficiaries, so section 11 of the Trusts of Land and Appointment of Trustees Act 1996 does not apply.

(b) In my will, "children":

(i) includes those who are legitimate, illegitimate or adopted; but

(ii) does not include step-children, nor natural children who have been adopted by another person;

and other terms describing family relationships are to be interpreted accordingly.

(c) My estate is to be divided as if any person who dies within one month of my death had predeceased me.

SIGNATURES

6–121

Signed by me on .... 20$/

Signature of Testator

Signed by $/ in our joint presence and then by us in $/{his$//hers$/}

Witness 1 Witness 2

Signature:

Full name:

Address:

Occupation:

111 Legacy to parents on discretionary trust, residue to siblings

Note: See the note to clause 110.

6–122

111a Complete powers

This is the last will of me $/ of $/.

1 REVOCATION

6–123

I revoke all former wills.

2 APPOINTMENT OF EXECUTORS

I appoint $/ $/[and $/$/] to be my $/{executor$//executors$/} but if $/{he is$// she is$//both of them are$//either of them is$//all of them are$//any of them is$/} unable or unwilling to act then I appoint $/ instead.

3 DISCRETIONARY TRUST

6–124

(a) In this clause, "my trustees" means my executors or the trustees for the time being of this clause.

(b) My trustees have all the powers given to executors by my will.

(c) In this clause "the beneficiaries" means:

(i) my parents, $/ and $/;

(ii) all descendants of either of my parents;

(iii) the spouses and former spouses of (ii); and

(iv) charities

(d) I give £$/ ("the trust fund") to my trustees on the following trusts:

(i) within 80 years of my death, to pay the capital to (or use it for the benefit of) any beneficiaries they think fit;

(ii) within 80 years of my death, to pay the income to (or use it for the benefit of) any beneficiaries they think fit, or within 21 years of my death to accumulate some or all of it.

(iii) my trustees must distribute the whole fund within 80 years of my death (which is the perpetuity period of this trust);

(iv) my trustees need not ensure equality among the beneficiaries, and are not liable to any beneficiary who they choose not to benefit;

(e) My trustees must exercise their discretions by deed of appointment. A deed of appointment may be revocable within 80 years of my death, or irrevocable.

(f) My backstop beneficiary is $/. If the above trusts fail entirely then my trustees must pay the trust fund to $/{him$//her$/} (or $/{his$//her$/} estate) absolutely.

(g) I express the wish (but without binding my executors) that they will treat my parents as the primary beneficiaries of this clause during their lifetimes.

6–125 4 BURDEN OF INHERITANCE TAX

If inheritance tax, or any other form of death duty, is payable on my free estate then my executors must pay it from the residue of my estate.

6–126 5 RESIDUE

I give to my executors:

(I) the rest of my estate, anywhere in the world; and

(II) any property over which I have a general power of appointment;

to hold it on trust:

(a) to pay my debts, taxes and funeral and testamentary expenses;

(b) to divide the residue equally between those of my brothers and sisters who are living at my death.

6–127 6 POWER OF INVESTMENT

My executors may invest my estate in any investments they could make if they owned my estate personally. In particular, they may:

(a) invest in unsecured loans, including interest-free loans to a beneficiary;

(b) invest in land, whether as an investment or as a residence for a beneficiary, and may improve and maintain it;

(c) invest jointly with another person;

(d) invest in wasting or non-income-producing assets;

(e) invest anywhere in the world; and

(f) choose not to diversify investments.

7 EXCLUSION OF THE APPORTIONMENT RULES   6–128

(a) My executors may treat income as arising on the day it is received.

(b) The Apportionment Act 1870 does not apply.

(c) The rules known as "the rule in *Howe v. Dartmouth*" and "the rule in *Allhusen v. Whittell*" do not apply.

8 EXCLUSION OF S.11 TLATA   6–129

My executors may exercise their powers without consulting beneficiaries, so section 11 of the Trusts of Land and Appointment of Trustees Act 1996 does not apply.

9 POWER OF APPROPRIATION   6–130

My executors may give specific assets of my estate to beneficiaries without requiring consent. (Section 41 of the Administration of Estates Act 1925 therefore applies subject to that amendment.)

10 POWER OF INSURANCE   6–131

My executors may:

(a) keep any assets of my estate insured, against any risk and in any amount;

(b) pay insurance premiums from the income or capital of that part of my estate which is held on the same trusts as the insured property; and

(c) treat any insurance money received as though it were the proceeds of sale of the insured property.

11 EXCLUSION OF EXECUTORS' LIABILITY   6–132

(a) Only a professional executor or trustee can be liable for any loss arising from:

　(i) exercising, or failing to exercise, any discretion or power;

　(ii) any improper investment made in good faith;

　(iii) the negligence or fraud of any agent employed by him, or by any other executor or trustee, even if the employment was not strictly necessary or expedient;

　(iv) any mistake or omission made in good faith;

　(v) any other matter, except willful and individual fraud on the part of the executor or trustee who is sought to be made liable.

(b) No executor can be liable for any loss, of any kind, if he has acted in accordance with the advice of Counsel of at least five years' standing.

6–133 12 TRUST CORPORATIONS

If a trust corporation is appointed as executor or trustee, it may:

(a) act by its proper officers;
(b) exercise all the powers given to executors or trustees by my will;
(c) charge under its published scale of fees, as amended from time to time;
(d) meet its charges out of capital or income, at its discretion.

6–134 13 POWER TO USE NOMINEES

My executors may vest any asset of my estate in the name of, or under the control of:

(a) one or more of their number; or
(b) any person (which may include a trust corporation), or people, as nominee(s).

6–135 14 POWER TO CHARGE FOR PROFESSIONAL SERVICES

Any of my executors who is engaged in a profession or business may charge fees for work done by him or her, or by his or her firm, in connection with my estate and its trusts, including acts which an executor or trustee not being in any profession or business could have done personally, and those charges shall be a first charge against my estate, without abatement.

6–136 15 COMMORIENTES

My estate is to be divided as if any person who dies within one month of my death had predeceased me.

6–137 16 POWER TO BORROW

(a) My executors may borrow money for any purpose.
(b) My executors may charge any assets of my estate as security for any liability.

6–138 17 POWER OF DELEGATION

My executors may delegate any of their functions, in writing, to:

(a) one or more of their number; or
(b) any other person;

and if they do so my executors are not personally liable to my estate for the defaults of that delegate.

18 INDEMNITIES 6–139

My executors may indemnify a retiring trustee, or any other person, against any liability concerning my estate. If they do so, then my estate (not my executors personally) will bear the liability of that indemnity. My executors may charge the indemnity on assets of my estate.

19 MINOR'S RECEIPT 6–140

where a person is a minor (that is:

(a) under 18; or
(b) 18 or over, but not of an age to be entitled to capital outright);

my executors may pay money to which he or she becomes entitled, whether:

(i) income or capital; or
(ii) as of right or under a power;

to any the following, and in each case their receipt is a complete discharge:

(A) the minor, if he or she has attained 16;
(B) the minor's parent or guardian, in which case my executors are under no further obligation to enquire into the use of the money; or
(C) a third party for the benefit of the minor;

or my executors may resolve to hold the money on trust for the minor absolutely (in which case the administrative provisions of my will continue to apply to the money).

20 CONFLICTS OF INTEREST 6–141

My executors may exercise (or fail to exercise) any powers in my will, even if one or more of them has a personal interest in the outcome.

21 USE OF EXECUTORS' POWERS 6–142

My executors may exercise any of their powers:

(a) from time to time; and
(b) at their absolute discretion.

22 DEFINITION OF "CHILDREN" 6–143

In my will, "children":

(a) includes those who are legitimate, illegitimate or adopted; but
(b) does not include step-children, nor natural children who have been adopted by another person;

and other terms describing family relationships are to be interpreted accordingly.

6–144 SIGNATURES

Signed by me on .... 20$/

Signature of Testator

Signed by $/ in our joint presence and then by us in $/{his$//hers$/}
                  Witness 1   Witness 2

Signature:

Full name:

Address:

Occupation:

111b Legacy to parents on discretionary trust, residue to siblings (STEP powers)

6–145 This is the last will of me $/ of $/.

6–146 1 REVOCATION

I revoke all former wills.

6–147 2 APPOINTMENT OF EXECUTORS

I appoint $/ $/[and $/$/] to be my $/{executor$//executors$/} but if $/{he is$// she is$//both of them are$//either of them is$//all of them are$//any of them is$/} unable or unwilling to act then I appoint $/ instead.

6–148 3 DISCRETIONARY TRUST

(a) In this clause, "my trustees" means my executors or the trustees for the time being of this clause.

(b) My trustees have all the powers given to executors by my will.

(c) In this clause "the beneficiaries" means:

    (i) my parents, $/ and $/;

    (ii) all descendants of either of my parents;

    (iii) the spouses and former spouses of (ii); and

    (iv) charities

(d) I give £$/ ("the trust fund") to my trustees on the following trusts:

    (i) within 80 years of my death, to pay the capital to (or use it for the benefit of) any beneficiaries they think fit;

    (ii) within 80 years of my death, to pay the income to (or use it for the benefit of) any beneficiaries they think fit, or within 21 years of my death to accumulate some or all of it.

    (iii) my trustees must distribute the whole fund within 80 years of my death (which is the perpetuity period of this trust);

(iv) my trustees need not ensure equality among the beneficiaries, and are not liable to any beneficiary who they choose not to benefit;

(e) My trustees must exercise their discretions by deed of appointment. A deed of appointment may be revocable within 80 years of my death, or irrevocable.

(f) My backstop beneficiary is $/. If the above trusts fail entirely then my trustees must pay the trust fund to $/{him$//her$/} (or $/{his$//her$/} estate) absolutely.

(g) I express the wish (but without binding my executors) that they will treat my parents as the primary beneficiaries of this clause during their lifetimes.

4 BURDEN OF INHERITANCE TAX

6–149

If inheritance tax, or any other form of death duty, is payable on my free estate then my executors must pay it from the residue of my estate.

5 RESIDUE

6–150

I give to my executors:

(I) the rest of my estate, anywhere in the world; and
(II) any property over which I have a general power of appointment;

to hold it on trust:

(a) to pay my debts, taxes and funeral and testamentary expenses;
(b) to divide the residue equally between those of my brothers and sisters who are living at my death.

6 TECHNICAL CLAUSES

6–151

(a) The Standard Provisions of the Society of Trust and Estate Practitioners (1st edition) apply, amended as follows:

(i) Standard provision 5 ("trust for sale") does not apply.
(ii) My executors may exercise their powers without consulting beneficiaries, so section 11 of the Trusts of Land and Appointment of Trustees Act 1996 does not apply.

(b) In my will, "children":

(i) includes those who are legitimate, illegitimate or adopted; but
(ii) does not include step-children, nor natural children who have been adopted by another person;

and other terms describing family relationships are to be interpreted accordingly.

(c) My estate is to be divided as if any person who dies within one month of my death had predeceased me.

6–152 SIGNATURES

Signed by me on . . . . 20$/

Signature of Testator

Signed by $/ in our joint presence and then by us in $/{his$//hers$/}

Witness 1   Witness 2

Signature:

Full name:

Address:

Occupation:

112 Annuity for parents with residue to siblings

6–153 *Note*:   See the note to clause 110.

112a Complete powers

This is the last will of me $/ of $/.

6–154 1 REVOCATION

I revoke all former wills.

6–155 2 APPOINTMENT OF EXECUTORS

I appoint $/ $/[and $/$/] to be my $/{executor$//executors$/} but if $/{he is$// she is$//both of them are$//either of them is$//all of them are$//any of them is$/} unable or unwilling to act then I appoint $/ instead.

6–156 3 GIFT OF ANNUITY

(a) I give to my parents $/ and $/, jointly, free of inheritance tax, a gross annuity of £$/ per annum.
(b) The annuity is to be paid net of any applicable taxes.
(c) The annuity will be paid by equal $/{monthly$//quarterly$//annual$/} payments, commencing on the date three months after my death.
(d) The annuity is not to be apportioned on the surviving annuitant's death (and accordingly the final payment will be the last one to fall due during his or her lifetime).

6–157 4 BURDEN OF INHERITANCE TAX

If inheritance tax, or any other form of death duty, is payable on my free estate then my executors must pay it from the residue of my estate.

5 RESIDUE

I give to my executors:

(I) the rest of my estate, anywhere in the world; and
(II) any property over which I have a general power of appointment;

to hold it on trust:

(a) to pay my debts, taxes and funeral and testamentary expenses;
(b) to divide the residue equally between those of my brothers and sisters who are living at my death.

6 POWER OF INVESTMENT

My executors may invest my estate in any investments they could make if they owned my estate personally. In particular, they may:

(a) invest in unsecured loans, including interest-free loans to a beneficiary;
(b) invest in land, whether as an investment or as a residence for a beneficiary, and may improve and maintain it;
(c) invest jointly with another person;
(d) invest in wasting or non-income-producing assets;
(e) invest anywhere in the world; and
(f) choose not to diversify investments.

7 EXCLUSION OF THE APPORTIONMENT RULES

(a) My executors may treat income as arising on the day it is received.
(b) The Apportionment Act 1870 does not apply.
(c) The rules known as "the rule in *Howe v. Dartmouth*" and "the rule in *Allhusen v. Whittell*" do not apply.

8 EXCLUSION OF S.11 TLATA

My executors may exercise their powers without consulting beneficiaries, so section 11 of the Trusts of Land and Appointment of Trustees Act 1996 does not apply.

9 POWER OF APPROPRIATION

My executors may give specific assets of my estate to beneficiaries without requiring consent. (Section 41 of the Administration of Estates Act 1925 therefore applies subject to that amendment.)

10 POWER OF INSURANCE

My executors may:

(a) keep any assets of my estate insured, against any risk and in any amount;
(b) pay insurance premiums from the income or capital of that part of my estate which is held on the same trusts as the insured property; and
(c) treat any insurance money received as though it were the proceeds of sale of the insured property.

6–164 11 EXCLUSION OF EXECUTORS' LIABILITY

(a) Only a professional executor or trustee can be liable for any loss arising from:

    (i) exercising, or failing to exercise, any discretion or power;

    (ii) any improper investment made in good faith;

    (iii) the negligence or fraud of any agent employed by him, or by any other executor or trustee, even if the employment was not strictly necessary or expedient;

    (iv) any mistake or omission made in good faith;

    (v) any other matter, except willful and individual fraud on the part of the executor or trustee who is sought to be made liable.

(b) No executor can be liable for any loss, of any kind, if he has acted in accordance with the advice of Counsel of at least five years' standing.

6–165 12 TRUST CORPORATIONS

If a trust corporation is appointed as executor or trustee, it may:

(a) act by its proper officers;

(b) exercise all the powers given to executors or trustees by my will;

(c) charge under its published scale of fees, as amended from time to time;

(d) meet its charges out of capital or income, at its discretion.

6–166 13 POWER TO USE NOMINEES

My executors may vest any asset of my estate in the name of, or under the control of:

(a) one or more of their number; or

(b) any person (which may include a trust corporation), or people, as nominee(s).

6–167 14 POWER TO CHARGE FOR PROFESSIONAL SERVICES

Any of my executors who is engaged in a profession or business may charge fees for work done by him or her, or by his or her firm, in connection with my estate and its trusts, including acts which an executor or trustee not being in any profession or business could have done personally, and those charges shall be a first charge against my estate, without abatement.

6–168 15 COMMORIENTES

My estate is to be divided as if any person who dies within one month of my death had predeceased me.

6–169 16 POWER TO BORROW

(a) My executors may borrow money for any purpose.

(b) My executors may charge any assets of my estate as security for any liability.

17 POWER OF DELEGATION 6–170

My executors may delegate any of their functions, in writing, to:

(a) one or more of their number; or
(b) any other person;

and if they do so my executors are not personally liable to my estate for the defaults of that delegate.

18 INDEMNITIES 6–171

My executors may indemnify a retiring trustee, or any other person, against any liability concerning my estate. If they do so, then my estate (not my executors personally) will bear the liability of that indemnity. My executors may charge the indemnity on assets of my estate.

19 CONFLICTS OF INTEREST 6–172

My executors may exercise (or fail to exercise) any powers in my will, even if one or more of them has a personal interest in the outcome.

20 USE OF EXECUTORS' POWERS 6–173

My executors may exercise any of their powers:

(a) from time to time; and
(b) at their absolute discretion.

21 POWER TO APPROPRIATE ANNUITY FUND 6–174

My executors may appropriate from my estate the sum which, in their view, is sufficient to satisfy the annuity given in my will. If they do so:

(a) My executors must take appropriate professional advice on the size and composition of the annuity fund.
(b) My executors may use the income and capital of the annuity fund to pay the annuity.
(c) If they believe that the annuity fund is, at any time, larger than is necessary to satisfy the annuity, my executors may hold the surplus as part of the residue of my estate.
(d) The annuitants have no further claim on my estate if, in the event, the annuity fund is inadequate to pay the annuity in full.
(e) On the death of the last annuitant, my executors must hold any balance of the annuity fund as part of the residue of my estate.

22 POWER TO PURCHASE ANNUITY 6–175

My executors may purchase an annuity from any insurance office, company or corporation as they think fit to satisfy the annuity given in my will. If they do so the annuitants have no further claim against my estate.

23 POWER TO COMMUTE AN ANNUITY 6–176

My executors may commute the annuity given in my will, by paying to the annuitants the capital amount which my executors consider reasonable. If they do so:

(a) My executors must take appropriate professional advice on the capital amount.

(b) The annuitants have no further claim on my estate.

6–177 24 DEFINITION OF "CHILDREN"

In my will, "children":

(a) includes those who are legitimate, illegitimate or adopted; but

(b) does not include step-children, nor natural children who have been adopted by another person;

and other terms describing family relationships are to be interpreted accordingly.

6–178 SIGNATURES

Signed by me on . . . . 20$/

Signature of Testator

Signed by $/ in our joint presence and then by us in $/{his$///hers$/}

           Witness 1   Witness 2

Signature:

Full name:

Address:

Occupation:

112b Annuity for parents with residue to siblings (STEP powers)

6–179 This is the last will of me $/ of $/.

6–180 1 REVOCATION

I revoke all former wills.

6–181 2 APPOINTMENT OF EXECUTORS

I appoint $/ $/[and $/$/] to be my $/{executor$///executors$/} but if $/{he is$///she is$//both of them are$//either of them is$//all of them are$//any of them is$/} unable or unwilling to act then I appoint $/ instead.

6–182 3 GIFT OF ANNUITY

(a) I give to my parents $/ and $/, jointly, free of inheritance tax, a gross annuity of £$/ per annum.

(b) The annuity is to be paid net of any applicable taxes.

(c) The annuity will be paid by equal $/{monthly$///quarterly$//annual$/} payments, commencing on the date three months after my death.

(d) The annuity is not to be apportioned on the surviving annuitant's death (and accordingly the final payment will be the last one to fall due during his or her lifetime).

4 BURDEN OF INHERITANCE TAX 6–183

If inheritance tax, or any other form of death duty, is payable on my free estate then my executors must pay it from the residue of my estate.

5 RESIDUE 6–184

I give to my executors:

(I) the rest of my estate, anywhere in the world; and
(II) any property over which I have a general power of appointment;

to hold it on trust:

(a) to pay my debts, taxes and funeral and testamentary expenses;
(b) to divide the residue equally between those of my brothers and sisters who are living at my death.

6 TECHNICAL CLAUSES 6–185

(a) The Standard Provisions of the Society of Trust and Estate Practitioners (1st edition) apply, amended as follows:

(i) Standard provision 5 ("trust for sale") does not apply.
(ii) My executors may exercise their powers without consulting beneficiaries, so section 11 of the Trusts of Land and Appointment of Trustees Act 1996 does not apply.

(b) In my will, "children":

(i) includes those who are legitimate, illegitimate or adopted; but
(ii) does not include step-children, nor natural children who have been adopted by another person;

and other terms describing family relationships are to be interpreted accordingly.

(c) My estate is to be divided as if any person who dies within one month of my death had predeceased me.

7 POWER TO APPROPRIATE ANNUITY FUND 6–186

My executors may appropriate from my estate the sum which, in their view, is sufficient to satisfy the annuity given in my will. If they do so:

(a) My executors must take appropriate professional advice on the size and composition of the annuity fund.
(b) My executors may use the income and capital of the annuity fund to pay the annuity.
(c) If they believe that the annuity fund is, at any time, larger than is necessary to satisfy the annuity, my executors may hold the surplus as part of the residue of my estate.

(d) The annuitants have no further claim on my estate if, in the event, the annuity fund is inadequate to pay the annuity in full.

(e) On the death of the last annuitant, my executors must hold any balance of the annuity fund as part of the residue of my estate.

6–187 8 POWER TO PURCHASE ANNUITY

My executors may purchase an annuity from any insurance office, company or corporation as they think fit to satisfy the annuity given in my will. If they do so the annuitants have no further claim against my estate.

6–188 9 POWER TO COMMUTE AN ANNUITY

My executors may commute the annuity given in my will, by paying to the annuitants the capital amount which my executors consider reasonable. If they do so:

(a) My executors must take appropriate professional advice on the capital amount.

(b) The annuitants have no further claim on my estate.

6–189 SIGNATURES

Signed by me on .... 20$/

Signature of Testator

Signed by $/ in our joint presence and then by us in $/{his$//hers$/}
           Witness 1   Witness 2

Signature:

Full name:

Address:

Occupation:

113 All to parents — substituting siblings

6–190 *Note*: See the note to clause 110.

113a Complete powers

This is the last will of me $/ of $/.

6–191 1 REVOCATION

I revoke all former wills.

2 APPOINTMENT OF EXECUTORS 6–192

I appoint $/ $/[and $/$/] to be my $/{executor$//executors$/} but if $/{he is$// she is$//both of them are$//either of them is$//all of them are$//any of them is$/} unable or unwilling to act then I appoint $/ instead.

3 BURDEN OF INHERITANCE TAX 6–193

If inheritance tax, or any other form of death duty, is payable on my free estate then my executors must pay it from the residue of my estate.

4 RESIDUE 6–194

I give to my executors:

(I) my estate, anywhere in the world; and
(II) any property over which I have a general power of appointment;

to hold it on trust:

(a) to pay my debts, taxes and funeral and testamentary expenses;
(b) to divide the residue equally between those of my parents $/ and $/, who are living at my death; but if the above trusts fail, then;
(c) to divide the residue equally between those of my brothers and sisters who are living at my death.

5 POWER OF INVESTMENT 6–195

My executors may invest my estate in any investments they could make if they owned my estate personally. In particular, they may:

(a) invest in unsecured loans, including interest-free loans to a beneficiary;
(b) invest in land, whether as an investment or as a residence for a beneficiary, and may improve and maintain it;
(c) invest jointly with another person;
(d) invest in wasting or non-income-producing assets;
(e) invest anywhere in the world; and
(f) choose not to diversify investments.

6 EXCLUSION OF S.11 TLATA 6–196

My executors may exercise their powers without consulting beneficiaries, so section 11 of the Trusts of Land and Appointment of Trustees Act 1996 does not apply.

7 POWER OF APPROPRIATION 6–197

My executors may give specific assets of my estate to beneficiaries without requiring consent. (Section 41 of the Administration of Estates Act 1925 therefore applies subject to that amendment.)

8 POWER OF INSURANCE 6–198

My executors may:

(a) keep any assets of my estate insured, against any risk and in any amount;

(b) pay insurance premiums from the income or capital of that part of my estate which is held on the same trusts as the insured property; and

(c) treat any insurance money received as though it were the proceeds of sale of the insured property.

6–199 9 EXCLUSION OF EXECUTORS' LIABILITY

(a) Only a professional executor or trustee can be liable for any loss arising from:

    (i) exercising, or failing to exercise, any discretion or power;

    (ii) any improper investment made in good faith;

    (iii) the negligence or fraud of any agent employed by him, or by any other executor or trustee, even if the employment was not strictly necessary or expedient;

    (iv) any mistake or omission made in good faith;

    (v) any other matter, except willful and individual fraud on the part of the executor or trustee who is sought to be made liable.

(b) No executor can be liable for any loss, of any kind, if he has acted in accordance with the advice of Counsel of at least five years' standing.

6–200 10 POWER TO USE NOMINEES

My executors may vest any asset of my estate in the name of, or under the control of:

(a) one or more of their number; or

(b) any person (which may include a trust corporation), or people, as nominee(s).

6–201 11 POWER TO CHARGE FOR PROFESSIONAL SERVICES

Any of my executors who is engaged in a profession or business may charge fees for work done by him or her, or by his or her firm, in connection with my estate and its trusts, including acts which an executor or trustee not being in any profession or business could have done personally, and those charges shall be a first charge against my estate, without abatement.

6–202 12 COMMORIENTES

My estate is to be divided as if any person who dies within one month of my death had predeceased me.

6–203 13 CONFLICTS OF INTEREST

My executors may exercise (or fail to exercise) any powers in my will, even if one or more of them has a personal interest in the outcome.

6–204 14 USE OF EXECUTORS' POWERS

My executors may exercise any of their powers:

(a) from time to time; and

(b) at their absolute discretion.

15 DEFINITION OF "CHILDREN" 6–205

In my will, "children":

(a) includes those who are legitimate, illegitimate or adopted; but

(b) does not include step-children, nor natural children who have been adopted by another person;

and other terms describing family relationships are to be interpreted accordingly.

SIGNATURES 6–206

Signed by me on . . . . 20$/
Signature of Testator

Signed by $/ in our joint presence and then by us in $/{his$//hers$/}
           Witness 1   Witness 2

Signature:

Full name:

Address:

Occupation:

113b All to parents — substituting siblings (STEP powers)

This is the last will of me $/ of $/. 6–207

1 REVOCATION 6–208

I revoke all former wills.

2 APPOINTMENT OF EXECUTORS 6–209

I appoint $/ $/[and $/$/] to be my $/{executor$//executors$/} but if $/{he is$// she is$//both of them are$//either of them is$//all of them are$//any of them is$/} unable or unwilling to act then I appoint $/ instead.

3 BURDEN OF INHERITANCE TAX 6–210

If inheritance tax, or any other form of death duty, is payable on my free estate then my executors must pay it from the residue of my estate.

4 RESIDUE 6–211

I give to my executors:

(I) my estate, anywhere in the world; and

(II) any property over which I have a general power of appointment;

to hold it on trust:

    (a) to pay my debts, taxes and funeral and testamentary expenses;

    (b) to divide the residue equally between those of my parents $/ and $/, who are living at my death; but if the above trusts fail, then;

    (c) to divide the residue equally between those of my brothers and sisters who are living at my death.

6–212   5   TECHNICAL CLAUSES

(a) The Standard Provisions of the Society of Trust and Estate Practitioners (1st edition) apply, amended as follows:

    (i) Standard provision 5 ("trust for sale") does not apply.

    (ii) My executors may exercise their powers without consulting beneficiaries, so section 11 of the Trusts of Land and Appointment of Trustees Act 1996 does not apply.

(b) My estate is to be divided as if any person who dies within one month of my death had predeceased me.

6–213   SIGNATURES

Signed by me on .... 20$/

Signature of Testator

Signed by $/ in our joint presence and then by us in $/{his$//hers$/}
                     Witness 1   Witness 2

Signature:

Full name:

Address:

Occupation:

114 Class gift to nieces and nephews on attaining a specified age

114a Complete powers

6–214   This is the last will of me $/ of $/.

6–215   1   REVOCATION

I revoke all former wills.

6–216   2   APPOINTMENT OF EXECUTORS

I appoint $/ $/[and $/$/] to be my $/{executor$//executors$/} but if $/{he is$// she is$//both of them are$//either of them is$//all of them are$//any of them is$/} unable or unwilling to act then I appoint $/ instead.

3 BURDEN OF INHERITANCE TAX   6–217

If inheritance tax, or any other form of death duty, is payable on my free estate then my executors must pay it from the residue of my estate.

4 RESIDUE   6–218

I give to my executors:

  (I) my estate, anywhere in the world; and
  (II) any property over which I have a general power of appointment;

to hold it on trust:

    (a) to pay my debts, taxes and funeral and testamentary expenses;
    (b) to divide the residue equally between those of my nieces and nephews who are living at my death $/[and attain $/{18$//21$//25$/}$/].

5 POWER OF INVESTMENT   6–219

My executors may invest my estate in any investments they could make if they owned my estate personally. In particular, they may:

    (a) invest in unsecured loans, including interest-free loans to a beneficiary;
    (b) invest in land, whether as an investment or as a residence for a beneficiary, and may improve and maintain it;
    (c) invest jointly with another person;
    (d) invest in wasting or non-income-producing assets;
    (e) invest anywhere in the world; and
    (f) choose not to diversify investments.

6 EXCLUSION OF S.11 TLATA   6–220

My executors may exercise their powers without consulting beneficiaries, so section 11 of the Trusts of Land and Appointment of Trustees Act 1996 does not apply.

7 POWER OF ADVANCEMENT   6–221

My executors may apply the share of any beneficiary for $/{his$//her$//his or her$/} benefit, and this power:

    (a) is in addition to any other powers my executors may have, in particular section 32 of the Trustee Act 1925;
    (b) applies to the whole or part of the beneficiary's share;
    (c) applies whether the beneficiary's right is vested, contingent, expectant or presumptive but not where another person is entitled in priority;
    (d) may be used for advancement, maintenance, education or any other benefit;
    (e) may be exercised by paying the share to a third party or, where appropriate, to the beneficiary direct.

8 POWER OF APPROPRIATION   6–222

My executors may give specific assets of my estate to beneficiaries without requiring consent. (Section 41 of the Administration of Estates Act 1925 therefore applies subject to that amendment.)

6–223 9 POWER OF INSURANCE

My executors may:

(a) keep any assets of my estate insured, against any risk and in any amount;

(b) pay insurance premiums from the income or capital of that part of my estate which is held on the same trusts as the insured property; and

(c) treat any insurance money received as though it were the proceeds of sale of the insured property.

6–224 10 EXCLUSION OF EXECUTORS' LIABILITY

(a) Only a professional executor or trustee can be liable for any loss arising from:

(i) exercising, or failing to exercise, any discretion or power;

(ii) any improper investment made in good faith;

(iii) the negligence or fraud of any agent employed by him, or by any other executor or trustee, even if the employment was not strictly necessary or expedient;

(iv) any mistake or omission made in good faith;

(v) any other matter, except willful and individual fraud on the part of the executor or trustee who is sought to be made liable.

(b) No executor can be liable for any loss, of any kind, if he has acted in accordance with the advice of Counsel of at least five years' standing.

6–225 11 TRUST CORPORATIONS

If a trust corporation is appointed as executor or trustee, it may:

(a) act by its proper officers;

(b) exercise all the powers given to executors or trustees by my will;

(c) charge under its published scale of fees, as amended from time to time;

(d) meet its charges out of capital or income, at its discretion.

6–226 12 POWER TO USE NOMINEES

My executors may vest any asset of my estate in the name of, or under the control of:

(a) one or more of their number; or

(b) any person (which may include a trust corporation), or people, as nominee(s).

6–227 13 POWER TO CHARGE FOR PROFESSIONAL SERVICES

Any of my executors who is engaged in a profession or business may charge fees for work done by him or her, or by his or her firm, in connection with my estate and its trusts, including acts which an executor or trustee not being in any profession or business could have done personally, and those charges shall be a first charge against my estate, without abatement.

14 COMMORIENTES 6–228

My estate is to be divided as if any person who dies within one month of my death had predeceased me.

15 ACCUMULATIONS OF INCOME 6–229

My executors may:

(a) within 21 years of my death, accumulate income to the extent that it is not paid to, or applied for the benefit of, any beneficiary; and
(b) apply accumulated income as if it were the income of the current year.

16 POWER OF DELEGATION 6–230

My executors may delegate any of their functions, in writing, to:

(a) one or more of their number; or
any other person;
(b) and if they do so my executors are not personally liable to my estate for the defaults of that delegate.

17 INDEMNITIES 6–231

My executors may indemnify a retiring trustee, or any other person, against any liability concerning my estate. If they do so, then my estate (not my executors personally) will bear the liability of that indemnity. My executors may charge the indemnity on assets of my estate.

18 MINOR'S RECEIPT 6–232

where a person is a minor (that is:

(I) under 18; or
(II) 18 or over, but not of an age to be entitled to capital outright);

my executors may pay money to which he or she becomes entitled, whether:

(i) income or capital; or
(ii) as of right or under a power;

to any the following, and in each case their receipt is a complete discharge:

(A) the minor, if he or she has attained 16;
(B) the minor's parent or guardian, in which case my executors are under no further obligation to enquire into the use of the money; or
(C) a third party for the benefit of the minor;

or my executors may resolve to hold the money on trust for the minor absolutely (in which case the administrative provisions of my will continue to apply to the money).

19 CONFLICTS OF INTEREST 6–233

My executors may exercise (or fail to exercise) any powers in my will, even if one or more of them has a personal interest in the outcome.

6–234 20 USE OF EXECUTORS' POWERS

My executors may exercise any of their powers:

(a) from time to time; and

(b) at their absolute discretion.

6–235 21 DEFINITION OF "CHILDREN"

In my will, "children":

(a) includes those who are legitimate, illegitimate or adopted; but

(b) does not include step-children, nor natural children who have been adopted by another person;

and other terms describing family relationships are to be interpreted accordingly.

6–236 SIGNATURES

Signed by me on . . . . 20$/

Signature of Testator

Signed by $/ in our joint presence and then by us in $/{his$//hers$/}
                 Witness 1   Witness 2

Signature:

Full name:

Address:

Occupation:

114b Class gift to nieces and nephews on attaining a specified age (step powers)

6–237 This is the last will of me $/ of $/.

6–238 1 REVOCATION

I revoke all former wills.

6–239 2 APPOINTMENT OF EXECUTORS

I appoint $/ $/[and $/$/] to be my $/{executor$//executors$/} but if $/{he is$// she is$//both of them are$//either of them is$//all of them are$//any of them is$/} unable or unwilling to act then I appoint $/ instead.

6–240 3 BURDEN OF INHERITANCE TAX

If inheritance tax, or any other form of death duty, is payable on my free estate then my executors must pay it from the residue of my estate.

4 RESIDUE

6–241

I give to my executors:
    (I) my estate, anywhere in the world; and
    (II) any property over which I have a general power of appointment;

to hold it on trust:

      (a) to pay my debts, taxes and funeral and testamentary expenses;
      (b) to divide the residue equally between those of my nieces and nephews who are living at my death $/[and attain $/{18$//21$//25$/}$/].

5 TECHNICAL CLAUSES

6–242

    (a) The Standard Provisions of the Society of Trust and Estate Practitioners (1st edition) apply, amended as follows:

      (i) Standard provision 5 ("trust for sale") does not apply.
      (ii) My executors may exercise their powers without consulting beneficiaries, so section 11 of the Trusts of Land and Appointment of Trustees Act 1996 does not apply.
    (b) My estate is to be divided as if any person who dies within one month of my death had predeceased me.

SIGNATURES

6–243

Signed by me on .... 20$/
Signature of Testator

Signed by $/ in our joint presence and then by us in $/{his$//hers$/}
               Witness 1   Witness 2

Signature:

Full name:

Address:

Occupation:

115 Nieces and nephews on flexible accumulation and maintenance trusts

115a Complete powers

This is the last will of me $/ of $/.

6–244

1 REVOCATION

6–245

I revoke all former wills.

6-246 2 APPOINTMENT OF EXECUTORS

I appoint $/ $/[and $/$/] to be my $/{executor$//executors$/} but if $/{he is$//
she is$//both of them are$//either of them is$//all of them are$//any of them
is$/} unable or unwilling to act then I appoint $/ instead.

6-247 3 BURDEN OF INHERITANCE TAX

If inheritance tax, or any other form of death duty, is payable on my free
estate then my executors must pay it from the residue of my estate.

6-248 4 RESIDUE

I give to my executors:

   (I) my estate, anywhere in the world; and
   (II) any property over which I have a general power of appointment;

to hold it on trust:

      (a) to pay my debts, taxes and funeral and testamentary expenses;
      (b) to pay the residue ("the trust fund") to the trustees of the
         settlement declared in clause (5) below.

6-249 5 FLEXIBLE ACCUMULATION AND MAINTENANCE TRUST

   (a) In this clause:
     "my trustees" means my executors or the trustees for the time being
     of this clause;
     "the primary beneficiaries" means those of my nieces and nephews
     who are either:

     (i) living at my death; or
     (ii) born after me but before the eldest living primary beneficiary
        attains 25;

     "the beneficiaries" means

     (i) the primary beneficiaries;
     (ii) all descendants of the primary beneficiaries;
     (iii) the spouses and former spouses of (i) and (ii);
     (iv) charities;

     "interest-in-possession" means the right to receive the current
     income from a share in the trust fund.
   (b) I give the trust fund to my trustees on the following trusts:

     (i) to divide the trust fund into one equal share for each primary
       beneficiary;
     (ii) while a primary beneficiary is under 25:

        (A) to apply the income from his or her share for his or her
           maintenance, education or benefit; or
        (B) within 21 years of my death, to accumulate any income not
           so applied;

(iii) as each primary beneficiary attains 25, to grant an interest-in-possession in his or her share, to him or her.

(c) The above trusts are subject to the following powers:

(i) while a primary beneficiary is under 25 my trustees may apply the income of his or her share for the benefit of any other primary beneficiary who is for the time being under 25;

(ii) my trustees may grant a primary beneficiary an interest-in-possession in his or her share at any age below 25;

(iii) if a primary beneficiary dies before attaining an interest-in-possession then my trustees may hold his or her share for the benefit of any of the beneficiaries they think fit.

(iv) once a primary beneficiary has attained an interest-in-possession, my trustees may hold his or her share for the benefit of any of the beneficiaries they think fit.

(v) if my trustees have the power to benefit any of the beneficiaries they think fit, their powers include:

(A) the power to pay to a primary beneficiary the capital of his or her share outright;

(B) the power to bring an interest-in-possession to an end, or to transfer it to another beneficiary;

(C) the power to use a share for the benefit of (or pay the capital from it to) a beneficiary other than the primary beneficiary whose share it was;

(D) the power to settle any part of the trust fund on the trustees of a separate trust if (and only if) the only possible beneficiaries of that trust are also beneficiaries of this clause;

(E) where a primary beneficiary has died, the power to redistribute his share among the shares of surviving primary beneficiaries.

(d) My trustees must exercise their discretions by deed of appointment. A deed of appointment may be revocable or irrevocable.

(e) My trustees have all the powers given to executors by my will.

6 POWER OF INVESTMENT 6–250

My executors may invest my estate in any investments they could make if they owned my estate personally. In particular, they may:

(a) invest in unsecured loans, including interest-free loans to a beneficiary;

(b) invest in land, whether as an investment or as a residence for a beneficiary, and may improve and maintain it;

(c) invest jointly with another person;

(d) invest in wasting or non-income-producing assets;

(e) invest anywhere in the world; and

(f) choose not to diversify investments.

6–251 7 EXCLUSION OF THE APPORTIONMENT RULES

(a) My executors may treat income as arising on the day it is received.

(b) The Apportionment Act 1870 does not apply.

(c) The rules known as "the rule in *Howe v. Dartmouth*" and "the rule in *Allhusen v. Whittell*" do not apply.

6–252 8 EXCLUSION OF S.11 TLATA

My executors may exercise their powers without consulting beneficiaries, so section 11 of the Trusts of Land and Appointment of Trustees Act 1996 does not apply.

6–253 9 POWER OF ADVANCEMENT

My executors may apply the share of any beneficiary for $/{his$//her$//his or her$/} benefit, and this power:

(a) is in addition to any other powers my executors may have, in particular section 32 of the Trustee Act 1925;

(b) applies to the whole or part of the beneficiary's share;

(c) applies whether the beneficiary's right is vested, contingent, expectant or presumptive but not where another person is entitled in priority;

(d) may be used for advancement, maintenance, education or any other benefit;

(e) may be exercised by paying the share to a third party or, where appropriate, to the beneficiary direct.

6–254 10 POWER OF APPROPRIATION

My executors may give specific assets of my estate to beneficiaries without requiring consent. (Section 41 of the Administration of Estates Act 1925 therefore applies subject to that amendment.)

6–255 11 POWER OF INSURANCE

My executors may:

(a) keep any assets of my estate insured, against any risk and in any amount;

(b) pay insurance premiums from the income or capital of that part of my estate which is held on the same trusts as the insured property; and

(c) treat any insurance money received as though it were the proceeds of sale of the insured property.

6–256 12 EXCLUSION OF EXECUTORS' LIABILITY

(a) Only a professional executor or trustee can be liable for any loss arising from:

    (i) exercising, or failing to exercise, any discretion or power;

    (ii) any improper investment made in good faith;

    (iii) the negligence or fraud of any agent employed by him, or by any other executor or trustee, even if the employment was not strictly necessary or expedient;

    (iv) any mistake or omission made in good faith;

    (v) any other matter, except willful and individual fraud on the part of the executor or trustee who is sought to be made liable.

(b) No executor can be liable for any loss, of any kind, if he has acted in accordance with the advice of Counsel of at least five years' standing.

13 TRUST CORPORATIONS 6–257

If a trust corporation is appointed as executor or trustee, it may:

(a) act by its proper officers;

(b) exercise all the powers given to executors or trustees by my will;

(c) charge under its published scale of fees, as amended from time to time;

(d) meet its charges out of capital or income, at its discretion.

14 POWER TO USE NOMINEES 6–258

My executors may vest any asset of my estate in the name of, or under the control of:

(a) one or more of their number; or

(b) any person (which may include a trust corporation), or people, as nominee(s).

15 POWER TO CHARGE FOR PROFESSIONAL SERVICES 6–259

Any of my executors who is engaged in a profession or business may charge fees for work done by him or her, or by his or her firm, in connection with my estate and its trusts, including acts which an executor or trustee not being in any profession or business could have done personally, and those charges shall be a first charge against my estate, without abatement.

16 COMMORIENTES 6–260

My estate is to be divided as if any person who dies within one month of my death had predeceased me.

17 ACCUMULATIONS OF INCOME 6–261

My executors may:

(a) within 21 years of my death, accumulate income to the extent that it is not paid to, or applied for the benefit of, any beneficiary; and

(b) apply accumulated income as if it were the income of the current year.

18 POWER TO BORROW 6–262

(a) My executors may borrow money for any purpose.

(b) My executors may charge any assets of my estate as security for any liability.

6–263 ## 19 POWER OF DELEGATION

My executors may delegate any of their functions, in writing, to:

(a) one or more of their number; or
(b) any other person;

and if they do so my executors are not personally liable to my estate for the defaults of that delegate.

6–264 ## 20 INDEMNITIES

My executors may indemnify a retiring trustee, or any other person, against any liability concerning my estate. If they do so, then my estate (not my executors personally) will bear the liability of that indemnity. My executors may charge the indemnity on assets of my estate.

6–265 ## 21 MINOR'S RECEIPT

where a person is a minor (that is:

(a) under 18; or
(b) 18 or over, but not of an age to be entitled to capital outright);

my executors may pay money to which he or she becomes entitled, whether:

(i) income or capital; or
(ii) as of right or under a power;

to any the following, and in each case their receipt is a complete discharge:

(A) the minor, if he or she has attained 16;
(B) the minor's parent or guardian, in which case my executors are under no further obligation to enquire into the use of the money; or
(C) a third party for the benefit of the minor;

or my executors may resolve to hold the money on trust for the minor absolutely (in which case the administrative provisions of my will continue to apply to the money).

6–266 ## 22 CONFLICTS OF INTEREST

My executors may exercise (or fail to exercise) any powers in my will, even if one or more of them has a personal interest in the outcome.

6–267 ## 23 USE OF EXECUTORS' POWERS

My executors may exercise any of their powers:

(a) from time to time; and
(b) at their absolute discretion.

6–268 ## 24 DEFINITION OF "CHILDREN"

In my will, "children":

(a) includes those who are legitimate, illegitimate or adopted; but

(b) does not include step-children, nor natural children who have been adopted by another person;

and other terms describing family relationships are to be interpreted accordingly.

SIGNATURES 6–269

Signed by me on .... 20$/

Signature of Testator

Signed by $/ in our joint presence and then by us in $/{his$//hers$/}

    Witness 1   Witness 2

Signature:

Full name:

Address:

Occupation:

115b Nieces and nephews on flexible accumulation and maintenance trusts (STEP powers)

This is the last will of me $/ of $/.   6–270

1 REVOCATION 6–271

I revoke all former wills.

2 APPOINTMENT OF EXECUTORS 6–272

I appoint $/ $/[and $/$/] to be my $/{executor$//executors$/} but if $/{he is$// she is$//both of them are$//either of them is$//all of them are$//any of them is$/} unable or unwilling to act then I appoint $/ instead.

3 BURDEN OF INHERITANCE TAX 6–273

If inheritance tax, or any other form of death duty, is payable on my free estate then my executors must pay it from the residue of my estate.

4 RESIDUE 6–274

I give to my executors:

(I) my estate, anywhere in the world; and

(II) any property over which I have a general power of appointment;

to hold it on trust:

(a) to pay my debts, taxes and funeral and testamentary expenses;

(b) to pay the residue ("the trust fund") to the trustees of the settlement declared in clause (5) below.

6–275 5 FLEXIBLE ACCUMULATION AND MAINTENANCE TRUST

In this clause:

"**my trustees**" means my executors or the trustees for the time being of this clause;

"**the primary beneficiaries**" means those of my nieces and nephews who are either:

(i) living at my death; or

(ii) born after me but before the eldest living primary beneficiary attains 25;

"**the beneficiaries**" means:

(i) the primary beneficiaries;

(ii) all descendants of the primary beneficiaries;

(iii) the spouses and former spouses of (i) and (ii);

(iv) charities;

"**interest-in-possession**" means the right to receive the income from a share in the trust fund.

(b) I give the trust fund to my trustees on the following trusts:

   (i) to divide the trust fund into one equal share for each primary beneficiary;

   (ii) while a primary beneficiary is under 25:

      (A) to apply the income from his or her share for his or her maintenance, education or benefit; or

      (B) within 21 years of my death, to accumulate any income not so applied;

   (iii) as each primary beneficiary attains 25, to grant an interest-in-possession in his or her share, to him or her.

(c) The above trusts are subject to the following powers:

   (i) while a primary beneficiary is under 25 my trustees may apply the income of his or her share for the benefit of any other primary beneficiary who is for the time being under 25;

   (ii) my trustees may grant a primary beneficiary an interest-in-possession in his or her share at any age below 25;

   (iii) if a primary beneficiary dies before attaining an interest-in-possession then my trustees may hold his or her share for the benefit of any of the beneficiaries they think fit.

   (iv) once a primary beneficiary has attained an interest-in-possession, my trustees may hold his or her share for the benefit of any of the beneficiaries they think fit.

   (v) if my trustees have the power to benefit any of the beneficiaries they think fit, their powers include:

(A) the power to pay to a primary beneficiary the capital of his or her share outright;

(B) the power to bring an interest-in-possession to an end, or to transfer it to another beneficiary;

(C) the power to use a share for the benefit of (or pay the capital from it to) a beneficiary other than the primary beneficiary whose share it was;

(D) the power to settle any part of the trust fund on the trustees of a separate trust if (and only if) the only possible beneficiaries of that trust are also beneficiaries of this clause;

(E) where a primary beneficiary has died, the power to redistribute his share among the shares of surviving primary beneficiaries.

(d) My trustees must exercise their discretions by deed of appointment. A deed of appointment may be revocable or irrevocable.

(e) My trustees have all the powers given to executors by my will.

6 TECHNICAL CLAUSES 6–276

(a) The Standard Provisions of the Society of Trust and Estate Practitioners (1st edition) apply, amended as follows:

(i) Standard provision 5 ("trust for sale") does not apply.

(ii) My executors may exercise their powers without consulting beneficiaries, so section 11 of the Trusts of Land and Appointment of Trustees Act 1996 does not apply.

(a) In my will, "children":

(i) includes those who are legitimate, illegitimate or adopted; but

(ii) does not include step-children, nor natural children who have been adopted by another person;

and other terms describing family relationships are to be interpreted accordingly.

(c) My estate is to be divided as if any person who dies within one month of my death had predeceased me.

SIGNATURES

Signed by me on . . . . 20$/
Signature of Testator

Signed by $/ in our joint presence and then by us in ${his$//hers$/}

| Witness 1 | Witness 2 |

Signature:

Full name:

Address:

Occupation:

116 Life interest for named beneficiary

116a Complete powers

6-278   This is the last will of me $/ of $/.

6-279 1 REVOCATION

I revoke all former wills.

6-280 2 APPOINTMENT OF EXECUTORS

I appoint $/ $/[and $/$/] to be my $/{executor$//executors$/} but if $/{he is$// she is$//both of them are$//either of them is$//all of them are$//any of them is$/} unable or unwilling to act then I appoint $/ instead.

6-281 3 BURDEN OF INHERITANCE TAX

If inheritance tax, or any other form of death duty, is payable on my free estate then my executors must pay it from the residue of my estate.

6-282 4 RESIDUE

I give to my executors:

> (I) my estate, anywhere in the world; and
> (II) any property over which I have a general power of appointment;

to hold it on trust:

>> (a) to pay my debts, taxes and funeral and testamentary expenses;
>> (b) to pay the residue ("the trust fund") to the trustees of the settlement declared in clause (5) below.

6-283 5 LIFE INTEREST TRUST

> (a) In this clause, "my trustees" means my executors or the trustees for the time being of this clause.
> (b) My trustees have all the powers given to executors by my will.
> (c) I give the trust fund to my trustees on trust to pay the income to $/ ("the life tenant") during $/{his$//her$/} lifetime; and subject to that:
> (d) to divide the residue equally between those of my $/{nieces$// nephews$//nieces and nephews$//cousins$/} who are living at the death of the survivor of:
>> (i) me; and
>> (ii) the life tenant;
> $/[and attain $/{18$//21$//25$/}$/].

6-284 6 POWER OF INVESTMENT

My executors may invest my estate in any investments they could make if they owned my estate personally. In particular, they may:

> (a) invest in unsecured loans, including interest-free loans to a beneficiary;

(b) invest in land, whether as an investment or as a residence for a beneficiary, and may improve and maintain it;

(c) invest jointly with another person;

(d) invest in wasting or non-income-producing assets;

(e) invest anywhere in the world; and

(f) choose not to diversify investments.

7 EXCLUSION OF THE APPORTIONMENT RULES   6–285

(a) My executors may treat income as arising on the day it is received.

(b) The Apportionment Act 1870 does not apply.

(c) The rules known as "the rule in *Howe v. Dartmouth*" and "the rule in *Allhusen v. Whittell*" do not apply.

8 EXCLUSION OF S.11 TLATA   6–286

My executors may exercise their powers without consulting beneficiaries, so section 11 of the Trusts of Land and Appointment of Trustees Act 1996 does not apply.

9 POWER OF ADVANCEMENT   6–287

My executors may apply the share of any beneficiary for $/{his$//her$//his or her$/} benefit, and this power:

(a) is in addition to any other powers my executors may have, in particular section 32 of the Trustee Act 1925;

(b) applies to the whole or part of the beneficiary's share;

(c) applies whether the beneficiary's right is vested, contingent, expectant or presumptive but not where another person is entitled in priority;

(d) may be used for advancement, maintenance, education or any other benefit;

(e) may be exercised by paying the share to a third party or, where appropriate, to the beneficiary direct.

10 POWER OF APPROPRIATION   6–288

My executors may give specific assets of my estate to beneficiaries without requiring consent. (Section 41 of the Administration of Estates Act 1925 therefore applies subject to that amendment.)

11 POWER OF INSURANCE   6–289

My executors may:

(a) keep any assets of my estate insured, against any risk and in any amount;

(b) pay insurance premiums from the income or capital of that part of my estate which is held on the same trusts as the insured property; and

(c) treat any insurance money received as though it were the proceeds of sale of the insured property.

12 EXCLUSION OF EXECUTORS' LIABILITY   6–290

(a) Only a professional executor or trustee can be liable for any loss arising from:

(i) exercising, or failing to exercise, any discretion or power;

(ii) any improper investment made in good faith;

(iii) the negligence or fraud of any agent employed by him, or by any other executor or trustee, even if the employment was not strictly necessary or expedient;

(iv) any mistake or omission made in good faith;

(v) any other matter, except willful and individual fraud on the part of the executor or trustee who is sought to be made liable.

(b) No executor can be liable for any loss, of any kind, if he has acted in accordance with the advice of Counsel of at least five years' standing.

6–291 13 TRUST CORPORATIONS

If a trust corporation is appointed as executor or trustee, it may:

(a) act by its proper officers;

(b) exercise all the powers given to executors or trustees by my will;

(c) charge under its published scale of fees, as amended from time to time;

(d) meet its charges out of capital or income, at its discretion.

6–292 14 POWER TO USE NOMINEES

My executors may vest any asset of my estate in the name of, or under the control of:

(a) one or more of their number; or

(b) any person (which may include a trust corporation), or people, as nominee(s).

6–293 15 POWER TO CHARGE FOR PROFESSIONAL SERVICES

Any of my executors who is engaged in a profession or business may charge fees for work done by him or her, or by his or her firm, in connection with my estate and its trusts, including acts which an executor or trustee not being in any profession or business could have done personally, and those charges shall be a first charge against my estate, without abatement.

6–294 16 COMMORIENTES

My estate is to be divided as if any person who dies within one month of my death had predeceased me.

6–295 17 ACCUMULATIONS OF INCOME

My executors may:

(a) within 21 years of my death, accumulate income to the extent that it is not paid to, or applied for the benefit of, any beneficiary; and

(b) apply accumulated income as if it were the income of the current year.

18 POWER TO BORROW 6–296

(a) My executors may borrow money for any purpose.
(b) My executors may charge any assets of my estate as security for any liability.

19 POWER OF DELEGATION 6–297

My executors may delegate any of their functions, in writing, to:

(a) one or more of their number; or
(b) any other person;

and if they do so my executors are not personally liable to my estate for the defaults of that delegate.

20 INDEMNITIES 6–298

My executors may indemnify a retiring trustee, or any other person, against any liability concerning my estate. If they do so, then my estate (not my executors personally) will bear the liability of that indemnity. My executors may charge the indemnity on assets of my estate.

21 MINOR'S RECEIPT 6–299

where a person is a minor (that is:

(a) under 18; or
(b) 18 or over, but not of an age to be entitled to capital outright);

my executors may pay money to which he or she becomes entitled, whether:

(i) income or capital; or
(ii) as of right or under a power;

to any the following, and in each case their receipt is a complete discharge:

(A) the minor, if he or she has attained 16;
(B) the minor's parent or guardian, in which case my executors are under no further obligation to enquire into the use of the money; or
(C) a third party for the benefit of the minor;

or my executors may resolve to hold the money on trust for the minor absolutely (in which case the administrative provisions of my will continue to apply to the money).

22 CONFLICTS OF INTEREST 6–300

My executors may exercise (or fail to exercise) any powers in my will, even if one or more of them has a personal interest in the outcome.

23 USE OF EXECUTORS' POWERS 6–301

My executors may exercise any of their powers:

(a) from time to time; and
(b) at their absolute discretion.

6–302 24 DEFINITION OF "CHILDREN"

In my will, "children":

(a) includes those who are legitimate, illegitimate or adopted; but

(b) does not include step-children, nor natural children who have been adopted by another person;

and other terms describing family relationships are to be interpreted accordingly.

6–303 SIGNATURES

Signed by me on . . . . 20$/

Signature of Testator

Signed by $/ in our joint presence and then by us in $/{his$//hers$/}
Witness 1   Witness 2

Signature:

Full name:

Address:

Occupation:

116b Life interest for named beneficiary (STEP powers)

6–304 This is the last will of me $/ of $/.

6–305 1 REVOCATION

I revoke all former wills.

6–306 2 APPOINTMENT OF EXECUTORS

I appoint $/ $/[and $/$/] to be my $/{executor$//executors$/} but if $/{he is$//she is$//both of them are$//either of them is$//all of them are$//any of them is$/} unable or unwilling to act then I appoint $/ instead.

6–307 3 BURDEN OF INHERITANCE TAX

If inheritance tax, or any other form of death duty, is payable on my free estate then my executors must pay it from the residue of my estate.

4 RESIDUE

I give to my executors:

    (I) my estate, anywhere in the world; and
    (II) any property over which I have a general power of appointment;

to hold it on trust:

      (a) to pay my debts, taxes and funeral and testamentary expenses;
      (b) to pay the residue ("the trust fund") to the trustees of the settlement declared in clause (5) below.

5 LIFE INTEREST TRUST

    (a) In this clause, "my trustees" means my executors or the trustees for the time being of this clause.
    (b) My trustees have all the powers given to executors by my will.
    (c) I give the trust fund to my trustees on trust to pay the income to $/ ("the life tenant") during $/{his$//her$/} lifetime; and subject to that:
    (d) to divide the residue equally between those of my $/{nieces$// nephews$//nieces and nephews$//cousins$/} who are living at the death of the survivor of:

      (i) me; and
      (ii) the life tenant;
      $/[and attain $/{18$//21$//25$/}$/].

6 TECHNICAL CLAUSES

    (a) The Standard Provisions of the Society of Trust and Estate Practitioners (1st edition) apply, amended as follows:

      (i) Standard provision 5 ("trust for sale") does not apply.
      (ii) My executors may exercise their powers without consulting beneficiaries, so section 11 of the Trusts of Land and Appointment of Trustees Act 1996 does not apply.

    (b) In my will, "children":

      (i) includes those who are legitimate, illegitimate or adopted; but
      (ii) does not include step-children, nor natural children who have been adopted by another person;

    and other terms describing family relationships are to be interpreted accordingly.
    (c) My estate is to be divided as if any person who dies within one month of my death had predeceased me.

6–311 SIGNATURES

Signed by me on .... 20$/

Signature of Testator

Signed by $/ in our joint presence and then by us in $/{his$//hers$/}

              Witness 1   Witness 2

Signature:

Full name:

Address:

Occupation:

117 Will to charity

117a Complete powers

6–312 This is the last will of me $/ of $/.

6–313 1 REVOCATION

I revoke all former wills.

6–314 2 APPOINTMENT OF EXECUTORS

I appoint $/ $/[and $/$/] to be my $/{executor$//executors$/} but if $/{he is$//she is$//both of them are$//either of them is$//all of them are$//any of them is$/} unable or unwilling to act then I appoint $/ instead.

6–315 3 BURDEN OF INHERITANCE TAX

If inheritance tax, or any other form of death duty, is payable on my free estate then my executors must pay it from the residue of my estate.

6–316 4 RESIDUE

I give to my executors:

   (I) my estate, anywhere in the world; and
  (II) any property over which I have a general power of appointment;

to hold it on trust:

   (a) to pay my debts, taxes and funeral and testamentary expenses;
  (b) to divide the residue equally between those of the following who are in existence at my death:

(i) $/ of $/ (registered charity number $/);
(ii) $/ of $/ (registered charity number $/); and
(iii) $/ of $/ (registered charity number $/).

5 CHARITIES' RECEIPT   6–317

My executors may accept, as a complete discharge, the receipt of any person who appears to be a proper officer of a charity.

6 POWER OF INVESTMENT   6–318

My executors may invest my estate in any investments they could make if they owned my estate personally. In particular, they may:

(a) invest in unsecured loans, including interest-free loans to a beneficiary;
(b) invest in land, whether as an investment or as a residence for a beneficiary, and may improve and maintain it;
(c) invest jointly with another person;
(d) invest in wasting or non-income-producing assets;
(e) invest anywhere in the world; and
(f) choose not to diversify investments.

7 EXCLUSION OF S.11 TLATA   6–319

My executors may exercise their powers without consulting beneficiaries, so section 11 of the Trusts of Land and Appointment of Trustees Act 1996 does not apply.

8 POWER OF APPROPRIATION   6–320

My executors may give specific assets of my estate to beneficiaries without requiring consent. (Section 41 of the Administration of Estates Act 1925 therefore applies subject to that amendment.)

9 POWER OF INSURANCE   6–321

My executors may:

(a) keep any assets of my estate insured, against any risk and in any amount;
(b) pay insurance premiums from the income or capital of that part of my estate which is held on the same trusts as the insured property; and
(c) treat any insurance money received as though it were the proceeds of sale of the insured property.

10 EXCLUSION OF EXECUTORS' LIABILITY   6–322

(a) Only a professional executor or trustee can be liable for any loss arising from:

(i) exercising, or failing to exercise, any discretion or power;
(ii) any improper investment made in good faith;
(iii) the negligence or fraud of any agent employed by him, or by any other executor or trustee, even if the employment was not strictly necessary or expedient;

    (iv) any mistake or omission made in good faith;

    (v) any other matter, except willful and individual fraud on the part of the executor or trustee who is sought to be made liable.

  (b) No executor can be liable for any loss, of any kind, if he has acted in accordance with the advice of Counsel of at least five years' standing.

6–323 11 POWER TO USE NOMINEES

My executors may vest any asset of my estate in the name of, or under the control of:

  (a) one or more of their number; or

  (b) any person (which may include a trust corporation), or people, as nominee(s).

6–324 12 POWER TO CHARGE FOR PROFESSIONAL SERVICES

Any of my executors who is engaged in a profession or business may charge fees for work done by him or her, or by his or her firm, in connection with my estate and its trusts, including acts which an executor or trustee not being in any profession or business could have done personally, and those charges shall be a first charge against my estate, without abatement.

6–325 13 COMMORIENTES

My estate is to be divided as if any person who dies within one month of my death had predeceased me.

6–326 14 CONFLICTS OF INTEREST

My executors may exercise (or fail to exercise) any powers in my will, even if one or more of them has a personal interest in the outcome.

6–327 15 USE OF EXECUTORS' POWERS

My executors may exercise any of their powers:

  (a) from time to time; and

  (b) at their absolute discretion.

SIGNATURES   6–328

Signed by me on . . . . 20$/
Signature of Testator

Signed by $/ in our joint presence and then by us in $/{his$//hers$/}
                    Witness 1   Witness 2

Signature:

Full name:

Address:

Occupation:

117b Will to charity (STEP powers)

This is the last will of me $/ of $/.   6–329

1 REVOCATION   6–330

I revoke all former wills.

2 APPOINTMENT OF EXECUTORS   6–331

I appoint $/ $/[and $/$/] to be my $/{executor$//executors$/} but if $/{he is$//
she is$//both of them are$//either of them is$//all of them are$//any of them
is$/} unable or unwilling to act then I appoint $/ instead.

3 BURDEN OF INHERITANCE TAX   6–332

If inheritance tax, or any other form of death duty, is payable on my free
estate then my executors must pay it from the residue of my estate.

4 RESIDUE   6–333

I give to my executors:
  (I) my estate, anywhere in the world; and
  (II) any property over which I have a general power of appointment;

to hold it on trust:

    (a) to pay my debts, taxes and funeral and testamentary expenses;
    (b) to divide the residue equally between those of the following who
          are in existence at my death:

        (i) $/ of $/ (registered charity number $/);
        (ii) $/ of $/ (registered charity number $/); and
        (iii) $/ of $/ (registered charity number $/).

5 CHARITIES' RECEIPT   6–334

My executors may accept, as a complete discharge, the receipt of any person
who appears to be a proper officer of a charity.

6–335 6 TECHNICAL CLAUSES

   (a) The Standard Provisions of the Society of Trust and Estate Practitioners (1st edition) apply, amended as follows:

     (i) Standard provision 5 ("trust for sale") does not apply.

     (ii) My executors may exercise their powers without consulting beneficiaries, so section 11 of the Trusts of Land and Appointment of Trustees Act 1996 does not apply.

   (b) My estate is to be divided as if any person who dies within one month of my death had predeceased me.

6–336 SIGNATURES

Signed by me on .... 20$/

Signature of Testator

Signed by $/ in our joint presence and then by us in $/{his$//hers$/}
              Witness 1   Witness 2

Signature:

Full name:

Address:

Occupation:

WILLS IN EXPECTATION OF MARRIAGE

6–337 This section gives four precedents, and as usual each precedent has an "a" and "b" type depending upon whether the STEP standard provisions are used.

    Precedents 118 and 119 are made in expectation of marriage, but only take effect when the marriage is solemnised. Precedents 120 and 121 take effect even if the death happens before the marriage.

    Clauses 118 and 120 predict the possibility of there being children of the marriage, whereas clauses 119 and 121 skip straight to the "gift over" on the spouse predeceasing and are more suitable, perhaps, for an older couple who know they will be childless.

118 Gift to future wife/husband in expectation of marriage, substituting potential children, with gift over — effective on marriage

118a Complete powers

6–338 This is the last will of me $/ of $/.

6–339 1 REVOCATION

I revoke all former wills.

192

2 EXPECTATION OF MARRIAGE 6–340

My will is not revoked if I marry $/.

3 APPOINTMENT OF EXECUTORS 6–341

I appoint $/ $/[and $/$/] to be my $/{executor$//executors$/} but if $/{he is$// she is$//both of them are$//either of them is$//all of them are$//any of them is$/} unable or unwilling to act then I appoint $/ instead.

4 BURDEN OF INHERITANCE TAX 6–342

If inheritance tax, or any other form of death duty, is payable on my free estate then my executors must pay it from the residue of my estate.

5 RESIDUE 6–343

I give to my executors:

(I) my estate, anywhere in the world; and
(II) any property over which I have a general power of appointment;

to hold it on trust:

(a) to pay my debts, taxes and funeral and testamentary expenses;
(b) If our marriage has been solemised at my death, then to pay the residue to the said $/ absolutely if $/{he$//she$/} survives me by 28 days; but if this gift fails
(c) to divide the residue equally between those of my children who are living at my death and attain $/{18$//21$/}; except:

(i) if any of my children dies before me, then to divide that child's share equally between those of his or her children who are living at my death and attain $/{18$//21$/}; and
(ii) if any of my children dies after me, but before attaining $/{18$//21$/}, then to divide that child's share equally between those of his or her children who are living at his or her death and attain $/{18$//21$/}.

if the above trusts fail, then:

(d) to pay the residue to $/ absolutely.

6 POWER OF INVESTMENT 6–344

My executors may invest my estate in any investments they could make if they owned my estate personally. In particular, they may:

(a) invest in unsecured loans, including interest-free loans to a beneficiary;
(b) invest in land, whether as an investment or as a residence for a beneficiary, and may improve and maintain it;
(c) invest jointly with another person;
(d) invest in wasting or non-income-producing assets;

(e) invest anywhere in the world; and

(f) choose not to diversify investments.

6-345 7 EXCLUSION OF S.11 TLATA

My executors may exercise their powers without consulting beneficiaries, so section 11 of the Trusts of Land and Appointment of Trustees Act 1996 does not apply.

6-346 8 POWER OF ADVANCEMENT

My executors may apply the share of any beneficiary for $/{his$//her$//his or her$/} benefit, and this power:

(a) is in addition to any other powers my executors may have, in particular section 32 of the Trustee Act 1925;

(b) applies to the whole or part of the beneficiary's share;

(c) applies whether the beneficiary's right is vested, contingent, expectant or presumptive but not where another person is entitled in priority;

(d) may be used for advancement, maintenance, education or any other benefit;

(e) may be exercised by paying the share to a third party or, where appropriate, to the beneficiary direct.

6-347 9 POWER OF APPROPRIATION

My executors may give specific assets of my estate to beneficiaries without requiring consent. (Section 41 of the Administration of Estates Act 1925 therefore applies subject to that amendment.)

6-348 10 POWER OF INSURANCE

My executors may:

(a) keep any assets of my estate insured, against any risk and in any amount;

(b) pay insurance premiums from the income or capital of that part of my estate which is held on the same trusts as the insured property; and

(c) treat any insurance money received as though it were the proceeds of sale of the insured property.

6-349 11 EXCLUSION OF EXECUTORS' LIABILITY

(a) Only a professional executor or trustee can be liable for any loss arising from:

(i) exercising, or failing to exercise, any discretion or power;

(ii) any improper investment made in good faith;

(iii) the negligence or fraud of any agent employed by him, or by any other executor or trustee, even if the employment was not strictly necessary or expedient;

(iv) any mistake or omission made in good faith;

(v) any other matter, except wilful and individual fraud on the part of the executor or trustee who is sought to be made liable.

(b) No executor can be liable for any loss, of any kind, if he has acted in accordance with the advice of Counsel of at least five years' standing.

12 TRUST CORPORATIONS   6–350

If a trust corporation is appointed as executor or trustee, it may:

(a) act by its proper officers;
(b) exercise all the powers given to executors or trustees by my will;
(c) charge under its published scale of fees, as amended from time to time;
(d) meet its charges out of capital or income, at its discretion.

13 POWER TO USE NOMINEES   6–351

My executors may vest any asset of my estate in the name of, or under the control of:

(a) one or more of their number; or
(b) any person (which may include a trust corporation), or people, as nominee(s).

14 POWER TO CHARGE FOR PROFESSIONAL SERVICES   6–352

Any of my executors who is engaged in a profession or business may charge fees for work done by him or her, or by his or her firm, in connection with my estate and its trusts, including acts which an executor or trustee not being in any profession or business could have done personally, and those charges shall be a first charge against my estate, without abatement.

15 COMMORIENTES   6–353

My estate is to be divided as if any person who dies within one month of my death had predeceased me.

16 ACCUMULATIONS OF INCOME   6–354

My executors may:

(a) within 21 years of my death, accumulate income to the extent that it is not paid to, or applied for the benefit of, any beneficiary; and
(b) apply accumulated income as if it were the income of the current year.

17 POWER OF DELEGATION   6–355

My executors may delegate any of their functions, in writing, to:

(a) one or more of their number; or
(b) any other person;

and if they do so my executors are not personally liable to my estate for the defaults of that delegate.

6–356 18 INDEMNITIES

My executors may indemnify a retiring trustee, or any other person, against any liability concerning my estate. If they do so, then my estate (not my executors personally) will bear the liability of that indemnity. My executors may charge the indemnity on assets of my estate.

6–357 19 MINOR'S RECEIPT

where a person is a minor (that is:

(a) under 18; or
(b) 18 or over, but not of an age to be entitled to capital outright);

my executors may pay money to which he or she becomes entitled, whether:

(i) income or capital; or
(ii) as of right or under a power;

to any the following, and in each case their receipt is a complete discharge:

(A) the minor, if he or she has attained 16;
(B) the minor's parent or guardian, in which case my executors are under no further obligation to enquire into the use of the money; or
(C) a third party for the benefit of the minor;

or my executors may resolve to hold the money on trust for the minor absolutely (in which case the administrative provisions of my will continue to apply to the money).

6–358 20 CONFLICTS OF INTEREST

My executors may exercise (or fail to exercise) any powers in my will, even if one or more of them has a personal interest in the outcome.

6–359 21 USE OF EXECUTORS' POWERS

My executors may exercise any of their powers:

(a) from time to time; and
(b) at their absolute discretion.

6–360 22 DEFINITION OF "CHILDREN"

In my will, "children":

(a) includes those who are legitimate, illegitimate or adopted; but
(b) does not include step-children, nor natural children who have been adopted by another person;

and other terms describing family relationships are to be interpreted accordingly.

SIGNATURES 6–361

Signed by me on .... 20$/

Signature of Testator

Signed by $/ in our joint presence and then by us in $/{his$//hers$/}
                    Witness 1   Witness 2

Signature:

Full name:

Address:

Occupation:

118b Gift to future wife/husband in expectation of marriage, substituting potential children, with gift over — effective on marriage (STEP powers)

This is the last will of me $/ of $/. 6–362

1 REVOCATION 6–363

I revoke all former wills.

2 EXPECTATION OF MARRIAGE 6–364

My will is not revoked if I marry $/.

3 APPOINTMENT OF EXECUTORS 6–365

I appoint $/ $/[and $/$/] to be my $/{executor$//executors$/} but if $/{he is$//she is$//both of them are$//either of them is$//all of them are$//any of them is$/} unable or unwilling to act then I appoint $/ instead.

4 BURDEN OF INHERITANCE TAX 6–366

If inheritance tax, or any other form of death duty, is payable on my free estate then my executors must pay it from the residue of my estate.

5 RESIDUE 6–367

I give to my executors:

    (I) my estate, anywhere in the world; and
    (II) any property over which I have a general power of appointment;

to hold it on trust:

        (a) to pay my debts, taxes and funeral and testamentary expenses;
        (b) If our marriage has been solemised at my death, then to pay the residue to the said $/ absolutely if $/{he$//she$/} survives me by 28 days; but if this gift fails

(c) to divide the residue equally between those of my children who are living at my death and attain $/{18$//21$/}; except:

    (i) if any of my children dies before me, then to divide that child's share equally between those of his or her children who are living at my death and attain $/{18$//21$/}; and

    (ii) if any of my children dies after me, but before attaining $/{18$//21$/}, then to divide that child's share equally between those of his or her children who are living at his or her death and attain $/{18$//21$/}.

if the above trusts fail, then:

(d) to pay the residue to $/ absolutely.

6–368 6 TECHNICAL CLAUSES

(a) The Standard Provisions of the Society of Trust and Estate Practitioners (1st edition) apply, amended as follows:

    (i) Standard provision 5 ("trust for sale") does not apply.

    (ii) My executors may exercise their powers without consulting beneficiaries, so section 11 of the Trusts of Land and Appointment of Trustees Act 1996 does not apply.

(b) In my will, "children":

    (i) includes those who are legitimate, illegitimate or adopted; but

    (ii) does not include step-children, nor natural children who have been adopted by another person;

and other terms describing family relationships are to be interpreted accordingly.

(c) My estate is to be divided as if any person who dies within one month of my death had predeceased me.

6–369 SIGNATURES

Signed by me on . . . . 20$/

Signature of Testator

Signed by $/ in our joint presence and then by us in $/{his$//hers$/}
             Witness 1   Witness 2

Signature:

Full name:

Address:

Occupation:

119 Gift to future wife/husband in expectation of marriage with gift over — effective on marriage

119a Complete powers

6–370 This is the last will of me $/ of $/.

1 REVOCATION

6–371

I revoke all former wills.

2 EXPECTATION OF MARRIAGE

6–372

My will is not revoked if I marry $/.

3 APPOINTMENT OF EXECUTORS

6–373

I appoint $/ $/[and $/$/] to be my $/{executor$//executors$/} but if $/{he is$// she is$//both of them are$//either of them is$//all of them are$//any of them is$/} unable or unwilling to act then I appoint $/ instead.

4 BURDEN OF INHERITANCE TAX

6–374

If inheritance tax, or any other form of death duty, is payable on my free estate then my executors must pay it from the residue of my estate.

5 RESIDUE

6–375

I give to my executors:

  (I) my estate, anywhere in the world; and
  (II) any property over which I have a general power of appointment;

to hold it on trust:

  (a) to pay my debts, taxes and funeral and testamentary expenses;
  (b) If our marriage has been solemised at my death, then to pay the residue to the said $/ absolutely if $/{he$//she$/} survives me by 28 days; but if this gift fails
  (c) to pay the residue to $/ absolutely.

6 POWER OF INVESTMENT

6–376

My executors may invest my estate in any investments they could make if they owned my estate personally. In particular, they may:

  (a) invest in unsecured loans, including interest-free loans to a beneficiary;
  (b) invest in land, whether as an investment or as a residence for a beneficiary, and may improve and maintain it;
  (c) invest jointly with another person;
  (d) invest in wasting or non-income-producing assets;
  (e) invest anywhere in the world; and
  (f) choose not to diversify investments.

7 EXCLUSION OF S.11 TLATA

6–377

My executors may exercise their powers without consulting beneficiaries, so section 11 of the Trusts of Land and Appointment of Trustees Act 1996 does not apply.

8 POWER OF APPROPRIATION

6–378

My executors may give specific assets of my estate to beneficiaries without requiring consent. (Section 41 of the Administration of Estates Act 1925 therefore applies subject to that amendment.)

6–379 9 POWER OF INSURANCE

My executors may:

(a) keep any assets of my estate insured, against any risk and in any amount;

(b) pay insurance premiums from the income or capital of that part of my estate which is held on the same trusts as the insured property; and

(c) treat any insurance money received as though it were the proceeds of sale of the insured property.

6–380 10 EXCLUSION OF EXECUTORS' LIABILITY

(a) Only a professional executor or trustee can be liable for any loss arising from:

    (i) exercising, or failing to exercise, any discretion or power;

    (ii) any improper investment made in good faith;

    (iii) the negligence or fraud of any agent employed by him, or by any other executor or trustee, even if the employment was not strictly necessary or expedient;

    (iv) any mistake or omission made in good faith;

    (v) any other matter, except wilful and individual fraud on the part of the executor or trustee who is sought to be made liable.

(b) No executor can be liable for any loss, of any kind, if he has acted in accordance with the advice of Counsel of at least five years' standing.

6–381 11 POWER TO USE NOMINEES

My executors may vest any asset of my estate in the name of, or under the control of:

(a) one or more of their number; or

(b) any person (which may include a trust corporation), or people, as nominee(s).

6–382 12 POWER TO CHARGE FOR PROFESSIONAL SERVICES

Any of my executors who is engaged in a profession or business may charge fees for work done by him or her, or by his or her firm, in connection with my estate and its trusts, including acts which an executor or trustee not being in any profession or business could have done personally, and those charges shall be a first charge against my estate, without abatement.

6–383 13 COMMORIENTES

My estate is to be divided as if any person who dies within one month of my death had predeceased me.

6–384 14 CONFLICTS OF INTEREST

My executors may exercise (or fail to exercise) any powers in my will, even if one or more of them has a personal interest in the outcome.

15 USE OF EXECUTORS' POWERS 6–385

My executors may exercise any of their powers:

(a) from time to time; and
(b) at their absolute discretion.

SIGNATURES 6–386

Signed by me on .... 20$/
Signature of Testator

Signed by $/ in our joint presence and then by us in $/{his$///hers$/}
               Witness 1   Witness 2

Signature:

Full name:

Address:

Occupation:

119b Gift to future wife/husband in expectation of marriage with gift over — effective on marriage (STEP powers)

This is the last will of me $/ of $/. 6–387

1 REVOCATION 6–388

I revoke all former wills.

2 EXPECTATION OF MARRIAGE 6–389

My will is not revoked if I marry $/.

3 APPOINTMENT OF EXECUTORS 6–390

I appoint $/ $/[and $/$/] to be my $/{executor$///executors$/} but if $/{he is$//she is$//both of them are$//either of them is$//all of them are$//any of them is$/} unable or unwilling to act then I appoint $/ instead.

4 BURDEN OF INHERITANCE TAX 6–391

If inheritance tax, or any other form of death duty, is payable on my free estate then my executors must pay it from the residue of my estate.

5 RESIDUE 6–392

I give to my executors:

(I) my estate, anywhere in the world; and

(II) any property over which I have a general power of appointment;

to hold it on trust:

(a) to pay my debts, taxes and funeral and testamentary expenses;

(b) If our marriage has been solemised at my death, then to pay the residue to the said $/ absolutely if $/{he$//she$/} survives me by 28 days; but if this gift fails:

(c) to pay the residue to $/ absolutely.

6–393 6 TECHNICAL CLAUSES

(a) The Standard Provisions of the Society of Trust and Estate Practitioners (1st edition) apply, amended as follows:

(i) Standard provision 5 ("trust for sale") does not apply.

(ii) My executors may exercise their powers without consulting beneficiaries, so section 11 of the Trusts of Land and Appointment of Trustees Act 1996 does not apply.

(b) My estate is to be divided as if any person who dies within one month of my death had predeceased me.

6–394 SIGNATURES

Signed by me on . . . . 20$/
Signature of Testator

Signed by $/ in our joint presence and then by us in $/{his$//hers$/}

Witness 1   Witness 2

Signature:

Full name:

Address:

Occupation:

120 Gift to future wife/husband in expectation of marriage, substituting potential children, with gift over — effective immediately

120a Complete powers

6–395 This is the last will of me $/ of $/.

6–396 1 REVOCATION

I revoke all former wills.

2 EXPECTATION OF MARRIAGE $\qquad$ 6–397

My will is not revoked if I marry $/.

3 APPOINTMENT OF EXECUTORS $\qquad$ 6–398

I appoint $/ $/[and $/$/] to be my $/{executor$//executors$/} but if $/{he is$// she is$//both of them are$//either of them is$//all of them are$//any of them is$/} unable or unwilling to act then I appoint $/ instead.

4 BURDEN OF INHERITANCE TAX $\qquad$ 6–399

If inheritance tax, or any other form of death duty, is payable on my free estate then my executors must pay it from the residue of my estate.

5 RESIDUE $\qquad$ 6–400

I give to my executors:
   (I) my estate, anywhere in the world; and
   (II) any property over which I have a general power of appointment;

to hold it on trust:

   (a) to pay my debts, taxes and funeral and testamentary expenses;
   (b) to pay the residue to the said $/ absolutely if $/{he$//she$/} survives me by 28 days; but if this gift fails
   (c) to divide the residue equally between those of my children who are living at my death and attain $/{18$//21$/}; except:

      (i) if any of my children dies before me, then to divide that child's share equally between those of his or her children who are living at my death and attain $/{18$//21$/}; and
      (ii) if any of my children dies after me, but before attaining $/{18$//21$/}, then to divide that child's share equally between those of his or her children who are living at his or her death and attain $/{18$//21$/}.

   if the above trusts fail, then:

   (d) to pay the residue to $/ absolutely.

6 POWER OF INVESTMENT $\qquad$ 6–401

My executors may invest my estate in any investments they could make if they owned my estate personally. In particular, they may:

   (a) invest in unsecured loans, including interest-free loans to a beneficiary;
   (b) invest in land, whether as an investment or as a residence for a beneficiary, and may improve and maintain it;
   (c) invest jointly with another person;
   (d) invest in wasting or non-income-producing assets;
   (e) invest anywhere in the world; and
   (f) choose not to diversify investments.

6–402 7 EXCLUSION OF S.11 TLATA

My executors may exercise their powers without consulting beneficiaries, so section 11 of the Trusts of Land and Appointment of Trustees Act 1996 does not apply.

6–403 8 POWER OF ADVANCEMENT

My executors may apply the share of any beneficiary for $/{his$//her$//his or her$/} benefit, and this power:

(a) is in addition to any other powers my executors may have, in particular section 32 of the Trustee Act 1925;
(b) applies to the whole or part of the beneficiary's share;
(c) applies whether the beneficiary's right is vested, contingent, expectant or presumptive but not where another person is entitled in priority;
(d) may be used for advancement, maintenance, education or any other benefit;
(e) may be exercised by paying the share to a third party or, where appropriate, to the beneficiary direct.

6–404 9 POWER OF APPROPRIATION

My executors may give specific assets of my estate to beneficiaries without requiring consent. (Section 41 of the Administration of Estates Act 1925 therefore applies subject to that amendment.)

6–405 10 POWER OF INSURANCE

My executors may:

(a) keep any assets of my estate insured, against any risk and in any amount;
(b) pay insurance premiums from the income or capital of that part of my estate which is held on the same trusts as the insured property; and
(c) treat any insurance money received as though it were the proceeds of sale of the insured property.

6–406 11 EXCLUSION OF EXECUTORS' LIABILITY

(a) Only a professional executor or trustee can be liable for any loss arising from:

    (i) exercising, or failing to exercise, any discretion or power;
    (ii) any improper investment made in good faith;
    (iii) the negligence or fraud of any agent employed by him, or by any other executor or trustee, even if the employment was not strictly necessary or expedient;
    (iv) any mistake or omission made in good faith;
    (v) any other matter, except wilful and individual fraud on the part of the executor or trustee who is sought to be made liable.

(b) No executor can be liable for any loss, of any kind, if he has acted in accordance with the advice of Counsel of at least five years' standing.

12 TRUST CORPORATIONS 6–407

If a trust corporation is appointed as executor or trustee, it may:

(a) act by its proper officers;
(b) exercise all the powers given to executors or trustees by my will;
(c) charge under its published scale of fees, as amended from time to time;
(d) meet its charges out of capital or income, at its discretion.

13 POWER TO USE NOMINEES 6–408

My executors may vest any asset of my estate in the name of, or under the control of:

(a) one or more of their number; or
(b) any person (which may include a trust corporation), or people, as nominee(s).

14 POWER TO CHARGE FOR PROFESSIONAL SERVICES 6–409

Any of my executors who is engaged in a profession or business may charge fees for work done by him or her, or by his or her firm, in connection with my estate and its trusts, including acts which an executor or trustee not being in any profession or business could have done personally, and those charges shall be a first charge against my estate, without abatement.

15 COMMORIENTES 6–410

My estate is to be divided as if any person who dies within one month of my death had predeceased me.

16 ACCUMULATIONS OF INCOME 6–411

My executors may:

(a) within 21 years of my death, accumulate income to the extent that it is not paid to, or applied for the benefit of, any beneficiary; and
(b) apply accumulated income as if it were the income of the current year.

17 POWER OF DELEGATION 6–412

My executors may delegate any of their functions, in writing, to:

(a) one or more of their number; or
any other person;
(b) and if they do so my executors are not personally liable to my estate for the defaults of that delegate.

6–413 18 INDEMNITIES

My executors may indemnify a retiring trustee, or any other person, against any liability concerning my estate. If they do so, then my estate (not my executors personally) will bear the liability of that indemnity. My executors may charge the indemnity on assets of my estate.

6–414 19 MINOR'S RECEIPT

where a person is a minor (that is:

(a) under 18; or
(b) 18 or over, but not of an age to be entitled to capital outright);

my executors may pay money to which he or she becomes entitled, whether:

(i) income or capital; or
(ii) as of right or under a power;

to any the following, and in each case their receipt is a complete discharge:

(A) the minor, if he or she has attained 16;
(B) the minor's parent or guardian, in which case my executors are under no further obligation to enquire into the use of the money; or
(C) a third party for the benefit of the minor;

or my executors may resolve to hold the money on trust for the minor absolutely (in which case the administrative provisions of my will continue to apply to the money).

6–415 20 CONFLICTS OF INTEREST

My executors may exercise (or fail to exercise) any powers in my will, even if one or more of them has a personal interest in the outcome.

6–416 21 USE OF EXECUTORS' POWERS

My executors may exercise any of their powers:

(a) from time to time; and
(b) at their absolute discretion.

6–417 22 DEFINITION OF "CHILDREN"

In my will, "children":

(a) includes those who are legitimate, illegitimate or adopted; but
(b) does not include step-children, nor natural children who have been adopted by another person;

and other terms describing family relationships are to be interpreted accordingly.

SIGNATURES 6–418

Signed by me on .... 20$/
Signature of Testator

Signed by $/ in our joint presence and then by us in $/{his$///hers$/}
           Witness 1   Witness 2

Signature:

Full name:

Address:

Occupation:

120b Gift to future wife/husband in expectation of marriage, substituting potential children, with gift over — effective immediately (STEP powers)

This is the last will of me $/ of $/.   6–419

1 REVOCATION 6–420

I revoke all former wills.

2 EXPECTATION OF MARRIAGE 6–421

My will is not revoked if I marry $/.

3 APPOINTMENT OF EXECUTORS 6–422

I appoint $/ $/[and $/$/] to be my $/{executor$///executors$/} but if $/{he is$///she is$///both of them are$///either of them is$///all of them are$///any of them is$/} unable or unwilling to act then I appoint $/ instead.

4 BURDEN OF INHERITANCE TAX 6–423

If inheritance tax, or any other form of death duty, is payable on my free estate then my executors must pay it from the residue of my estate.

5 RESIDUE 6–424

I give to my executors:
    (I) my estate, anywhere in the world; and
    (II) any property over which I have a general power of appointment;

to hold it on trust:
    (a) to pay my debts, taxes and funeral and testamentary expenses;
    (b) to pay the residue to the said $/ absolutely if $/{he$///she$/} survives me by 28 days; but if this gift fails
    (c) to divide the residue equally between those of my children who are living at my death and attain $/{18$///21$/}; except:

(i) if any of my children dies before me, then to divide that child's share equally between those of his or her children who are living at my death and attain $/{18$//21$/}; and

(ii) if any of my children dies after me, but before attaining $/{18$//21$/}, then to divide that child's share equally between those of his or her children who are living at his or her death and attain $/{18$//21$/}.

if the above trusts fail, then:

(d) to pay the residue to $/ absolutely.

6–425 6 TECHNICAL CLAUSES

(a) The Standard Provisions of the Society of Trust and Estate Practitioners (1st edition apply, amended as follows:

   (i) Standard provision 5 ("trust for sale") does not apply.

   (ii) My executors may exercise their powers without consulting beneficiaries, so section 11 of the Trusts of Land and Appointment of Trustees Act 1996 does not apply.

(b) In my will, "children":

   (i) includes those who are legitimate, illegitimate or adopted; but

   (ii) does not include step-children, nor natural children who have been adopted by another person;

and other terms describing family relationships are to be interpreted accordingly.

(c) My estate is to be divided as if any person who dies within one month of my death had predeceased me.

6–426 SIGNATURES

Signed by me on .... 20$/

Signature of Testator

Signed by $/ in our joint presence and then by us in $/{his$//hers$/}
                  Witness 1   Witness 2

Signature:

Full name:

Address:

Occupation:

121 Gift to future wife/husband in expectation of marriage, with gift over — effective immediately

121a Complete powers

This is the last will of me $/ of $/.   6–427

1 REVOCATION   6–428

I revoke all former wills.

2 EXPECTATION OF MARRIAGE   6–429

My will is not revoked if I marry $/.

3 APPOINTMENT OF EXECUTORS   6–430

I appoint $/ $/[and $/$/] to be my $/{executor$//executors$/} but if $/{he is$// she is$//both of them are$//either of them is$//all of them are$//any of them is$/} unable or unwilling to act then I appoint $/ instead.

4 BURDEN OF INHERITANCE TAX   6–431

If inheritance tax, or any other form of death duty, is payable on my free estate then my executors must pay it from the residue of my estate.

5 RESIDUE   6–432

I give to my executors:

   (I) my estate, anywhere in the world; and
  (II) any property over which I have a general power of appointment;

to hold it on trust:

   (a) to pay my debts, taxes and funeral and testamentary expenses;
   (b) to pay the residue to the said $/ absolutely if $/{he$//she$/} survives me by 28 days; but if this gift fails
   (c) to pay the residue to $/ absolutely.

6 POWER OF INVESTMENT   6–433

My executors may invest my estate in any investments they could make if they owned my estate personally. In particular, they may:

   (a) invest in unsecured loans, including interest-free loans to a beneficiary;
   (b) invest in land, whether as an investment or as a residence for a beneficiary, and may improve and maintain it;
   (c) invest jointly with another person;
   (d) invest in wasting or non-income-producing assets;
   (e) invest anywhere in the world; and
   (f) choose not to diversify investments.

7 EXCLUSION OF S.11 TLATA   6–434

My executors may exercise their powers without consulting beneficiaries, so section 11 of the Trusts of Land and Appointment of Trustees Act 1996 does not apply.

6–435 8 POWER OF APPROPRIATION

My executors may give specific assets of my estate to beneficiaries without requiring consent. (Section 41 of the Administration of Estates Act 1925 therefore applies subject to that amendment.)

6–436 9 POWER OF INSURANCE

My executors may:

(a) keep any assets of my estate insured, against any risk and in any amount;

(b) pay insurance premiums from the income or capital of that part of my estate which is held on the same trusts as the insured property; and

(c) treat any insurance money received as though it were the proceeds of sale of the insured property.

6–437 10 EXCLUSION OF EXECUTORS' LIABILITY

(a) Only a professional executor or trustee can be liable for any loss arising from:

(i) exercising, or failing to exercise, any discretion or power;

(ii) any improper investment made in good faith;

(iii) the negligence or fraud of any agent employed by him, or by any other executor or trustee, even if the employment was not strictly necessary or expedient;

(iv) any mistake or omission made in good faith;

(v) any other matter, except wilful and individual fraud on the part of the executor or trustee who is sought to be made liable.

(b) No executor can be liable for any loss, of any kind, if he has acted in accordance with the advice of Counsel of at least five years' standing.

6–438 11 POWER TO USE NOMINEES

My executors may vest any asset of my estate in the name of, or under the control of:

(a) one or more of their number; or

(b) any person (which may include a trust corporation), or people, as nominee(s).

6–439 12 POWER TO CHARGE FOR PROFESSIONAL SERVICES

Any of my executors who is engaged in a profession or business may charge fees for work done by him or her, or by his or her firm, in connection with my estate and its trusts, including acts which an executor or trustee not being in any profession or business could have done personally, and those charges shall be a first charge against my estate, without abatement.

6–440 13 COMMORIENTES

My estate is to be divided as if any person who dies within one month of my death had predeceased me.

14 CONFLICTS OF INTEREST 6–441

My executors may exercise (or fail to exercise) any powers in my will, even if one or more of them has a personal interest in the outcome.

15 USE OF EXECUTORS' POWERS 6–442

My executors may exercise any of their powers:

(a) from time to time; and
(b) at their absolute discretion.

SIGNATURES 6–443

Signed by me on .... 20$/

Signature of Testator

Signed by $/ in our joint presence and then by us in $/{his$//hers$/}
     Witness 1   Witness 2

Signature:

Full name:

Address:

Occupation:

121b Gift to future wife/husband in expectation of marriage, with gift over — effective immediately (STEP powers)

This is the last will of me $/ of $/.   6–444

1 REVOCATION 6–445

I revoke all former wills.

2 EXPECTATION OF MARRIAGE 6–446

My will is not revoked if I marry $/.

3 APPOINTMENT OF EXECUTORS 6–447

I appoint $/ $/[and $/$/] to be my $/{executor$//executors$/} but if $/{he is$// she is$//both of them are$//either of them is$//all of them are$//any of them is$/} unable or unwilling to act then I appoint $/ instead.

4 BURDEN OF INHERITANCE TAX 6–448

If inheritance tax, or any other form of death duty, is payable on my free estate then my executors must pay it from the residue of my estate.

6–449 5 RESIDUE

I give to my executors:

(I) my estate, anywhere in the world; and

(II) any property over which I have a general power of appointment;

to hold it on trust:

(a) to pay my debts, taxes and funeral and testamentary expenses;

(b) to pay the residue to the said $/ absolutely if $/{he$//she$/} survives me by 28 days; but if this gift fails

(c) to pay the residue to $/ absolutely.

6–450 6 TECHNICAL CLAUSES

(a) The Standard Provisions of the Society of Trust and Estate Practitioners (1st edition) apply, amended as follows:

(i) Standard provision 5 ("trust for sale") does not apply.

(ii) My executors may exercise their powers without consulting beneficiaries, so section 11 of the Trusts of Land and Appointment of Trustees Act 1996 does not apply.

(b) My estate is to be divided as if any person who dies within one month of my death had predeceased me.

6–451 SIGNATURES

Signed by me on .... 20$/

Signature of Testator

Signed by $/ in our joint presence and then by us in $/{his$//hers$/}

         Witness 1   Witness 2

Signature:

Full name:

Address:

Occupation:

MARRIED COUPLES

122 Will to husband/wife absolutely, then to children on second death with a substitution of grandchildren and a gift over

122a Complete powers

6–452 This is the last will of me $/ of $/.

1 REVOCATION
6–453

I revoke all former wills.

2 APPOINTMENT OF EXECUTORS
6–454

I appoint $/ $/[and $/$/] to be my $/{executor$//executors$/} but if $/{he is$//she is$//both of them are$//either of them is$//all of them are$//any of them is$/} unable or unwilling to act then I appoint $/ instead.

3 APPOINTMENT OF GUARDIANS
6–455

(a) If at my death I am the sole surviving parent, I appoint $/ $/[and $/ $/] to be the $/{guardian$//guardians$/} of any of my children who are under 18

(b) If $/{he is$//she is$//either of them is$//both of them are$//any of them is$//all of them are$/} unable or unwilling to act then I appoint $/ $/[and $/ $/] instead

4 BURDEN OF INHERITANCE TAX
6–456

If inheritance tax, or any other form of death duty, is payable on my free estate then my executors must pay it from the residue of my estate.

5 RESIDUE
6–457

I give to my executors:

(I) my estate, anywhere in the world; and

(II) any property over which I have a general power of appointment;

to hold it on trust:

(a) to pay my debts, taxes and funeral and testamentary expenses;

(b) to pay the residue to my $/{husband$//wife$/} $/ absolutely if $/{he$//she$/} survives me by 28 days; but if this gift fails

(c) to divide the residue equally between those of my children who are living at my death and attain $/{18$//21$/}; except:

(i) if any of my children dies before me, then to divide that child's share equally between those of his or her children who are living at my death and attain $/{18$//21$/}; and

(ii) if any of my children dies after me, but before attaining $/{18$//21$/}, then to divide that child's share equally between those of his or her children who are living at his or her death and attain $/{18$//21$/}.

if the above trusts fail, then:

(d) to pay the residue to $/ absolutely.

6 POWER OF INVESTMENT
6–458

My executors may invest my estate in any investments they could make if they owned my estate personally. In particular, they may:

(a) invest in unsecured loans, including interest-free loans to a beneficiary;

(b) invest in land, whether as an investment or as a residence for a beneficiary, and may improve and maintain it;

(c) invest jointly with another person;

(d) invest in wasting or non-income-producing assets;

(e) invest anywhere in the world; and

(f) choose not to diversify investments.

6–459 7 EXCLUSION OF S.11 TLATA

My executors may exercise their powers without consulting beneficiaries, so section 11 of the Trusts of Land and Appointment of Trustees Act 1996 does not apply.

6–460 8 POWER OF ADVANCEMENT

My executors may apply the share of any beneficiary for $/{his$//her$//his or her$/} benefit, and this power:

(a) is in addition to any other powers my executors may have, in particular section 32 of the Trustee Act 1925;

(b) applies to the whole or part of the beneficiary's share;

(c) applies whether the beneficiary's right is vested, contingent, expectant or presumptive but not where another person is entitled in priority;

(d) may be used for advancement, maintenance, education or any other benefit;

(e) may be exercised by paying the share to a third party or, where appropriate, to the beneficiary direct.

6–461 9 POWER OF APPROPRIATION

My executors may give specific assets of my estate to beneficiaries without requiring consent. (Section 41 of the Administration of Estates Act 1925 therefore applies subject to that amendment.)

6–462 10 POWER OF INSURANCE

My executors may:

(a) keep any assets of my estate insured, against any risk and in any amount;

(b) pay insurance premiums from the income or capital of that part of my estate which is held on the same trusts as the insured property; and

(c) treat any insurance money received as though it were the proceeds of sale of the insured property.

6–463 11 EXCLUSION OF EXECUTORS' LIABILITY

(a) Only a professional executor or trustee can be liable for any loss arising from:

(i) exercising, or failing to exercise, any discretion or power;

(ii) any improper investment made in good faith;

(iii) the negligence or fraud of any agent employed by him, or by any other executor or trustee, even if the employment was not strictly necessary or expedient;

(iv) any mistake or omission made in good faith;

(v) any other matter, except wilful and individual fraud on the part of the executor or trustee who is sought to be made liable.

(b) No executor can be liable for any loss, of any kind, if he has acted in accordance with the advice of Counsel of at least five years' standing.

12 TRUST CORPORATIONS 6–464

If a trust corporation is appointed as executor or trustee, it may:

(a) act by its proper officers;

(b) exercise all the powers given to executors or trustees by my will;

(c) charge under its published scale of fees, as amended from time to time;

(d) meet its charges out of capital or income, at its discretion.

13 POWER TO USE NOMINEES 6–465

My executors may vest any asset of my estate in the name of, or under the control of:

(a) one or more of their number; or

(b) any person (which may include a trust corporation), or people, as nominee(s).

14 POWER TO CHARGE FOR PROFESSIONAL SERVICES 6–466

Any of my executors who is engaged in a profession or business may charge fees for work done by him or her, or by his or her firm, in connection with my estate and its trusts, including acts which an executor or trustee not being in any profession or business could have done personally, and those charges shall be a first charge against my estate, without abatement.

15 COMMORIENTES 6–467

My estate is to be divided as if any person who dies within one month of my death had predeceased me.

16 ACCUMULATIONS OF INCOME 6–468

My executors may:

(a) within 21 years of my death, accumulate income to the extent that it is not paid to, or applied for the benefit of, any beneficiary; and

(b) apply accumulated income as if it were the income of the current year.

6-469 17 POWER OF DELEGATION

My executors may delegate any of their functions, in writing, to:

(a) one or more of their number; or

(b) any other person;

and if they do so my executors are not personally liable to my estate for the defaults of that delegate.

6-470 18 INDEMNITIES

My executors may indemnify a retiring trustee, or any other person, against any liability concerning my estate. If they do so, then my estate (not my executors personally) will bear the liability of that indemnity. My executors may charge the indemnity on assets of my estate.

6-471 19 MINOR'S RECEIPT

where a person is a minor (that is:

(I) under 18; or

(II) 18 or over, but not of an age to be entitled to capital outright);

my executors may pay money to which he or she becomes entitled, whether:

(i) income or capital; or

(ii) as of right or under a power;

to any the following, and in each case their receipt is a complete discharge:

(A) the minor, if he or she has attained 16;

(B) the minor's parent or guardian, in which case my executors are under no further obligation to enquire into the use of the money; or

(C) a third party for the benefit of the minor;

or my executors may resolve to hold the money on trust for the minor absolutely (in which case the administrative provisions of my will continue to apply to the money).

6-472 20 CONFLICTS OF INTEREST

My executors may exercise (or fail to exercise) any powers in my will, even if one or more of them has a personal interest in the outcome.

6-473 21 USE OF EXECUTORS' POWERS

My executors may exercise any of their powers:

(a) from time to time; and

(b) at their absolute discretion.

6-474 22 DEFINITION OF "CHILDREN"

In my will, "children":

(a) includes those who are legitimate, illegitimate or adopted; but

(b) does not include step-children, nor natural children who have been adopted by another person;

and other terms describing family relationships are to be interpreted accordingly.

SIGNATURES 6–475

Signed by me on .... 20$/

Signature of Testator

Signed by $/ in our joint presence and then by us in $/{his$//hers$/}
             Witness 1   Witness 2

Signature:

Full name:

Address:

Occupation:

122b Will to husband/wife absolutely, then to children on second death with a substitution of grandchildren and a gift over (STEP powers)

This is the last will of me $/ of $/. 6–476

1 REVOCATION 6–477

I revoke all former wills.

2 APPOINTMENT OF EXECUTORS 6–478

I appoint $/ $/[and $/$/] to be my $/{executor$//executors$/} but if $/{he is$//she is$//both of them are$//either of them is$//all of them are$//any of them is$/} unable or unwilling to act then I appoint $/ instead.

3 APPOINTMENT OF GUARDIANS 6–479

(a) If at my death I am the sole surviving parent, I appoint $/ $/[and $/ $/] to be the $/{guardian$//guardians$/} of any of my children who are under 18

(b) If $/{he is$//she is$//either of them is$//both of them are$//any of them is$//all of them are$/} unable or unwilling to act then I appoint $/ $/[and $/ $/] instead

4 BURDEN OF INHERITANCE TAX 6–480

If inheritance tax, or any other form of death duty, is payable on my free estate then my executors must pay it from the residue of my estate.

6–481 5 RESIDUE

I give to my executors:

(I) my estate, anywhere in the world; and
(II) any property over which I have a general power of appointment;

to hold it on trust:

(a) to pay my debts, taxes and funeral and testamentary expenses;
(b) to pay the residue to my $/{husband$//wife$/} $/ absolutely if $/{he$//she$/} survives me by 28 days; but if this gift fails
(c) to divide the residue equally between those of my children who are living at my death and attain $/{18$//21$/}; except:

(i) if any of my children dies before me, then to divide that child's share equally between those of his or her children who are living at my death and attain $/{18$//21$/}; and
(ii) if any of my children dies after me, but before attaining $/{18$//21$/}, then to divide that child's share equally between those of his or her children who are living at his or her death and attain $/{18$//21$/}.

if the above trusts fail, then:

(d) to pay the residue to $/ absolutely.

6–482 6 TECHNICAL CLAUSES

(a) The Standard Provisions of the Society of Trust and Estate Practitioners (1st edition) apply, amended as follows:

(i) Standard provision 5 ("trust for sale") does not apply.
(ii) My executors may exercise their powers without consulting beneficiaries, so section 11 of the Trusts of Land and Appointment of Trustees Act 1996 does not apply.

(b) In my will, "children":

(i) includes those who are legitimate, illegitimate or adopted; but
(ii) does not include step-children, nor natural children who have been adopted by another person;

and other terms describing family relationships are to be interpreted accordingly.

(c) My estate is to be divided as if any person who dies within one month of my death had predeceased me.

SIGNATURES 6–483

Signed by me on . . . . 20$/

Signature of Testator

Signed by $/ in our joint presence and then by us in $/{his$//hers$/}

Witness 1   Witness 2

Signature:

Full name:

Address:

Occupation:

123 Basic will for married couple (similar to 122) incorporating nil-band discretionary trust

123a Complete powers

This is the last will of me $/ of $/. 6–484

1 REVOCATION 6–485

I revoke all former wills.

2 APPOINTMENT OF EXECUTORS 6–486

I appoint $/ $/[and $/$/] to be my $/{executor$//executors$/} but if $/{he is$//she is$//both of them are$//either of them is$//all of them are$//any of them is$/} unable or unwilling to act then I appoint $/ instead.

3 APPOINTMENT OF GUARDIANS 6–487

(a) If at my death I am the sole surviving parent, I appoint $/ $/[and $/ $/] to be the $/{guardian$//guardians$/} of any of my children who are under 18.

(b) If $/{he is$//she is$//either of them is$//both of them are$//any of them is$//all of them are$/} unable or unwilling to act then I appoint $/ $/[and $/ $/] instead.

4 GIFT OF CHATTELS 6–488

(a) In this clause, "personal chattels" has the meaning given in section 55(1)(x) of the Administration of Estates Act 1925, but does not include chattels which are the subject of specific gifts.

(b) I give all my personal chattels to my $/{husband$//wife$/}.

5 NIL-BAND DISCRETIONARY TRUST 6–489

(a) In this clause and the next (6):

"the nil-band sum" means the lower of:

(i) the maximum sum which I could give to a non-exempt beneficiary by this clause, without inheritance tax becoming payable on my death;

(ii) the upper limit of the nil per cent rate band in Schedule 1 to the Inheritance Tax Act 1984, as it is applicable on my death; or

(iii) nil if:

(A) inheritance tax has been abolished at my death;

(B) I am not married at my death; or

(C) the nil-band sum would otherwise be less than £10,000;

"the nil-band fund" means:

(i) the nil-band sum; and

(ii) the assets from time to time representing it.

"my trustees" means:

(i) my executors; and

(ii) the trustees for the time being of this clause

"the beneficiaries" means:

(i) my $/{husband$//wife$/};

(ii) all descendants of any of my grandparents;

(iii) all descendants of any of my $/{husband's$//wife's$/} grandparents;

(iv) the spouses and former spouses of (ii) and (iii);

(v) charities

(b) I give the nil-band sum to my trustees on the following trusts:

(i) within 80 years of my death, to pay the capital to (or use it for the benefit of) any beneficiaries they think fit;

(ii) within 80 years of my death, to pay the income to (or use it for the benefit of) any beneficiaries they think fit, or within 21 years of my death to accumulate some or all of it.

(iii) my trustees must distribute the whole fund within 80 years of my death (which is the perpetuity period of this trust);

(iv) my trustees need not ensure equality among the beneficiaries, and are not liable to any beneficiary who they choose not to benefit;

(c) My backstop beneficiary is $/. If the above trusts fail entirely then my trustees must pay the nil-band fund to $/{him$//her$/} (or $/{his$//her$/} estate) absolutely.

6-490 6 TRUSTEES' POWERS ANCILLARY TO THE NIL-BAND DISCRETIONARY TRUST

(a) My trustees have all the powers given to executors by my will.

(b) My trustees must exercise their discretions by deed of appointment. A deed of appointment may be revocable within 80 years of my death, or irrevocable.

(c) My executors may require my trustees to accept:

(i) a binding promise of payment made by my $/{husband$//wife$/}; or

220

    (ii) a charge over any property given to my $/{husband$//wife$/} by my will or any codicil;

in place of all or part of the nil-band fund, and this power may be exercised even if my executors and my trustees are, at that time, the same people. My executors are under no further liability to ensure that the trustees receive the sum promised or charged.

(d) If my executors exercise their power to charge property given to my $/{husband$//wife$/} they may make an assent of the property, subject to the charge, without my $/{husband$//wife$/} becoming personally liable for the sum charged.

(e) My trustees may lend any of the nil-band fund to my $/{husband$//wife$/}.

(f) Any promise made by my $/{husband$//wife$/}, or loan made to my $/{husband$//wife$/}, may be made subject to such terms as to repayment and security as my trustees think fit.

7 BURDEN OF INHERITANCE TAX   6–491

If inheritance tax, or any other form of death duty, is payable on my free estate then my executors must pay it from the residue of my estate.

8 RESIDUE   6–492

I give to my executors:
    (I) the rest of my estate, anywhere in the world; and
    (II) any property over which I have a general power of appointment;

to hold it on trust:

    (a) to pay my debts, taxes and funeral and testamentary expenses;

    (b) to pay the residue to my $/{husband$//wife$/} $/ absolutely if $/{he$//she$/} survives me by 28 days; but if this gift fails

    (c) to divide the residue equally between those of my children who are living at my death and attain $/{18$//21$/}; except:

        (i) if any of my children dies before me, then to divide that child's share equally between those of his or her children who are living at my death and attain $/{18$//21$/}; and

        (a) if any of my children dies after me, but before attaining $/{18$//21$/}, then to divide that child's share equally between those of his or her children who are living at his or her death and attain $/{18$//21$/}.

if the above trusts fail, then:

    (d) to pay the residue to $/ absolutely.

9 POWER OF INVESTMENT   6–493

My executors may invest my estate in any investments they could make if they owned my estate personally. In particular, they may:

    (a) invest in unsecured loans, including interest-free loans to a beneficiary;

(b) invest in land, whether as an investment or as a residence for a beneficiary, and may improve and maintain it;

(c) invest jointly with another person;

(d) invest in wasting or non-income-producing assets;

(e) invest anywhere in the world; and

(f) choose not to diversify investments.

6–494   10 EXCLUSION OF THE APPORTIONMENT RULES

(a) My executors may treat income as arising on the day it is received.

(b) The Apportionment Act 1870 does not apply.

(c) The rules known as "the rule in *Howe v. Dartmouth*" and "the rule in *Allhusen v. Whittell*" do not apply.

6–495   11 EXCLUSION OF S.11 TLATA

My executors may exercise their powers without consulting beneficiaries, so section 11 of the Trusts of Land and Appointment of Trustees Act 1996 does not apply.

6–496   12 POWER OF ADVANCEMENT

My executors may apply the share of any beneficiary for $/{his$//her$//his or her$/} benefit, and this power:

(a) is in addition to any other powers my executors may have, in particular section 32 of the Trustee Act 1925;

(b) applies to the whole or part of the beneficiary's share;

(c) applies whether the beneficiary's right is vested, contingent, expectant or presumptive but not where another person is entitled in priority;

(d) may be used for advancement, maintenance, education or any other benefit;

(e) may be exercised by paying the share to a third party or, where appropriate, to the beneficiary direct.

6–497   13 POWER OF APPROPRIATION

My executors may give specific assets of my estate to beneficiaries without requiring consent. (Section 41 of the Administration of Estates Act 1925 therefore applies subject to that amendment.)

6–498   14 POWER OF INSURANCE

My executors may:

(a) keep any assets of my estate insured, against any risk and in any amount;

(b) pay insurance premiums from the income or capital of that part of my estate which is held on the same trusts as the insured property; and

(c) treat any insurance money received as though it were the proceeds of sale of the insured property.

15 EXCLUSION OF EXECUTORS' LIABILITY   6–499

(a) Only a professional executor or trustee can be liable for any loss arising from:

   (i) exercising, or failing to exercise, any discretion or power;
   (ii) any improper investment made in good faith;
   (iii) the negligence or fraud of any agent employed by him, or by any other executor or trustee, even if the employment was not strictly necessary or expedient;
   (iv) any mistake or omission made in good faith;
   (v) any other matter, except wilful and individual fraud on the part of the executor or trustee who is sought to be made liable.

(b) No executor can be liable for any loss, of any kind, if he has acted in accordance with the advice of Counsel of at least five years' standing.

16 TRUST CORPORATIONS   6–500

If a trust corporation is appointed as executor or trustee, it may:

(a) act by its proper officers;
(b) exercise all the powers given to executors or trustees by my will;
(c) charge under its published scale of fees, as amended from time to time;
(d) meet its charges out of capital or income, at its discretion.

17 POWER TO USE NOMINEES   6–501

My executors may vest any asset of my estate in the name of, or under the control of:

(a) one or more of their number; or
(b) any person (which may include a trust corporation), or people, as nominee(s).

18 POWER TO CHARGE FOR PROFESSIONAL SERVICES   6–502

Any of my executors who is engaged in a profession or business may charge fees for work done by him or her, or by his or her firm, in connection with my estate and its trusts, including acts which an executor or trustee not being in any profession or business could have done personally, and those charges shall be a first charge against my estate, without abatement.

19 COMMORIENTES   6–503

My estate is to be divided as if any person who dies within one month of my death had predeceased me.

20 ACCUMULATIONS OF INCOME   6–504

My executors may:

(a) within 21 years of my death, accumulate income to the extent that it is not paid to, or applied for the benefit of, any beneficiary; and

(b) apply accumulated income as if it were the income of the current year.

6–505 21 POWER TO BORROW

(a) My executors may borrow money for any purpose.
(b) My executors may charge any assets of my estate as security for any liability.

6–506 22 POWER OF DELEGATION

My executors may delegate any of their functions, in writing, to:

(a) one or more of their number; or
  any other person;
(b) and if they do so my executors are not personally liable to my estate for the defaults of that delegate.

6–507 23 INDEMNITIES

My executors may indemnify a retiring trustee, or any other person, against any liability concerning my estate. If they do so, then my estate (not my executors personally) will bear the liability of that indemnity. My executors may charge the indemnity on assets of my estate.

6–508 24 MINOR'S RECEIPT

where a person is a minor (that is:
  (I) under 18; or
  (II) 18 or over, but not of an age to be entitled to capital outright);

  my executors may pay money to which he or she becomes entitled, whether:

  (i) income or capital; or
  (ii) as of right or under a power;

to any the following, and in each case their receipt is a complete discharge:

  (A) the minor, if he or she has attained 16;
  (B) the minor's parent or guardian, in which case my executors are under no further obligation to enquire into the use of the money; or
  (C) a third party for the benefit of the minor;

or my executors may resolve to hold the money on trust for the minor absolutely (in which case the administrative provisions of my will continue to apply to the money).

6–509 25 CONFLICTS OF INTEREST

My executors may exercise (or fail to exercise) any powers in my will, even if one or more of them has a personal interest in the outcome.

6–510 26 USE OF EXECUTORS' POWERS

My executors may exercise any of their powers:

(a) from time to time; and

(b) at their absolute discretion.

27 DEFINITION OF "CHILDREN" 6–511

In my will, "children":

(a) includes those who are legitimate, illegitimate or adopted; but

(b) does not include step-children, nor natural children who have been adopted by another person;

and other terms describing family relationships are to be interpreted accordingly.

SIGNATURES 6–512

Signed by me on .... 20$/

Signature of Testator

Signed by $/ in our joint presence and then by us in $/{his$//hers$/}

           Witness 1   Witness 2

Signature:

Full name:

Address:

Occupation:

123b Basic will for married couple (similar to 122) incorporating nil-band discretionary trust (STEP powers)

This is the last will of me $/ of $/. 6–513

1 REVOCATION 6–514

I revoke all former wills.

2 APPOINTMENT OF EXECUTORS 6–515

I appoint $/ $/[and $/$/] to be my $/{executor$//executors$/} but if $/{he is$//she is$//both of them are$//either of them is$//all of them are$//any of them is$/} unable or unwilling to act then I appoint $/ instead.

3 APPOINTMENT OF GUARDIANS 6–516

(a) If at my death I am the sole surviving parent, I appoint $/ $/[and $/ $/] to be the $/{guardian$//guardians$/} of any of my children who are under 18

(b) If $/{he is$//she is$//either of them is$//both of them are$//any of them is$//all of them are$/} unable or unwilling to act then I appoint $/ $/[and $/ $/] instead

6–517 4 GIFT OF CHATTELS

(a) In this clause, "personal chattels" has the meaning given in section 55(1)(x) of the Administration of Estates Act 1925, but does not include chattels which are the subject of specific gifts.

(b) I give all my personal chattels to my $/{husband$//wife$/}.

6–518 5 NIL-BAND DISCRETIONARY TRUST

(a) In this clause and the next (6):

"the nil-band sum" means the lower of:

(i) the maximum sum which I could give to a non-exempt beneficiary by this clause, without inheritance tax becoming payable on my death;

(ii) the upper limit of the nil per cent rate band in Schedule 1 to the Inheritance Tax Act 1984, as it is applicable on my death; or

(iii) nil if:

    (A) inheritance tax has been abolished at my death;

    (B) I am not married at my death; or

    (C) the nil-band sum would otherwise be less than £10,000;

"the nil-band fund" means:

(i) the nil-band sum; and

(ii) the assets from time to time representing it.

"my trustees" means:

(i) my executors; and

(ii) the trustees for the time being of this clause

"the beneficiaries" means:

(i) my $/{husband$//wife$/};

(ii) all descendants of any of my grandparents;

(iii) all descendants of any of my $/{husband's$//wife's$/} grandparents;

(iv) the spouses and former spouses of (ii) and (iii);

(v) charities

(b) I give the nil-band sum to my trustees on the following trusts:

(i) within 80 years of my death, to pay the capital to (or use it for the benefit of) any beneficiaries they think fit;

(ii) within 80 years of my death, to pay the income to (or use it for the benefit of) any beneficiaries they think fit, or within 21 years of my death to accumulate some or all of it.

(iii) my trustees must distribute the whole fund within 80 years of my death (which is the perpetuity period of this trust);

(iv) my trustees need not ensure equality among the beneficiaries, and are not liable to any beneficiary who they choose not to benefit;

(c) My backstop beneficiary is $/. If the above trusts fail entirely then my trustees must pay the nil-band fund to $/{him$//her$/} (or $/{his$//her$/} estate) absolutely.

6 TRUSTEES' POWERS ANCILLARY TO THE NIL-BAND DISCRETIONARY TRUST

6–519

(a) My trustees have all the powers given to executors by my will.

(b) My trustees must exercise their discretions by deed of appointment. A deed of appointment may be revocable within 80 years of my death, or irrevocable.

(c) My executors may require my trustees to accept:

  (i) a binding promise of payment made by my $/{husband$//wife$/};
  or

  (ii) a charge over any property given to my $/{husband$//wife$/} by my will or any codicil;

  in place of all or part of the nil-band fund, and this power may be exercised even if my executors and my trustees are, at that time, the same people. My executors are under no further liability to ensure that the trustees receive the sum promised or charged.

(d) If my executors exercise their power to charge property given to my $/{husband$//wife$/} they may make an assent of the property, subject to the charge, without my $/{husband$//wife$/} becoming personally liable for the sum charged.

(e) My trustees may lend any of the nil-band fund to my $/{husband$// wife$/}.

(f) Any promise made by my $/{husband$//wife$/}, or loan made to my $/{husband$//wife$/}, may be made subject to such terms as to repayment and security as my trustees think fit.

7 BURDEN OF INHERITANCE TAX

6–520

If inheritance tax, or any other form of death duty, is payable on my free estate then my executors must pay it from the residue of my estate.

8 RESIDUE

6–521

I give to my executors:

  (I) the rest of my estate, anywhere in the world; and

  (II) any property over which I have a general power of appointment;

to hold it on trust:

(a) to pay my debts, taxes and funeral and testamentary expenses;

(b) to pay the residue to my $/{husband$//wife$/} $/ absolutely if $/{he$//she$/} survives me by 28 days; but if this gift fails

(c) to divide the residue equally between those of my children who are living at my death and attain $/{18$//21$/}; except:

  (i) if any of my children dies before me, then to divide that child's share equally between those of his or her children who are living at my death and attain $/{18$//21$/}; and

  (ii) if any of my children dies after me, but before attaining $/{18$//21$/}, then to divide that child's share equally between those of his or her children who are living at his or her death and attain $/{18$//21$/}.

if the above trusts fail, then:

(d) to pay the residue to $/ absolutely.

6–522 9 TECHNICAL CLAUSES

(a) The Standard Provisions of the Society of Trust and Estate Practitioners (1st edition) apply, amended as follows:

(i) Standard provision 5 ("trust for sale") does not apply.

(ii) My executors may exercise their powers without consulting beneficiaries, so section 11 of the Trusts of Land and Appointment of Trustees Act 1996 does not apply.

(b) In my will, "children":

(i) includes those who are legitimate, illegitimate or adopted; but

(ii) does not include step-children, nor natural children who have been adopted by another person;

and other terms describing family relationships are to be interpreted accordingly.

(c) My estate is to be divided as if any person who dies within one month of my death had predeceased me.

6–523 SIGNATURES

Signed by me on . . . . 20$/

Signature of Testator

Signed by $/ in our joint presence and then by us in $/{his$//hers$/}

	Witness 1	Witness 2

Signature:

Full name:

Address:

Occupation:

124 Life interest to surviving spouse with remainder to children

124a Complete powers

6–524 This is the last will of me $/ of $/.

6–525 1 REVOCATION

I revoke all former wills.

6–526 2 APPOINTMENT OF EXECUTORS

I appoint $/ $/[and $/$/] to be my $/{executor$//executors$/} but if $/{he is$// she is$//both of them are$//either of them is$//all of them are$//any of them is$/} unable or unwilling to act then I appoint $/ instead.

3 APPOINTMENT OF GUARDIANS 6–527

(a) If at my death I am the sole surviving parent, I appoint $/ $/[and $/ $/]
to be the $/{guardian$//guardians$/} of any of my children who are
under 18

(b) If $/{he is$//she is$//either of them is$//both of them are$//any of them
is$//all of them are$/} unable or unwilling to act then I appoint $/
$/[and $/ $/] instead

4 BURDEN OF INHERITANCE TAX 6–528

If inheritance tax, or any other form of death duty, is payable on my free
estate then my executors must pay it from the residue of my estate.

5 RESIDUE 6–529

I give to my executors:

(I) my estate, anywhere in the world; and

(II) any property over which I have a general power of appointment;

to hold it on trust:

(a) to pay my debts, taxes and funeral and testamentary expenses;

(b) to pay the residue ("the trust fund") to the trustees of the
settlement declared in clause (6) below.

6 LIFE INTEREST TRUST 6–530

(a) In this clause, "my trustees" means my executors or the trustees for
the time being of this clause.

(b) My trustees have all the powers given to executors by my will.

(c) I give the trust fund to my trustees on trust to pay the income to my
$/{husband$//wife$/} ("the Life Tenant") during $/{his$//her$/} lifetime $/[or until $/{he$//she$/} remarries$/]; and subject to that:

(d) to divide the residue equally between those of my children who are
living at the death of the survivor of:

(i) me; and

(ii) the life tenant;

and attain $/{18$//21$/}; except:

(A) if any of my children dies before the survivor of me and the
life tenant, then to divide that child's share equally between
those of his or her children who are living at the death of
the survivor of me and the life tenant, and attain
$/{18$//21$/}; and

(B) if any of my children dies after the survivor of me and the
life tenant, but before attaining $/{18$//21$/}, then to divide
that child's share equally between those of his or her
children who are living at his or her death and attain
$/{18$//21$/}.

(e) $/[If the determining event was the remarriage of the life tenant, then
the provisions describing the remainder interest are to be interpreted
as if the life tenant had died at the date of that remarriage.$/]

6–531 7 POWER OF INVESTMENT

My executors may invest my estate in any investments they could make if they owned my estate personally. In particular, they may:

(a) invest in unsecured loans, including interest-free loans to a beneficiary;
(b) invest in land, whether as an investment or as a residence for a beneficiary, and may improve and maintain it;
(c) invest jointly with another person;
(d) invest in wasting or non-income-producing assets;
(e) invest anywhere in the world; and
(f) choose not to diversify investments.

6–532 8 EXCLUSION OF THE APPORTIONMENT RULES

(a) My executors may treat income as arising on the day it is received.
(b) The Apportionment Act 1870 does not apply.
(c) The rules known as "the rule in *Howe v. Dartmouth*" and "the rule in *Allhusen v. Whittell*" do not apply.

6–533 9 EXCLUSION OF S.11 TLATA

My executors may exercise their powers without consulting beneficiaries, so section 11 of the Trusts of Land and Appointment of Trustees Act 1996 does not apply.

6–534 10 POWER OF ADVANCEMENT

My executors may apply the share of any beneficiary for $/{his$//her$//his or her$/} benefit, and this power:

(a) is in addition to any other powers my executors may have, in particular section 32 of the Trustee Act 1925;
(b) applies to the whole or part of the beneficiary's share;
(c) applies whether the beneficiary's right is vested, contingent, expectant or presumptive but not where another person is entitled in priority;
(d) may be used for advancement, maintenance, education or any other benefit;
(e) may be exercised by paying the share to a third party or, where appropriate, to the beneficiary direct.

6–535 11 POWER OF APPROPRIATION

My executors may give specific assets of my estate to beneficiaries without requiring consent. (Section 41 of the Administration of Estates Act 1925 therefore applies subject to that amendment.)

6–536 12 POWER OF INSURANCE

My executors may:

(a) keep any assets of my estate insured, against any risk and in any amount;

(b) pay insurance premiums from the income or capital of that part of my estate which is held on the same trusts as the insured property; and

(c) treat any insurance money received as though it were the proceeds of sale of the insured property.

13 EXCLUSION OF EXECUTORS' LIABILITY 6–537

(a) Only a professional executor or trustee can be liable for any loss arising from:

    (i) exercising, or failing to exercise, any discretion or power;

    (ii) any improper investment made in good faith;

    (iii) the negligence or fraud of any agent employed by him, or by any other executor or trustee, even if the employment was not strictly necessary or expedient;

    (iv) any mistake or omission made in good faith;

    (v) any other matter, except wilful and individual fraud on the part of the executor or trustee who is sought to be made liable.

(b) No executor can be liable for any loss, of any kind, if he has acted in accordance with the advice of Counsel of at least five years' standing.

14 TRUST CORPORATIONS 6–538

If a trust corporation is appointed as executor or trustee, it may:

(a) act by its proper officers;

(b) exercise all the powers given to executors or trustees by my will;

(c) charge under its published scale of fees, as amended from time to time;

(d) meet its charges out of capital or income, at its discretion.

15 POWER TO USE NOMINEES 6–539

My executors may vest any asset of my estate in the name of, or under the control of:

(a) one or more of their number; or

(b) any person (which may include a trust corporation), or people, as nominee(s).

16 POWER TO CHARGE FOR PROFESSIONAL SERVICES 6–540

Any of my executors who is engaged in a profession or business may charge fees for work done by him or her, or by his or her firm, in connection with my estate and its trusts, including acts which an executor or trustee not being in any profession or business could have done personally, and those charges shall be a first charge against my estate, without abatement.

17 COMMORIENTES 6–541

My estate is to be divided as if any person who dies within one month of my death had predeceased me.

6–542 18 ACCUMULATIONS OF INCOME

My executors may:

(a) within 21 years of my death, accumulate income to the extent that it is not paid to, or applied for the benefit of, any beneficiary; and

(b) apply accumulated income as if it were the income of the current year.

6–543 19 POWER TO BORROW

(a) My executors may borrow money for any purpose.

(b) My executors may charge any assets of my estate as security for any liability.

6–544 20 POWER OF DELEGATION

My executors may delegate any of their functions, in writing, to:

(a) one or more of their number; or

(b) any other person;

and if they do so my executors are not personally liable to my estate for the defaults of that delegate.

6–545 21 INDEMNITIES

My executors may indemnify a retiring trustee, or any other person, against any liability concerning my estate. If they do so, then my estate (not my executors personally) will bear the liability of that indemnity. My executors may charge the indemnity on assets of my estate.

6–546 22 MINOR'S RECEIPT

where a person is a minor (that is:

(a) under 18; or

(b) 18 or over, but not of an age to be entitled to capital outright);

my executors may pay money to which he or she becomes entitled, whether:

(i) income or capital; or

(ii) as of right or under a power;

to any the following, and in each case their receipt is a complete discharge:

(A) the minor, if he or she has attained 16;

(B) the minor's parent or guardian, in which case my executors are under no further obligation to enquire into the use of the money; or

(C) a third party for the benefit of the minor;

or my executors may resolve to hold the money on trust for the minor absolutely (in which case the administrative provisions of my will continue to apply to the money).

6–547 23 CONFLICTS OF INTEREST

My executors may exercise (or fail to exercise) any powers in my will, even if one or more of them has a personal interest in the outcome.

24 USE OF EXECUTORS' POWERS   6–548

My executors may exercise any of their powers:

    (a) from time to time; and

    (b) at their absolute discretion.

25 DEFINITION OF "CHILDREN"   6–549

In my will, "children":

    (a) includes those who are legitimate, illegitimate or adopted; but

    (b) does not include step-children, nor natural children who have been adopted by another person;

and other terms describing family relationships are to be interpreted accordingly.

SIGNATURES   6–550

Signed by me on . . . . 20$/

Signature of Testator

Signed by $/ in our joint presence and then by us in $/{his$///hers$/}
               Witness 1   Witness 2

Signature:

Full name:

Address:

Occupation:

124b Life interest to surviving spouse with remainder to children (STEP powers)

This is the last will of me $/ of $/.   6–551

1 REVOCATION   6–552

I revoke all former wills.

2 APPOINTMENT OF EXECUTORS   6–553

I appoint $/ $/[and $/$/] to be my $/{executor$///executors$/} but if $/{he is$///she is$///both of them are$///either of them is$///all of them are$///any of them is$/} unable or unwilling to act then I appoint $/ instead.

3 APPOINTMENT OF GUARDIANS   6–554

    (a) If at my death I am the sole surviving parent, I appoint $/ $/[and $/ $/] to be the $/{guardian$///guardians$/} of any of my children who are under 18

(b) If $/{he is$//she is$//either of them is$//both of them are$//any of them is$//all of them are$/} unable or unwilling to act then I appoint $/ $/[and $/ $/] instead

6–555 4 BURDEN OF INHERITANCE TAX

If inheritance tax, or any other form of death duty, is payable on my free estate then my executors must pay it from the residue of my estate.

6–556 5 RESIDUE

I give to my executors:
  (I) my estate, anywhere in the world; and
  (II) any property over which I have a general power of appointment;

to hold it on trust:

  (a) to pay my debts, taxes and funeral and testamentary expenses;
  (b) to pay the residue ("the trust fund") to the trustees of the settlement declared in clause (6) below.

6–557 6 LIFE INTEREST TRUST

  (a) In this clause, "my trustees" means my executors or the trustees for the time being of this clause.
  (b) My trustees have all the powers given to executors by my will.
  (c) I give the trust fund to my trustees on trust to pay the income to my $/{husband$//wife$/} ("the Life Tenant") during $/{his$//her$/} lifetime $/[or until $/{he$//she$/} remarries$/]; and subject to that:
  (d) to divide the residue equally between those of my children who are living at the death of the survivor of:

  (i) me; and
  (ii) the life tenant;

and attain $/{18$//21$/}; except:

  (A) if any of my children dies before the survivor of me and the life tenant, then to divide that child's share equally between those of his or her children who are living at the death of the survivor of me and the life tenant, and attain $/{18$//21$/}; and
  (B) if any of my children dies after the survivor of me and the life tenant, but before attaining $/{18$//21$/}, then to divide that child's share equally between those of his or her children who are living at his or her death and attain $/{18$//21$/}.

  (e) $/[If the determining event was the remarriage of the life tenant, then the provisions describing the remainder interest are to be interpreted as if the life tenant had died at the date of that remarriage.$/]

6–558 7 TECHNICAL CLAUSES

  (a) The Standard Provisions of the Society of Trust and Estate Practitioners (1st edition) apply, amended as follows:

(i) Standard provision 5 ("trust for sale") does not apply.

(ii) My executors may exercise their powers without consulting beneficiaries, so section 11 of the Trusts of Land and Appointment of Trustees Act 1996 does not apply.

(b) In my will, "children":

(i) includes those who are legitimate, illegitimate or adopted; but

(ii) does not include step-children, nor natural children who have been adopted by another person;

and other terms describing family relationships are to be interpreted accordingly.

(c) My estate is to be divided as if any person who dies within one month of my death had predeceased me.

SIGNATURES 6–559

Signed by me on . . . . 20$/
Signature of Testator

Signed by $/ in our joint presence and then by us in $/{his$///hers$/}
           Witness 1   Witness 2

Signature:

Full name:

Address:

Occupation:

125 Will suitable for younger couple — residue to survivor, then potential children, then respective families

125a Complete powers

This is the last will of me $/ of $/.   6–560

1 REVOCATION 6–561

I revoke all former wills.

2 APPOINTMENT OF EXECUTORS 6–562

I appoint $/ $/[and $/$/] to be my $/{executor$///executors$/} but if $/{he is$// she is$//both of them are$//either of them is$//all of them are$//any of them is$/} unable or unwilling to act then I appoint $/ instead.

3 APPOINTMENT OF GUARDIANS 6–563

(a) If at my death I am the sole surviving parent, I appoint $/ $/[and $/ $/] to be the $/{guardian$///guardians$/} of any of my children who are under 18

235

(b) If $/{he is$//she is$//either of them is$//both of them are$//any of them is$//all of them are$/} unable or unwilling to act then I appoint $/ $/[and $/ $/] instead

6–564 4 BURDEN OF INHERITANCE TAX

If inheritance tax, or any other form of death duty, is payable on my free estate then my executors must pay it from the residue of my estate.

6–565 5 RESIDUE

I give to my executors:

(I) my estate, anywhere in the world; and
(II) any property over which I have a general power of appointment;

to hold it on trust:

(a) to pay my debts, taxes and funeral and testamentary expenses;
(b) to pay the residue to my $/{husband$//wife$/} $/ absolutely if $/{he$//she$/} survives me by 28 days $/[; but if this gift fails$/]
(c) to divide the residue equally between those of my children who are living at my death and attain $/{18$//21$/}; except:

(i) if any of my children dies before me, then to divide that child's share equally between those of his or her children who are living at my death and attain $/{18$//21$/}; and
(ii) if any of my children dies after me, but before attaining $/{18$//21$/}, then to divide that child's share equally between those of his or her children who are living at his or her death and attain $/{18$//21$/}.

if the above trusts fail, then:

(d) to divide the residue into two equal shares and to pay:

(i) one share:

(A) to those of my parents who survive me, jointly, but if this gift fails:
(B) to those of my brothers and sisters who survive me equally; and

(ii) one share:

(A) to those of my $/{husband's$//wife's$/} parents who survive me, jointly, but if this gift fails:
(B) to those of my $/{husband's$//wife's$/} brothers and sisters who survive me equally.

(e) If either of the above shares fail, the failed share accrues to the other.

6–566 6 POWER OF INVESTMENT

My executors may invest my estate in any investments they could make if they owned my estate personally. In particular, they may:

(a) invest in unsecured loans, including interest-free loans to a beneficiary;
(b) invest in land, whether as an investment or as a residence for a beneficiary, and may improve and maintain it;
(c) invest jointly with another person;
(d) invest in wasting or non-income-producing assets;
(e) invest anywhere in the world; and
(f) choose not to diversify investments.

7 EXCLUSION OF S.11 TLATA   6–567

My executors may exercise their powers without consulting beneficiaries, so section 11 of the Trusts of Land and Appointment of Trustees Act 1996 does not apply.

8 POWER OF ADVANCEMENT   6–568

My executors may apply the share of any beneficiary for $/{his$//her$//his or her$/} benefit, and this power:

(a) is in addition to any other powers my executors may have, in particular section 32 of the Trustee Act 1925;
(b) applies to the whole or part of the beneficiary's share;
(c) applies whether the beneficiary's right is vested, contingent, expectant or presumptive but not where another person is entitled in priority;
(d) may be used for advancement, maintenance, education or any other benefit;
(e) may be exercised by paying the share to a third party or, where appropriate, to the beneficiary direct.

9 POWER OF APPROPRIATION   6–569

My executors may give specific assets of my estate to beneficiaries without requiring consent. (Section 41 of the Administration of Estates Act 1925 therefore applies subject to that amendment.)

10 POWER OF INSURANCE   6–570

My executors may:

(a) keep any assets of my estate insured, against any risk and in any amount;
(b) pay insurance premiums from the income or capital of that part of my estate which is held on the same trusts as the insured property; and
(c) treat any insurance money received as though it were the proceeds of sale of the insured property.

11 EXCLUSION OF EXECUTORS' LIABILITY   6–571

(a) Only a professional executor or trustee can be liable for any loss arising from:

  (i) exercising, or failing to exercise, any discretion or power;
  (ii) any improper investment made in good faith;

(iii) the negligence or fraud of any agent employed by him, or by any other executor or trustee, even if the employment was not strictly necessary or expedient;

(iv) any mistake or omission made in good faith;

(v) any other matter, except wilful and individual fraud on the part of the executor or trustee who is sought to be made liable.

(b) No executor can be liable for any loss, of any kind, if he has acted in accordance with the advice of Counsel of at least five years' standing.

6–572 12 TRUST CORPORATIONS

If a trust corporation is appointed as executor or trustee, it may:

(a) act by its proper officers;

(b) exercise all the powers given to executors or trustees by my will;

(c) charge under its published scale of fees, as amended from time to time;

(d) meet its charges out of capital or income, at its discretion.

6–573 13 POWER TO USE NOMINEES

My executors may vest any asset of my estate in the name of, or under the control of:

(a) one or more of their number; or

(b) any person (which may include a trust corporation), or people, as nominee(s).

6–574 14 POWER TO CHARGE FOR PROFESSIONAL SERVICES

Any of my executors who is engaged in a profession or business may charge fees for work done by him or her, or by his or her firm, in connection with my estate and its trusts, including acts which an executor or trustee not being in any profession or business could have done personally, and those charges shall be a first charge against my estate, without abatement.

6–575 15 COMMORIENTES

My estate is to be divided as if any person who dies within one month of my death had predeceased me.

6–576 16 ACCUMULATIONS OF INCOME

My executors may:

(a) within 21 years of my death, accumulate income to the extent that it is not paid to, or applied for the benefit of, any beneficiary; and

(b) apply accumulated income as if it were the income of the current year.

6–577 17 POWER OF DELEGATION

My executors may delegate any of their functions, in writing, to:

(a) one or more of their number; or

(b) any other person;

and if they do so my executors are not personally liable to my estate for the defaults of that delegate.

18 INDEMNITIES 6–578

My executors may indemnify a retiring trustee, or any other person, against any liability concerning my estate. If they do so, then my estate (not my executors personally) will bear the liability of that indemnity. My executors may charge the indemnity on assets of my estate.

19 MINOR'S RECEIPT 6–579

where a person is a minor (that is:

(a) under 18; or
(b) 18 or over, but not of an age to be entitled to capital outright);

my executors may pay money to which he or she becomes entitled, whether:

(i) income or capital; or
(ii) as of right or under a power;

to any the following, and in each case their receipt is a complete discharge:

(A) the minor, if he or she has attained 16;
(B) the minor's parent or guardian, in which case my executors are under no further obligation to enquire into the use of the money; or
(C) a third party for the benefit of the minor;

or my executors may resolve to hold the money on trust for the minor absolutely (in which case the administrative provisions of my will continue to apply to the money).

20 CONFLICTS OF INTEREST 6–580

My executors may exercise (or fail to exercise) any powers in my will, even if one or more of them has a personal interest in the outcome.

21 USE OF EXECUTORS' POWERS 6–581

My executors may exercise any of their powers:

(a) from time to time; and
(b) at their absolute discretion.

22 DEFINITION OF "CHILDREN" 6–582

In my will, "children":

(a) includes those who are legitimate, illegitimate or adopted; but
(b) does not include step-children, nor natural children who have been adopted by another person;
and other terms describing family relationships are to be interpreted accordingly.

6–583 SIGNATURES

Signed by me on .... 20$/

Signature of Testator

Signed by $/ in our joint presence and then by us in $/{his$//hers$/}

| Witness 1 | Witness 2 |

Signature:

Full name:

Address:

Occupation:

125b Will suitable for younger couple — residue to survivor, then potential children, then respective families (STEP powers)

6–584 This is the last will of me $/ of $/.

6–585 1 REVOCATION

I revoke all former wills.

6–586 2 APPOINTMENT OF EXECUTORS

I appoint $/ $/[and $/$/] to be my $/{executor$//executors$/} but if $/{he is$//she is$//both of them are$//either of them is$//all of them are$//any of them is$/} unable or unwilling to act then I appoint $/ instead.

6–587/8 3 APPOINTMENT OF GUARDIANS

   (a) If at my death I am the sole surviving parent, I appoint $/ $/[and $/ $/] to be the $/{guardian$//guardians$/} of any of my children who are under 18

   (b) If $/{he is$//she is$//either of them is$//both of them are$//any of them is$//all of them are$/} unable or unwilling to act then I appoint $/ $/[and $/ $/] instead

6–589 4 BURDEN OF INHERITANCE TAX

If inheritance tax, or any other form of death duty, is payable on my free estate then my executors must pay it from the residue of my estate.

6–590 5 RESIDUE

I give to my executors:

   (I) my estate, anywhere in the world; and

   (II) any property over which I have a general power of appointment;

to hold it on trust:

- (a) to pay my debts, taxes and funeral and testamentary expenses;
- (b) to pay the residue to my $/{husband$//wife$/} $/ absolutely if $/{he$//she$/} survives me by 28 days; but if this gift fails
- (c) to divide the residue equally between those of my children who are living at my death and attain $/{18$//21$/}; except:
  - (i) if any of my children dies before me, then to divide that child's share equally between those of his or her children who are living at my death and attain $/{18$//21$/}; and
  - (ii) if any of my children dies after me, but before attaining $/{18$//21$/}, then to divide that child's share equally between those of his or her children who are living at his or her death and attain $/{18$//21$/}.

  if the above trusts fail, then:
- (d) to divide the residue into two equal shares and to pay:
  - (i) one share:
    - (A) to those of my parents who survive me, jointly, but if this gift fails:
    - (B) to those of my brothers and sisters who survive me equally; and
  - (ii) one share:
    - (A) to those of my $/{husband's$//wife's$/} parents who survive me, jointly, but if this gift fails:
    - (B) to those of my $/{husband's$//wife's$/} brothers and sisters who survive me equally.
- (e) If either of the above shares fail, the failed share accrues to the other.

6 TECHNICAL CLAUSES 6–591

- (a) The Standard Provisions of the Society of Trust and Estate Practitioners (1st edition) apply, amended as follows:
  - (i) Standard provision 5 ("trust for sale") does not apply.
  - (ii) My executors may exercise their powers without consulting beneficiaries, so section 11 of the Trusts of Land and Appointment of Trustees Act 1996 does not apply.
- (b) In my will, "children":
  - (i) includes those who are legitimate, illegitimate or adopted; but
  - (ii) does not include step-children, nor natural children who have been adopted by another person;

  and other terms describing family relationships are to be interpreted accordingly.
- (c) My estate is to be divided as if any person who dies within one month of my death had predeceased me.

6–592 SIGNATURES

Signed by me on . . . . 20$/

Signature of Testator

Signed by $/ in our joint presence and then by us in $/{his$//hers$/}

               Witness 1   Witness 2

Signature:

Full name:

Address:

Occupation:

126 Childless couple benefiting survivor, then charities on second death

126a Complete powers

6–593 This is the last will of me $/ of $/.

6–594 1 REVOCATION

I revoke all former wills.

6–595 2 APPOINTMENT OF EXECUTORS

I appoint $/ $/[and $/$/] to be my $/{executor$//executors$/} but if $/{he is$// she is$//both of them are$//either of them is$//all of them are$//any of them is$/} unable or unwilling to act then I appoint $/ instead.

6–596 3 BURDEN OF INHERITANCE TAX

If inheritance tax, or any other form of death duty, is payable on my free estate then my executors must pay it from the residue of my estate.

6–597 4 RESIDUE

I give to my executors:

    (I) my estate, anywhere in the world; and

    (II) any property over which I have a general power of appointment;

to hold it on trust:

        (a) to pay my debts, taxes and funeral and testamentary expenses;

    (b) to pay the residue to my $/{husband$//wife$/} $/ absolutely if $/{he$//she$/} survives me by 28 days; but if this gift fails

    (c) to divide the residue equally between those of the following who are in existence at my death:

        (i) $/ of $/ (registered charity number $/);

        (ii) $/ of $/ (registered charity number $/); and

        (iii) $/ of $/ (registered charity number $/).

5 CHARITIES' RECEIPT   6–598

My executors may accept, as a complete discharge, the receipt of any person who appears to be a proper officer of a charity.

6 POWER OF INVESTMENT   6–599

My executors may invest my estate in any investments they could make if they owned my estate personally. In particular, they may:

    (a) invest in unsecured loans, including interest-free loans to a beneficiary;

    (b) invest in land, whether as an investment or as a residence for a beneficiary, and may improve and maintain it;

    (c) invest jointly with another person;

    (d) invest in wasting or non-income-producing assets;

    (e) invest anywhere in the world; and

    (f) choose not to diversify investments.

7 EXCLUSION OF S.11 TLATA   6–600

My executors may exercise their powers without consulting beneficiaries, so section 11 of the Trusts of Land and Appointment of Trustees Act 1996 does not apply.

8 POWER OF APPROPRIATION   6–601

My executors may give specific assets of my estate to beneficiaries without requiring consent. (Section 41 of the Administration of Estates Act 1925 therefore applies subject to that amendment.)

9 POWER OF INSURANCE   6–602

My executors may:

    (a) keep any assets of my estate insured, against any risk and in any amount;

    (b) pay insurance premiums from the income or capital of that part of my estate which is held on the same trusts as the insured property; and

    (c) treat any insurance money received as though it were the proceeds of sale of the insured property.

6–603 10 EXCLUSION OF EXECUTORS' LIABILITY

(a) Only a professional executor or trustee can be liable for any loss arising from:

    (i) exercising, or failing to exercise, any discretion or power;

    (ii) any improper investment made in good faith;

    (iii) the negligence or fraud of any agent employed by him, or by any other executor or trustee, even if the employment was not strictly necessary or expedient;

    (iv) any mistake or omission made in good faith;

    (v) any other matter, except willful and individual fraud on the part of the executor or trustee who is sought to be made liable.

(b) No executor can be liable for any loss, of any kind, if he has acted in accordance with the advice of Counsel of at least five years' standing.

6–604 11 POWER TO USE NOMINEES

My executors may vest any asset of my estate in the name of, or under the control of:

(a) one or more of their number; or

(b) any person (which may include a trust corporation), or people, as nominee(s).

6–605 12 POWER TO CHARGE FOR PROFESSIONAL SERVICES

Any of my executors who is engaged in a profession or business may charge fees for work done by him or her, or by his or her firm, in connection with my estate and its trusts, including acts which an executor or trustee not being in any profession or business could have done personally, and those charges shall be a first charge against my estate, without abatement.

6–606 13 COMMORIENTES

My estate is to be divided as if any person who dies within one month of my death had predeceased me.

6–607 14 CONFLICTS OF INTEREST

My executors may exercise (or fail to exercise) any powers in my will, even if one or more of them has a personal interest in the outcome.

6–608 15 USE OF EXECUTORS' POWERS

My executors may exercise any of their powers:

(a) from time to time; and

(b) at their absolute discretion.

SIGNATURES 6–609

Signed by me on .... 20$/

Signature of Testator

Signed by $/ in our joint presence and then by us in $/{his$///hers$/}

             Witness 1   Witness 2

Signature:

Full name:

Address:

Occupation:

126b Childless couple benefiting survivor, then charities on second death (STEP powers)

This is the last will of me $/ of $/. 6–610

1 REVOCATION 6–611

I revoke all former wills.

2 APPOINTMENT OF EXECUTORS 6–612

I appoint $/ $/[and $/$/] to be my $/{executor$///executors$/} but if $/{he is$///she is$///both of them are$///either of them is$///all of them are$///any of them is$/} unable or unwilling to act then I appoint $/ instead.

3 BURDEN OF INHERITANCE TAX 6–613

If inheritance tax, or any other form of death duty, is payable on my free estate then my executors must pay it from the residue of my estate.

4 RESIDUE 6–614

I give to my executors:

(I) my estate, anywhere in the world; and
(II) any property over which I have a general power of appointment;

to hold it on trust:

    (a) to pay my debts, taxes and funeral and testamentary expenses;
    (b) to pay the residue to my $/{husband$///wife$/} $/ absolutely if $/{he$///she$/} survives me by 28 days; but if this gift fails
    (c) to divide the residue equally between those of the following who are in existence at my death:

        (i) $/ of $/ (registered charity number $/);

(ii) $/ of $/ (registered charity number $/); and

(iii) $/ of $/ (registered charity number $/).

6–615 5 CHARITIES' RECEIPT

My executors may accept, as a complete discharge, the receipt of any person who appears to be a proper officer of a charity.

6–616 6 TECHNICAL CLAUSES

(a) The Standard Provisions of the Society of Trust and Estate Practitioners (1st edition) apply, amended as follows:

(i) Standard provision 5 ("trust for sale") does not apply.

(ii) My executors may exercise their powers without consulting beneficiaries, so section 11 of the Trusts of Land and Appointment of Trustees Act 1996 does not apply.

(b) My estate is to be divided as if any person who dies within one month of my death had predeceased me.

6–617 SIGNATURES

Signed by me on . . . . 20$/

Signature of Testator

Signed by $/ in our joint presence and then by us in $/{his$//hers$/}

Witness 1   Witness 2

Signature:

Full name:

Address:

Occupation:

SINGLE PARENTS AND SEPARATED CLIENTS

127 Will to children, with gift over

127a Complete powers

6–618 This is the last will of me $/ of $/.

6–619 1 REVOCATION

I revoke all former wills.

2 APPOINTMENT OF EXECUTORS 6–620

I appoint $/ $/[and $/$/] to be my $/{executor$//executors$/} but if $/{he is$// she is$//both of them are$//either of them is$//all of them are$//any of them is$/} unable or unwilling to act then I appoint $/ instead.

3 APPOINTMENT OF GUARDIANS 6–621

(a) I appoint $/ $/[and $/ $/] to be the $/{guardian$//guardians$/} of any of my children who are under 18.

(b) If $/{he is$//she is$//either of them is$//both of them are$//any of them is$//all of them are$/} unable or unwilling to act then I appoint $/ $/[and $/ $/] instead.

4 BURDEN OF INHERITANCE TAX 6–622

If inheritance tax, or any other form of death duty, is payable on my free estate then my executors must pay it from the residue of my estate.

5 RESIDUE 6–623

I give to my executors:

(I) my estate, anywhere in the world; and

(II) any property over which I have a general power of appointment;

to hold it on trust:

(a) to pay my debts, taxes and funeral and testamentary expenses;

(b) to divide the residue equally between those of my children who are living at my death and attain $/{18$//21$/}; except:

(i) if any of my children dies before me, then to divide that child's share equally between those of his or her children who are living at my death and attain $/{18$//21$/}; and

(ii) if any of my children dies after me, but before attaining $/{18$//21$/}, then to divide that child's share equally between those of his or her children who are living at his or her death and attain $/{18$//21$/}.

if the above trusts fail, then:

(c) to pay the residue to $/ absolutely.

6 POWER OF INVESTMENT 6–624

My executors may invest my estate in any investments they could make if they owned my estate personally. In particular, they may:

(a) invest in unsecured loans, including interest-free loans to a beneficiary;

(b) invest in land, whether as an investment or as a residence for a beneficiary, and may improve and maintain it;

(c) invest jointly with another person;

(d) invest in wasting or non-income-producing assets;

(e) invest anywhere in the world; and

(f) choose not to diversify investments.

6–625 7 EXCLUSION OF S.11 TLATA

My executors may exercise their powers without consulting beneficiaries, so section 11 of the Trusts of Land and Appointment of Trustees Act 1996 does not apply.

6–626 8 POWER OF ADVANCEMENT

My executors may apply the share of any beneficiary for $/{his$//her$//his or her$/} benefit, and this power:

(a) is in addition to any other powers my executors may have, in particular section 32 of the Trustee Act 1925;

(b) applies to the whole or part of the beneficiary's share;

(c) applies whether the beneficiary's right is vested, contingent, expectant or presumptive but not where another person is entitled in priority;

(d) may be used for advancement, maintenance, education or any other benefit;

(e) may be exercised by paying the share to a third party or, where appropriate, to the beneficiary direct.

6–627 9 POWER OF APPROPRIATION

My executors may give specific assets of my estate to beneficiaries without requiring consent. (Section 41 of the Administration of Estates Act 1925 therefore applies subject to that amendment.)

6–628 10 POWER OF INSURANCE

My executors may:

(a) keep any assets of my estate insured, against any risk and in any amount;

(b) pay insurance premiums from the income or capital of that part of my estate which is held on the same trusts as the insured property; and

(c) treat any insurance money received as though it were the proceeds of sale of the insured property.

6–629 11 EXCLUSION OF EXECUTORS' LIABILITY

(a) Only a professional executor or trustee can be liable for any loss arising from:

(i) exercising, or failing to exercise, any discretion or power;

(ii) any improper investment made in good faith;

(iii) the negligence or fraud of any agent employed by him, or by any other executor or trustee, even if the employment was not strictly necessary or expedient;

(iv) any mistake or omission made in good faith;

(v) any other matter, except wilful and individual fraud on the part of the executor or trustee who is sought to be made liable.

(b) No executor can be liable for any loss, of any kind, if he has acted in accordance with the advice of Counsel of at least five years' standing.

12 TRUST CORPORATIONS 6–630

If a trust corporation is appointed as executor or trustee, it may:

(a) act by its proper officers;
(b) exercise all the powers given to executors or trustees by my will;
(c) charge under its published scale of fees, as amended from time to time;
(d) meet its charges out of capital or income, at its discretion.

13 POWER TO USE NOMINEES 6–631

My executors may vest any asset of my estate in the name of, or under the control of:

(a) one or more of their number; or
(b) any person (which may include a trust corporation), or people, as nominee(s).

14 POWER TO CHARGE FOR PROFESSIONAL SERVICES 6–632

Any of my executors who is engaged in a profession or business may charge fees for work done by him or her, or by his or her firm, in connection with my estate and its trusts, including acts which an executor or trustee not being in any profession or business could have done personally, and those charges shall be a first charge against my estate, without abatement.

15 COMMORIENTES 6–633

My estate is to be divided as if any person who dies within one month of my death had predeceased me.

16 ACCUMULATIONS OF INCOME 6–634

My executors may:

(a) within 21 years of my death, accumulate income to the extent that it is not paid to, or applied for the benefit of, any beneficiary; and

(a) apply accumulated income as if it were the income of the current year.

17 POWER OF DELEGATION 6–635

My executors may delegate any of their functions, in writing, to:

(a) one or more of their number; or
(b) any other person;

and if they do so my executors are not personally liable to my estate for the defaults of that delegate.

18 INDEMNITIES 6–636

My executors may indemnify a retiring trustee, or any other person, against any liability concerning my estate. If they do so, then my estate (not my executors personally) will bear the liability of that indemnity. My executors may charge the indemnity on assets of my estate.

6–637 19 MINOR'S RECEIPT

where a person is a minor (that is:

- (a) under 18; or
- (b) 18 or over, but not of an age to be entitled to capital outright);

my executors may pay money to which he or she becomes entitled, whether:

- (i) income or capital; or
- (ii) as of right or under a power;

to any the following, and in each case their receipt is a complete discharge:

- (A) the minor, if he or she has attained 16;
- (B) the minor's parent or guardian, in which case my executors are under no further obligation to enquire into the use of the money; or
- (C) a third party for the benefit of the minor;

or my executors may resolve to hold the money on trust for the minor absolutely (in which case the administrative provisions of my will continue to apply to the money).

6–638 20 CONFLICTS OF INTEREST

My executors may exercise (or fail to exercise) any powers in my will, even if one or more of them has a personal interest in the outcome.

6–639 21 USE OF EXECUTORS' POWERS

My executors may exercise any of their powers:

- (a) from time to time; and
- (b) at their absolute discretion.

6–640 22 DEFINITION OF "CHILDREN"

In my will, "children":

- (a) includes those who are legitimate, illegitimate or adopted; but
- (b) does not include step-children, nor natural children who have been adopted by another person;

and other terms describing family relationships are to be interpreted accordingly.

SIGNATURES 6–641

Signed by me on .... 20$/

Signature of Testator

Signed by $/ in our joint presence and then by us in $/{his$//hers$/}
                Witness 1   Witness 2

Signature:

Full name:

Address:

Occupation:

127b Will to children, with gift over (STEP powers)

This is the last will of me $/ of $/.   6–642

1 REVOCATION 6–643

I revoke all former wills.

2 APPOINTMENT OF EXECUTORS 6–644

I appoint $/ $/[and $/$/] to be my $/{executor$//executors$/} but if $/{he is$//
she is$//both of them are$//either of them is$//all of them are$//any of them
is$/} unable or unwilling to act then I appoint $/ instead.

3 APPOINTMENT OF GUARDIANS 6–645

(a) I appoint $/ $/[and $/ $/] to be the $/{guardian$//guardians$/} of any of
my children who are under 18.

(b) If $/{he is$//she is$//either of them is$//both of them are$//any of them
is$//all of them are$/} unable or unwilling to act then I appoint $/
$/[and $/ $/] instead.

4 BURDEN OF INHERITANCE TAX 6–646

If inheritance tax, or any other form of death duty, is payable on my free
estate then my executors must pay it from the residue of my estate.

5 RESIDUE 6–647

I give to my executors:

(I) my estate, anywhere in the world; and

(II) any property over which I have a general power of appointment;

to hold it on trust:

(a) to pay my debts, taxes and funeral and testamentary expenses;

    (b) to divide the residue equally between those of my children who are living at my death and attain $/{18$//21$/}; except:

        (i) if any of my children dies before me, then to divide that child's share equally between those of his or her children who are living at my death and attain $/{18$//21$/}; and

        (ii) if any of my children dies after me, but before attaining $/{18$//21$/}, then to divide that child's share equally between those of his or her children who are living at his or her death and attain $/{18$//21$/}.

    if the above trusts fail, then:

    (a) to pay the residue to $/ absolutely.

6–648 6 TECHNICAL CLAUSES

    (a) The Standard Provisions of the Society of Trust and Estate Practitioners (1st edition) apply, amended as follows:

        (i) Standard provision 5 ("trust for sale") does not apply.

        (ii) My executors may exercise their powers without consulting beneficiaries, so section 11 of the Trusts of Land and Appointment of Trustees Act 1996 does not apply.

    (b) In my will, "children":

        (i) includes those who are legitimate, illegitimate or adopted; but

        (ii) does not include step-children, nor natural children who have been adopted by another person;

    and other terms describing family relationships are to be interpreted accordingly.

    (c) My estate is to be divided as if any person who dies within one month of my death had predeceased me.

6–649 SIGNATURES

Signed by me on . . . . 20$/

Signature of Testator

Signed by $/ in our joint presence and then by us in $/{his$//hers$/}
               Witness 1   Witness 2

Signature:

Full name:

Address:

Occupation:

128 Division by shares between former partner and present partner, substituting respective families, with forfeiture clause

6–650 *Note*: These precedents require amendment if either:

(a) the testator wants the substitution to be to the children of both himself and the predeceased beneficiary; or

(b) the forfeiture is intended to cut out the children of the potential claimant, also.

128a Complete powers

This is the last will of me $/ of $/.

1 REVOCATION

6–651

I revoke all former wills.

2 APPOINTMENT OF EXECUTORS

6–652

I appoint $/ $/[and $/$/] to be my $/{executor$//executors$/} but if $/{he is$// she is$//both of them are$//either of them is$//all of them are$//any of them is$/} unable or unwilling to act then I appoint $/ instead.

3 APPOINTMENT OF GUARDIANS

6–653

(a) I appoint $/ $/[and $/ $/] to be the $/{guardian$//guardians$/} of any of my children who are under 18

(b) If $/{he is$//she is$//either of them is$//both of them are$//any of them is$//all of them are$/} unable or unwilling to act then I appoint $/ $/[and $/ $/] instead

4 BURDEN OF INHERITANCE TAX

6–654

If inheritance tax, or any other form of death duty, is payable on my free estate then my executors must pay it from the residue of my estate.

5 RESIDUE

6–655

I give to my executors:

(I) my estate, anywhere in the world; and

(II) any property over which I have a general power of appointment;

to hold it on trust:

(a) to pay my debts, taxes and funeral and testamentary expenses;

(b) to divide the residue into $/ equal shares and to pay:

(i) $/ $/{share$//shares$/} to $/ if $/{he$//she$/} survives me but if $/{he$//she$/} does not then to those of $/{his$//her$/} children who survive me $/[and attain $/{18$//21$/}$/]; and

(ii) $/ $/{share$//shares$/} to $/ if $/{he$//she$/} survives me but if $/{he$//she$/} does not then to those of $/{his$//her$/} children who survive me $/[and attain $/{18$//21$/}$/].

(c) If either of the above shares fail, the failed share accrues to the other.

6 FORFEITURE

6–656

All benefits given to $/ by this will are forfeited (and my estate divided as if $/{he$//she$/} had died before me) if

(a) $/[$/{he$//she$/} is remarried at my death; or$/]

(b) $/{he$//she$/} makes any application to the court, whether:

    (i) under the Inheritance (Provision for Family and Dependants) Act 1975; or

    (ii) relying on any other ground;

the effect of which, if successful, would be to alter any of the terms of my will.

My executors must not pay any benefits to $/{him$//her$/} until either:

(a) $/{he$//she$/} has given a binding undertaking to accept the terms of my will; or

(b) the last date upon which $/{he$//she$/} could make a claim under the Inheritance (Provision for Family and Dependants) Act 1975 has passed, without a claim being made.

6–657 7 POWER OF INVESTMENT

My executors may invest my estate in any investments they could make if they owned my estate personally. In particular, they may:

(a) invest in unsecured loans, including interest-free loans to a beneficiary;

(b) invest in land, whether as an investment or as a residence for a beneficiary, and may improve and maintain it;

(c) invest jointly with another person;

(d) invest in wasting or non-income-producing assets;

(e) invest anywhere in the world; and

(f) choose not to diversify investments.

6–658 8 EXCLUSION OF S.11 TLATA

My executors may exercise their powers without consulting beneficiaries, so section 11 of the Trusts of Land and Appointment of Trustees Act 1996 does not apply.

6–659 9 POWER OF ADVANCEMENT

My executors may apply the share of any beneficiary for $/{his$//her$//his or her$/} benefit, and this power:

(a) is in addition to any other powers my executors may have, in particular section 32 of the Trustee Act 1925;

(b) applies to the whole or part of the beneficiary's share;

(c) applies whether the beneficiary's right is vested, contingent, expectant or presumptive but not where another person is entitled in priority;

(d) may be used for advancement, maintenance, education or any other benefit;

(e) may be exercised by paying the share to a third party or, where appropriate, to the beneficiary direct.

6–660 10 POWER OF APPROPRIATION

My executors may give specific assets of my estate to beneficiaries without requiring consent. (Section 41 of the Administration of Estates Act 1925 therefore applies subject to that amendment.)

11 POWER OF INSURANCE 6–661

My executors may:

(a) keep any assets of my estate insured, against any risk and in any amount;

(b) pay insurance premiums from the income or capital of that part of my estate which is held on the same trusts as the insured property; and

(c) treat any insurance money received as though it were the proceeds of sale of the insured property.

12 EXCLUSION OF EXECUTORS' LIABILITY 6–662

(a) Only a professional executor or trustee can be liable for any loss arising from:

  (i) exercising, or failing to exercise, any discretion or power;

  (ii) any improper investment made in good faith;

  (iii) the negligence or fraud of any agent employed by him, or by any other executor or trustee, even if the employment was not strictly necessary or expedient;

  (iv) any mistake or omission made in good faith;

  (v) any other matter, except wilful and individual fraud on the part of the executor or trustee who is sought to be made liable.

(b) No executor can be liable for any loss, of any kind, if he has acted in accordance with the advice of Counsel of at least five years' standing.

13 TRUST CORPORATIONS 6–663

If a trust corporation is appointed as executor or trustee, it may:

(a) act by its proper officers;

(b) exercise all the powers given to executors or trustees by my will;

(c) charge under its published scale of fees, as amended from time to time;

(d) meet its charges out of capital or income, at its discretion.

14 POWER TO USE NOMINEES 6–664

My executors may vest any asset of my estate in the name of, or under the control of:

(a) one or more of their number; or

(b) any person (which may include a trust corporation), or people, as nominee(s).

15 POWER TO CHARGE FOR PROFESSIONAL SERVICES 6–665

Any of my executors who is engaged in a profession or business may charge fees for work done by him or her, or by his or her firm, in connection with my estate and its trusts, including acts which an executor or trustee not being in any profession or business could have done personally, and those charges shall be a first charge against my estate, without abatement.

6–666 16 COMMORIENTES

My estate is to be divided as if any person who dies within one month of my death had predeceased me.

6–667 17 ACCUMULATIONS OF INCOME

My executors may:

(a) within 21 years of my death, accumulate income to the extent that it is not paid to, or applied for the benefit of, any beneficiary; and

(b) apply accumulated income as if it were the income of the current year.

6–668 18 POWER OF DELEGATION

My executors may delegate any of their functions, in writing, to:

(a) one or more of their number; or

(b) any other person;

and if they do so my executors are not personally liable to my estate for the defaults of that delegate.

6–669 19 INDEMNITIES

My executors may indemnify a retiring trustee, or any other person, against any liability concerning my estate. If they do so, then my estate (not my executors personally) will bear the liability of that indemnity. My executors may charge the indemnity on assets of my estate.

6–670 20 MINOR'S RECEIPT

where a person is a minor (that is:

(a) under 18; or

(b) 18 or over, but not of an age to be entitled to capital outright);

my executors may pay money to which he or she becomes entitled, whether:

(i) income or capital; or

(ii) as of right or under a power;

to any the following, and in each case their receipt is a complete discharge:

(A) the minor, if he or she has attained 16;

(B) the minor's parent or guardian, in which case my executors are under no further obligation to enquire into the use of the money; or

(C) a third party for the benefit of the minor;

or my executors may resolve to hold the money on trust for the minor absolutely (in which case the administrative provisions of my will continue to apply to the money).

6–671 21 CONFLICTS OF INTEREST

My executors may exercise (or fail to exercise) any powers in my will, even if one or more of them has a personal interest in the outcome.

22 USE OF EXECUTORS' POWERS

6–672

My executors may exercise any of their powers:

  (a) from time to time; and
  (b) at their absolute discretion.

23 DEFINITION OF "CHILDREN"

6–673

In my will, "children":

  (a) includes those who are legitimate, illegitimate or adopted; but
  (b) does not include step-children, nor natural children who have been adopted by another person;

and other terms describing family relationships are to be interpreted accordingly.

SIGNATURES

6–674

Signed by me on .... 20$/

Signature of Testator

Signed by $/ in our joint presence and then by us in $/{his$//hers$/}
                  Witness 1   Witness 2

Signature:

Full name:

Address:

Occupation:

128b Division by shares between former partner and present partner, substituting respective families, with forfeiture clause (STEP powers)

This is the last will of me $/ of $/.   6–675

1 REVOCATION   6–676

I revoke all former wills.

2 APPOINTMENT OF EXECUTORS   6–677

I appoint $/ $/[and $/$/] to be my $/{executor$//executors$/} but if $/{he is$// she is$//both of them are$//either of them is$//all of them are$//any of them is$/} unable or unwilling to act then I appoint $/ instead.

3 APPOINTMENT OF GUARDIANS   6–678

  (a) I appoint $/ $/[and $/ $/] to be the $/{guardian$//guardians$/} of any of my children who are under 18

(b) If $/{he is$//she is$//either of them is$//both of them are$//any of them is$//all of them are$/} unable or unwilling to act then I appoint $/ $/[and $/ $/] instead

6–679 4 BURDEN OF INHERITANCE TAX

If inheritance tax, or any other form of death duty, is payable on my free estate then my executors must pay it from the residue of my estate.

6–680 5 RESIDUE

I give to my executors:

(I) my estate, anywhere in the world; and
(II) any property over which I have a general power of appointment;

to hold it on trust:

(a) to pay my debts, taxes and funeral and testamentary expenses;
(b) to divide the residue into $/ equal shares and to pay:

(i) $/ $/{share$//shares$/} to $/ if $/{he$//she$/} survives me but if $/{he$//she$/} does not then to those of $/{his$//her$/} children who survive me $/[and attain $/{18$//21$/}$/]; and
(ii) $/ $/{share$//shares$/} to $/ if $/{he$//she$/} survives me but if $/{he$//she$/} does not then to those of $/{his$//her$/} children who survive me $/[and attain $/{18$//21$/}$/].

(c) If either of the above shares fail, the failed share accrues to the other.

6–681 6 FORFEITURE

All benefits given to $/ by this will are forfeited (and my estate divided as if $/{he$//she$/} had died before me) if

(a) $/[$/{he$//she$/} is remarried at my death; or$/]
(b) $/{he$//she$/} makes any application to the court, whether:

(i) under the Inheritance (Provision for Family and Dependants) Act 1975; or
(ii) relying on any other ground;
the effect of which, if successful, would be to alter any of the terms of my will.

My executors must not pay any benefits to $/{him$//her$/} until either:

(a) $/{he$//she$/} has given a binding undertaking to accept the terms of my will; or
(b) the last date upon which $/{he$//she$/} could make a claim under the Inheritance (Provision for Family and Dependants) Act 1975 has passed, without a claim being made.

6–682 7 TECHNICAL CLAUSES

(a) The Standard Provisions of the Society of Trust and Estate Practitioners (1st edition) apply, amended as follows:

(i) Standard provision 5 ("trust for sale") does not apply.

(ii) My executors may exercise their powers without consulting beneficiaries, so section 11 of the Trusts of Land and Appointment of Trustees Act 1996 does not apply.

(b) In my will, "children":

(i) includes those who are legitimate, illegitimate or adopted; but

(ii) does not include step-children, nor natural children who have been adopted by another person;

and other terms describing family relationships are to be interpreted accordingly.

(c) My estate is to be divided as if any person who dies within one month of my death had predeceased me.

SIGNATURES

6–683

Signed by me on .... 20$/

Signature of Testator

Signed by $/ in our joint presence and then by us in $/{his$//hers$/}

      Witness 1   Witness 2

Signature:

Full name:

Address:

Occupation:

SECOND FAMILIES

While there are infinite varieties possible in wills, it is thought that there are **6–684** realistically four solutions to the "second family problem". The problem arises where two people who have children from former relationships marry or cohabit together, but are fearful that if the first of them to die leaves everything to the survivor, that survivor may change his or her will so as to benefit his or her own children only, leaving the children of the first to die unprovided for. The four solutions to this problem can be described as follows:

(a) *Trusting the survivor.* While in many ways unsatisfactory, we find that in practice this is often the course preferred by testators. Options (b) and (c) are often so complex as concepts, and so unattractive for other reasons, that option (a) is often fallen back on. Only testators of considerable means are satisfied by option (d) below. By trusting the survivor, we mean simply an outright gift to the survivor with residue shared between the two families on second death, and an unenforceable assumption that the survivor will in all probability not change his or her will, having inherited from the first to die.

(b) *Mutual wills.* We have chosen not to embark upon a detailed discussion of mutual wills in this book, our aim being to discourage rather than encourage their use. In summary, a mutual will is a normal will on the same terms as in (a) above, but with a contract, enforceable by one set of executors against the other, that the survivor will not change his or her will after the death of the first. Wills of this kind create numerous problems, particularly where (as often happens in practice) the survivor does in fact change his or her will.

(c) *A life interest to the survivor, with remainder to the testator's own children.* This is rarely acceptable to families without substantial wealth, who are naturally inclined to feel that the income from their assets is unlikely to be adequate by itself to provide for the survivor, even taking into account the survivor's absolute ownership of his or her assets. Setting tax issues aside, however, this might be the most appropriate approach for families where there is adequate wealth. An alternative which is sometimes acceptable to the less wealthy where they are (or can become) tenants in common of the property, is to give a life interest in the home, with residue outright to the survivor.

(d) *Providing for the testator's own children on first death.* The testator gives a legacy to his or her own children on the first death. Residue is then given to the survivor, who may make any arrangements he or she chooses, without having any moral obligation to the family of the first to die. Again, this approach is often only suitable for the reasonably wealthy since the survivor must be capable of maintaining his or her lifestyle without access to the money which is the subject matter of the legacy.

129 All to survivor with second death split between both families

129a Complete powers

6–685 This is the last will of me $/ of $/.

6–686 1 REVOCATION

I revoke all former wills.

6–687 2 APPOINTMENT OF EXECUTORS

I appoint $/ $/[and $/$/] to be my $/{executor$//executors$/} but if $/{he is$// she is$//both of them are$//either of them is$//all of them are$//any of them is$/} unable or unwilling to act then I appoint $/ instead.

3 BURDEN OF INHERITANCE TAX   6–688

If inheritance tax, or any other form of death duty, is payable on my free estate then my executors must pay it from the residue of my estate.

4 RESIDUE   6–689

I give to my executors:

(I) my estate, anywhere in the world; and
(II) any property over which I have a general power of appointment;

to hold it on trust:

(a) to pay my debts, taxes and funeral and testamentary expenses;
(b) to pay the residue to my $/{husband$//wife$/} $/ absolutely if $/{he$//she$/} survives me by 28 days; but if this gift fails
(c) to divide the residue into two equal shares and to pay;

    (i) one share to those of my children who are living at my death$/[and attain $/{18$//21$/} $/]; and
    (ii) one share to those of the children of my $/{husband$//wife$/} who are living at my death $/[and attain $/{18$//21$/}$/]; except

(d) if any of the beneficiaries above die before me, then to divide his or her share equally between those of his or her children who are living at my death and attain $/{18$//21$/}; and
(e) if any of them dies after me, but before attaining $/{18$//21$/}then to divide his or her share equally between those of her or her children who are living at his or her death and attain $/{18$//21$/};
(f) if either of the above shares fails entirely then the failed share accrues to the other.

5 POWER OF INVESTMENT   6–690

My executors may invest my estate in any investments they could make if they owned my estate personally. In particular, they may:

(a) invest in unsecured loans, including interest-free loans to a beneficiary;
(b) invest in land, whether as an investment or as a residence for a beneficiary, and may improve and maintain it;
(c) invest jointly with another person;
(d) invest in wasting or non-income-producing assets;
(e) invest anywhere in the world; and
(f) choose not to diversify investments.

6 EXCLUSION OF S.11 TLATA   6–691

My executors may exercise their powers without consulting beneficiaries, so section 11 of the Trusts of Land and Appointment of Trustees Act 1996 does not apply.

6–692 7 POWER OF ADVANCEMENT

My executors may apply the share of any beneficiary for $/{his$//her$//his or her$/} benefit, and this power:

(a) is in addition to any other powers my executors may have, in particular section 32 of the Trustee Act 1925;

(b) applies to the whole or part of the beneficiary's share;

(c) applies whether the beneficiary's right is vested, contingent, expectant or presumptive but not where another person is entitled in priority;

(d) may be used for advancement, maintenance, education or any other benefit;

(e) may be exercised by paying the share to a third party or, where appropriate, to the beneficiary direct.

6–693 8 POWER OF APPROPRIATION

My executors may give specific assets of my estate to beneficiaries without requiring consent. (Section 41 of the Administration of Estates Act 1925 therefore applies subject to that amendment.)

6–694 9 POWER OF INSURANCE

My executors may:

(a) keep any assets of my estate insured, against any risk and in any amount;

(b) pay insurance premiums from the income or capital of that part of my estate which is held on the same trusts as the insured property; and

(c) treat any insurance money received as though it were the proceeds of sale of the insured property.

6–695 10 EXCLUSION OF EXECUTORS' LIABILITY

(a) Only a professional executor or trustee can be liable for any loss arising from:

    (i) exercising, or failing to exercise, any discretion or power;

    (ii) any improper investment made in good faith;

    (iii) the negligence or fraud of any agent employed by him, or by any other executor or trustee, even if the employment was not strictly necessary or expedient;

    (iv) any mistake or omission made in good faith;

    (v) any other matter, except wilful and individual fraud on the part of the executor or trustee who is sought to be made liable.

(b) No executor can be liable for any loss, of any kind, if he has acted in accordance with the advice of Counsel of at least five years' standing.

11 TRUST CORPORATIONS 6–696

If a trust corporation is appointed as executor or trustee, it may:

(a) act by its proper officers;
(b) exercise all the powers given to executors or trustees by my will;
(c) charge under its published scale of fees, as amended from time to time;
(d) meet its charges out of capital or income, at its discretion.

12 POWER TO USE NOMINEES 6–697

My executors may vest any asset of my estate in the name of, or under the control of:

(a) one or more of their number; or
(b) any person (which may include a trust corporation), or people, as nominee(s).

13 POWER TO CHARGE FOR PROFESSIONAL SERVICES 6–698

Any of my executors who is engaged in a profession or business may charge fees for work done by him or her, or by his or her firm, in connection with my estate and its trusts, including acts which an executor or trustee not being in any profession or business could have done personally, and those charges shall be a first charge against my estate, without abatement.

14 COMMORIENTES 6–699

My estate is to be divided as if any person who dies within one month of my death had predeceased me.

15 ACCUMULATIONS OF INCOME 6–700

My executors may:

(a) within 21 years of my death, accumulate income to the extent that it is not paid to, or applied for the benefit of, any beneficiary; and
(b) apply accumulated income as if it were the income of the current year.

16 POWER OF DELEGATION 6–701

My executors may delegate any of their functions, in writing, to:

(a) one or more of their number; or
any other person;
(b) and if they do so my executors are not personally liable to my estate for the defaults of that delegate.

17 INDEMNITIES 6–702

My executors may indemnify a retiring trustee, or any other person, against any liability concerning my estate. If they do so, then my estate (not my executors personally) will bear the liability of that indemnity. My executors may charge the indemnity on assets of my estate.

6–703 ## 18 MINOR'S RECEIPT

where a person is a minor (that is:

    (a) under 18; or

    (b) 18 or over, but not of an age to be entitled to capital outright);

my executors may pay money to which he or she becomes entitled, whether:

        (i) income or capital; or

        (ii) as of right or under a power;

to any the following, and in each case their receipt is a complete discharge:

            (A) the minor, if he or she has attained 16;

            (B) the minor's parent or guardian, in which case my executors are under no further obligation to enquire into the use of the money; or

            (C) a third party for the benefit of the minor;

or my executors may resolve to hold the money on trust for the minor absolutely (in which case the administrative provisions of my will continue to apply to the money).

6–704 ## 19 CONFLICTS OF INTEREST

My executors may exercise (or fail to exercise) any powers in my will, even if one or more of them has a personal interest in the outcome.

6–705 ## 20 USE OF EXECUTORS' POWERS

My executors may exercise any of their powers:

    (a) from time to time; and

    (b) at their absolute discretion.

6–706 ## 21 DEFINITION OF "CHILDREN"

In my will, "children":

    (a) includes those who are legitimate, illegitimate or adopted; but

    (b) does not include step-children, nor natural children who have been adopted by another person;

and other terms describing family relationships are to be interpreted accordingly.

SIGNATURES 6–707

Signed by me on .... 20$/

Signature of Testator

Signed by $/ in our joint presence and then by us in $/{his$//hers$/}
        Witness 1   Witness 2

Signature:

Full name:

Address:

Occupation:

129b All to survivor with second death split between both families (STEP powers)

This is the last will of me $/ of $/.   6–708

1 REVOCATION 6–709

I revoke all former wills.

2 APPOINTMENT OF EXECUTORS 6–710

I appoint $/ $/[and $/$/] to be my $/{executor$//executors$/} but if $/{he is$// she is$//both of them are$//either of them is$//all of them are$//any of them is$/} unable or unwilling to act then I appoint $/ instead.

3 BURDEN OF INHERITANCE TAX 6–711

If inheritance tax, or any other form of death duty, is payable on my free estate then my executors must pay it from the residue of my estate.

4 RESIDUE 6–712

I give to my executors:

    (I) my estate, anywhere in the world; and
    (II) any property over which I have a general power of appointment;

to hold it on trust:

        (a) to pay my debts, taxes and funeral and testamentary expenses;
        (b) to pay the residue to my $/{husband$//wife$/} $/ absolutely if $/{he$//she$/} survives me by 28 days; but if this gift fails
        (c) to divide the residue into two equal shares and to pay;

            (i) one share to those of my children who are living at my death$/[and attain $/{18$//21$/} $/]; and

(ii) one share to those of the children of my $/{husband$//wife$/} who are living at my death $/[and attain $/{18$//21$/}$/]; except

(d) if any of the beneficiaries above die before me, then to divide his or her share equally between those of his or her children who are living at my death and attain $/{18$//21$/}; and

(e) if any of them dies after me, but before attaining $/{18$//21$/}then to divide his or her share equally between those of her or her children who are living at his or her death and attain $/{18$//21$/};

(f) if either of the above shares fails entirely then the failed share accrues to the other.

6–713 5 TECHNICAL CLAUSES

(a) The Standard Provisions of the Society of Trust and Estate Practitioners (1st edition) apply, amended as follows:

(i) Standard provision 5 ("trust for sale") does not apply.

(ii) My executors may exercise their powers without consulting beneficiaries, so section 11 of the Trusts of Land and Appointment of Trustees Act 1996 does not apply.

(b) In my will, "children":

(i) includes those who are legitimate, illegitimate or adopted; but

(ii) does not include step-children, nor natural children who have been adopted by another person;

and other terms describing family relationships are to be interpreted accordingly.

(c) My estate is to be divided as if any person who dies within one month of my death had predeceased me.

6–714 SIGNATURES

Signed by me on . . . . 20$/

Signature of Testator

Signed by $/ in our joint presence and then by us in $/{his$//hers$/}

Witness 1   Witness 2

Signature:

Full name:

Address:

Occupation:

130 All to survivor with second death split to both families, with mutual wills

130a Complete powers

6–715 This is the last will of me $/ of $/.

1 REVOCATION

6–716

I revoke all former wills.

2 APPOINTMENT OF EXECUTORS

6–717

I appoint $/ $/[and $/$/] to be my $/{executor$//executors$/} but if $/{he is$// she is$//both of them are$//either of them is$//all of them are$//any of them is$/} unable or unwilling to act then I appoint $/ instead.

3 MUTUAL WILLS

6–718

I have made this will on the same day as $/ has made $/{his$//her$/} will. It is our intention that the wills should be mutual. That is, we agree that if the first of us dies without having changed the will made today, the survivor will be bound to stand by the terms of his or her will made today. We agree that this agreement is to be enforceable against the survivor of us, and his or her executors. $/ has acknowledged this agreement by signing the following declaration on the face of my will.

DECLARATION

I, $/, acknowledge the agreement set out above. I agree that if $/ dies before me without having changed this will, I am bound to honour the terms of my will signed today. This agreement binds me and my executors.

. . . .

Signature of $/

---

4 BURDEN OF INHERITANCE TAX

6–719

If inheritance tax, or any other form of death duty, is payable on my free estate then my executors must pay it from the residue of my estate.

5 RESIDUE

6–720

I give to my executors:
    (I) my estate, anywhere in the world; and
    (II) any property over which I have a general power of appointment;

to hold it on trust:

    (a) to pay my debts, taxes and funeral and testamentary expenses;
    (b) to pay the residue to my $/{husband$//wife$/} $/ absolutely if $/{he$//she$/} survives me by 28 days; but if this gift fails
    (c) to divide the residue into two equal shares and to pay;

        (i) one share to those of my children who are living at my death$/[and attain $/{18$//21$/}$/]; and

(ii) one share to those of the children of my $/{husband$//
wife$/} who are living at my death $/[and attain
$/{18$//21$/}$/]; except

(d) if any of the beneficiaries above die before me, then to divide his
or her share equally between those of his or her children who are
living at my death and attain $/{18$//21$/}; and

(e) if any of them dies after me, but before attaining $/{18$//21$/}then
to divide his or her share equally between those of her or her
children who are living at his or her death and attain $/{18$//21$/};

(f) if either of the above shares fails entirely then the failed share
accrues to the other.

6–721 6 POWER OF INVESTMENT

My executors may invest my estate in any investments they could make if
they owned my estate personally. In particular, they may:

(a) invest in unsecured loans, including interest-free loans to a beneficiary;
(b) invest in land, whether as an investment or as a residence for a
beneficiary, and may improve and maintain it;
(c) invest jointly with another person;
(d) invest in wasting or non-income-producing assets;
(e) invest anywhere in the world; and
(f) choose not to diversify investments.

6–722 7 EXCLUSION OF S.11 TLATA

My executors may exercise their powers without consulting beneficiaries, so
section 11 of the Trusts of Land and Appointment of Trustees Act 1996 does
not apply.

6–723 8 POWER OF ADVANCEMENT

My executors may apply the share of any beneficiary for $/{his$//her$//his or
her$/} benefit, and this power:

(a) is in addition to any other powers my executors may have, in particular
section 32 of the Trustee Act 1925;
(b) applies to the whole or part of the beneficiary's share;
(c) applies whether the beneficiary's right is vested, contingent, expectant
or presumptive but not where another person is entitled in priority;
(d) may be used for advancement, maintenance, education or any other
benefit;
(e) may be exercised by paying the share to a third party or, where
appropriate, to the beneficiary direct.

6–724 9 POWER OF APPROPRIATION

My executors may give specific assets of my estate to beneficiaries without
requiring consent. (Section 41 of the Administration of Estates Act 1925
therefore applies subject to that amendment.)

10 POWER OF INSURANCE 6–725

My executors may:

(a) keep any assets of my estate insured, against any risk and in any amount;

(b) pay insurance premiums from the income or capital of that part of my estate which is held on the same trusts as the insured property; and

(c) treat any insurance money received as though it were the proceeds of sale of the insured property.

11 EXCLUSION OF EXECUTORS' LIABILITY 6–726

(a) Only a professional executor or trustee can be liable for any loss arising from:

(i) exercising, or failing to exercise, any discretion or power;

(ii) any improper investment made in good faith;

(iii) the negligence or fraud of any agent employed by him, or by any other executor or trustee, even if the employment was not strictly necessary or expedient;

(iv) any mistake or omission made in good faith;

(v) any other matter, except wilful and individual fraud on the part of the executor or trustee who is sought to be made liable.

(b) No executor can be liable for any loss, of any kind, if he has acted in accordance with the advice of Counsel of at least five years' standing.

12 TRUST CORPORATIONS 6–727

If a trust corporation is appointed as executor or trustee, it may:

(a) act by its proper officers;

(b) exercise all the powers given to executors or trustees by my will;

(c) charge under its published scale of fees, as amended from time to time;

(d) meet its charges out of capital or income, at its discretion.

13 POWER TO USE NOMINEES 6–728

My executors may vest any asset of my estate in the name of, or under the control of:

(a) one or more of their number; or

(b) any person (which may include a trust corporation), or people, as nominee(s).

14 POWER TO CHARGE FOR PROFESSIONAL SERVICES 6–729

Any of my executors who is engaged in a profession or business may charge fees for work done by him or her, or by his or her firm, in connection with my estate and its trusts, including acts which an executor or trustee not being in any profession or business could have done personally, and those charges shall be a first charge against my estate, without abatement.

6–730 15 COMMORIENTES

My estate is to be divided as if any person who dies within one month of my death had predeceased me.

6–731 16 ACCUMULATIONS OF INCOME

My executors may:

    (a) within 21 years of my death, accumulate income to the extent that it is not paid to, or applied for the benefit of, any beneficiary; and

    (b) apply accumulated income as if it were the income of the current year.

6–732 17 POWER OF DELEGATION

My executors may delegate any of their functions, in writing, to:

    (a) one or more of their number; or

    (b) any other person;

and if they do so my executors are not personally liable to my estate for the defaults of that delegate.

6–733 18 INDEMNITIES

My executors may indemnify a retiring trustee, or any other person, against any liability concerning my estate. If they do so, then my estate (not my executors personally) will bear the liability of that indemnity. My executors may charge the indemnity on assets of my estate.

6–734 19 MINOR'S RECEIPT

where a person is a minor (that is:

    (a) under 18; or

    (b) 18 or over, but not of an age to be entitled to capital outright);

my executors may pay money to which he or she becomes entitled, whether:

        (i) income or capital; or

        (ii) as of right or under a power;

to any the following, and in each case their receipt is a complete discharge:

        (A) the minor, if he or she has attained 16;

        (B) the minor's parent or guardian, in which case my executors are under no further obligation to enquire into the use of the money; or

        (C) a third party for the benefit of the minor;

or my executors may resolve to hold the money on trust for the minor absolutely (in which case the administrative provisions of my will continue to apply to the money).

6–735 20 CONFLICTS OF INTEREST

My executors may exercise (or fail to exercise) any powers in my will, even if one or more of them has a personal interest in the outcome.

21 USE OF EXECUTORS' POWERS 6–736

My executors may exercise any of their powers:

    (a) from time to time; and

    (b) at their absolute discretion.

22 DEFINITION OF "CHILDREN" 6–737

In my will, "children":

    (a) includes those who are legitimate, illegitimate or adopted; but

    (b) does not include step-children, nor natural children who have been adopted by another person;

and other terms describing family relationships are to be interpreted accordingly.

SIGNATURES 6–738

Signed by me on . . . . 20$/
Signature of Testator

Signed by $/ in our joint presence and then by us in $/{his$//hers$/}
               Witness 1   Witness 2

Signature:

Full name:

Address:

Occupation:

130b All to survivor with second death split to both families, with mutual wills (STEP powers)

This is the last will of me $/ of $/. 6–739

1 REVOCATION 6–740

I revoke all former wills.

2 APPOINTMENT OF EXECUTORS 6–741

I appoint $/ $/[and $/$/] to be my $/{executor$//executors$/} but if $/{he is$// she is$//both of them are$//either of them is$//all of them are$//any of them is$/} unable or unwilling to act then I appoint $/ instead.

3 MUTUAL WILLS 6–742

I have made this will on the same day as $/ has made $/{his$//her$/} will. It is our intention that the wills should be mutual. That is, we agree that if the first of us dies without having changed the will made today, the survivor will be bound to stand by the terms of his or her will made today. We agree that this agreement is to be enforceable against the survivor of us, and his or her executors. $/ has acknowledged this agreement by signing the following declaration on the face of my will.

DECLARATION

I, $/, acknowledge the agreement set out above. I agree that if $/ dies before me without having changed this will, I am bound to honour the terms of my will signed today. This agreement binds me and my executors.

. . . .
Signature of $/

6–743 4 BURDEN OF INHERITANCE TAX

If inheritance tax, or any other form of death duty, is payable on my free estate then my executors must pay it from the residue of my estate.

6–744 5 RESIDUE

I give to my executors:
   (I) my estate, anywhere in the world; and
   (II) any property over which I have a general power of appointment;

to hold it on trust:

     (a) to pay my debts, taxes and funeral and testamentary expenses;
     (b) to pay the residue to my $/{husband$//wife$/} $/ absolutely if $/{he$//she$/} survives me by 28 days; but if this gift fails
     (c) to divide the residue into two equal shares and to pay;

        (i) one share to those of my children who are living at my death$/[and attain $/{18$//21$/}$/]; and
        (ii) one share to those of the children of my $/{husband$//wife$/} who are living at my death $/[and attain $/{18$//21$/}$/]; except

     (d) if any of the beneficiaries above die before me, then to divide his or her share equally between those of his or her children who are living at my death and attain $/{18$//21$/}; and
     (e) if any of them dies after me, but before attaining $/{18$//21$/}then to divide his or her share equally between those of her or her children who are living at his or her death and attain $/{18$//21$/};
     (f) if either of the above shares fails entirely then the failed share accrues to the other.

6 TECHNICAL CLAUSES 6–745

(a) The Standard Provisions of the Society of Trust and Estate Practitioners (1st edition) apply, amended as follows:

(i) Standard provision 5 ("trust for sale") does not apply.

(ii) My executors may exercise their powers without consulting beneficiaries, so section 11 of the Trusts of Land and Appointment of Trustees Act 1996 does not apply.

(b) In my will, "children":

(i) includes those who are legitimate, illegitimate or adopted; but

(ii) does not include step-children, nor natural children who have been adopted by another person;

and other terms describing family relationships are to be interpreted accordingly.

(c) My estate is to be divided as if any person who dies within one month of my death had predeceased me.

SIGNATURES 6–746

Signed by me on .... 20$/

Signature of Testator

Signed by $/ in our joint presence and then by us in $/{his$//hers$/}
      Witness 1   Witness 2

Signature:

Full name:

Address:

Occupation:

131 Life interest in residue to survivor, with remainder to testator's own children

131a Complete powers

This is the last will of me $/ of $/. 6–747

1 REVOCATION 6–748

I revoke all former wills.

2 APPOINTMENT OF EXECUTORS 6–749

I appoint $/ $/[and $/$/] to be my $/{executor$//executors$/} but if $/{he is$// she is$//both of them are$//either of them is$//all of them are$//any of them is$/} unable or unwilling to act then I appoint $/ instead.

6–750 3 BURDEN OF INHERITANCE TAX

If inheritance tax, or any other form of death duty, is payable on my free estate then my executors must pay it from the residue of my estate.

6–751 4 RESIDUE

I give to my executors:
  (I) my estate, anywhere in the world; and
  (II) any property over which I have a general power of appointment;

to hold it on trust:

> (a) to pay my debts, taxes and funeral and testamentary expenses;
> (b) to pay the residue ("the trust fund") to the trustees of the settlement declared in clause (5) below.

6–752 5 LIFE INTEREST TRUST

(a) In this clause, "my trustees" means my executors or the trustees for the time being of this clause.
(b) My trustees have all the powers given to executors by my will.
(c) I give the trust fund to my trustees on trust to pay the income to my $/{husband$//wife$/} during $/{his$//her$/} lifetime; and subject to that:
(d) to divide the residue equally between those of my children who are living at the death of the survivor of:

  (i) me; and
  (ii) my $/{husband$//wife$/}

(e) if any of my children dies before the survivor of me and my $/{husband$//wife$/}, then to divide that child's share equally between those of his or her children who are living at the death of the survivor of me and my $/{husband$//wife$/}$/[and attain $/{18$//21$/}$/].

6–753 6 POWER OF INVESTMENT

My executors may invest my estate in any investments they could make if they owned my estate personally. In particular, they may:

(a) invest in unsecured loans, including interest-free loans to a beneficiary;
(b) invest in land, whether as an investment or as a residence for a beneficiary, and may improve and maintain it;
(c) invest jointly with another person;
(d) invest in wasting or non-income-producing assets;
(e) invest anywhere in the world; and
(f) choose not to diversify investments.

6–754 7 EXCLUSION OF THE APPORTIONMENT RULES

(a) My executors may treat income as arising on the day it is received.
(b) The Apportionment Act 1870 does not apply.
(c) The rules known as "the rule in *Howe v. Dartmouth*" and "the rule in *Allhusen v. Whittell*" do not apply.

8 EXCLUSION OF S.11 TLATA 6–755

My executors may exercise their powers without consulting beneficiaries, so section 11 of the Trusts of Land and Appointment of Trustees Act 1996 does not apply.

9 POWER OF ADVANCEMENT 6–756

My executors may apply the share of any beneficiary for $/{his$//her$//his or her$/} benefit, and this power:

(a) is in addition to any other powers my executors may have, in particular section 32 of the Trustee Act 1925;

(b) applies to the whole or part of the beneficiary's share;

(c) applies whether the beneficiary's right is vested, contingent, expectant or presumptive but not where another person is entitled in priority;

(d) may be used for advancement, maintenance, education or any other benefit;

(e) may be exercised by paying the share to a third party or, where appropriate, to the beneficiary direct.

10 POWER OF APPROPRIATION 6–757

My executors may give specific assets of my estate to beneficiaries without requiring consent. (Section 41 of the Administration of Estates Act 1925 therefore applies subject to that amendment.)

11 POWER OF INSURANCE 6–758

My executors may:

(a) keep any assets of my estate insured, against any risk and in any amount;

(b) pay insurance premiums from the income or capital of that part of my estate which is held on the same trusts as the insured property; and

(c) treat any insurance money received as though it were the proceeds of sale of the insured property.

12 EXCLUSION OF EXECUTORS' LIABILITY 6–759

(a) Only a professional executor or trustee can be liable for any loss arising from:

  (i) exercising, or failing to exercise, any discretion or power;

  (ii) any improper investment made in good faith;

  (iii) the negligence or fraud of any agent employed by him, or by any other executor or trustee, even if the employment was not strictly necessary or expedient;

  (iv) any mistake or omission made in good faith;

  (v) any other matter, except wilful and individual fraud on the part of the executor or trustee who is sought to be made liable.

(b) No executor can be liable for any loss, of any kind, if he has acted in accordance with the advice of Counsel of at least five years' standing.

6–760 13 TRUST CORPORATIONS

If a trust corporation is appointed as executor or trustee, it may:

(a) act by its proper officers;

(b) exercise all the powers given to executors or trustees by my will;

(c) charge under its published scale of fees, as amended from time to time;

(d) meet its charges out of capital or income, at its discretion.

6–761 14 POWER TO USE NOMINEES

My executors may vest any asset of my estate in the name of, or under the control of:

(a) one or more of their number; or

(b) any person (which may include a trust corporation), or people, as nominee(s).

6–762 15 POWER TO CHARGE FOR PROFESSIONAL SERVICES

Any of my executors who is engaged in a profession or business may charge fees for work done by him or her, or by his or her firm, in connection with my estate and its trusts, including acts which an executor or trustee not being in any profession or business could have done personally, and those charges shall be a first charge against my estate, without abatement.

6–763 16 COMMORIENTES

My estate is to be divided as if any person who dies within one month of my death had predeceased me.

6–764 17 ACCUMULATIONS OF INCOME

My executors may:

(a) within 21 years of my death, accumulate income to the extent that it is not paid to, or applied for the benefit of, any beneficiary; and

(b) apply accumulated income as if it were the income of the current year.

6–765 18 POWER TO BORROW

(a) My executors may borrow money for any purpose.

(b) My executors may charge any assets of my estate as security for any liability.

6–766 19 POWER OF DELEGATION

My executors may delegate any of their functions, in writing, to:

(a) one or more of their number; or

(b) any other person;

and if they do so my executors are not personally liable to my estate for the defaults of that delegate.

20 INDEMNITIES 6–767

My executors may indemnify a retiring trustee, or any other person, against any liability concerning my estate. If they do so, then my estate (not my executors personally) will bear the liability of that indemnity. My executors may charge the indemnity on assets of my estate.

21 MINOR'S RECEIPT 6–768

where a person is a minor (that is:

(a) under 18; or
(b) 18 or over, but not of an age to be entitled to capital outright);

my executors may pay money to which he or she becomes entitled, whether:

(i) income or capital; or
(ii) as of right or under a power;

to any the following, and in each case their receipt is a complete discharge:

(A) the minor, if he or she has attained 16;
(B) the minor's parent or guardian, in which case my executors are under no further obligation to enquire into the use of the money; or
(C) a third party for the benefit of the minor;

or my executors may resolve to hold the money on trust for the minor absolutely (in which case the administrative provisions of my will continue to apply to the money).

22 CONFLICTS OF INTEREST 6–769

My executors may exercise (or fail to exercise) any powers in my will, even if one or more of them has a personal interest in the outcome.

23 USE OF EXECUTORS' POWERS 6–770

My executors may exercise any of their powers:

(a) from time to time; and
(b) at their absolute discretion.

24 DEFINITION OF "CHILDREN" 6–771

In my will, "children":

(a) includes those who are legitimate, illegitimate or adopted; but
(b) does not include step-children, nor natural children who have been adopted by another person;

and other terms describing family relationships are to be interpreted accordingly.

6–772 SIGNATURES

Signed by me on .... 20$/

Signature of Testator

Signed by $/ in our joint presence and then by us in $/{his$///hers$/}

              Witness 1   Witness 2

Signature:

Full name:

Address:

Occupation:

131b Life interest in residue to survivor, with remainder to testator's own children (STEP powers)

6–773 This is the last will of me $/ of $/.

6–774 1 REVOCATION

I revoke all former wills.

6–775 2 APPOINTMENT OF EXECUTORS

I appoint $/ $/[and $/$/] to be my $/{executor$///executors$/} but if $/{he is$///she is$///both of them are$///either of them is$///all of them are$///any of them is$/} unable or unwilling to act then I appoint $/ instead.

6–776 3 BURDEN OF INHERITANCE TAX

If inheritance tax, or any other form of death duty, is payable on my free estate then my executors must pay it from the residue of my estate.

6–777 4 RESIDUE

I give to my executors:

    (I) my estate, anywhere in the world; and
    (II) any property over which I have a general power of appointment;

to hold it on trust:

        (a) to pay my debts, taxes and funeral and testamentary expenses;
        (b) to pay the residue ("the trust fund") to the trustees of the settlement declared in clause (5) below.

6–778 5 LIFE INTEREST TRUST

    (a) In this clause, "my trustees" means my executors or the trustees for the time being of this clause.

(b) My trustees have all the powers given to executors by my will.

(c) I give the trust fund to my trustees on trust to pay the income to my $/{husband$//wife$/} during $/{his$//her$/} lifetime; and subject to that:

(d) to divide the residue equally between those of my children who are living at the death of the survivor of:

   (i) me; and

   (ii) my $/{husband$//wife$/}

(e) if any of my children dies before the survivor of me and my $/{husband$//wife$/}, then to divide that child's share equally between those of his or her children who are living at the death of the survivor of me and my $/{husband$//wife$/}$/[and attain $/{18$//21$/}$/].

6 TECHNICAL CLAUSES   6–779

(a) The Standard Provisions of the Society of Trust and Estate Practitioners (1st edition) apply, amended as follows:

   (i) Standard provision 5 ("trust for sale") does not apply.

   (ii) My executors may exercise their powers without consulting beneficiaries, so section 11 of the Trusts of Land and Appointment of Trustees Act 1996 does not apply.

(b) In my will, "children":

   (i) includes those who are legitimate, illegitimate or adopted; but

   (ii) does not include step-children, nor natural children who have been adopted by another person;

and other terms describing family relationships are to be interpreted accordingly.

(c) My estate is to be divided as if any person who dies within one month of my death had predeceased me.

SIGNATURES   6–780

Signed by me on .... 20$/

Signature of Testator

Signed by $/ in our joint presence and then by us in $/{his$//hers$/}
          Witness 1   Witness 2

Signature:

Full name:

Address:

Occupation:

132 Life interest in house, remainder to testator's own children, residue to survivor substituting families half and half

132a Complete powers

6–781 This is the last will of me $/ of $/.

6–782 1 REVOCATION

I revoke all former wills.

6–783 2 APPOINTMENT OF EXECUTORS

I appoint $/ $/[and $/$/] to be my $/{executor$//executors$/} but if $/{he is$// she is$//both of them are$//either of them is$//all of them are$//any of them is$/} unable or unwilling to act then I appoint $/ instead.

6–784 3 GIFT OF CONTENTS

(a) In this clause and the next (4):

   (i) "the life tenant" means $/;

   (ii) "the property" means $/ or any other property which I own as my main residence at my death; and

   (iii) "personal chattels" has the meaning given in section 55(1)(x) of the Administration of Estates Act 1925, but does not include chattels which are the subject of specific gifts.

(b) I give all my personal chattels which are situated in the property at my death to the life tenant.

6–785 4 LIFE INTEREST IN HOUSE

(a) In this clause:

   (i) "my trustees" means my executors or the trustees for the time being of this clause; and

   (ii) "the trust fund" means all my interest in the property, and the assets representing it from time to time.

(b) My trustees have all the powers given to executors by my will.

(c) I give the trust fund to my trustees on trust to pay the income to the life tenant during $/{his$//her$/} lifetime.

(d) While the trust fund contains a dwelling occupied by the life tenant as a home, the life tenant must comply with the following conditions:

   (i) the life tenant must pay all outgoings;

   (ii) the life tenant must keep the dwelling in good repair;

   (iii) the life tenant must keep the dwelling insured to its full reinstatement value, with an insurance company approved by my trustees, at the life tenant's expense.

(e) On the failure of the above trusts, my executors must hold the trust fund:

(f) to divide the residue equally between those of my children who are living at the death of the survivor of:

    (i) me; and

    (ii) the life tenant

except:

(g) if any of my children dies before the survivor of me and the life tenant, then to divide that child's share equally between those of his or her children who are living at the death of the survivor of me and the life tenant and attain $/{18$//21$/}

5 BURDEN OF INHERITANCE TAX 6–786

If inheritance tax, or any other form of death duty, is payable on my free estate then my executors must pay it from the residue of my estate.

6 RESIDUE 6–787

I give to my executors:

    (I) the rest of my estate, anywhere in the world; and

    (II) any property over which I have a general power of appointment;

to hold it on trust:

(a) to pay my debts, taxes and funeral and testamentary expenses;

(b) to pay the residue to my $/{husband$//wife$/} $/ absolutely if $/{he$//she$/} survives me by 28 days; but if this gift fails

(c) to divide the residue into two equal shares and to pay;

    (i) one share to those of my children who are living at my death $/[and attain $/{18$//21$/}$/]; and

    (ii) one share to those of the children of my $/{husband$// wife$/} who are living at my death$/[and attain $/{18$//21$/} $/]; except

(d) if any of the beneficiaries above die before me, then to divide his or her share equally between those of his or her children who are living at my death and attain $/{18$//21$/}; and

(e) if any of them dies after me, but before attaining $/{18$//21$/}then to divide his or her share equally between those of his or her children who are living at his or her death and attain $/{18$//21$/}

(f) if either of the above shares fails entirely then the failed share accrues to the other.

7 POWER OF INVESTMENT 6–788

My executors may invest my estate in any investments they could make if they owned my estate personally. In particular, they may:

(a) invest in unsecured loans, including interest-free loans to a beneficiary;

(b) invest in land, whether as an investment or as a residence for a beneficiary, and may improve and maintain it;

(c) invest jointly with another person;

(d) invest in wasting or non-income-producing assets;

(e) invest anywhere in the world; and

(f) choose not to diversify investments.

6–789 8 EXCLUSION OF THE APPORTIONMENT RULES

(a) My executors may treat income as arising on the day it is received.
(b) The Apportionment Act 1870 does not apply.
(c) The rules known as "the rule in *Howe v. Dartmouth*" and "the rule in *Allhusen v. Whittell*" do not apply.

6–790 9 EXCLUSION OF S.11 TLATA

My executors may exercise their powers without consulting beneficiaries, so section 11 of the Trusts of Land and Appointment of Trustees Act 1996 does not apply.

6–791 10 POWER OF ADVANCEMENT

My executors may apply the share of any beneficiary for $/{his$//her$//his or her$/} benefit, and this power:

(a) is in addition to any other powers my executors may have, in particular section 32 of the Trustee Act 1925;
(b) applies to the whole or part of the beneficiary's share;
(c) applies whether the beneficiary's right is vested, contingent, expectant or presumptive but not where another person is entitled in priority;
(d) may be used for advancement, maintenance, education or any other benefit;
(e) may be exercised by paying the share to a third party or, where appropriate, to the beneficiary direct.

6–792 11 POWER OF APPROPRIATION

My executors may give specific assets of my estate to beneficiaries without requiring consent. (Section 41 of the Administration of Estates Act 1925 therefore applies subject to that amendment.)

6–793 12 POWER OF INSURANCE

My executors may:

(a) keep any assets of my estate insured, against any risk and in any amount;
(b) pay insurance premiums from the income or capital of that part of my estate which is held on the same trusts as the insured property; and
(c) treat any insurance money received as though it were the proceeds of sale of the insured property.

6–794 13 EXCLUSION OF EXECUTORS' LIABILITY

(a) Only a professional executor or trustee can be liable for any loss arising from:

(i) exercising, or failing to exercise, any discretion or power;

282

    (ii) any improper investment made in good faith;

    (iii) the negligence or fraud of any agent employed by him, or by any other executor or trustee, even if the employment was not strictly necessary or expedient;

    (iv) any mistake or omission made in good faith;

    (v) any other matter, except wilful and individual fraud on the part of the executor or trustee who is sought to be made liable.

(b) No executor can be liable for any loss, of any kind, if he has acted in accordance with the advice of Counsel of at least five years' standing.

14 TRUST CORPORATIONS 6–795

If a trust corporation is appointed as executor or trustee, it may:

(a) act by its proper officers;

(b) exercise all the powers given to executors or trustees by my will;

(c) charge under its published scale of fees, as amended from time to time;

(d) meet its charges out of capital or income, at its discretion.

15 POWER TO USE NOMINEES 6–796

My executors may vest any asset of my estate in the name of, or under the control of:

(a) one or more of their number; or

(b) any person (which may include a trust corporation), or people, as nominee(s).

16 POWER TO CHARGE FOR PROFESSIONAL SERVICES 6–797

Any of my executors who is engaged in a profession or business may charge fees for work done by him or her, or by his or her firm, in connection with my estate and its trusts, including acts which an executor or trustee not being in any profession or business could have done personally, and those charges shall be a first charge against my estate, without abatement.

17 COMMORIENTES 6–798

My estate is to be divided as if any person who dies within one month of my death had predeceased me.

18 ACCUMULATIONS OF INCOME 6–799

My executors may:

(a) within 21 years of my death, accumulate income to the extent that it is not paid to, or applied for the benefit of, any beneficiary; and

(b) apply accumulated income as if it were the income of the current year.

6–800 19 POWER TO BORROW

(a) My executors may borrow money for any purpose.
(b) My executors may charge any assets of my estate as security for any liability.

6–801 20 POWER OF DELEGATION

My executors may delegate any of their functions, in writing, to:

(a) one or more of their number; or
(b) any other person;

and if they do so my executors are not personally liable to my estate for the defaults of that delegate.

6–802 21 INDEMNITIES

My executors may indemnify a retiring trustee, or any other person, against any liability concerning my estate. If they do so, then my estate (not my executors personally) will bear the liability of that indemnity. My executors may charge the indemnity on assets of my estate.

6–803 22 MINOR'S RECEIPT

where a person is a minor (that is:

(I)   under 18; or
(II) 18 or over, but not of an age to be entitled to capital outright);

my executors may pay money to which he or she becomes entitled, whether:

(i) income or capital; or
(ii) as of right or under a power;

to any the following, and in each case their receipt is a complete discharge:

(A) the minor, if he or she has attained 16;
(B) the minor's parent or guardian, in which case my executors are under no further obligation to enquire into the use of the money; or
(C) a third party for the benefit of the minor;

or my executors may resolve to hold the money on trust for the minor absolutely (in which case the administrative provisions of my will continue to apply to the money).

6–804 23 CONFLICTS OF INTEREST

My executors may exercise (or fail to exercise) any powers in my will, even if one or more of them has a personal interest in the outcome.

6–805 24 USE OF EXECUTORS' POWERS

My executors may exercise any of their powers:

(a) from time to time; and
(b) at their absolute discretion.

25 DEFINITION OF "CHILDREN" 6–806

In my will, "children":

    (a) includes those who are legitimate, illegitimate or adopted; but

    (b) does not include step-children, nor natural children who have been adopted by another person;

and other terms describing family relationships are to be interpreted accordingly.

SIGNATURES 6–807

Signed by me on .... 20$/

Signature of Testator

Signed by $/ in our joint presence and then by us in $/{his$///hers$/}
                   Witness 1   Witness 2

Signature:

Full name:

Address:

Occupation:

132b Life interest in house, remainder to testator's own children, residue to survivor substituting families half and half (STEP powers)

This is the last will of me $/ of $/.   6–808

1 REVOCATION 6–809

I revoke all former wills.

2 APPOINTMENT OF EXECUTORS 6–810

I appoint $/ $/[and $/$/] to be my $/{executor$///executors$/} but if $/{he is$/// she is$///both of them are$///either of them is$///all of them are$///any of them is$/} unable or unwilling to act then I appoint $/ instead.

3 GIFT OF CONTENTS 6–811

    (a) In this clause and the next (4):

        (i) "the life tenant" means $/;

        (ii) "the property" means $/ or any other property which I own as my main residence at my death; and

        (iii) "personal chattels" has the meaning given in section 55(1)(x) of the Administration of Estates Act 1925, but does not include chattels which are the subject of specific gifts.

(b) I give all my personal chattels which are situated in the property at my death to the life tenant.

6–812 4 LIFE INTEREST IN HOUSE

(a) In this clause:
  (i) "my trustees" means my executors or the trustees for the time being of this clause; and
  (ii) "the trust fund" means all my interest in the property, and the assets representing it from time to time.

(b) My trustees have all the powers given to executors by my will.

(c) I give the trust fund to my trustees on trust to pay the income to the life tenant during $/{his$//her$/} lifetime.

(d) While the trust fund contains a dwelling occupied by the life tenant as a home, the life tenant must comply with the following conditions:
  (i) the life tenant must pay all outgoings;
  (ii) the life tenant must keep the dwelling in good repair;
  (iii) the life tenant must keep the dwelling insured to its full reinstatement value, with an insurance company approved by my trustees, at the life tenant's expense.

(e) On the failure of the above trusts, my executors must hold the trust fund:

(f) to divide the residue equally between those of my children who are living at the death of the survivor of:
  (i) me; and
  (ii) the life tenant

  except:

(g) if any of my children dies before the survivor of me and the life tenant, then to divide that child's share equally between those of his or her children who are living at the death of the survivor of me and the life tenant and attain $/{18$//21$/}

6–813 5 BURDEN OF INHERITANCE TAX

If inheritance tax, or any other form of death duty, is payable on my free estate then my executors must pay it from the residue of my estate.

6–814 6 RESIDUE

I give to my executors:
  (I) the rest of my estate, anywhere in the world; and
  (II) any property over which I have a general power of appointment;
to hold it on trust:

  (a) to pay my debts, taxes and funeral and testamentary expenses;
  (b) to pay the residue to my $/{husband$//wife$/} $/ absolutely if $/{he$//she$/} survives me by 28 days; but if this gift fails
  (c) to divide the residue into two equal shares and to pay;

    (i) one share to those of my children who are living at my death $/[and attain $/{18$//21$/}$/]; and

286

(ii) one share to those of the children of my $/{husband$// wife$/} who are living at my death$/[and attain $/{18$//21$/} $/]; except

(d) if any of the beneficiaries above die before me, then to divide his or her share equally between those of his or her children who are living at my death and attain $/{18$//21$/}; and

(e) if any of them dies after me, but before attaining $/{18$//21$/}then to divide his or her share equally between those of his or her children who are living at his or her death and attain $/{18$//21$/};

(f) if either of the above shares fails entirely then the failed share accrues to the other.

7 TECHNICAL CLAUSES 6–815

(a) The Standard Provisions of the Society of Trust and Estate Practitioners (1st edition) apply, amended as follows:

(i) Standard provision 5 ("trust for sale") does not apply.
(ii) My executors may exercise their powers without consulting beneficiaries, so section 11 of the Trusts of Land and Appointment of Trustees Act 1996 does not apply.

(b) In my will, "children":

(i) includes those who are legitimate, illegitimate or adopted; but
(ii) does not include step-children, nor natural children who have been adopted by another person;

and other terms describing family relationships are to be interpreted accordingly.

(c) My estate is to be divided as if any person who dies within one month of my death had predeceased me.

SIGNATURES 6–816

Signed by me on .... 20$/
Signature of Testator

Signed by $/ in our joint presence and then by us in $/{his$//hers$/}
      Witness 1   Witness 2

Signature:

Full name:

Address:

Occupation:

133 Legacy to testator's own children, residue to survivor, substitution of both families equally

133a Complete powers

6–817 This is the last will of me $/ of $/.

6–818 1 REVOCATION

I revoke all former wills.

6–819 2 APPOINTMENT OF EXECUTORS

I appoint $/ $/[and $/$/] to be my $/{executor$//executors$/} but if $/{he is$// she is$//both of them are$//either of them is$//all of them are$//any of them is$/} unable or unwilling to act then I appoint $/ instead.

6–820 3 LEGACIES

(a) I give, free of inheritance tax, the sum of £$/ to those of my children who are living at my death equally; except

(b) If any of my children dies before me then to divide that child's share equally between those of his or her children who are living at my death and attain $/{18$//21$//25$/}.

6–821 4 BURDEN OF INHERITANCE TAX

If inheritance tax, or any other form of death duty, is payable on my free estate then my executors must pay it from the residue of my estate.

6–822 5 RESIDUE

I give to my executors:

(I) the rest of my estate, anywhere in the world; and

(II) any property over which I have a general power of appointment;

to hold it on trust:

(a) to pay my debts, taxes and funeral and testamentary expenses;

(b) to pay the residue to my $/{husband$//wife$/} $/ absolutely if $/{he$//she$/} survives me by 28 days; but if this gift fails

(c) to divide the residue into two equal shares and to pay;

(i) one share to those of my children who are living at my death; and

(ii) one share to those of the children of my $/{husband$// wife$/} who are living at my death; except

(d) if any of the beneficiaries above die before me, then to divide his or her share equally between those of his or her children who are living at my death and attain $/{18$//21$/};

(e) if either of the above shares fails entirely then the failed share accrues to the other;

6 POWER OF INVESTMENT 6–823

My executors may invest my estate in any investments they could make if they owned my estate personally. In particular, they may:

(a) invest in unsecured loans, including interest-free loans to a beneficiary;
(b) invest in land, whether as an investment or as a residence for a beneficiary, and may improve and maintain it;
(c) invest jointly with another person;
(d) invest in wasting or non-income-producing assets;
(e) invest anywhere in the world; and
(f) choose not to diversify investments.

7 EXCLUSION OF S.11 TLATA 6–824

My executors may exercise their powers without consulting beneficiaries, so section 11 of the Trusts of Land and Appointment of Trustees Act 1996 does not apply.

8 POWER OF ADVANCEMENT 6–825

My executors may apply the share of any beneficiary for $/{his$//her$//his or her$/} benefit, and this power:

(a) is in addition to any other powers my executors may have, in particular section 32 of the Trustee Act 1925;
(b) applies to the whole or part of the beneficiary's share;
(c) applies whether the beneficiary's right is vested, contingent, expectant or presumptive but not where another person is entitled in priority;
(d) may be used for advancement, maintenance, education or any other benefit;
(e) may be exercised by paying the share to a third party or, where appropriate, to the beneficiary direct.

9 POWER OF APPROPRIATION 6–826

My executors may give specific assets of my estate to beneficiaries without requiring consent. (Section 41 of the Administration of Estates Act 1925 therefore applies subject to that amendment.)

10 POWER OF INSURANCE 6–827

My executors may:

(a) keep any assets of my estate insured, against any risk and in any amount;
(b) pay insurance premiums from the income or capital of that part of my estate which is held on the same trusts as the insured property; and
(c) treat any insurance money received as though it were the proceeds of sale of the insured property.

6–828 11 EXCLUSION OF EXECUTORS' LIABILITY

   (a) Only a professional executor or trustee can be liable for any loss arising from:

      (i) exercising, or failing to exercise, any discretion or power;

      (ii) any improper investment made in good faith;

      (iii) the negligence or fraud of any agent employed by him, or by any other executor or trustee, even if the employment was not strictly necessary or expedient;

      (iv) any mistake or omission made in good faith;

      (v) any other matter, except wilful and individual fraud on the part of the executor or trustee who is sought to be made liable.

   (b) No executor can be liable for any loss, of any kind, if he has acted in accordance with the advice of Counsel of at least five years' standing.

6–829 12 TRUST CORPORATIONS

If a trust corporation is appointed as executor or trustee, it may:

   (a) act by its proper officers;

   (b) exercise all the powers given to executors or trustees by my will;

   (c) charge under its published scale of fees, as amended from time to time;

   (d) meet its charges out of capital or income, at its discretion.

6–830 13 POWER TO USE NOMINEES

My executors may vest any asset of my estate in the name of, or under the control of:

   (a) one or more of their number; or

   (b) any person (which may include a trust corporation), or people, as nominee(s).

6–831 14 POWER TO CHARGE FOR PROFESSIONAL SERVICES

Any of my executors who is engaged in a profession or business may charge fees for work done by him or her, or by his or her firm, in connection with my estate and its trusts, including acts which an executor or trustee not being in any profession or business could have done personally, and those charges shall be a first charge against my estate, without abatement.

6–832 15 COMMORIENTES

My estate is to be divided as if any person who dies within one month of my death had predeceased me.

6–833 16 ACCUMULATIONS OF INCOME

My executors may:

   (a) within 21 years of my death, accumulate income to the extent that it is not paid to, or applied for the benefit of, any beneficiary; and

(b) apply accumulated income as if it were the income of the current year.

17 POWER OF DELEGATION 6–834

My executors may delegate any of their functions, in writing, to:

(a) one or more of their number; or
(b) any other person;

and if they do so my executors are not personally liable to my estate for the defaults of that delegate.

18 INDEMNITIES 6–835

My executors may indemnify a retiring trustee, or any other person, against any liability concerning my estate. If they do so, then my estate (not my executors personally) will bear the liability of that indemnity. My executors may charge the indemnity on assets of my estate.

19 MINOR'S RECEIPT 6–836

where a person is a minor (that is:
(I) under 18; or
(II) 18 or over, but not of an age to be entitled to capital outright);

my executors may pay money to which he or she becomes entitled, whether:

(i) income or capital; or
(ii) as of right or under a power;

to any the following, and in each case their receipt is a complete discharge:

(A) the minor, if he or she has attained 16;
(B) the minor's parent or guardian, in which case my executors are under no further obligation to enquire into the use of the money; or
(C) a third party for the benefit of the minor;

or my executors may resolve to hold the money on trust for the minor absolutely (in which case the administrative provisions of my will continue to apply to the money).

20 CONFLICTS OF INTEREST 6–837

My executors may exercise (or fail to exercise) any powers in my will, even if one or more of them has a personal interest in the outcome.

21 USE OF EXECUTORS' POWERS 6–838

My executors may exercise any of their powers:

(a) from time to time; and
(b) at their absolute discretion.

6–839 22 DEFINITION OF "CHILDREN"

In my will, "children":

(a) includes those who are legitimate, illegitimate or adopted; but
(b) does not include step-children, nor natural children who have been adopted by another person;

and other terms describing family relationships are to be interpreted accordingly.

6–840 SIGNATURES

Signed by me on .... 20$/

Signature of Testator

Signed by $/ in our joint presence and then by us in $/{his$//hers$/}
        Witness 1   Witness 2

Signature:

Full name:

Address:

Occupation:

133b Legacy to testator's own children, residue to survivor, substitution of both families equally (STEP powers)

6–841 This is the last will of me $/ of $/.

6–842 1 REVOCATION

I revoke all former wills.

6–843 2 APPOINTMENT OF EXECUTORS

I appoint $/ $/[and $/$/] to be my $/{executor$//executors$/} but if $/{he is$// she is$//both of them are$//either of them is$//all of them are$//any of them is$/} unable or unwilling to act then I appoint $/ instead.

6–844 3 LEGACIES

(a) I give, free of inheritance tax, the sum of £$/ to those of my children who are living at my death equally; except
(b) If any of my children dies before me then to divide that child's share equally between those of his or her children who are living at my death and attain $/{18$//21$//25$/}.

6–845 4 BURDEN OF INHERITANCE TAX

If inheritance tax, or any other form of death duty, is payable on my free estate then my executors must pay it from the residue of my estate.

5 RESIDUE 6–846

I give to my executors:

(I) the rest of my estate, anywhere in the world; and
(II) any property over which I have a general power of appointment;

to hold it on trust:
    (a) to pay my debts, taxes and funeral and testamentary expenses;
    (b) to pay the residue to my $/{husband$//wife$/} $/ absolutely if $/{he$//she$/} survives me by 28 days; but if this gift fails
    (c) to divide the residue into two equal shares and to pay;

        (i) one share to those of my children who are living at my death; and
        (ii) one share to those of the children of my $/{husband$//wife$/} who are living at my death; except

    (d) if any of the beneficiaries above die before me, then to divide his or her share equally between those of his or her children who are living at my death and attain $/{18$//21$/};
    (e) if either of the above shares fails entirely then the failed share accrues to the other;

6 TECHNICAL CLAUSES 6–847

    (a) The Standard Provisions of the Society of Trust and Estate Practitioners (1st edition) apply, amended as follows:

        (i) Standard provision 5 ("trust for sale") does not apply.
        (ii) My executors may exercise their powers without consulting beneficiaries, so section 11 of the Trusts of Land and Appointment of Trustees Act 1996 does not apply.

    (b) In my will, "children":

        (i) includes those who are legitimate, illegitimate or adopted; but
        (ii) does not include step-children, nor natural children who have been adopted by another person;

    and other terms describing family relationships are to be interpreted accordingly.
    (c) My estate is to be divided as if any person who dies within one month of my death had predeceased me.

6–848 SIGNATURES

Signed by me on .... 20$/

Signature of Testator

Signed by $/ in our joint presence and then by us in $/{his$//hers$/}

	Witness 1	Witness 2

Signature:

Full name:

Address:

Occupation:

PART 7

WILLS OF BUSINESSMEN

WILLS OF BUSINESSMEN

134 Legacy of business subject to various charges

Note: The situation we envisage here is that of a testator who wants to pass **7–001** his or her business on to one of the children (who intends actively to run it) but who wishes to subject the business to various charges for the benefit of other members of the family.

The type of charges which could be applied are:

(a) a delayed legacy to a member of the family, for one of two purposes:

   (i) as necessary provision (for example, with a surviving spouse); or

   (ii) as compensation (for example to another child who is not receiving an interest in the business);

(b) an annuity to the surviving spouse to provide for her ongoing maintenance; or

(c) an interest in the business to be given to a child who has not yet attained his majority.

When drafting using this precedent it is necessary to delete some of "the charges on the business" as defined the will.

It is also important for the testator to consider how much financial burden he can put on his business in this way. The underlying purpose of the clause will in reality be defeated if the charges prove too much for the business to bear and it is forced to fold.

134a Legacy of business subject to various charges (complete powers)

This is the last will of me $/ of $/.   **7–002**

1 REVOCATION   **7–003**

I revoke all former wills.

2 APPOINTMENT OF EXECUTORS   **7–004**

I appoint $/ $/[and $/$/] to be my $/{executor$//executors$/} but if $/{he is$// she is$//both of them are$//either of them is$//all of them are$//any of them is$/} unable or unwilling to act then I appoint $/ instead.

7–005 3 APPOINTMENT OF GUARDIANS

(a) $/[If at my death I am the sole surviving parent, $/] I appoint $/ $/[and $/ $/] to be the ${guardian$//guardians$/} of any of my children who are under 18

(b) If ${he is$//she is$//either of them is$//both of them are$//any of them is$//all of them are$/} unable or unwilling to act then I appoint $/ $/[and $/ $/] instead

7–006 4 DEFINITIONS

In the next clause (headed "Gift of Business Subject to Charges"):

(a) **"the business"** means;

  (i) ${my business of $/ carried on by me at $/$//$/ Ltd.$//all my shares in $/ Ltd.$/};

  (ii) all assets of mine used in the business;

  (iii) $/[all my interest in the premesis at $/$/]; and

  (iv) all loans due to my from the ${business$//company$/}

(b) **"the charges on the business"** means

  (i) a gross annuity of £$/ per annum payable to $/.

  (ii) the sum of £$/ payable to $/ within $/ ${months$//years$/} of my death.

  (iii) a sum equal to $/% of the net value of the business at the date of payment, payable to $/ within $/ ${months$//years$/} of my death.

  (iv) a sum equal to $/% of the net value of the business at the date of payment, payable to $/ if ${he$//she$/} attains ${18$//21$//25$/}.

  (v) a sum equal to $/% of the net value of the business at the date of payment, payable to $/ if ${he$//she$/} attains ${18$//21$//25$/} or, at $/'s discretion, the option for $/ to enter the business as an ${equal$//$/%$/} ${partner$//shareholder$/}.

$/[Where, above, a value is required at "the date of payment", a valuation must be made by my executors, taking appropriate professional advice, and if there is no material change in the circumstances of the business such a valuation will be deemed to be the true valuation for three months from the date on which it is made. $/]

7–007 5 GIFT OF BUSINESS SUBJECT TO CHARGES

I give the business to $/ absolutely if (and only if) ${he enters$//she enters$// they enter$/} into a deed of covenant or contract which will, to the reasonable satisfaction of my executors, secure the charges on the business.

7–008 6 BURDEN OF INHERITANCE TAX

If inheritance tax, or any other form of death duty, is payable on my free estate then my executors must pay it from the residue of my estate.

7 RESIDUE   7–009

I give to my executors:
    (I) the rest of my estate, anywhere in the world; and
    (II) any property over which I have a general power of appointment;

to hold it on trust:

    (a) to pay my debts, taxes and funeral and testamentary expenses;
    (b) to pay the residue to my $/{husband$//wife$/} $/ absolutely if $/{he$//she$/} survives me by 28 days; but if this gift fails
    (c) to divide the residue equally between those of my children who are living at my death and attain $/{18$//21$/}; except:

        (i) if any of my children dies before me, then to divide that child's share equally between those of his or her children who are living at my death and attain $/{18$//21$/}; and
        (ii) if any of my children dies after me, but before attaining $/{18$//21$/}, then to divide that child's share equally between those of his or her children who are living at his or her death and attain $/{18$//21$/}.

8 POWER OF INVESTMENT   7–010

My executors may invest my estate in any investments they could make if they owned my estate personally. In particular, they may:

    (a) invest in unsecured loans, including interest-free loans to a beneficiary;
    (b) invest in land, whether as an investment or as a residence for a beneficiary, and may improve and maintain it;
    (c) invest jointly with another person;
    (d) invest in wasting or non-income-producing assets;
    (e) invest anywhere in the world; and
    (f) choose not to diversify investments.

9 EXCLUSION OF S.11 TLATA   7–011

My executors may exercise their powers without consulting beneficiaries, so section 11 of the Trusts of Land and Appointment of Trustees Act 1996 does not apply.

10 POWER OF ADVANCEMENT   7–012

My executors may apply the share of any beneficiary for $/{his$//her$//his or her$/} benefit, and this power:

    (a) is in addition to any other powers my executors may have, in particular section 32 of the Trustee Act 1925;
    (b) applies to the whole or part of the beneficiary's share;
    (c) applies whether the beneficiary's right is vested, contingent, expectant or presumptive but not where another person is entitled in priority;
    (d) may be used for advancement, maintenance, education or any other benefit;

(e) may be exercised by paying the share to a third party or, where appropriate, to the beneficiary direct.

7–013 11 POWER OF APPROPRIATION

My executors may give specific assets of my estate to beneficiaries without requiring consent. (Section 41 of the Administration of Estates Act 1925 therefore applies subject to that amendment.)

7–014 12 POWER OF INSURANCE

My executors may:

(a) keep any assets of my estate insured, against any risk and in any amount;
(b) pay insurance premiums from the income or capital of that part of my estate which is held on the same trusts as the insured property; and
(c) treat any insurance money received as though it were the proceeds of sale of the insured property.

7–015 13 EXCLUSION OF EXECUTORS' LIABILITY

(a) Only a professional executor or trustee can be liable for any loss arising from:
   (i) exercising, or failing to exercise, any discretion or power;
   (ii) any improper investment made in good faith;
   (iii) the negligence or fraud of any agent employed by him, or by any other executor or trustee, even if the employment was not strictly necessary or expedient;
   (iv) any mistake or omission made in good faith;
   (v) any other matter, except wilful and individual fraud on the part of the executor or trustee who is sought to be made liable.

(b) No executor can be liable for any loss, of any kind, if he has acted in accordance with the advice of Counsel of at least five years' standing.

7–016 14 TRUST CORPORATIONS

If a trust corporation is appointed as executor or trustee, it may:

(a) act by its proper officers;
(b) exercise all the powers given to executors or trustees by my will;
(c) charge under its published scale of fees, as amended from time to time;
(d) meet its charges out of capital or income, at its discretion.

7–017 15 POWER TO USE NOMINEES

My executors may vest any asset of my estate in the name of, or under the control of:

(a) one or more of their number; or
(b) any person (which may include a trust corporation), or people, as nominee(s).

16 POWER TO CHARGE FOR PROFESSIONAL SERVICES 7–018

Any of my executors who is engaged in a profession or business may charge fees for work done by him or her, or by his or her firm, in connection with my estate and its trusts, including acts which an executor or trustee not being in any profession or business could have done personally, and those charges shall be a first charge against my estate, without abatement.

17 COMMORIENTES 7–019

My estate is to be divided as if any person who dies within one month of my death had predeceased me.

18 ACCUMULATIONS OF INCOME 7–020

My executors may:

(a) within 21 years of my death, accumulate income to the extent that it is not paid to, or applied for the benefit of, any beneficiary; and
(b) apply accumulated income as if it were the income of the current year.

19 POWER OF DELEGATION 7–021

My executors may delegate any of their functions, in writing, to:

(a) one or more of their number; or
    any other person;
(b) and if they do so my executors are not personally liable to my estate for the defaults of that delegate.

20 INDEMNITIES 7–022

My executors may indemnify a retiring trustee, or any other person, against any liability concerning my estate. If they do so, then my estate (not my executors personally) will bear the liability of that indemnity. My executors may charge the indemnity on assets of my estate.

21 MINOR'S RECEIPT 7–023

where a person is a minor (that is:

(a) under 18; or
(b) 18 or over, but not of an age to be entitled to capital outright);

my executors may pay money to which he or she becomes entitled, whether:

(i) income or capital; or
(ii) as of right or under a power;

to any the following, and in each case their receipt is a complete discharge:

(A) the minor, if he or she has attained 16;
(B) the minor's parent or guardian, in which case my executors are under no further obligation to enquire into the use of the money; or

(C) a third party for the benefit of the minor;

or my executors may resolve to hold the money on trust for the minor absolutely (in which case the administrative provisions of my will continue to apply to the money).

7–024   22 CONFLICT OF INTEREST

My executors may exercise (or fail to exercise) any powers in my will, even if one or more of them has a personal interest in the outcome.

7–025   23 USE OF EXECUTORS' POWERS

My executors may exercise any of their powers:

(a) from time to time; and
(b) at their absolute discretion.

7–026   24 POWER NOT TO INTERFERE IN THE MANAGEMENT OF A BUSINESS

My executors may choose not to interfere in the management (or conduct) of any business, company or corporation over which my executors have any level of control. If they are not aware of any wrongdoing on the part of the directors of a company, my executors may leave:

(a) the conduct of the business; and
(b) the decision whether to declare a dividend, and its amount;

to those directors. My executors are not liable to my estate for any action they take, or fail to take, in reliance on this clause.

7–027   25 POWER TO ACT AS OFFICER OR EMPLOYEE

Any executor may act personally as an officer, or employee, of any company in which my estate is interested. An executor who does so may retain personally any remuneration received. This is so even if:

(a) my executor having chosen to exercise (or not to exercise) rights over shares in my estate may have been instrumental in procuring the position as officer or employee; or
(b) my executor's qualifications for the position may be constituted (in part or in whole) by the holding in my estate.

7–028   26 POWER TO RUN A BUSINESS

My executors may carry on any business in which I am engaged at my death. If they do so then they may:

(a) carry on the business either alone or in partnership with any other people (and whether as general partners or limited partners);
(b) act upon such terms as they think fit, and as if they were the beneficial owners absolutely entitled;
(c) employ any of the capital of my estate in the business, including capitalising financing (by loans, guarantees or otherwise);

(d) employ anyone in connection with the business on such terms as they think fit;

(e) promote a company or corporation in any part of the world to acquire the business (or part of it) by the issue to my trustees of shares or securities or otherwise;

(f) pay, out of any property held upon the same trusts as the business, the cost of promoting such a company or corporation, and of the transfer of the business to it;

and my executors are indemnified, out of any property held upon the same trusts as the business, against any personal liability which they incur in connection with the business (unless that liability arose by reason of their own wilful and individual fraud or wrongdoing)

27 TREATMENT OF BUSINESS PROFITS 7–029

The net profits of any business in my estate are to be treated *as if* they were the income which would arise from investments representing the proceeds of sale of the business, if it were sold.

28 DEFINITION OF "CHILDREN" 7–030

In my will, "children":

(a) includes those who are legitimate, illegitimate or adopted; but

(b) does not include step-children, nor natural children who have been adopted by another person;

and other terms describing family relationships are to be interpreted accordingly.

SIGNATURES 7–031

Signed by me on . . . . 20$/

Signature of Testator

Signed by $/ in our joint presence and then by us in $/{his$//hers$/}
                Witness 1   Witness 2

Signature:

Full name:

Address:

Occupation:

134b Legacy of business subject to various charges (STEP powers)

This is the last will of me $/ of $/. 7–032

1 REVOCATION 7–033

I revoke all former wills.

7–034 2 APPOINTMENT OF EXECUTORS

I appoint $/ $/[and $/$/] to be my $/{executor$//executors$/} but if $/{he is$// she is$//both of them are$//either of them is$//all of them are$//any of them is$/} unable or unwilling to act then I appoint $/ instead.

7–035 3 APPOINTMENT OF GUARDIANS

(a) $/[If at my death I am the sole surviving parent, $/] I appoint $/ $/[and $/ $/] to be the $/{guardian$//guardians$/} of any of my children who are under 18

(b) If $/{he is$//she is$//either of them is$//both of them are$//any of them is$//all of them are$/} unable or unwilling to act then I appoint $/ $/[and $/ $/] instead

7–036 4 DEFINITIONS

In the next clause (headed "Gift of Business Subject to Charges"):

(a) "the business" means;

(i) $/{my business of $/ carried on by me at $/$//$/ Ltd.$//all my shares in $/ Ltd.$/};

(ii) all assets of mine used in the business;

(iii) $/[all my interest in the premesis at $/$/]; and

(iv) all loans due to my from the $/{business$//company$/}

(b) "the charges on the business" means

(i) a gross annuity of £$/ per annum payable to $/.

(ii) the sum of £$/ payable to $/ within $/ $/{months$//years$/} of my death.

(iii) a sum equal to $/% of the net value of the business at the date of payment, payable to $/ within $/ $/{months$//years$/} of my death.

(iv) a sum equal to $/% of the net value of the business at the date of payment, payable to $/ if $/{he$//she$/} attains $/{18$//21$//25$/}.

(v) a sum equal to $/% of the net value of the business at the date of payment, payable to $/ if $/{he$//she$/} attains $/{18$//21$//25$/} or, at $/'s discretion, the option for $/ to enter the business as an $/{equal$//$/%$/} $/{partner$//shareholder$/}.

$/[Where, above, a value is required at "the date of payment", a valuation must be made by my executors, taking appropriate professional advice, and if there is no material change in the circumstances of the business such a valuation will be deemed to be the true valuation for three months from the date on which it is made. $/]

7–037 5 GIFT OF BUSINESS SUBJECT TO CHARGES

I give the business to $/ absolutely if (and only if) $/{he enters$//she enters$// they enter$/} into a deed of covenant or contract which will, to the reasonable satisfaction of my executors, secure the charges on the business.

7–038 6 BURDEN OF INHERITANCE TAX

If inheritance tax, or any other form of death duty, is payable on my free estate then my executors must pay it from the residue of my estate.

7 RESIDUE

7–039

I give to my executors:
- (I) the rest of my estate, anywhere in the world; and
- (II) any property over which I have a general power of appointment;

to hold it on trust:
- (a) to pay my debts, taxes and funeral and testamentary expenses;
- (b) to pay the residue to my $/{husband$//wife$/} $/ absolutely if $/{he$//she$/} survives me by 28 days; but if this gift fails
- (c) to divide the residue equally between those of my children who are living at my death and attain $/{18$//21$/}; except:
    - (i) if any of my children dies before me, then to divide that child's share equally between those of his or her children who are living at my death and attain $/{18$//21$/}; and
    - (ii) if any of my children dies after me, but before attaining $/{18$//21$/}, then to divide that child's share equally between those of his or her children who are living at his or her death and attain $/{18$//21$/}.

8 TECHNICAL CLAUSES

7–040

- (a) The Standard Provisions of the Society of Trust and Estate Practitioners (1st edition) apply, amended as follows:
    - (i) Standard provision 5 ("trust for sale") does not apply.
    - (ii) My executors may exercise their powers without consulting beneficiaries, so section 11 of the Trusts of Land and Appointment of Trustees Act 1996 does not apply.

- (b) In my will, "children":
    - (i) includes those who are legitimate, illegitimate or adopted; but
    - (ii) does not include step-children, nor natural children who have been adopted by another person;

    and other terms describing family relationships are to be interpreted accordingly.

- (c) My estate is to be divided as if any person who dies within one month of my death had predeceased me.

9 POWER TO ACT AS OFFICER OR EMPLOYEE

7–041

Any executor may act personally as an officer, or employee, of any company in which my estate is interested. An executor who does so may retain personally any remuneration received. This is so even if:

- (a) my executor having chosen to exercise (or not to exercise) rights over shares in my estate may have been instrumental in procuring the position as officer or employee; or
- (b) my executor's qualifications for the position may be constituted (in part or in whole) by the holding in my estate.

7-042 10 POWER TO RUN A BUSINESS

My executors may carry on any business in which I am engaged at my death. If they do so then they may:

(a) carry on the business either alone or in partnership with any other people (and whether as general partners or limited partners);

(b) act upon such terms as they think fit, and as if they were the beneficial owners absolutely entitled;

(c) employ any of the capital of my estate in the business, including capitalising financing (by loans, guarantees or otherwise);

(d) employ anyone in connection with the business on such terms as they think fit;

(e) promote a company or corporation in any part of the world to acquire the business (or part of it) by the issue to my trustees of shares or securities or otherwise;

(f) pay, out of any property held upon the same trusts as the business, the cost of promoting such a company or corporation, and of the transfer of the business to it;

and my executors are indemnified, out of any property held upon the same trusts as the business, against any personal liability which they incur in connection with the business (unless that liability arose by reason of their own wilful and individual fraud or wrongdoing)

7-043 11 TREATMENT OF BUSINESS PROFITS

The net profits of any business in my estate are to be treated as if they were the income which would arise from investments representing the proceeds of sale of the business, if it were sold.

7-044 SIGNATURES

Signed by me on .... 20$/

Signature of Testator

Signed by $/ in our joint presence and then by us in $/{his$//hers$/}
Witness 1   Witness 2

Signature:

Full name:

Address:

Occupation:

135 Legacy of business outright

135a Complete powers

7-045 This is the last will of me $/ of $/.

1 REVOCATION

I revoke all former wills.

2 APPOINTMENT OF EXECUTORS

I appoint $/ $/[and $/$/] to be my $/{executor$//executors$/} but if $/{he is$//she is$//both of them are$//either of them is$//all of them are$//any of them is$/} unable or unwilling to act then I appoint $/ instead.

3 APPOINTMENT OF GUARDIANS

(a) $/[If at my death I am the sole surviving parent, $/] I appoint $/ $/[and $/ $/] to be the $/{guardian$//guardians$/} of any of my children who are under 18

(b) If $/{he is$//she is$//either of them is$//both of them are$//any of them is$//all of them are$/} unable or unwilling to act then I appoint $/ $/[and $/ $/] instead

4 GIFT OF BUSINESS

(a) I give my business to $/ absolutely.

(b) In this clause "my business" means;

(i) $/{my business of $/ carried on by me at $/$//$/ Ltd.$//all my shares in $/ Ltd.$/};

(ii) all assets of mine used in the business;

(iii) $/[all my interest in the premises at $/$/]; and

(iv) all loans due to my from the $/{business$//company$/}.

5 BURDEN OF INHERITANCE TAX

If inheritance tax, or any other form of death duty, is payable on my free estate then my executors must pay it from the residue of my estate.

6 RESIDUE

I give to my executors:

(I) the rest of my estate, anywhere in the world; and

(II) any property over which I have a general power of appointment;

to hold it on trust:

(a) to pay my debts, taxes and funeral and testamentary expenses;

(b) to pay the residue to my $/{husband$//wife$/} $/ absolutely if $/{he$//she$/} survives me by 28 days; but if this gift fails

(c) to divide the residue equally between those of my children who are living at my death and attain $/{18$//21$/}; except:

(i) if any of my children dies before me, then to divide that child's share equally between those of his or her children who are living at my death and attain $/{18$//21$/}; and

(ii) if any of my children dies after me, but before attaining $/{18$//21$/}, then to divide that child's share equally between those of his or her children who are living at his or her death and attain $/{18$//21$/}.

7–052 7 POWER OF INVESTMENT

My executors may invest my estate in any investments they could make if they owned my estate personally. In particular, they may:

(a) invest in unsecured loans, including interest-free loans to a beneficiary;
(b) invest in land, whether as an investment or as a residence for a beneficiary, and may improve and maintain it;
(c) invest jointly with another person;
(d) invest in wasting or non-income-producing assets;
(e) invest anywhere in the world; and
(f) choose not to diversify investments.

7–053 8 EXCLUSION OF S.11 TLATA

My executors may exercise their powers without consulting beneficiaries, so section 11 of the Trusts of Land and Appointment of Trustees Act 1996 does not apply.

7–054 9 POWER OF ADVANCEMENT

My executors may apply the share of any beneficiary for $/{his$//her$//his or her$/} benefit, and this power:

(a) is in addition to any other powers my executors may have, in particular section 32 of the Trustee Act 1925;
(b) applies to the whole or part of the beneficiary's share;
(c) applies whether the beneficiary's right is vested, contingent, expectant or presumptive but not where another person is entitled in priority;
(d) may be used for advancement, maintenance, education or any other benefit;
(e) may be exercised by paying the share to a third party or, where appropriate, to the beneficiary direct.

7–055 10 POWER OF APPROPRIATION

My executors may give specific assets of my estate to beneficiaries without requiring consent. (Section 41 of the Administration of Estates Act 1925 therefore applies subject to that amendment.)

7–056 11 POWER OF INSURANCE

My executors may:

(a) keep any assets of my estate insured, against any risk and in any amount;
(b) pay insurance premiums from the income or capital of that part of my estate which is held on the same trusts as the insured property; and
(c) treat any insurance money received as though it were the proceeds of sale of the insured property.

12 EXCLUSION OF EXECUTORS' LIABILITY   7–057

(a) Only a professional executor or trustee can be liable for any loss arising from:

    (i) exercising, or failing to exercise, any discretion or power;

    (ii) any improper investment made in good faith;

    (iii) the negligence or fraud of any agent employed by him, or by any other executor or trustee, even if the employment was not strictly necessary or expedient;

    (iv) any mistake or omission made in good faith;

    (v) any other matter, except wilful and individual fraud on the part of the executor or trustee who is sought to be made liable.

(b) No executor can be liable for any loss, of any kind, if he has acted in accordance with the advice of Counsel of at least five years' standing.

13 TRUST CORPORATIONS   7–058

If a trust corporation is appointed as executor or trustee, it may:

(a) act by its proper officers;

(b) exercise all the powers given to executors or trustees by my will;

(c) charge under its published scale of fees, as amended from time to time;

(d) meet its charges out of capital or income, at its discretion.

14 POWER TO USE NOMINEES   7–059

My executors may vest any asset of my estate in the name of, or under the control of:

(a) one or more of their number; or

(b) any person (which may include a trust corporation), or people, as nominee(s).

15 POWER TO CHARGE FOR PROFESSIONAL SERVICES   7–060

Any of my executors who is engaged in a profession or business may charge fees for work done by him or her, or by his or her firm, in connection with my estate and its trusts, including acts which an executor or trustee not being in any profession or business could have done personally, and those charges shall be a first charge against my estate, without abatement.

16 COMMORIENTES   7–061

My estate is to be divided as if any person who dies within one month of my death had predeceased me.

17 ACCUMULATIONS OF INCOME   7–062

My executors may:

(a) within 21 years of my death, accumulate income to the extent that it is not paid to, or applied for the benefit of, any beneficiary; and

(b) apply accumulated income as if it were the income of the current year.

7–063 18 POWER OF DELEGATION

My executors may delegate any of their functions, in writing, to:

(a) one or more of their number; or
(b) any other person;

and if they do so my executors are not personally liable to my estate for the defaults of that delegate.

7–064 19 INDEMNITIES

My executors may indemnify a retiring trustee, or any other person, against any liability concerning my estate. If they do so, then my estate (not my executors personally) will bear the liability of that indemnity. My executors may charge the indemnity on assets of my estate.

7–065 20 MINOR'S RECEIPT

where a person is a minor (that is:

(a) under 18; or
(b) 18 or over, but not of an age to be entitled to capital outright);

my executors may pay money to which he or she becomes entitled, whether:

(i) income or capital; or
(ii) as of right or under a power;

to any the following, and in each case their receipt is a complete discharge:

(A) the minor, if he or she has attained 16;
(B) the minor's parent or guardian, in which case my executors are under no further obligation to enquire into the use of the money; or
(C) a third party for the benefit of the minor;

or my executors may resolve to hold the money on trust for the minor absolutely (in which case the administrative provisions of my will continue to apply to the money).

7–066 21 CONFLICT OF INTEREST

My executors may exercise (or fail to exercise) any powers in my will, even if one or more of them has a personal interest in the outcome.

7–067 22 USE OF EXECUTORS' POWERS

My executors may exercise any of their powers:

(a) from time to time; and
(b) at their absolute discretion.

23 POWER NOT TO INTERFERE IN THE MANAGEMENT OF A BUSINESS

My executors may choose not to interfere in the management (or conduct) of any business, company or corporation over which my executors have any level of control. If they are not aware of any wrongdoing on the part of the directors of a company, my executors may leave:

(a) the conduct of the business; and

(b) the decision whether to declare a dividend, and its amount;

to those directors. My executors are not liable to my estate for any action they take, or fail to take, in reliance on this clause.

24 POWER TO ACT AS OFFICER OR EMPLOYEE

Any executor may act personally as an officer, or employee, of any company in which my estate is interested. An executor who does so may retain personally any remuneration received. This is so even if:

(a) my executor having chosen to exercise (or not to exercise) rights over shares in my estate may have been instrumental in procuring the position as officer or employee; or

(b) my executor's qualifications for the position may be constituted (in part or in whole) by the holding in my estate.

25 POWER TO RUN A BUSINESS

My executors may carry on any business in which I am engaged at my death. If they do so then they may:

(a) carry on the business either alone or in partnership with any other people (and whether as general partners or limited partners);

(b) act upon such terms as they think fit, and as if they were the beneficial owners absolutely entitled;

(c) employ any of the capital of my estate in the business, including capitalising financing (by loans, guarantees or otherwise);

(d) employ anyone in connection with the business on such terms as they think fit;

(e) promote a company or corporation in any part of the world to acquire the business (or part of it) by the issue to my trustees of shares or securities or otherwise;

(f) pay, out of any property held upon the same trusts as the business, the cost of promoting such a company or corporation, and of the transfer of the business to it;

and my executors are indemnified, out of any property held upon the same trusts as the business, against any personal liability which they incur in connection with the business (unless that liability arose by reason of their own wilful and individual fraud or wrongdoing)

26 TREATMENT OF BUSINESS PROFITS

The net profits of any business in my estate are to be treated *as if* they were the income which would arise from investments representing the proceeds of sale of the business, if it were sold.

7–072 27 DEFINITION OF "CHILDREN"

In my will, "children":

(a) includes those who are legitimate, illegitimate or adopted; but

(b) does not include step-children, nor natural children who have been adopted by another person;

and other terms describing family relationships are to be interpreted accordingly.

7–073 SIGNATURES

Signed by me on .... 20$/

Signature of Testator

Signed by $/ in our joint presence and then by us in $/{his$//hers$/}
                 Witness 1   Witness 2

Signature:

Full name:

Address:

Occupation:

135b Legacy of business outright (STEP powers)

7–074 This is the last will of me $/ of $/.

7–075 1 REVOCATION

I revoke all former wills.

7–076 2 APPOINTMENT OF EXECUTORS

I appoint $/ $/[and $/$/] to be my $/{executor$//executors$/} but if $/{he is$//she is$//both of them are$//either of them is$//all of them are$//any of them is$/} unable or unwilling to act then I appoint $/ instead.

7–077 3 APPOINTMENT OF GUARDIANS

(a) $/[If at my death I am the sole surviving parent, $/] I appoint $/ $/[and $/ $/] to be the $/{guardian$//guardians$/} of any of my children who are under 18

(b) If $/{he is$//she is$//either of them is$//both of them are$//any of them is$//all of them are$/} unable or unwilling to act then I appoint $/ $/[and $/ $/] instead

4 GIFT OF BUSINESS 7–078

(a) I give my business to $/ absolutely.
(b) In this clause "my business" means;

    (i) $/{my business of $/ carried on by me at $/$//$/ Ltd.$//all my shares in $/ Ltd.$/};
    (ii) all assets of mine used in the business;
    (iii) $/[all my interest in the premises at $/$/]; and
    (iv) all loans due to my from the $/{business$//company$/}.

5 BURDEN OF INHERITANCE TAX 7–079

If inheritance tax, or any other form of death duty, is payable on my free estate then my executors must pay it from the residue of my estate.

6 RESIDUE 7–080

I give to my executors:

    (I) the rest of my estate, anywhere in the world; and
    (II) any property over which I have a general power of appointment;

to hold it on trust:

    (a) to pay my debts, taxes and funeral and testamentary expenses;
    (b) to pay the residue to my $/{husband$//wife$/} $/ absolutely if $/{he$//she$/} survives me by 28 days; but if this gift fails
    (c) to divide the residue equally between those of my children who are living at my death and attain $/{18$//21$/}; except:

        (i) if any of my children dies before me, then to divide that child's share equally between those of his or her children who are living at my death and attain $/{18$//21$/}; and
        (ii) if any of my children dies after me, but before attaining $/{18$//21$/}, then to divide that child's share equally between those of his or her children who are living at his or her death and attain $/{18$//21$/}.

7 TECHNICAL CLAUSES 7–081

(a) The Standard Provisions of the Society of Trust and Estate Practitioners (1st edition) apply, amended as follows:

    (i) Standard provision 5 ("trust for sale") does not apply.
    (ii) My executors may exercise their powers without consulting beneficiaries, so section 11 of the Trusts of Land and Appointment of Trustees Act 1996 does not apply.

(b) In my will, "children":

    (i) includes those who are legitimate, illegitimate or adopted; but

(ii) does not include step-children, nor natural children who have been adopted by another person;

and other terms describing family relationships are to be interpreted accordingly.

(c) My estate is to be divided as if any person who dies within one month of my death had predeceased me.

7–082 8 POWER TO ACT AS OFFICER OR EMPLOYEE

Any executor may act personally as an officer, or employee, of any company in which my estate is interested. An executor who does so may retain personally any remuneration received. This is so even if:

(a) my executor having chosen to exercise (or not to exercise) rights over shares in my estate may have been instrumental in procuring the position as officer or employee; or

(b) my executor's qualifications for the position may be constituted (in part or in whole) by the holding in my estate.

7–083 9 POWER TO RUN A BUSINESS

My executors may carry on any business in which I am engaged at my death. If they do so then they may:

(a) carry on the business either alone or in partnership with any other people (and whether as general partners or limited partners);

(b) act upon such terms as they think fit, and as if they were the beneficial owners absolutely entitled;

(c) employ any of the capital of my estate in the business, including capitalising financing (by loans, guarantees or otherwise);

(d) employ anyone in connection with the business on such terms as they think fit;

(e) promote a company or corporation in any part of the world to acquire the business (or part of it) by the issue to my trustees of shares or securities or otherwise;

(f) pay, out of any property held upon the same trusts as the business, the cost of promoting such a company or corporation, and of the transfer of the business to it;

and my executors are indemnified, out of any property held upon the same trusts as the business, against any personal liability which they incur in connection with the business (unless that liability arose by reason of their own wilful and individual fraud or wrongdoing)

7–084 10 TREATMENT OF BUSINESS PROFITS

The net profits of any business in my estate are to be treated *as if* they were the income which would arise from investments representing the proceeds of sale of the business, if it were sold.

SIGNATURES 7–085

Signed by me on .... 20$/

Signature of Testator

Signed by $/ in our joint presence and then by us in $/{his$//hers$/}

         Witness 1   Witness 2

Signature:

Full name:

Address:

Occupation:

PART 8

CODICILS

CODICILS

CLAUSES

136 Commencement for first codicil

This is a codicil to the will of me, $/ of $/.

1 MY WILL   8–001

I made my will on $/.

137 Commencement for Second Codicil

This is a second codicil to the will of me, $/ of $/.

1 PREVIOUS DOCUMENTS   8–002

(a) I made my will on $/
(b) I made the first codicil to my will on $/.

138 Commencement for third or subsequent codicils

This is a $/{third$//fourth$/} codicil to the will of me, $/ of $/.

2 PREVIOUS DOCUMENTS   8–003

(a) I made my will on $/
(b) I have made previous codicils to my will, as follows:
    (i) a first codicil on $/;
    (ii) a second codicil on $/;
    (iii) $/[a third codicil on $/.$/]

139 Ending

3 CONFIRMATION   8–004

In all other respects I confirm my will $/[and $/{my first codicil$//my first and second codicils$//my first, second and third codicils$/}$/].

8–005 SIGNATURES

Signed by me on .... 20$/

Signature of Testator

Signed by $/ in our joint presence and then by us in $/{his$//hers$/}
         Witness 1   Witness 2

Signature:

Full name:

Address:

Occupation:

140 Background leader ("first style")

8–006 1 BACKGROUND

In my will:

141 Tails for "first style" leader

141a Legacy

8–007   (a) I gave $/ to $/.

141b Executor

(a) I appointed $/ to be $/{my executor$//one of my executors$//a substitute executor$/}.

141c Guardian

(a) I appointed $/ to be a guardian of my minor children.

141d "Complex"

(a) by clause $/, I made various provisions for the benefit of $/.

141e Residue

(a) I gave $/[a share in $/]the residue of my estate to $/.

142 Background leader ("second style")

8–008 Since the date of my Will:

143 Tails for "Second Style" Leader

143a . . . has died.

    (a) $/ has died.   **8–009**

143b I no longer wish to appoint . . .

    (a) I have decided that I no longer wish to appoint $/.

143c I no longer have minor children

    (a) I no longer have any minor children.

143d "catch all"

    (a) I have decided that I wish the terms set out below to apply.

144 Revoking legacy

1 REVOKING LEGACY   **8–010**

I revoke the legacy of $/ given to $/ by my will.

145 Replacing legacy

1 CHANGING LEGACY   **8–011**

    (a) I revoke the legacy of $/ given to $/ by my will.
    (b) Instead, I give $/ to $/.

146 Replacing executor

1 APPOINTMENT OF EXECUTORS   **8–012**

    (a) I revoke the appointment of $/ as executor.
    (b) I appoint $/ to be my executor $/[to act together with $/$/].

147 Replacing executor with firm of solicitors

1 APPOINTMENT OF EXECUTORS   **8–013**

    (a) I revoke the appointment of $/ as executor.
    (b) I appoint as my executors the partners at my death in the firm of $/ (solicitors) of $/ $/[to act together with $/ $/].
    (c) If at my death that firm no longer exists, I appoint the firm which carries on its practice.
    (d) I wish no more than two people to act as my executors.

148 Replacing executor with firm of solicitors and introducing charging clause

8–014 **1 APPOINTMENT OF EXECUTORS**

> (a) I revoke the appointment of $/ as executor.
> (b) I appoint as my executors the partners at my death in the firm of $/ (solicitors) of $/ $/[to act together with $/ $/].
> (c) If at my death that firm no longer exists, I appoint the firm which carries on its practice.
> (d) I wish no more than two people to act as my executors.

8–015 **2 POWER TO CHARGE FOR PROFESSIONAL SERVICES**

> Any of my executors who is engaged in a profession or business may charge fees for work done by him or her, or by his or her firm, in connection with my estate and its trusts, including acts which an executor or trustee not being in any profession or business could have done personally, and those charges shall be a first charge against my estate, without abatement.

149 Replacing guardian

8–016 **1 APPOINTMENT OF GUARDIAN**

> (a) I revoke the appointment of $/ as guardian.
> (b) $/[If at my death I am the sole surviving parent, $/] I appoint $/ $/[and $/ $/] to be the $/{guardian$//guardians$/} of any of my children who are under 18.

150 Revoking guardian

8–017 **1 REVOKING APPOINTMENT OF GUARDIAN**

> I revoke the appointment of $/ as guardian.

COMPLETE CODICILS

151 Codicil reciting death of a legatee (and therefore revoking a legacy) and increasing another legacy

> *Note*: A will and its codicils become a public documents on being proved. It is therefore usually inadvisable to reduce or revoke legacies to living beneficiaries by codicil, and where feelings are to be spared, a new will is preferable.

8–018 This is a codicil to the will of me, $/ of $/.

8–019 **1 MY WILL**

> I made my will on $/.

2 BACKGROUND

In my will:
   (a) I gave £$/ to $/.
   (b) I gave £$/ to $/.

Since the date of my Will, $/ has died.

3 REVOKING LEGACY

I revoke the legacy of £$/ given to $/ by my will.

4 CHANGING LEGACY

   (a) I revoke the legacy of £$/ given to $/ by my will.
   (b) Instead, I give £$/ to $/.

5 CONFIRMATION

In all other respects I confirm my will.

SIGNATURES

Signed by me on . . . . 20$/

Signature of Testator

Signed by $/ in our joint presence and then by us in $/{his$//hers$/}
          Witness 1   Witness 2

Signature:

Full name:

Address:

Occupation:

152 "Catch all" codicil replacing executor

Note: This codicil is suitable for "bulk" changes of executor, of the kind **8–025**
       which occur when a firm of solicitors is taken over, or breaks up, or
       where a fee-earner is "followed" to a new firm.

This is a codicil to the will of me, $/ of $/.

1 MY WILL

I made my will on $/.

8–027 2 BACKGROUND

By my will I appointed the partners at my death in the firm of $/ (Solicitors) of $/ to be my executors.

8–028 3 CHANGE OF EXECUTORS

(a) I revoke the appointment of $/.
(b) I appoint as my executors the partners at my death in the firm of $/ (solicitors) of $/.
(c) The partners of $/ are to take office in the same circumstances, and on the same terms and conditions, as the partners of $/ were appointed in my will.
(d) If at my death that firm no longer exists, I appoint the firm which carries on its practice.
(e) I wish no more than two people to act as my executors.

7-029 4 POWER TO CHARGE FOR PROFESSIONAL SERVICES

Any of my executors who is engaged in a profession or business may charge fees for work done by him or her, or by his or her firm, in connection with my estate and its trusts, including acts which an executor or trustee not being in any profession or business could have done personally, and those charges shall be a first charge against my estate, without abatement.

8–030 5 CONFIRMATION

In all other respects I confirm my will.

8–031 SIGNATURES

Signed by me on . . . . 20$/

Signature of Testator

Signed by $/ in our joint presence and then by us in $/{his$//hers$/}
　　　　　　　　Witness 1　　　　　　　　　　　　Witness 2

Signature:

Full name:

Address:

Occupation:

PART 9

DISCLAIMERS AND DEEDS OF VARIATION

DISCLAIMERS AND DEEDS OF VARIATION

Introduction

A number of situations can arise whereby the devolution either on intestacy **9–001** or under a will is varied without such variation being deemed a transfer of value for inheritance tax purposes, it being treated as taking effect at the date of death.

A variation under the Inheritance (Provision for Family and Dependants) Act 1975 is deemed both by section 19 of the Act and by section 146 of the Inheritance Tax Act 1984 to have effect from the date of death. Note however, that out of Court settlements will not fall within these provisions although might conceivably be embodied in a Deed of Variation, but by section 146(6) of the IHTA 1984 a compromise of claims under the Act embodied in Tomlin Orders to the extent that the terms agreed could have been embodied in an Order under the Act, are treated as if they were provisions of such an Order.

If a surviving spouse elects under section 47(a) of the Administration of **9–002** Estates Act 1925 to redeem his or her life interest in the residuary estate on intestacy, the redemption is not a transfer of value but the surviving spouse is treated as having been entitled to that capital value instead of the life interest.

The distribution by a legatee in accordance with the testator's express wishes, if made within two years of the date of death, are relieved by sections 17(b) and 143 of the IHTA 1984. The most common situation arises where a testator gives chattels to an executor or some other person intending that they should distribute some or all of those items in accordance with a Letter of Wishes or Memorandum. The wishes are not legally binding and need not be expressed in writing, and the provision is not restricted to chattels, although the use of the word "legatee" in section 146 implies that it does not extend to freehold land. Similarly, a distribution made out of a testamentary discretionary trust is relieved by section 144 of the IHTA 1984. The two remaining cases are Disclaimers and Deeds of Variation.

Disclaimers

A disclaimer is a unilateral act by an intended beneficiary whereby a proffered **9–003** gift is refused. Having disclaimed, the beneficiary cannot direct the gift elsewhere and his involvement ends.

By virtue of the IHTA 1984, section 142(1) and (3) the disclaimer must be made in writing within two years of the death, and must not be made for any consideration in money or money's worth except the making of another disclaimer or variation which is treated as made by the deceased. A minor cannot disclaim although the Court can do so for him.

Whilst there is no authority on the point, it does appear that the whole interest must be disclaimed and there cannot be a partial disclaimer, *e.g.* part of a legacy.

9–004   The effect of disclaiming an absolute gift (other than residue) is that the gift so disclaimed falls into residue. The effect of the disclaimer on residue or a share of residue is to cause an intestacy as to the benefit disclaimed. Thus before disclaiming, the beneficiary should be made aware of the consequences as they may be entirely unexpected. A beneficiary cannot properly disclaim if he has taken any benefit from the gift.

Deeds of variation

9–005   Section 142 of the Inheritance Tax Act 1984 provides that where within the period of two years after a person's death, any of the dispositions (whether effected by will, the laws of intestacy or otherwise) of the property comprised in his estate before death are varied by an instrument in writing made by the persons (or any of them) who benefit or who would benefit under the dispositions, the variation is not a transfer of value and takes effect for the purposes of inheritance tax as if the variation had been effected by the deceased.

It should be noted that the section is directed to, and only direct to, inheritance tax. Thus if a parent directs his testamentary benefit to his infant child, the income during the child's minority will be deemed to be the parents for income tax purposes. If a legatee is insolvent, he cannot avoid the effect of the bankruptcy laws on his estate by executing a Deed of Variation in favour of his wife.

Who may vary?

9–006   Except in the case of persons under a disability anyone can vary who benefits directly or has in fact become entitled under a disclaimer or variation. An important opportunity to vary that should not be overlooked is where a beneficiary under one estate dies shortly after the death of the first deceased. Assume for example, that a husband dies leaving an estate of £300,000 to his wife, and she dies six months later leaving an estate of £100,000 to her two children. A variation of husband's estate by substituting the children will prevent the aggregation of husbands and wives estates on her death for inheritance tax purposes.

What may be varied?

9–007   The variation can apply to any of the dispositions of the property comprised in a deceased's estate and the definition is extended to include "excluded property", *e.g.* a reversionary interest. The "or otherwise" provision in the legislation permits, *e.g.* the post death severing of a joint tenancy.

Considerable care should be taken to ensure that any interest is only varied once. A second variation which further redirects any item or any part of an item that has already been redirected by an earlier instrument will not fall within IHT 1984, section 142.[1] Rectification will be allowed[2] and in *Matthews v. Martin and Others*[3] an order for rectification was granted because the original deed did not reflect the agreement reached between the parties because of errors in the preparation of the draft for execution.

Consideration

There must be no consideration in money or money's worth "other than **9–008** consideration consisting of the making, in respect of another of the dispositions, of a variation or disclaimer" to fall within the section. Thus if by will Blackacre is given to A and Whiteacre to B, they can exchange their gifts but there can be no payment by way of equality of exchange.

Parties

The variation must be made by the person or persons who would, apart from **9–009** the variation, have benefited. It is convenient, though not necessary, for the deceased's personal representatives to join in so as to give their consent to the election referred to below, where necessary, and it is usual, though unnecessary for the donee to be a party where he merely accepts the gift in place of the donor, but if the instrument creates trusts, the trustees will have to join in.

Where the original beneficiary has died his personal representatives may enter into a variation and sign an election.[4]

Election

The variation will not take effect under the section unless the persons making **9–010** the instrument and, if the variation causes extra tax to be payable, the personal representatives, give written notice of election that the variation shall take effect to the revenue within six months after the date of execution of the variation or such longer time as the revenue may allow. It is common practice to insert the election in the deed itself and the notice of election must refer to the appropriate statutory provisions. The Revenue's attention must specifically be drawn to the election contained within the instrument. If there is additional tax payable the deceased's personal representatives can only refuse to join in the election if there are insufficient assets in the Estate to meet the additional tax.

Income

Until the execution of the Deed of Variation the income is that of the original **9–011** beneficiary.

---

[1] *Russell v. I.R.C.* [1988] S.T.C. 195.
[2] *Lake v. Lake* [1989] S.T.C. 865.
[3] CLD 1990 [1991] BTC 8048.
[4] Revenue Tax Bulletin, February 1995, page 194.

153 Disclaimer of legacy or life interest

9–012   *Note:*   Here the assumption is that there is a gift of personal chattels and a pecuniary legacy to the testator's widow and she has a life interest in the residue remainder to the testator's children. She wishes to retain the chattels but give up the rest of her entitlement. The effect would be that the legacy disclaimed will fall into the residuary estate which will pass in its entirety to the children.

9–013   THIS DEED OF DISCLAIMER is made the (day) day of (month) 20(year) by me (A) of (address) whereas:

1. By his will dated the (day) day of (month) 20(year) (B) of (address) (hereinafter called "the testator") by clause 2 gave to me absolutely all his chattels as therein described by clause 3 he gave me absolutely the sum of £10,000 and by clause 4 he provided that the trustees of his will should pay the income of his residuary estate therein referred to as the "trust fund" to me during my lifetime.
2. The testator died on the (day) day of (month) 20(year) and his will was duly proved by myself and (C) the executors named therein on the (day) day of (month) 20(year) in the [Principal] [District] Probate Registry of the Family Division of the High Court of Justice.
3. I have not entered in any way into possession or enjoyment of capital or income of the trust fund nor received the said sum of £10,000 nor any part thereof.

9–014   NOW THIS DEED WITNESSES that I hereby irrevocably disclaim.

1. The said legacy of £10,000 given to me by clause 3 of the will.
2. All the interest in the trust fund given to me by the said will but I do not disclaim the gift to me in clause 2 of the said will.

9–015   IN WITNESS whereof I have hereunto set my hand the day and year first above written.

SIGNED and DELIVERED as a Deed by
the said (A)
in the presence of:

154 Disclaimer of residue under will and share of residue under resulting intestacy

9–016   *Note:*   The disclaimer of a share of residue under a will does not affect the beneficiary's right to inherit under the resulting intestacy. It is said that there can be no disclaimer of a part of a gift but this is becoming increasingly doubtful and even more so in the case of residue. The following disclaimer is by a widow who under the rules of intestacy would as surviving spouse be entitled to three separate interests namely a statutory legacy of the chattels, a statutory pecuniary legacy and a life interest. There would not appear to be any objection to the disclaimer of one or more of those interests.

THIS DEED OF DISCLAIMER is made on the (day) day of (month) **9–017** 20(year) by me (A) of (address):

WHEREAS

1. (B) (my husband) died on the (day) day of (month) having by his will dated the (day) of (month) 20(year) appointed me to be his sole Executrix and giving me the whole of his estate both real and personal.
2. His will was duly proved by me on the (day) of (month) 20(year) in the [Principal] [District] Probate Registry of the Family Division of the High Court of Justice.
3. I have not in any way entered into beneficial possession or enjoyment of the capital or income of the deceased's Estate.

NOW THIS DEED WITNESSES that I hereby disclaim all interest in the deceased's estate given to me by the said will and all rights title and interest arising on intestacy in the said estate

IN WITNESS, *etc.*

155 Deed of disclaimer and variation by widow giving up her interest in the residue for the benefit of minor children

Note: The testator has given the whole of his estate to his widow and there **9–018** are minor children of the marriage. She decides to give up the interest under the Will in favour of the children. If any of them die before attaining majority his or her estate will pass on intestacy back to the widow and she can then disclaim. The opportunity is taken to appoint a co-trustee as she had been appointed the sole executor.

Notice of election must be given to the CTO if the Deed is to be effective for IHT purposes and in some cases it will be necessary to claim for capital gains tax purposes under TCGA, section 62(6). Stamp duty is not payable (Finance Act 1985, section 84).

THIS DEED OF DISCLAIMER AND VARIATION is made the (day) day **9–019** of (month) 20(year) BETWEEN CAROL SMITH of (address) (hereinafter called "the wife") of the one part and PETER JONES of (address) solicitor (hereinafter called "Mr. Jones") of the other part.

WHEREAS:

1. David Smith (the husband of the wife) (hereinafter called "the testator") died on the (day) of (month) 20(year) having by his will dated (day) of (month) 20(year) appointed the wife to be his sole executrix and given to her the whole of his estate both real and personal absolutely

2. The will of the testator was duly proved by the wife on the (day) of (month) 20(year) in the [Principal] [District] Probate Registry of the Family Division of the High Court of Justice

3. There are three children of the marriage of the testator and the wife namely James who was born on the (day) of (month) 20(year) Lucinda who was born on the (day) of (month) 20(year) and Thomas who was born on the (day) of (month) 20(year)

4. All the debts and liabilities of the testator's estate have been paid and discharged and the trust fund (as defined by the will) is now represented by the assets and securities specified in the first schedule hereto (except the personal chattels herein referred to)

5. The wife wishes to disclaim all her interest in the testator's estate (save as herein provided) for the benefit of the said three children and to make provision for the administration thereof pending their attainment of majority

6. In pursuance of her desire she wishes to appoint her solicitor Mr Jones to act as co-trustee with her (which he has been agreed to)

9–020 NOW THIS DEED WITNESSES:

1. The wife hereby declares that the provisions of the Second Schedule hereto shall be substituted for the dispositive provisions of the testator's will save as to the personal chattels as defined in paragraph 1 thereof (which she accepts) she hereby disclaims all benefit in the testator's estate whether under the will or on his intestacy

2. The wife hereby declares that she holds the trust fund on the trusts in accordance with the provisions of the Second Schedule hereto and in exercise of the statutory power in that behalf and of every other power her enabling she hereby appoints Mr. Jones to be a Trustee of the will (as varied aforesaid) and to act jointly with her in the trusts thereof

3. The parties hereto hereby give notice to the Board of Inland Revenue pursuant to section 142(2) of the Inheritance Taxes Act 1984 that this deed shall take effect as a variation under section 142(1) of the said Act

IN WITNESS, *etc.*

THE FIRST SCHEDULE

9–021 [List of property and securities constituting the trust fund]

THE SECOND SCHEDULE

9–022 1. I give to my wife Carol Smith all my personal chattels as defined by section 55(1)(x) of the Administration of Estates Act 1925 absolutely

2. Subject as aforesaid I give all my residuary estate (after payment there out of my debts funeral and testamentary expenses and any inheritance tax payable in respect thereof) (hereinafter referred as the trust fund) unto my executrix upon trust for my three children James Lucinda and Thomas in equal shares and subject to the following provisions

3. My executrix shall during her lifetime have power to appoint new or additional trustees of the trust fund

4. My trustees shall have power to pay any income of the share of any child of mine to my wife or his or her guardian for his or her maintenance education and benefit without seeing to the application thereof

5. In addition to all other powers conferred by law my trustees may at any time raise the whole or any part of the share of any child of mine during his or her minority and pay the sum to or apply the same for the advancement maintenance education or otherwise for the benefit of such beneficiary

6. Any monies requiring investment hereunder may be laid out in or upon the acquisition or security of any property of whatsoever and nature wheresoever situate to the intent that my trustees shall have the same powers in all respects as if the were absolute owners beneficially entitled

IN WITNESS, *etc.*

156 Deed of variation by widow passing the nil-rate band onto her two adult children and the infant son of a deceased child

Note: It is assumed that having surrendered the nil-rate band the widow's **9–023** total assets are sufficient for her purposes and this is an exercise of pure tax planning. The nil-rate band available is that prevailing at the date of the testator's death. This is currently £250,000 and the widow decides to divide it unequally. There being no additional tax arising as a result of the deed the executors are not required to join in

THIS DEED OF VARIATION is made the (day) day of (month) 20(year) by **9–024** SUSAN SMITH of (address) (hereinafter called "Mrs Smith")

WHEREAS: **9–025**
1. (David Smith) (hereinafter called "the Testator") died on the (day) of (month) 20(year) having by his will dated (day) of (month) 20(year) appointed Peter Wilson of (address) and John White of (address) to be the executors and trustees thereof
2. The said will was duly proved by the executors on the (day) day of (month) 20(year) in the [Principal] [District] Probate Registry of the Family Division of the High Court of Justice.
3. By his will the testator gave his net residuary estate to Mrs Smith absolutely.
4. Mrs Smith wishes to vary the Will in the manner hereinafter provided.

NOW THIS DEED WITNESSES **9–026**
1. The Will shall be read and construed and take effect as if prior to the gift of the residuary estate to Mrs Smith the following clause had been inserted:

   (a) "I give to each of them my son Toby and my daughter Gillian the sum of £70,000 free of inheritance tax
   (b) I give to my trustees the sum of £75,000 upon trust for such of them my grandchildren Philip Smith and Jane Smith (the children of my deceased son Colin Smith) as shall attain the age of twenty one years

and if more than one in equal shares absolutely and so that the trusts declared in this sub-clause shall carry the intermediate income"

2. I hereby give notice, *etc.*
IN WITNESS, *etc.*

157 Deed of variation by widow and issue whereby the widow gives up her life interest for a capital sum remainder to issue being contingent

9–027 *Note*: Perhaps the most common form of will is varied here namely a life interest to widow with remainder to children who survive both parents with substitution of grandchildren for any predeceasing child. The difficulty is that the ultimate beneficiaries cannot be ascertained until the death of the wife and even if the children are getting on, there is no way of being sure as a matter of strict law that another grandchild may not come into existence. Strictly an application to the court should be made under the Variation of Trusts Act 1958.

This is however, an expensive and potentially time consuming exercise and the parties may be willing to take a risk. They might also consider insuring the wife's life.

In any event, under the general law there is a power to advance up to one half of each contingent share if the trustees think that such an advance is proper and many modern wills permit such an advance up to the entirety of the fund. The trustees will need to be indemnified and as each grandchild attains full age he should agree under seal to the terms for the Deed.

9–028 THIS DEED OF VARIATION is made the (day) day of (month) 20(year) BETWEEN PAULINE JONES of (address) (hereinafter called "the wife") of the first part HENRY JONES of (address) (hereinafter called "Henry") of the second part HARRIET JONES of (address) (hereinafter called "Harriet") of the third part CHARLOTTE JONES of (address) (hereinafter called "Charlotte") of the fourth part and HENRY and HARRIET (hereinafter together called "the trustees") of the fifth part

9–029 WHEREAS:
1. Frederick Jones (hereinafter called "the Testator") died on the (day) of (month) 20(year) having by his will ("the will") dated the (day) day of (month) 20(year) appointed the trustees to be the executors and trustees thereof.
2. The will was duly proved by the trustees on the (day) of (month) 20(year) in the Oxford District Probate Registry of the Family Division of the High Court of Justice.
3. By the will and in the events which have happened the testator gave his net residuary estate to the trustees to hold the same upon trust to pay the income thereof to the wife for life and subject thereto in trust for such of them Henry, Harriet and Charlotte as shall survive himself and his wife and if more than one in equal shares provided that if any of them should predecease the

survivor of himself and his wife leaving a child or children who should survive himself and his wife then such child or children should take and if more than one in equal shares the share of the net residuary Estate which his her or their parent would have taken had he or she survived the testator and the wife.

4. The parties hereto of the first second third and fourth parts are of the opinion that it is in the best interests of the testator's family that the arrangements herein provided should be made and the trustees are satisfied that so far as may be necessary they should concur therein by the exercise of their powers of advancement.

NOW THIS DEED WITNESSES **9–030**

1. The parties hereto of the first second third and fourth parts hereby declare that the following provisions with regard to the testator's net residuary estate shall take effect in lieu of the provisions with regard thereto in the will (that is to say):

The testators net residuary estate shall be held upon trust:

(a) To pay to the wife the sum of £(X)

(b) To pay thereout any inheritance tax exigible on the net residuary Estate as a result of this deed

(c) Subject thereto in trust absolutely for Henry, Harriet and Charlotte in equal shares

2. Accordingly the parties hereto of the first second third and fourth parts hereby surrender all their rights titles and interests in the testator's net residuary estate as originally provided by the testator's will.

3. The trustees in exercise of their powers of appointment hereby and with the consent of the wife appoint the capital of the testator's net residuary estate to Henry Harriet and Charlotte in equal shares.

4. Each of them Henry, Harriet and Charlotte hereby covenants with the trustees and each of them that he or she will indemnify the trustees and each of them against any claim by or liability to any child or children of him or her (the covenantor) by reason of the execution or implementation of this deed

5. We hereby give notice, *etc.*

IN WITNESS, *etc.*

158 Deed of variation by widow and children whereby widow gives up life interest of capital sum and a daughter receives a capital sum

Note: The assumption here is that the testator, a farmer, has by his will given **9–031** his wife a life interest in his estate with remainder to their three children, two sons who farm the land and a daughter who does not. It is agreed that the daughter will take her share in cash and the wife will take a sum agreed between the parties (which may be greater or less than the actual capitalised value of her interest). The family are aware that at the present time 100 per cent agricultural property relief is available and this may not be available on the death of the wife.

9–032 THIS DEED OF VARIATION is made the (day) day of (month) 20(year) BETWEEN AMY BROWN of (address) (hereinafter called "the wife") of the first part JOHN BROWN of (address) (hereinafter called "John") of the second part WILLIAM BROWN of (address) (hereinafter called "William") of the third part JANE SMITH of (address) (hereinafter called "Jane") of the fourth part and AMY and WILLIAM (hereinafter together called "the Trustees") of the fifth part

9–033 WHEREAS:

1. Charles Brown (hereinafter called "the testator") died on the (day) of (month) 20(year) having by his will ("the will") dated the (day) of (month) 20(year) appointed the trustees to be the executors and trustees thereof.

2. The will was proved by the trustees on the (day) day of (month) 20(year) in the Oxford District Probate Registry of the Family Division of the High Court of Justice.

3. By his will and in the events which have happened the testator gave his net residuary estate to his trustees to hold the same upon trust to pay the income thereof to the wife during her life and subject thereto in trust for his children John, William and Jane in equal shares.

4. The parties hereto have agreed to vary the terms of the will and to distribute the net residuary estate in the manner hereinafter provided

9–034 NOW THIS DEED WITNESSES

1. The wife has upon the execution hereof been paid the sum of £(X) (the receipt of which is hereby acknowledged) in satisfaction of her life interest in the net residuary estate and accordingly she hereby disclaims and surrenders all her right title and interest in the net residuary estate

2. Jane has upon the execution hereof been paid the sum of £(X) (the receipt whereof is hereby acknowledged) in satisfaction of her share of the capital of the net residuary estate and accordingly she hereby disclaims all her right title and interest in the net residuary estate

3. In the premises it is hereby agreed and declared by all parties hereto that the net residuary estate now belongs to John and William in equal shares absolutely and John and William hereby covenant jointly and severally with the wife and Jane to indemnify them and their representatives against all debts and liabilities (including any inheritance tax payable in respect of the testator's estate) of the testator or his estate

4. The parties hereto hereby give notice, etc.

IN WITNESS, *etc.*

159 Deed of variation after death of beneficiary

9–035 *Note*: In this case husband has died and within two years of his death his wife has now died. By his will he gave his estate to her if she survived (which she did) and by her will she passes her estate to the children, the result of all of this is that husband's nil-rate band for inheritance tax purposes has been lost and it is now wished to vary husband's estate to dispose of his nil-rate band and effect a tax saving.

The wife's personal representative must be a party to the Deed as he is legally entitled to the benefits on the death of husband.

THIS DEED OF VARIATION is made the (day) day of (month) 20(year) **9–036** BETWEEN (A) of (address) (hereinafter called "Jane's executor") of the first part (B) of (address) and (C) of (address) (hereinafter called "the beneficiaries") of the second part

WHEREAS: **9–037**

1. Albert Smith (hereinafter called "Albert") died on the (day) day of (month) 20(year) and by his will ("the will") dated the (day) day of (month) 20(year) appointed his wife Jane Smith and Albert's executor to be the executors and trustees thereof
2. The will was proved by the trustees thereof on the (day) day of (month) 20(year) in the Principal Probate Registry of the Family Division of the High Court of Justice.
3. By the will and in the events which have happened Albert gave the whole of his estate to his wife absolutely
4. Jane Smith (hereinafter called "Jane") died on the (day) day of (month) 20(year) and by her will dated the (day) day of (month) 20(year) appointed Jane's executor to be the executor and trustee thereof and Jane's executor has applied to the Principal Probate Registry for Probate thereof
5. By Jane's will and in the events which have happened she gave the whole of her estate to the beneficiaries in equal shares.
6. Jane's executor and the beneficiaries have agreed to vary the will of Albert in the manner hereinafter appearing

NOW THIS DEED WITNESSES

1. Jane's executor and the beneficiaries hereby agree and declare that in lieu of **9–038** clause . . . of the will [the clause giving the estate to Jane] the clause set forth in the schedule hereto shall be substituted
2. The parties hereto hereby give notice, *etc.*

THE SCHEDULE

"I give the sum of £(X) [the then nil-rate band] to my children in equal shares absolutely and subject thereto I give all my estate by real and person to my wife Jane absolutely"

IN WITNESS, *etc.*

PART 10

LIVING WILLS

LIVING WILLS

A "living will" (or "advance directive") is not a true will at all, but is instead a **10–001** letter aimed at the doctors who may be treating you in the future, in circumstances where you yourself are unable to make (or communicate) informed medical decisions.

A living will can give any directions you wish about your medical treatment. The most common use is an advance refusal of any treatment which will prolong your life in circumstances where there can be no quality of life. Another common use is to express (usually religious) objections to blood transfusion, organ transplants or amputation.

In practice, we have often found it useful to refer clients to the Terrence Higgins Trust and the Voluntary Euthanasia Society. Both organisations produce draft living wills, and accompanying information packs, and any practitioner intending to advise on living wills would be well advised to use their literature as a starting point.

160 Living will

Note: Much of the following text is optional, so we have chosen not to put **10–002** stop-codes around everything that could be removed. Remember that it would be a very rare client who wanted every word included.

1 LIVING WILL

This is the living will of me, $/ of $/.

1 BACKGROUND   10–003

In the event that I am incapable of making, or communicating, decisions to my doctors, I would like them to act in accordance with my following wishes.

2 CONSULTATION   10–004

I would like my doctors to consult with $/ regarding my medical treatment.

3 ADVANCE REFUSAL   10–005

I refuse the following treatment:

   (a) any treatment aimed at prolonging my life if two doctors are of the opinion that I am unlikely to recover from a condition involving severe distress;

(b) any treatment aimed at prolonging my life if two doctors are of the opinion that I am unlikely to recover from a condition making me incapable of rational existence;

(c) blood transfusions;

(d) transplant surgery;

(e) amputation of any part of my body.

10–006 4 ADVANCE CONSENT

I consent to the following treatment:

(a) any treatment intended to reduce my pain or to control any distressing symptoms of my condition$/[, even if the effect of such treatment may be to shorten my life$/].

(b) any treatment proposed with the intention of complying with the wishes set out in this living will, and I absolve my doctors from any liability which they might otherwise incur in giving such treatment.

10–007 SIGNATURES

Signed by me on . . . . 20$/

Signature of $/

	Witness 1	Witness 2
Signature:		
Full name:		
Address:		
Occupation:		

APPENDIX I

WILL INSTRUCTIONS/ QUESTIONNAIRE

WILL INSTRUCTIONS/QUESTIONNAIRE

In order that we may prepare a will which suits your circumstances, we should be grateful if you could complete as far as possible the following questionnaire. Please continue on a separate sheet if necessary, indicating the section to which the information relates. Copies of existing wills and other relevant documents should be provided, if possible.

PARTICULARS OF YOU AND YOUR FAMILY

1.	**Personal Details**	
1.1	Full Name	
1.2	Address	
1.3	Day time telephone number	
1.4	Home telephone number	
1.5	Occupation	
1.6	Date of birth	
1.7	Country of residence	
1.8	Location of any previous will	
1.9	Marital Status	Single Divorced Engaged Remarried Married Widowed Separated

2.	**Details of any Spouse/Partner**	
2.1	Name	
2.2	Address	
2.3	Status	Spouse/Partner

3.	**Details of any children**			
	Full name	Address	Date of birth	Status. Indicate children not from present relationship
				Natural Adopted Step Child Illegitimate

4.	Details of any Grand-children			
	Full name	Address	Date of birth	Name of Parent

CONTENTS OF WILL

5.	**Funeral/burial/cremation requirements/organs for medical use**			

		Name	Address	Relationship to you
6.	**Particulars of Executors and Guardians**			
6.1	Executors			
6.2	Your solicitors as Executors — sole executors — jointly with Executors named — substitute executors	YES/NO YES/NO YES/NO		
6.2	Guardian(s)			

Consider a substitute if one dies or is unable to act.

If it is intended to leave a gift to any of the above please include the details in sections 8 or 9 below and indicate whether the gift is conditional on acceptance of the appointment.

7.	**Specific gifts**		
	Beneficiary	Address	Description of Gift
7.1	Business or agricultural property		
7.2	Other specific gifts (jewellery, antiques etc.)		
7.3	Separate list to be prepared for Executors to carry out wishes		

8.	**Gifts of money**		
	Beneficiary	Address	Amount

9.	**The rest of your estate**		
	Beneficiary	Interest absolute or restricted, *e.g.* life interest only	Proportion of residuary estate

10.	**Who will inherit your estate if neither your family nor those listed in 10 above survive you?**	

11.	Additional comments or relevant information	

12.	Please indicate if any of the following apply and if so complete **PARTICULARS OF YOUR PROPERTY**	
12.1	Your total assets exceed £200,000	YES/NO
12.2	You have children from a previous relationship	YES/NO
12.3	You pay maintenance to a former spouse or children of a previous relationship	YES/NO

PARTICULARS OF YOUR PROPERTY

13.	**Details of your Estate**			
		Brief details	Value of your interest	Value of your spouse/ Partner's interest
13.1	Main residence, any outstanding mortgage secured on it, and location of title documents			
13.2	Stocks and shares			
13.3	Unit Trusts			
13.4	Bank accoaunts			
13.5	Building Society accounts			
13.6	Natinal Savings accounts			

13.	**Details of your Estate** —*cont.*			
		Brief details	Value of your interest	Value of your spouse/ Partner's interest
13.7	Life Policies			
13.8	Business property			
13.9	Agricultural property			
13.10	Foreign property			
13.11	Property in trusts of which you are a beneficiary and in trusts in which you have general power of attorney			
13.12	Lifetime gifts, to whom and when made			

13.	**Details of your Estate** —*cont.*			
		Brief details	Value of your interest	Value of your spouse/ Partner's interest
13.3	Pensions — self employed, personal or occupational. Brief Details of arrangements for nominating death benefits (*e.g.* letter of wishes)			

APPENDIX II

STEP STANDARD PROVISIONS

SOCIETY OF TRUST AND ESTATE PRACTITIONERS STANDARD PROVISIONS: 1st EDITION

1. INTRODUCTORY

1(1) These Provisions may be called the standard provisions of the Society of Trust and Estate Practitioners (1st Edition).

1(2) These Provisions may be incorporated in a document by the words:—

The standard provisions of the Society of Trust and Estate Practitioners (1st Edition) shall apply or in any manner indicating an intention to incorporate them.

2. INTERPRETATION

2(1) In these Provisions, unless the context otherwise requires:—

   (a) **Income Beneficiary,** in relation to Trust Property, means a Person to whom income of the Trust Property is payable (as of right or at the discretion of the Trustees).
   (b) **Person** includes a person anywhere in the world and includes a Trustee.
   (c) **The Principal Document** means the document in which these Provisions are incorporated.
   (d) **The Settlement** means any settlement created by the Principal Document and an estate of a deceased Person to which the Principal Document relates.
   (e) **The Trustees** means the personal representatives or trustees of the Settlement for the time being.
   (f) **The Trust Fund** means the property comprised in the Settlement for the time being.
   (g) **Trust Property** means any property comprised in the Trust Fund.
   (h) **A Professional Trustee** means a Trustee who is or has been carrying on a business which consists of or includes the management of trusts or the administration of estates.

2(2) These Provisions have effect subject to the provisions of the Principal Document.

3. ADMINISTRATIVE POWERS

The Trustees shall have the following powers:

3(1) Investment

   (a) The Trustees may invest Trust Property in any manner as if they were beneficial owners. In particular the Trustees may invest in unsecured loans.

(b) The Trustees may decide not to diversify the Trust Fund.

3(2) Management

The Trustees may effect any transaction relating to the management administration or disposition of Trust Property as if they were beneficial owners. In particular:

(a) The Trustees may repair and maintain Trust Property.
(b) The Trustees may develop or improve Trust Property.

3(3) Joint Property

The Trustees may acquire property jointly with any Person.

3(4) Income and Capital

The Trustees may decide not to hold a balance between conflicting interests of Persons interested in Trust Property. In particular:

(a) The Trustees may acquire

   (i) wasting assets and
   (ii) assets which yield little or no income

   for investment or any other purpose.
(b) The Trustees may decide not to procure distributions from a company in which they are interested.
(c) The Trustees may pay taxes and other expenses out of income although they would otherwise be paid out of capital.

3(5) Accumulated Income

The Trustees may apply accumulated income as if it were income arising in the current year.

3(6) Use of Trust Property

The Trustees may permit an Income Beneficiary to occupy or enjoy the use of Trust Property on such terms as they think fit. The Trustees may acquire any property for this purpose.

3(7) Application of Trust Capital

The Trustees may:—

(a) lend money which is Trust Property to an Income Beneficiary without security, on such terms as they think fit,
(b) charge Trust Property as security for debts or obligations of an Income Beneficiary, or
(c) pay money which is Trust Property to an Income Beneficiary as his income, for the purpose of augmenting his income
Provided that:—
(i) the Trustees have power to transfer such Property to that Beneficiary absolutely; or
(ii) the Trustees have power to do so with the consent of another Person and the Trustees act with the written consent of that Person.

3(8) Trade

The Trustees may carry on a trade, in any part of the world, alone or in partnership.

3(9) Borrowing

The Trustees may borrow money for investment or any other purpose. Money borrowed shall be treated as Trust Property.

3(10) Insurance

The Trustees may insure Trust Property for any amount against any risk.

3(11) Delegation

A Trustee may delegate in writing any of his functions to any Person. A Trustee shall not be responsible for the default of that Person (even if the delegation was not strictly necessary or expedient) provided that he took reasonable care in his selection and supervision.

3(12) Deposit of Documents

The Trustees may deposit documents relating to the Settlement (including bearer securities) with any Person.

3(13) Nominees

The Trustees may vest Trust Property in any Person as nominee, and may place Trust Property in the possession or control of any Person.

3(14) Offshore administration

The Trustees may carry on the administration of the trusts of the Settlement outside the United Kingdom.

3(15) Payment of tax

The Trustees may pay tax liabilities of the Settlement (and interest on such tax) even though such liabilities are not enforceable against the Trustees.

3(16) Indemnities

The Trustees may indemnify any Person for any liability properly chargeable against Trust Property.

3(17) Security

The Trustees may charge Trust Property as security for any liability properly incurred by them as Trustees.

3(18) Supervision of Company

The Trustees are under no duty to enquire into the conduct of a company in which they are interested, unless they have knowledge of circumstances which call for enquiry.

3(19) Appropriation

The Trustees may appropriate Trust Property to any Person or class of Persons in or towards the satisfaction of their interest in the Trust Fund.

3(20) Receipt by Charities

Where Trust Property is to be paid or transferred to a charity, the receipt of the treasurer or appropriate officer of the charity shall be a complete discharge to the Trustees.

3(21) Release of Powers

The Trustees may by deed release any of their powers wholly or in part so as to bind future trustees.

3(22) Ancillary Powers

The Trustees may do anything which is incidental or conducive to the exercise of their functions.

4. POWERS OF MAINTENANCE AND ADVANCEMENT

Sections 31 and 32 Trustee Act 1925 shall apply with the following modifications:—

(a) The Proviso to section 31(1) shall be deleted.
*(b)*The words one-half of in section 32(1)(a) shall be deleted.

5. TRUST FOR SALE

The Trustees shall hold land in England and Wales on trust for sale.

6. MINORS

6(1) Where the Trustees may apply income for the benefit of a minor, they may do so by paying the income to the minor's parent or guardian on behalf of the minor, or to the minor if he has attained the age of 16. The Trustees are under no duty to enquire into the use of the income unless they have knowledge of circumstances which call for enquiry.

6(2) Where the Trustees may apply income for the benefit of a minor, they may do so by resolving that they hold that income on trust for the minor absolutely and:

(a) The Trustees may apply that income for the benefit of the minor during his minority.
(b) The Trustees shall transfer the residue of that income to the minor on attaining the age of 18.
(c) For investment and other administrative purposes that income shall be treated as Trust Property.

7. DISCLAIMER

A Person may disclaim his interest under the Settlement wholly or in part.

8. APPORTIONMENT

Income and expenditure shall be treated as arising when payable, and not from day to day, so that no apportionment shall take place.

9. CONFLICTS OF INTEREST

9(1) In this paragraph:

    (a) **A Fiduciary** means a Person subject to fiduciary duties under the Settlement.

    (b) **An Independent Trustee,** in relation to a Person, means a Trustee who is not:

        (i) a brother, sister, ancestor, descendant or dependent of the Person;

        (ii) a spouse of the Person or of (i) above; or

        (iii) a company controlled by one or more of any of the above.

9(2) A Fiduciary may:

    (a) enter into a transaction with the Trustees, or

    (b) be interested in an arrangement in which the Trustees are or might have been interested, or

    (c) act (or not act) in any other circumstances

even though his fiduciary duty under the Settlement conflicts with other duties or with his personal interest;

Provided that:—

    (i) The Fiduciary first discloses to the Trustees the nature and extent of any material interest conflicting with his fiduciary duties, and

    (ii) there is an Independent Trustee in respect of whom there is no conflict of interest, and he considers that the transaction arrangement or action is not contrary to the general interest of the Settlement.

9(3) The powers of the Trustees may be used to benefit a Trustee (to the same extent as if he were not a Trustee) provided that there is an Independent Trustee in respect of whom there is no conflict of interest.

10. POWERS OF TRUSTEES

The powers of the Trustees may be exercised:

(a) at their absolute discretion; and

(b) from time to time as occasion requires.

11. TRUSTEE REMUNERATION

11(1) A Trustee who is a solicitor or an accountant or who is engaged in a business may charge for work done by him or his firm in connection with the Settlement, including work not requiring professional assistance. This has priority to any disposition made in the Principal Document.

11(2) The Trustees may make arrangements to remunerate themselves for work done for a company connected with the Trust Fund.

12. LIABILITY OF TRUSTEES

12(1) A Trustee (other than a Professional Trustee) shall not be liable for a loss to the Trust Fund unless that loss was caused by his own fraud or negligence.

12(2) A Trustee shall not be liable for acting in accordance with the advice of Counsel of at least five years standing, with respect to the Settlement, unless, when he does so:—

(a) he knows or has reasonable cause to suspect that the advice was given in ignorance of material facts; or

(b) proceedings are pending to obtain the decision of the court on the matter.

13. APPOINTMENT AND RETIREMENT OF TRUSTEES

13(1) A Person may be appointed trustee of the Settlement even though he has no connection with the United Kingdom.

13(2) A Professional Trustee who is an individual who has reached the age of 65 shall retire if:—

(a) he is requested to do so by his co-trustees, or by a Person interested in Trust Property; and

(b) he is effectually indemnified against liabilities properly incurred as Trustee.

On that retirement a new Trustee shall be appointed if necessary to ensure that there will be two individuals or a Trust Corporation to act as Trustee.

In this sub-paragraph Trust Corporation has the same meaning as in the Trustee Act 1925.

This sub-paragraph does not apply to a Professional Trustee who is:—

(a) a personal representative

(b) the settlor of the Settlement

(c) a spouse or former spouse of the settlor or testator.

14. PROTECTION FOR INTEREST IN POSSESSION AND ACCUMULATION AND MAINTENANCE SETTLEMENTS

These Provisions shall not have effect:—

(a) so as to prevent a Person from being entitled to an interest in possession in Trust Property (within the meaning of the Inheritance Tax Act 1984);

(b) so as to cause the Settlement to be an accumulation or discretionary settlement (within the meaning of section 5 Taxation of Chargeable Gains Act 1992);

(c) so as to prevent the conditions of section 71(1) Inheritance Tax Act 1984 from applying to Trust Property.

APPENDIX III

STEP STANDARD PROVISIONS: COMMENTARY BY JAMES KESSLER, BARRISTER

STEP STANDARD PROVISIONS:
COMMENTARY BY JAMES KESSLER, Barrister

(This commentary does not form part of the Standard Provisions)

INTRODUCTION TO THE STANDARD PROVISIONS

Any properly drafted will or settlement must contain a large amount of text dealing with routine administrative matters. In the past it has been necessary to set this out in full in each will. STEP has condensed this material into its Standard Provisions.

Use of the Standard Provisions offers many advantages. The final document is much shorter. Drafters and client can concentrate on the beneficial provisions which matter most. The risk of unfortunate omissions is avoided; and the reader familiar with the standard form will save a considerable amount of time.

There is no doubt that the lot of many beneficiaries under short wills would be substantially improved if their wills included the STEP Provisions by incorporation. This led Professor John Adams to describe the publication of the Provisions as "quite the most exciting development for private client draftsmen for several decades;" and Ralph Ray to describe them as "an enormous asset".

How should the Standard Provisions be incorporated?

No difficulty arises if a will or settlement simply incorporates the STEP Provisions in their present form, using the short form set out in clause 1(2) of the Standard Provisions:

The Standard Provisions of the Society of Trust and Estate Practitioners (1st Edition) shall apply.

However, the Trusts of Land and Appointment of Trustees Act 1996 makes two amendments appropriate:
(1) Delete Standard Provision clause 5 (trust for sale). While this clause certainly does no harm, it has now become unnecessary.
(2) Exclude Section 11 of the TLATA 1996 (which imposes duties of consultation inappropriate to a substantive trust).

The following is therefore suggested as a standard form in the light of the new legislation:

Administrative provisions
The Standard Provisions of the Society of Trust and Estate Practi-
tioners (1st Edition) shall apply with the deletion of paragraph 5.
Section 11 Trust of Land and Appointment of Trustees Act 1996
(consultation with beneficiaries) shall not apply.

When should the Standard Provisions be used?

The Standard Provisions form a comprehensive code of administrative provisions, and are suitable for inclusion in any normal will or settlement.

What should one tell the client?

For clients who do not want a detailed explanation of the Standard Provisions, it is sufficient to say: "This is the standard way of providing the executors with technical and routine provisions they need to administer the estate properly. In particular, this authorises professional executors or trustees to charge for their work."

Procedure for obtaining probate

When it comes to obtaining a grant of probate, it is not necessary to prove the Standard Provisions as well as the Will.[1]

Duplication of the Provisions

The Standard Provisions may be duplicated or published in any manner.

CLAUSE BY CLAUSE COMMENTARY

Clause 1 Introductory

This is self-explanatory.

Clause 2 Interpretation

Clause 2(1) sets out some definitions which are used in the Provisions. It should be noted that "Trustees" includes personal representatives as well as trustees; and "Trust Property" includes property in a deceased's estate as well as property in a settlement.
Clause 2(2) provides that in the event of a conflict between the Provisions and the will or deed in which the Provisions are incorporated, the terms of the will or deed should prevail.

Clause 3 Administrative Provisions

This clause provides the trustees with the powers they should have to manage the trust fund in the best way in the interest of the beneficiaries.

---

[1] Practice Direction of the Principal Registry of the Family Division, April 10, 1995; Circular of the Secretary of the Principal Registry, May 17, 1995.

3(1) Investment

This gives the trustees a power of investment slightly wider than that of the Trustee Act 2000. See *Drafting Trusts and Will Trusts* 6th ed., 20.22.

The second sentence is only for the avoidance of doubt. There is no general rule which requires trustees to diversify trust investments. The rule is that trustees must consider the need for diversification. See Trustee Act 2000, s.4(3)(b). Trustees may — if they are satisfied it is appropriate to do so — invest the trust fund in a single asset.

3(2) Management

Trustees should be allowed to manage trust property without restrictions; this is the effect of clause 3(2). The powers conferred by the general law are not quite comprehensive. See *Drafting Trusts and Will Trusts* 6th ed., 20.25.

3(3) Joint Property

Trustees may wish to acquire property jointly with others and this needs express authorisation: *Webb v. Jones* See *Drafting Trusts and Will Trusts*[2] 6th ed. 20.24.

3(4) Income and Capital

This would allow trustees if they thought fit:

— to acquire wasting assets or capital growth assets;
— to pay capital expenses out of income.

The general trust law normally requires trustees to hold a balance between the interests of life tenant and remainderman. That is, trustees should normally invest trust funds so as to produce a reasonable amount of income *and* to protect capital values.[3]

It is easy to foresee occasions where, for good reasons, trustees would like to increase the income of the life tenant at the expense of the remainderman.[4]

It seems to the STEP Technical Committee that decisions on this balance are best left to the good sense of the trustees. The trustees are, in principle, persons chosen by the testator; he may be taken to have some faith in them; and in a typical case, the testator's first wish is that his widow should be provided for, in priority to other beneficiaries.

Nevertheless, the point has rightly been made that the existence of this power will be contrary to the intention of some testators. A testator may have very firm views that his widow's income should not in any circumstances be increased at the expense of the remainderman. This is particularly likely in

---

[2] (1888) 36 Ch.D. 660.
[3] For exceptions, see *Drafting Trusts & Will Trusts,* 6th ed., para 15–033.
[4] Conversely, it may be desired to invest in non-income-producing assets even completely depriving the life tenant of her income. This may be because the life tenant has sufficient income for her needs, or, for instance, the widow may be in state residential accommodation and find that all her trust income is taken to pay the cost of her care.

circumstances where the remaindermen are not the children of the widow; *e.g.* a will trust:

(1) to the widow for life, remainder to charity; or
(2) to the widow for life, remainder to children of an earlier marriage of the testator.

In such cases it would be appropriate for the drafter to exclude this paragraph of the STEP Standard Provisions.[5]

It should be noted that this power does not permit income to be accumulated after the expiry of the accumulation period: *Re Rochford*[6] This power is permitted in an interest in possession settlement and in an accumulation and maintenance settlement: see *Pearson v. IRC*[7] *Inglewood v. IRC*[8] See *Drafting Trusts and Will Trusts* 6th ed., 20.27 ff.

3(5) Accumulated Income

This clause authorises trustees to apply accumulated income as if it were income. This may be necessary to obtain the tax credit under Income and Corporation Taxes Act 1988, s.687. See *Drafting Trusts and Will Trusts* 6th ed., 20.29.

3(6) Use of Trust Property

This authorises trustees to acquire, in particular, a dwelling-house, for a beneficiary. The powers conferred by the general law are too narrow: see *Drafting Trusts and Will Trusts,* 6th ed., 20.35.

3(7) Application of Trust Property

Trustees will generally have power to transfer trust property to some of the beneficiaries. Where this is the case, the claim allows trustees three alternatives to a simple transfer of trust capital. They may:

— lend money to the beneficiary interest free;
— allow the beneficiary to borrow from a bank on the security of the trust property;
— transfer the trust property to the beneficiary as his income rather than as capital.

(This may offer tax advantages). See *Drafting Trusts and Will Trusts* 6th ed., 20.37.

3(8) Trade

This permits trustees to carry on a trade. See *Drafting Trusts and Will Trusts* 6th ed., 20.40.

---

[5] This may be done by the following form: "The Standard Provisions of the Society of Trust and Estate Practitioners (1st Edition) shall apply with the deletion of paragraphs 3(4) and 5."
[6] [1965] Ch. 111.
[7] [1980] S.T.C. 318.
[8] [1983] S.T.C. 133.

3(9) Borrowing

This clause gives the trustees unrestricted power to borrow. The general law gives trustees power to borrow for restricted purposes but not (*inter alia*) for investment purposes: *Re Suensen Taylor*[9] See *Drafting Trusts and Will Trusts* 6th ed., 20.41.

3(10) Insurance

This permits trustees to insure trust property, but this is now conferred by the general law: s.19 TA 1925 as amended by s.34 TA 2000.

3(11) Delegation

This extends the statutory power. See *Drafting Trusts and Will Trusts*, 6th ed., 20.42.

3(12) Deposit of documents

This slightly extends the statutory power: Trustee Act 2000, ss.16–21. See Drafting Trusts and Will Trusts 6th ed., 20.43.

3(13) Nominees

This strictly extends the statutory power. See *Drafting Trusts and Will Trusts* 6th ed., 20.43.

3(14) Offshore administration

If trustees are to be non-UK resident, for CGT purposes, it is generally necessary to administer the trusts abroad. This clause permits this in terms which echo the statutory provision: Taxation of Chargeable Gains Act 1992, s.69. See *Drafting Trusts and Will Trusts* 6th ed., 27.5.

3(15) Payment of Tax

In the absence of express power, the trustees are only entitled to pay foreign taxes in limited circumstances: *Re Lord Cable*.[10]

3(16) Indemnities

Where the trustees grant appropriate indemnities, they can also:

— reimburse themselves out of the Trust Fund if the indemnity is called upon; and
— secure the indemnity on the Trust Fund: see clause 3(17).
See *Drafting Trusts and Will Trusts* 6th ed., 20.44.

---

[9] [1974] 1 W.L.R. 1280.
[10] [1977] 1 W.L.R. 7.

3(17) Security

The general law allows trustees to mortgage trust property for certain purposes only; but if trustees are to be trusted with power to borrow, they should also have power to give security for their borrowing. See *Drafting Trusts and Will Trusts* 6th ed., 20.45.

3(18) Supervision of Company

This requires trustees to take action only if they have knowledge of circumstances which call for enquiry. In the absence of such a provision, it is the duty of trustees to keep a close eye on the running of a trust company: *Bartlett v. Barclays Trust Co. (No. 1).*[11] See *Drafting Trusts and Will Trusts* 6th ed., 5.29.

3(19) Appropriation

This gives trustees power to arrange a rational division of the trust fund, if it is to be shared out between beneficiaries. The power conferred by the general law is more restricted: Administration of Estates Act 1925, s.41. See *Drafting Trusts and Will Trusts* 6th ed., 20.46.

3(20) Receipt by Charities

This form solves a possible administrative difficulty where trust property is payable to a charitable trust or an unincorporated charitable association. In such cases trustees would otherwise need to investigate who could give them a valid receipt. See *Drafting Trusts and Will Trusts* 6th ed., 20.47.

3(21) Release of Powers

This allows trustees to release their powers. See *Drafting Trusts and Will Trusts* 6th ed., 20.48.

3(22) Ancillary Powers

This fall-back form is intended to prevent a narrow construction of trustees' powers. See *Drafting Trusts and Will Trusts* 6th ed., 20.49.

Clause 4 Powers of Maintenance and Advancement

This provides two standard amendments to sections 31 and 32 of the Trustee Act 1925. The effect is to increase slightly trustees' powers of maintenance and advancement. See *Drafting Trusts and Will Trusts* 6th ed., 10.8 and 15.21.

Clause 5 Trust for Sale

This imposes a trust for sale on land. Its purpose was to prevent the application of the Settled Land Act 1925. Now the Trust of Land and

---

[11] [1980] Ch. 515.

Appointment of Trustees Act 1996 has abolished the SLA 1925 for new settlements, this provision is obsolete. See *Drafting Trusts and Will Trusts* 6th ed., 2.27.

Clause 6 Minors

Where income is to be applied for a child under 18, trustees will often pay the income to a parent on behalf of the child. This clause relieves the trustees of the duty to monitor the parent's use of the money. This will simplify trust administration: the sums involved are usually small. Where the trustees are dealing with trust capital, it remains their duty to ensure that the capital is properly applied.

It might occasionally be convenient to allow an older child to receive funds directly, and this is authorised if the child is 16.

Clause 6(2) allows trustees to retain trust income on behalf of a minor. Instead, the income will be paid to the child once he is 18. See *Drafting Trusts and Will Trusts* 6th ed., 20.50.

Clause 7 Disclaimer

This clause authorises partial disclaimer (which the general law would not allow). This may help to take full advantage of section 93 of the Inheritance Act 1984 (disclaimers). See *Drafting Trusts and Will Trusts* 6th ed., 20.53.

Clause 8 Apportionment

This clause excludes the operation of the Apportionment Act 1870, which would otherwise require the trustees to make time-consuming calculations over small amounts of income. See *Drafting Trusts and Will Trusts* 6th ed., 20.54.

Clause 9 Conflicts of Interest

The general rule is that trustees may not enter into any transaction which gives rise to a conflict of interest. This clause relaxes the general rule, but with a safeguard: there must be at least one independent person to watch over the interests of the trust. The qualifications of the independent trustee are set out in clause 9(1)(b). The Fiduciary must disclose the position to the trustees, and the independent trustee must consent: clause 9(2). See *Drafting Trusts and Will Trusts* 6th ed., 5.13.

Clause 9(3)

This deals with the different problem which may arise where a beneficiary is a trustee, and wishes, say, to appoint property to himself. He may do so if there is an independent trustee.

In the rare case where a settlor is both trustee and the principal beneficiary of a settlement, it may be desired to relax this clause.

Clause 10 Powers of Trustees

Clause 10 contains two general provisions relating to trustees' powers:

— trustees' powers may be exercised at their absolute discretion.
— trustees' powers may be exercised from time to time as occasion requires. This will apply to the powers conferred in the will or settlement as well as to the powers in the Standard Provisions.

These general provisions make it unnecessary to specify whenever trustees are given powers that they may exercise the powers

(1) "at their absolute discretion;"

(2) "as they shall think fit;"

(3) "as they shall in their absolute discretion think fit;"

(4) "at any time or times;" or

(5) "from time to time;"

so a certain amount of verbiage can be avoided in the rest of the will or settlement.

The clause does not allow trustees to exercise their powers improperly: see *Gisborne v. Gisborne.*[12] See *Drafting Trusts and Will Trusts* 6th ed., 6.7 ff.

Clause 11 Trustee Remuneration

This slightly extends the statutory power; see *Drafting Trusts and Will Trusts,* 6th ed., 20.55 ff. The Trustee remuneration was given priority to dispositions in the will or settlement, so as to prevent the executors' remuneration abating jointly with other legacies, but this is now no longer necessary.

Clause 11(2) authorises trustees to charge for work done for a company held by the trust. See *Drafting Trusts and Will Trusts* 6th ed., 20.65.

Clause 12 Liability of Trustees

Trustees are not liable for breach of trust when they have acted honestly and reasonably and ought fairly to be excused: Trustee Act 1925, s.61. This clause relieves trustees from liability for breach of trust in two further circumstances:

— Where the trustee is not a professional trustee (defined in clause 1) and is not guilty of negligence.
— Where the trustees are acting on the opinion of Counsel.
Wider trustee relieving provisions are sometimes found, which purport to exclude trustees' liability for any act except fraud or wilful default. Such forms raise serious difficulties (in particular there are professional conduct implications where the draftsman's firm is acting as trustee); they should only be

---

[12] (1877) 2 App. Cas. 300.

used in special circumstances. See *Drafting Trusts and Will Trusts* 6th ed., 5.17 ff.

Clause 13 Appointment and Retirement of Trustees

Clause 13(1) authorises the appointment of foreign trustees: the extent to which this can be done without express authority is unclear.

Clause 13(2) allows a professional trustee (defined in clause 1) to be retired on attaining retirement age. A retirement date is set for virtually every office and employment. However trust law does not impose a retirement date. This clause avoids difficulties which occasionally arise. See *Drafting Trusts and Will Trusts* 6th ed., 5.33 ff.

Clause 14 Protection for Interest in Possession and Accumulation and Maintenance Settlement

This clause ensures (for the avoidance of doubt only) that none of the Standard Provisions will have undesirable tax effects. See *Drafting Trusts and Will Trusts* 6th ed., 18.17. Clause 14(2) is now obsolete following the FA 1998, but its retention does no harm.

FURTHER READING

The Standard Provisions are derived from *Drafting Trusts & Will Trusts* by James Kessler (6th ed., Sweet & Maxwell, 2002) which contains a much fuller commentary than is possible here.

APPENDIX IV

HOW TO USE "BRIGHOUSE'S PRECEDENTS OF WILLS" CD

HOW TO USE
"BRIGHOUSE'S PRECEDENTS OF WILLS" CD

THE COMPANION CD

Instructions for Use

Introduction

These notes are provided for guidance only. They should be read and interpreted in the context of your own computer system and operational procedures. It is assumed that you have a basic knowledge of WINDOWS. However, if there is any problem please contact our help line on 020 7393 7266 who will be happy to help you.

CD Format and Contents

To run this CD you need at least:
- IBM compatible PC with Pentium processor
- 8MB RAM
- CD-ROM drive
- Microsoft Windows 95

This CD contains data files of the clauses in this book. It does not contain software or commentary.

Installation

The following instructions make the assumption that you will copy the data files to a single directory on your hard disk (e.g. C:\Brighouse).

Open your **CD ROM drive,** select and double click on **setup.exe** and follow the instructions. The files will be unzipped to your **C drive** and you will be able to open them up from the new **C:\Brighouse** folder there.

Setting up

If you have followed the instructions at the back of the book, the Brighouse precedents will all be situated in a folder on your c:\drive.

The other useful thing that you can do is to place the documents called "Brighouse Template" in your own Templates folder. This is done as follows:

1. From "My Computer" on the Windows Desktop, find c:\Brighouse.

2. Find "Brighouse Template.tmp", right click it, and choose "copy" from the pop-up menu.

3. Again from "My Computer" go into your own templates directory. If you have a fairly ordinary set-up that will probably be "C:\Program Files\Microsoft Office\Templates", or "C:\Microsoft Office\Templates". (A way of checking whether you are in the right folder is to look for a document called "normal". If you find it you are in the right place).

4. Choose "Copy" from the edit menu.

5. Close the "Templates" box.

6. A way of checking whether this has worked correctly is to go into Word, and choose "New" from the "File" menu. In the "General" tab you should see "Brighouse Template" next to "Blank Document".

Inserting Files

Brighouse is written so that Wills can be "built" clause by clause. This is done as follows:

1. From within Word, choose "New" from the "File" menu.

2. Click on the "General" tab.

3. Double click "Brighouse Template". This produces a blank document. The Brighouse Template also has a toolbar of its own called "Brighouse" which will probably have appeared automatically on your screen. If it has not, then right click your toolbars and choose "Brighouse" from the drop down menu.

4. Insert the first clause that you need. There are three different ways of inserting a file:

   (a) You can choose "file" from the "insert" menu.
   (b) There is an "insert file" button on some Word toolbars.
   (c) The best method, if you intending to use Brighouse precedents regularly, is to learn the keyboard shortcut which is ALT+I+L. (This reduces inserting a clause to six or seven keystrokes, which can take less than a second, and does not involve moving your hands from the keyboard to the mouse.)

5. In the "insert file" dialog box, select the file where your precedents are kept (probably C:\Brighouse) from the "look in" drop-down list. The next time you choose the "insert file" command you will already be in the right place.

6. Select the clause you want in one of two ways:

   (a) Find it in the large box in the middle of the screen and double click it.
   (b) Type its name in the "file name" box and press return. Once you are used to it this is far quicker than option (a). The files names are just numbers — which was done deliberately to reduce the

number of keystrokes — and these correspond with the equivalent precedent numbers in the book.

7. Repeat this operation for each precedent clause you need.

Stop-Codes

Perhaps the most confusing item in Brighouse, for those who have not used it before, is the use of the "stop-code".

A stop-code appears as "$/" on the screen, and that rather unusual choice of characters was made because it is unlikely to appear in a document just by accident.

There are three different types of stop-code:

(a) A plain stop-code, which simply marks where information needs to be filled in. For example:

I give £$/ to $/.

can become:

I give £45 to my brother Frederick Williams.

(b) Optional text stop codes, marked with [ ], indicate text that might — or might not — be required. For example:

to pay the income to my husband during his lifetime $/[or until he remarries$/].

can become:

to pay the income to my husband during his lifetime.

or:

to pay the income to my husband during his lifetime or until he remarries.

(c) Choice stop codes, marked with { }, indicate a set of options, For example:

to pay the residue to my $/{husband$//wife$/} absolutely.

can become:

to pay the residue to my husband absolutely.

or:

to pay the residue to my wife absolutely.

381

It is possible for stop codes to sit inside other stop codes, and although this looks "mad" on the page, it can in fact be quite useful. For example:

Those of my children who survive me $/[and attain $/{18$//21$//25$/}$/]

can become:

Those of my children who survive me

Those of my children who survive me and attain 18

Those of my children who survive me and attain 21

or:

Those of my children who survive me and attain 25

Leaders, Sub-Leaders and "Tails"

The Brighouse precedents are written so that they "string together" to make complete Wills. Each precedent clause is therefore not necessarily an isolated clause of the Will which would stand alone in its own right, and this is particularly noticeable:

(a) In precedents which have been deliberately broken up into their "building blocks", particularly in the legacies section of Part 2, and in the Chapter on Codicils.

(b) In the "residue" of all Wills. Instead of drafting complete residue clauses, we have give a "residue commencement" — suitable for every Will — followed by a series of "residue continuations" which trail on from the residue commencement. Each of these ends with an optional phrase along the lines of "if these trusts fail" or "subject to that", allowing you to string another residue continuation after the first, and another, and another, until you have dealt with as many levels of substitution as your particular client wants. Also, most precedents in the "trusts" chapter are available in a form called "residue continuation", which works in the same way.

(c) In the life interests section of the trusts chapter, we have deliberately separated life interests from remainders. To produce a complete life interest trust you need to choose two precedents and string them together. We believe that with appropriate modification it is fairly easy to adapt our clauses for successive life interests, also.

These terms "leader" and "sub-leader", as used in the book, are best explained by example:

1 LEGACIES

   (a) I give, free of inheritance tax:

      (i) all my jewellery to my daughter **Alice Smith**

      (ii) to my son **Adam Smith**:

         (A) my late husband's collection of model racing cars; and

         (B) two thousand pounds.

Line "(a)" is a leader. Line (ii) is a sub-leader because although it is a leader itself (it leads clauses "(A)" and "(B))", it also follows a leader (line "(a)").

Outline

We have developed a set of "outline numbered" "styles" in Word. (The terms in quotation marks in the previous sentence are technical terms within Word, and you will be able to look them up in your own Word textbook). The precedents are easiest to use if you actually **accept our style of numbering, rather than attempting to fight against it!** Obviously, there are ways of changing the numbering, indents, fonts, etc., but the book was written on the assumption that you will not want to do so. If you accept our formatting, the precedents are relatively easy to use, and buttons on the toolbar (explained below) send any piece of text straight to its appropriate level in the outline.

At its simplest the outline looks like this:

Text

1   LEVEL 1

   Text at level 1

   (a) Level 2

      Text at level 2

      (i) Level 3

         Text at level 3

         (A) Level 4

            (I) Level 5

As you will notice when using the precedents, most of the text is written in "text at level 1" or "level 2". Level 1 is used only for clause headings, and is always in bold capitals.

The Brighouse Toolbar

The following buttons appear on the Brighouse toolbar:

(a) *Restart Numbering.* This is a standard word command, and therefore not explained in this guide.

(b) *Continue Numbering.* This is a standard word command, and therefore not explained in this guide.

(c) *Stop-Code.* This finds, and highlights, the next stop code in the text for you.

(d) The next nine buttons, taken together, are used to shift text between the outline levels explained above. The pictures on the first five are just characters: 1, a, i, A, I. These take you to the levels of the outline which have that number formatting. (Pressing "i", for example, numbers the current paragraphs, as i, ii, iii etc., as appropriate. The next four buttons have the word "text" written across them in red, and they put text at the indicated level, without a letter or number.

Perhaps the easiest way of learning to use these buttons is to type a short sentence onto a blank document created with the Brighouse template, then pushing the buttons to watch what happens to your text. We think it is reasonably intuitive with a little practice.

INDEX

405

THE COMPANION CD-ROM
Instructions for Use

Introduction

These notes are provided for guidance only. They should be read and interpreted in the context of your own computer system and operational procedures. It is assumed that you have a basic knowledge of WINDOWS. However, if there is any problem please contact our help line on 020 7393 7266 who will be happy to help you.

CD Format and Contents

To run this CD you need at least:

- IBM compatible PC with Pentium processor
- 8mb RAM
- CD-ROM drive
- Microsoft Windows 95

The CD contains data files of Precedent material. It does not contain software or commentary.

Installation

The following instructions make the assumption that you will copy the data files to a single directory on your hard disk (e.g. C:\Brighouse).

Open your **CD ROM drive,** select and double click on **setup.exe** and follow the instructions. The files will be unzipped to your **C drive** and you will be able to open them up from the new **C:\Brighouse** folder there.

LICENCE AGREEMENT

Definitions

1. The following terms will have the following meanings:
"The PUBLISHERS" means Sweet & Maxwell of 100 Avenue Road, London NW3 3PF (which expression shall, where the context admits, include the PUBLISHERS' assigns or successors in business as the case may be) of the other part on behalf of Thomson Books Limited of Cheriton House, North Way, Andover SP10 5BE.
"The LICENSEE" means the purchaser of the title containing the Licensed Material.
"Licensed Material" means the data included on the disk;
"Licence" means a single user licence;
"Computer" means an IBM-PC compatible computer.

Grant of Licence; Back up copies

2. (1) The PUBLISHERS hereby grant to the LICENSEE, a non-exclusive, non-transferable licence to use the Licensed Material in accordance with these terms and conditions.

(2) The LICENSEE may install the Licensed Material for use on one computer only at any one time.

(3) The LICENSEE may make one back-up copy of the Licensed Material only, to be kept in the LICENSEE's control and possession.

Proprietary Rights

3. (1) All rights not expressly granted herein are reserved.

(2) The Licensed Material is not sold to the LICENSEE who shall not acquire any right, title or interest in the Licensed Material or in the media upon which the Licensed Material is supplied.

(3) The LICENSEE shall not erase, remove, deface or cover any trademark, copyright notice, guarantee or other statement on any media containing the Licensed Material.

(4) The LICENSEE shall only use the Licensed Material in the normal course of its business and shall not use the Licensed Material for the purpose of operating a bureau or similar service or any online service whatsoever.

(5) Permission is hereby granted to LICENSEES who are members of the legal profession (which expression does not include individuals or organisations engaged in the supply of services to the legal profession) to reproduce, transmit and store small quantities of text for the purpose of enabling them to provide legal advice to or to draft documents or conduct proceedings on behalf of their clients.

(6) The LICENSEE shall not sublicense the Licensed Material to others and this Licence Agreement may not be transferred, sublicensed, assigned or otherwise disposed of in whole or in part.

(7) The LICENSEE shall inform the PUBLISHERS on becoming aware of any unauthorised use of the Licensed Material.

Warranties

4. (1) The PUBLISHERS warrant that they have obtained all necessary rights to grant this licence.

(2) Whilst reasonable care is taken to ensure the accuracy and completeness of the Licensed Material supplied, the PUBLISHERS make no representations or warranties, express or implied, that the Licensed Material is free from errors or omissions.

(3) The Licensed Material is supplied to the LICENSEE on an "as is" basis and has not been supplied to meet the LICENSEE'S individual requirements. It is the sole responsibility of the LICENSEE to satisfy itself prior to entering this Licence Agreement that the Licensed Material will meet the LICENSEE's requirements and be compatible with the LICENSEE's hardware/software configuration. No failure of any part of the Licensed Material to be suitable for the LICENSEE's requirements will give rise to any claim against the PUBLISHERS.

(4) In the event of any material inherent defects in the physical media on which the licensed material may be supplied, other than caused by accident abuse or misuse by the LICENSEE, the PUBLISHERS will replace the defective original media free of charge provided it is returned to the place of purchase within 90 days of the purchase date.

The PUBLISHERS' enure liability and the LICENSEE's exclusive remedy shall be the replacement of such defective media.

(5) Whilst all reasonable care has been taken to exclude computer viruses, no warranty is made that the Licensed Material is virus free. The LICENSEE shall be responsible to ensure that no virus is introduced to any computer or network and shall not hold the PUBLISHERS responsible.

(6) The warranties set out herein are exclusive of and in lieu of all other conditions and warranties, either express or implied, statutory or otherwise.

(7) All other conditions and warranties, either express or implied, statutory or otherwise, which relate in the condition and fitness for any purpose of the Licensed Material are hereby excluded and the PUBLISHERS' shall not be liable in contract or in tort for any loss of any kind suffered by reason of any defect in the Licensed Material (whether or not caused by the negligence of the PUBLISHERS).

Limitation of Liability and Indemnity

5. (1) The LICENSEE shall accept sole responsibility for and the PUBLISHERS shall not be liable for the use of the Licensed Material by the LICENSEE, its agents and employees and the LICENSEE shall hold the PUBLISHERS harmless and fully indemnified against any claims, costs, damages, loss and liabilities arising out of any such use.

(2) The PUBLISHERS shall not be liable for any indirect or consequential loss suffered by the LICENSEE (including without limitation loss of profits, goodwill or data) in connection with the Licensed Material howsoever arising.

(3) The PUBLISHERS will have no liability whatsoever for any liability of the LICENSEE or any third party which might arise.

(4) The LICENSEE hereby agrees that
(a) the LICENSEE is best placed to foresee and evaluate any loss that might be suffered in connection with this Licence Agreement;
(b) that the cost of supply of the Licensed Material has been calculated on the basis of the limitations and exclusions contained herein; and
(c) the LICENSEE will effect such insurance as is suitable having regard to the LICENSEE's circumstances.

(5) The aggregate maximum liability of the PUBLISHERS in respect of any direct loss or any other loss (to the extent that such loss is not excluded by this Licence Agreement or otherwise) whether such a claim arises in contract or tort shall not exceed a sum equal to that paid as the price for the title containing the Licensed Material.

Termination

6. (1) In the event of any breach of this Agreement including any violation of any copyright in the Licensed Material, whether held by the PUBLISHERS or others in the Licensed Material, the Licence Agreement shall automatically terminate immediately, without notice and without prejudice to any claim which the PUBLISHERS may have either for moneys due and/or damages and/or otherwise.

(2) Clauses 3 to S shall survive the termination for whatsoever reason of this Licence Agreement.

(3) In the event of termination of this Licence Agreement the LICENSEE will remove the Licensed Material.

Miscellaneous

7. (1) Any delay or forbearance by the PUBLISHERS in enforcing any provisions of this Licence Agreement shall not be construed as a waiver of such provision or an agreement thereafter not to enforce the said provision.

(2) This Licence Agreement shall be governed by the laws of England and Wales, If any difference shall arise between the Parties touching the meaning of this Licence Agreement or the rights and liabilities of the parties thereto, the same shall be referred to arbitration in accordance with the provisions of the Arbitration Act 1996, or any amending or substituting statute for the time being in force.

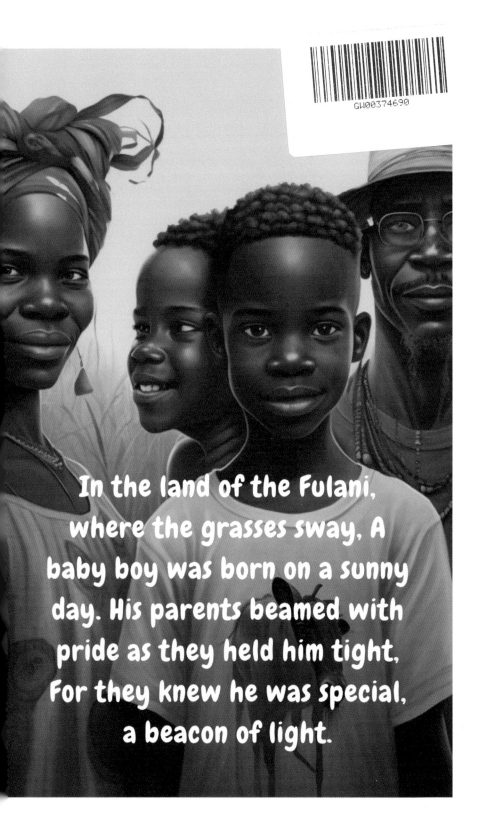

In the land of the Fulani,
where the grasses sway, A
baby boy was born on a sunny
day. His parents beamed with
pride as they held him tight,
For they knew he was special,
a beacon of light.

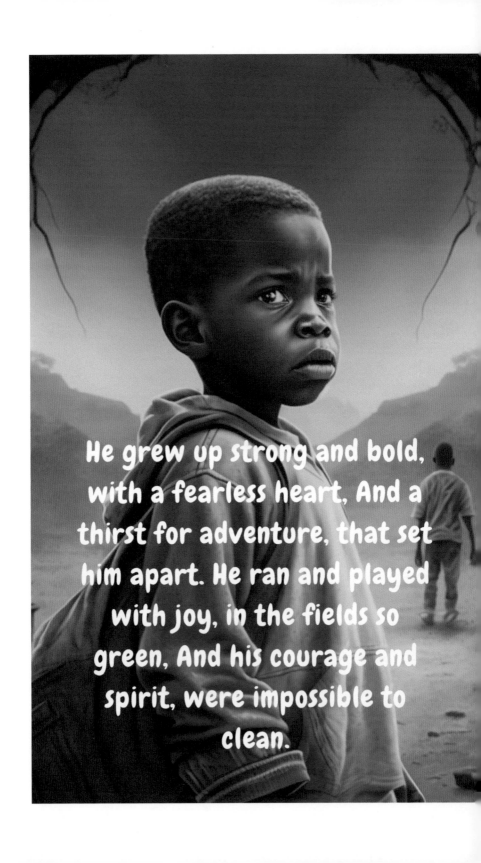

He grew up strong and bold, with a fearless heart, And a thirst for adventure, that set him apart. He ran and played with joy, in the fields so green, And his courage and spirit, were impossible to clean.

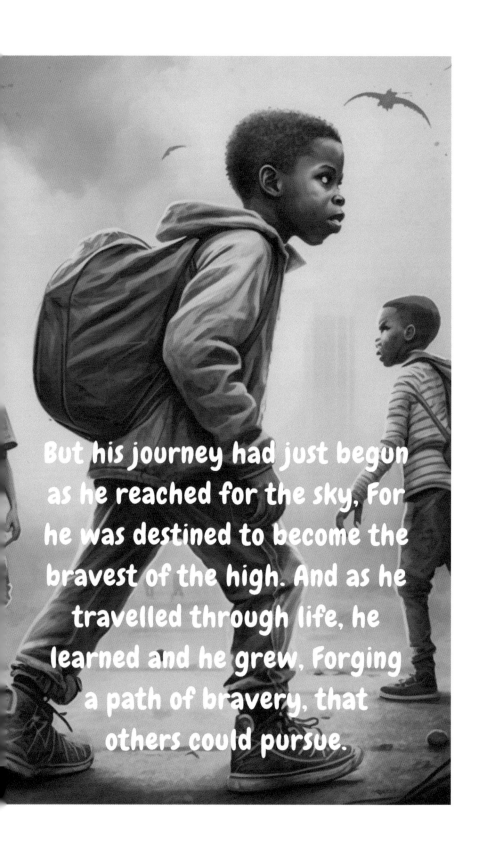

But his journey had just begun as he reached for the sky, For he was destined to become the bravest of the high. And as he travelled through life, he learned and he grew, Forging a path of bravery, that others could pursue.

And so it was written that the birth of this brave, Would inspire generations, and the world would be saved. The brave Fulani boy will always be remembered, As a shining example of strength and surrender.

As the boy grew older, he was put to the test. Challenges came his way, and he had to impress. He faced trials and hardships, but he did not back down, For he was determined, to wear the bravest crown.

He learned to stand up tall in the face of fear and keep moving forward, despite what was near. For he knew that challenges were opportunities, To grow and become more robust, with each victory.

And so he pushed on through
the storms and the rain and
learned that courage is not
about fame. But about
standing tall in the face of
the fray, And being true to
oneself, come what may.

And with each test he passed, he grew bold, And his spirit of bravery never grew cold. For he was a true warrior of the Fulani kind, And his limits were boundless, with a strength of mind.

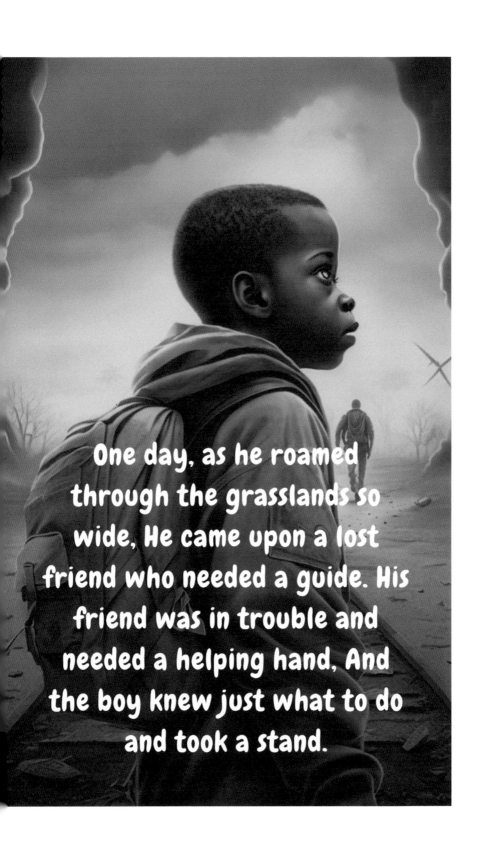

One day, as he roamed through the grasslands so wide, He came upon a lost friend who needed a guide. His friend was in trouble and needed a helping hand, And the boy knew just what to do and took a stand.

He stood by his friend with a heart full of love, And together they faced the challenges above. For he knew that a friend is a treasure to hold And that helping others is worth more than gold.

And so they set out, on a journey as one, With the boy leading the way until the work was done. And when the task was complete and their friend was at peace, The boy learned the value of compassion and release.

And from that day on, he carried a cheerful heart, For he knew that kindness could conquer any fight. And with his friend by his side, he continued to roam, A true warrior of the Fulani with a heart made of stone.

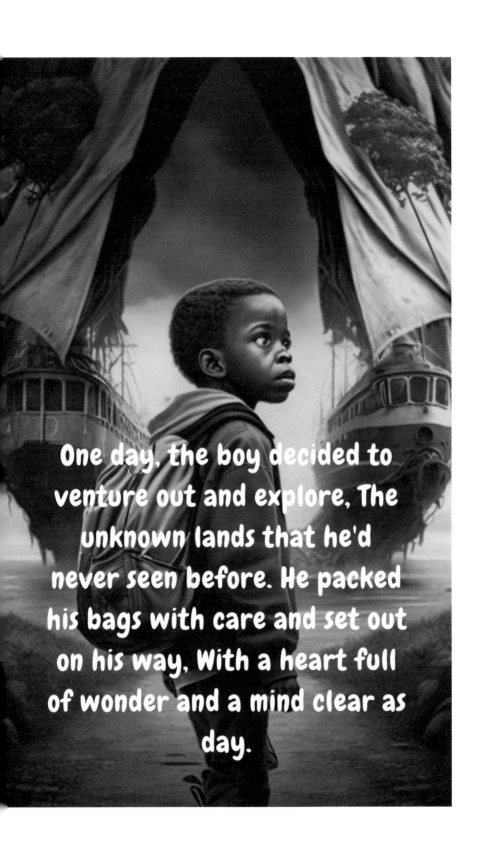

One day, the boy decided to venture out and explore, The unknown lands that he'd never seen before. He packed his bags with care and set out on his way, With a heart full of wonder and a mind clear as day.

He encountered obstacles and dangers on his quest, But he kept moving forward, with his courage at its best. For he knew that fear was just an illusion in his mind, And he was determined to leave it all behind.

And as he ventured deeper into the unknown, He discovered secrets that had never been shown. He marvelled at the beauty of the world around him, And he knew that his bravery would never be dimmed.

And when his journey was over, and he'd seen all he sought, He returned to his home with stories he brought. And he shared his tales of adventure and delight, Inspiring others to venture out into the night.

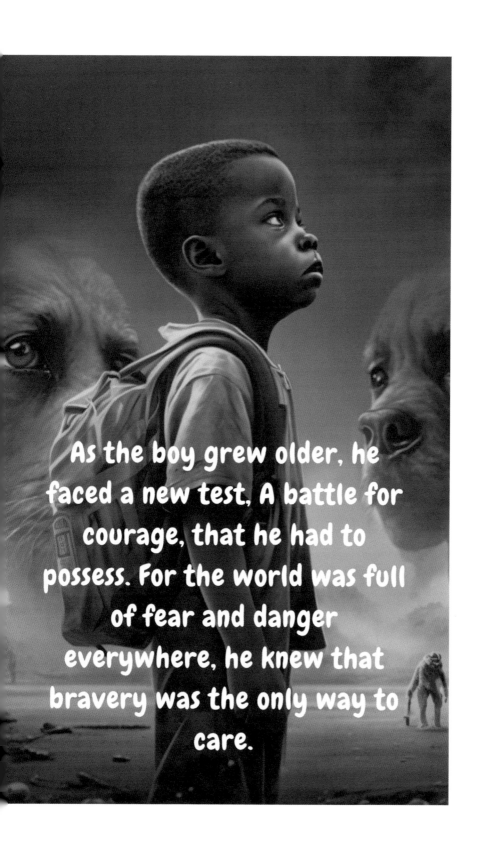

As the boy grew older, he faced a new test, A battle for courage, that he had to possess. For the world was full of fear and danger everywhere, he knew that bravery was the only way to care.

He trained and prepared for the fight ahead, sharpening his skills until they shone like lead. For he knew that courage was not just about might, But about standing up for what's right.

And when the day arrived for the battle, He took to the field with a heart full of sin. And he fought with all his might, against the forces of fear, With a courage that shone, so bright and clear.

And in the end, he emerged, as the victor of the fight, With a heart full of bravery and a soul full of light. And he proved to the world that courage could conquer all, And that bravery would never fall.

And so the boy became a hero of his land, With a heart full of bravery, and a spirit so grand. He roamed the grasslands with strength so true, And he inspired others to be brave just like he grew.

People came from far and wide to hear his tales and see the bravery that shone from his sails. And as he travelled, he spread his message with care, That courage is within us, and it's always there.

And so he emerged, as a
leader of his kind, With a
heart full of courage and a
spirit so divine. And his legend
grew, with each passing day,
Of the brave Fulani boy who
showed us the way.

And though he may have left this world far behind, His legacy lives on in the hearts of humanity. He was a hero, who inspired us all, And his bravery will never fall.

And so the story ends, of the brave Fulani boy, Who roamed the grasslands with a heart full of joy. His legacy lives on in the hearts of the young, And his bravery will always be sung.

For he showed us how to be strong and bold, And to conquer our fears with a heart made of gold. And he proved that courage is within us all, And that bravery can beat any fall.

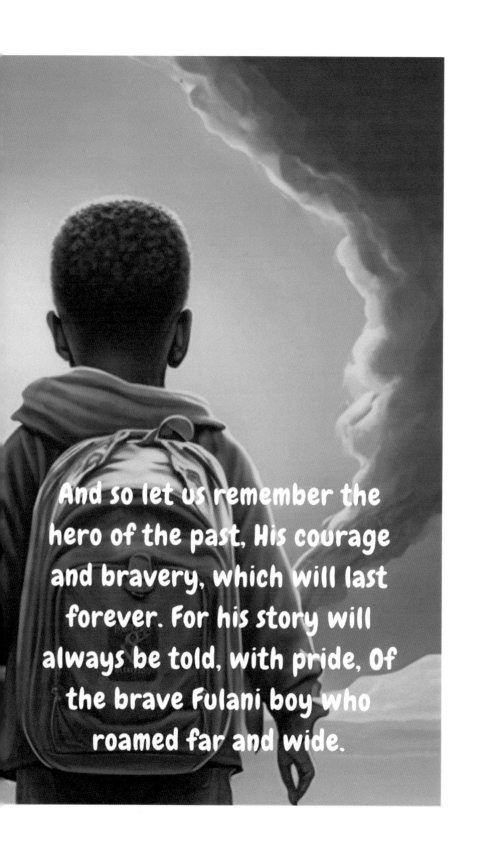

And so let us remember the hero of the past, His courage and bravery, which will last forever. For his story will always be told, with pride, Of the brave Fulani boy who roamed far and wide.

And as we continue on our
journey through life, Let us
be inspired by the bravery of
the brave Fulani boy, And let
us carry on his legacy with
care, For his courage and
bravery, will always be
there.

Printed in Great Britain
by Amazon